Women Theorists *on* Society *and* Politics

Lynn McDonald,
editor

Wilfrid Laurier University Press

This book has been published with the help of a grant from the Humanities and Social Sciences Federation of Canada, using funds provided by the Social Sciences and Humanities Research Council of Canada.

We acknowledge the financial support of the Government of Canada through the Book Publishing Industry Development Program for our publishing activities.

Canadian Cataloguing in Publication Data

Main entry under title:

Women theorists on society and politics

Includes bibliographical references and index.
ISBN 0-88920-316-4 (pbk.)

1. Social sciences – Philosophy – History.   2. Political science – History.   3. Women social scientists – History.   4. Women political scientists – History.   I. McDonald, Lynn, 1940-   .

H31.W65 1998   300'.9   C98-930586-4

Copyright © 1998
WILFRID LAURIER UNIVERSITY PRESS
Waterloo, Ontario, Canada N2L 3C5

Cover design by Leslie Macredie

Printed in Canada

***Women Theorists on Society and Politics* has been produced from a manuscript supplied in camera-ready form by the editor.**

All rights reserved. No part of this work covered by the copyrights hereon may be reproduced or used in any form or by any means—graphic, electronic, or mechanical—without the prior written permission of the publisher. Any request for photocopying, recording, taping, or reproducing in information storage and retrieval systems of any part of this book shall be directed in writing to the Canadian Reprography Collective, 214 King Street West, Suite 312, Toronto, Ontario M5H 3S6.

Dedicated to
Thelma McCormack

Professor Emerita at the Department of Sociology, York University, and founding director of the York Graduate Programme in Women's Studies, Thelma McCormack has encouraged, assisted, aided and abetted a whole generation of women scholars. I am one of many who has benefited from her advice, practical help and friendship.

Table of Contents

Dedication iii

Preface vii

Acknowledgements ix

CHAPTER 1
Introduction 1

CHAPTER 2
Early Theorists: Christine de Pisan, Mary Astell,
Emilie du Châtelet, Mary Wortley Montagu, Sophia 9

CHAPTER 3
Theorists on Revolution: Catharine Macaulay,
Mary Wollstonecraft, Mary Hays, Marie Jeanne-Roland,
Germaine de Staël, Sophie Grouchy de Condorcet 47

CHAPTER 4
Theorists on Social Reform: Flora Tristan, Harriet Martineau,
Florence Nightingale, Helen Taylor, Beatrice Webb 129

CHAPTER 5
Theorists on Gender and Violence: Josephine Butler,
Elizabeth Blackwell, Frances Power Cobbe 231

CHAPTER 6
Theorists on Peace, War and Militarism: Jane Addams,
Bertha von Suttner, Olive Schreiner, Catherine E. Marshall,
Emily Greene Balch 259

CHAPTER 7
An Afterword 295

Manuscript Sources 299

Bibliography 301

Index 315

Preface

Women Theorists on Society and Politics represents the end of a long intellectual journey, to find and publish the great women theorists who have been so unjustly excluded from textbooks and courses on theory, in spite of the high quality of their contributions. My *Early Origins of the Social Sciences*, 1993, included women theorists along with many more men, while *The Women Founders of the Social Sciences*, 1994, was devoted entirely to reporting the women's work. Most of the theorists included in this anthology appeared at least in the *Women Founders*, but the focus there was on their methodological contribution, with only secondary attention to social and political theory.

Women Theorists on Society and Politics now provides the opportunity to relate the enormously interesting social and political writing of these theorists, with biographical background on their no less exciting lives. The quality of these theorists' contributions will speak for itself. I merely recount my own experience of being constantly amazed at how prescient they were, how often they "anticipated" the work of better-known men and how lively and witty their writing was.

A significant phase of "unlearning" was required to get me past a well-ingrained deference to leading male theorists to see the originality and relevance of the women's work. In some cases the women theorists were saying something quite different, material that deserves to be read for its distinctive contribution. In other cases their position was not greatly different from that of more prominent men, but they nonetheless brought insights, experience and nuance worth considering. Readers of conventional histories of social and political theory and students and professors in conventional courses, which still deal virtually exclusively with men theorists, are the losers for the absence of these women.

Growing numbers of scholars have taken up these women theorists, so that the work is no longer lonely. Especially helpful were the sessions on women theorists at the International Sociological Association, History of Sociology, meeting in Amsterdam, 1996, a session on women theorists at the American Sociological Association meetings, Toronto, 1997 and the founding of the Harriet Martineau Sociological Association at the Amsterdam meetings, with its first working meeting at Mackinac Island, 1997 (a special thanks to Michael Hill and Mary Jo Deegan for organizing it). I appreciated also Charles Camic's encouragement to pursue the women theorists, by including my paper at his mini-conference on theory at the American Sociological Association meetings in Washington, D.C., 1994, later published in his *Reclaiming the Sociological Classics*, 1997.

Another happy indicator of interest is the coming together of a group of scholars to prepare a collected works of Florence Nightingale, in my view the most exciting of the women theorists included here. This work is now in progress, with first publication anticipated, with Wilfrid Laurier University Press. (This will include complete publication in electronic form of Nightingale's work, selective publication in print, with myself as the project director/chief editor.)

Lynn McDonald
University of Guelph

Acknowledgements

As well as the persons cited above, many others assisted in the preparation of this book. I especially acknowledge the role of Sandra Woolfrey, director of Wilfrid Laurier University Press, and Joanne Duncan-Robinson, technical assistant at the Department of Sociology and Anthropology, University of Guelph. Faults and errors that remain are, of course, my own.

This book has been published with the help of a grant from the Humanities and Social Sciences Federation of Canada, using funds provided by the Social Sciences and Humanities Research Council of Canada.

I gratefully acknowledge permission by Jean Hawkes to reproduce material from her translation of *The London Journal of Flora Tristan*, permission of the British Library of Political and Economic Science to publish material from the Mill-Taylor collection and the Passfield Papers and the assistance of the Charles Woodward Memorial Room, Woodward Biomedical Library, University of British Columbia for supplying previously unpublished Nightingale letters.

The British Library Students' Manuscript Room, the Wellcome Institute for the History of Medicine, Contemporary Medical Archives and Claydon House are all gratefully acknowledged for providing access to previously unpublished Nightingale manuscripts. Appreciation is due to the Henry Bonham Carter Will Trust for treating Nightingale material as public domain and generally facilitating scholarly access.

Chapter 1

Introduction

The recovery of writing by women scholars is now high on the feminist agenda for social and political theory. In the past feminist scholars devoted their efforts to the exposure of sexist bias in scholarly research and discussed the possibility of a new feminist paradigm. Women's studies programmes have resulted in considerable publication, some very impressive, on women's history and literature, and issues of the status of women and gender roles. Dale Spender's *Women of Ideas*, 1982, and *Feminist Theorists*, 1983, are excellent examples (and there are others, both by Spender and others) of this work of recovery, but focusing on status of women issues. The great works by women theorists on mainstream social and political issues have remained in obscurity. Little attention has been paid to *women's contributions themselves*, even those of great originality and importance at the time, and by very well known women. Women political theorists are absent from political science texts as they are from histories and textbooks of "sociological thought" or social theory. Yet women have, for centuries, written on such central issues as the nature of the social bond, social contract, individual rights versus social obligation, the role of government, the welfare state, socialism, constitutional change, slavery and revolution.

This book is directed to filling, as much as one anthology can, that gap of missing contributions. It presents, with critical introductions, texts on society and politics by a diverse range of women scholars. The time period covered is effectively the eighteenth century to World War II, with a small amount of material from the Renaissance (one writer, Christine de Pisan) and the late seventeenth century (Mary Astell). The bulk of the work, however, comes from the mid- to late eighteenth century (especially Emilie du Châtelet, Catharine Macaulay, Mary Wollstonecraft, Germaine de Staël, Marie-Jeanne Roland) and the nineteenth century (notably Florence Nightingale, Harriet Martineau, Elizabeth Blackwell, Frances Power Cobbe, Helen Taylor, Jane Addams and Beatrice Webb).

Work on more recent writers is much more available and the need for its inclusion here correspondingly less. Earlier writing, although there is much less of it, of course, enjoys no such readership, but would have presented other problems. The little early material that is included is difficult to read for non-specialists. To do justice to the theorists selected it seemed best to limit the time period to the three hundred years from the early French Enlightenment (du Châtelet) to the American sociologist Emily Greene Balch. There is writing as late as the 1940s, but a theorist had to have begun publishing before 1900 to be included.

Many of the texts are effectively unavailable to any but the intrepid user of British and French research collections and archives. Some have never been published before (especially work by Florence Nightingale). Some items have not appeared before in English (du Châtelet and de Staël). Many of the published texts could be had only in old editions with unfamiliar scripts and outmoded punctuation and spelling (especially the work of Pisan, Astell and Macaulay). Yet most of the material was published, and a very full anthology only of *published* material would have been possible. The work being presented here, in other words, is largely work that need not have fallen into obscurity. Some of the women were indeed famous in their time, their work not only published but reprinted in numerous editions and translated. This is work that never made it into the scholarly canon, was never taught at universities and rarely attracted a graduate student. It was work that was lost effectively, and had to be recovered, but gems that were always there for the looking.

In the analysis attention is paid to the issue of similarities and differences with writing by, usually better known, male theorists of the same time. There is correspondence with two American presidents, George Washington and Thomas Jefferson. The presentation will also make possible the identification of comparisons and contrasts with work today on the same subjects. Many of the controversies contemporary feminist scholars deal with are variations on earlier themes. The texts presented will show that women's writing has never been monolithic, but there are some patterns and tendencies. Active collaboration and other links among the women will be indicated.

That women's contributions to social and political theory have been substantial and original I learned in the course of researching my last two books. *Early Origins of the Social Sciences*, 1993, includes women, albeit as a minority among many more men. *Women Founders of the Social Sciences*, 1994, relates the work of the women only and in greater detail. A number of the women whose work was discussed in these two books are presented again here, now with the focus on their *social and political theory*: Astell, Wortley Montagu, Macaulay, Roland, Wollstonecraft, Hays, Tristan, de Staël, Martineau, Nightingale, Webb and Addams. In addition there is work from Josephine Butler, Helen Taylor, Frances Power Cobbe, Elizabeth Blackwell, Bertha von Suttner, Olive Schreiner, Catherine Marshall and Emily Greene Balch, all of

Introduction

whom wrote on social and political theory but were not included earlier because they did not work on the foundations of the social sciences or their methodology.

Curiously, it seems that contemporary women interested in political theory have chosen to concentrate on the failings of male theorists (an embarrassment of riches!) rather than the accomplishments (albeit less impressive) of the women. Recent decades have seen a substantial critical literature emerge on the oversights, prejudice, ignorance and inconsistencies of major male political theorists.[1] This has doubtless helped to open the eyes and hone the judgment of a new generation of scholars and is certainly a welcome addition to the literature. This criticism has been aimed at the most progressive of liberal political theorists, like **John Locke** and even the feminist **John Stuart Mill**, as well as the illiberal **Thomas Hobbes** and anti-democratic **Jean-Jacques Rousseau**. The women theorists themselves to be presented below did make choices, however, approving of some of the leading male theorists and rejecting others. Male theorists who contributed ideas that helped the women in their struggles, whatever their failings in the eyes of contemporary feminists, were cited with approval, their ideas fleshed out and used.

The purpose of this book is to report on the considerable accomplishments of women theorists themselves rather than dwell on recent critiques. The subjects include such central issues as the social contract, individual rights and social obligation. There are contributions on the principles of the welfare state and socialism, including work on the related subjects of the rights of labour, the labour theory of value and inequality. There are analyses of the French and American Revolutions, slavery and the American Civil War. British imperialism is addressed in relation to Ireland and India. Some early observations on racism are included. There is theoretical work on the rule of law and democratic process. There is practical advice on public administration from national and local to international government. Specific topics include the establishment of public health care and unemployment insurance. A distinctive women's perspective on ecology and the human/nature bond appears. Women's views on peace, war and militarism are presented, with work as early as the fifteenth

---

[1] Lorenne M.G. Clark and Lynda Lange, eds. *The Sexism of Social and Political Theory*; Diana H. Coole, *Women in Political Theory*; Josephine Donovan, *Feminist Theory*; Jean Bethke Elshtain, *Public Man, Private Woman*; Jean Grimshaw, *Philosophy and Feminist Thinking*; Virginia Held, *Feminist Morality*; Nancy J. Hirschmann, *Rethinking Obligation*; Kathleen B. Jones and Anna G. Jonasdottir, eds., *The Political Interests of Gender*; Terry R. Kandal, *The Woman Question in Classical Sociological Theory*; Ellen Kennedy and Susan Mendus, eds., *Women in Western Political Theory*; Angela R. Miles and Geraldine Finn, eds., *Feminism from Pressure to Politics*; Andrea Nye, *Feminist Theory and the Philosophies of Man*; Susan Moller Okin, *Women in Western Political Thought*; Martha Lee Osborne, ed., *Woman in Western Thought*; Carole Pateman and Elizabeth Gross, eds., *Feminist Challenges*; Maja Pellikaan-Engle, ed., *Against Patriarchal Thinking*; Arlene W. Saxonhouse, *Women in the History of Political Thought*; Janet Siltanen and Michelle Stanworth, eds., *Women and the Public Sphere*; Nancy Tuana, *Woman and the History of Philosophy*.

century to as late as the reorganization of the United Nations after World War II. (This last subject, incidentally, is the only one for which there is substantial coverage in other anthologies, listed in Chapter 6; even so material came to light which is not otherwise available.) The subject of gender relations is itself given some coverage on two subjects: violence against women and the regulation of prostitution.

I wish to argue no less than that the social sciences would be different now if the work of these women had been given the attention it merited.[2] The loss of their distinctive contributions has resulted in a skewing of the field. There would have been a more positive approach to the social contract, and less enthusiasm for the models of Hobbes and Rousseau, if the women were seriously read. Writing on such prosaic subjects as to how to make government work, on how the social classes can make the necessary compromises to live and work together, would form a greater and more esteemed part of the political science oeuvre. Evaluative studies on government programs would have become common. Applied social science itself would have had greater respectability. The routine use of statistics and evaluation in the field of health would have resulted in more emphasis on health promotion and preventive medicine, and less on treatment of disease after the fact. There would have been less reverence for the double standard of sexual morality. Work on prostitution—its institutions, causes and measures for its control—would have been very different if a number of these women theorists had been listened to. (For starters there would have been no compulsory examination of women and pimping would have been treated as a serious crime.)

In international relations more attention would have been accorded to the development of institutions for the peaceful settlement of conflicts; there would have been less glorification of war and military virtues. There would have been more early work on the little discussed subject of the links between society and nature. There would have been less insistence on a radical separation between humans and other species. Similarities across the species would have been paid more heed and human *responsibility* for animals instead of *rights* over them would have been more often asserted.

In other respects the loss of women's contributions has not resulted in a skewing of the field, but simple impoverishment. There have been excellent essays, letters and books by women on the welfare state, class relations, inequality, socialism, republican principles, the French and American Revolutions, British imperialism (India and Ireland) and the anti-slavery movement. The selections to come will show interesting analyses and perspectives, short of being substantively different from those of male theorists of the same time.

---

[2] See my chapter, "Classical Social Theory with the Women Founders Included" in Charles Camic, ed., *Reclaiming the Sociological Classics*, 1998.

Introduction

The book is organized chronologically, by author. The short Chapter 2 reports the work of early theorists (Pisan, Astell and du Châtelet). Chapter 3 deals with the French Enlightenment and the great revolutions, French and American. The lengthy Chapter 4 covers social conditions and social reform, reporting the work of nineteenth-century mainstream sociologists (Tristan, Martineau, Nightingale, Taylor and Webb). The last two chapters are again on nineteenth-century theorists, now with several running into the twentieth century. These short chapters deal with gender and violence (Chapter 5) and peace, war and militarism (Chapter 6). Chapter 6 notably picks up on work reported by the first theorist, Pisan, and relates to themes on the benign or violent qualities of basic human nature raised in all the previous chapters.

In no case is all the work of the theorist in question presented (that would require an encyclopedia-length work). For each selections were made of material that corresponds with major themes in social and political theory. These themes are identified and introductory material not only sets the context for the writer herself but relates it to other work reported. A major theme is the *social bond*, a major general and positive term to that of *social contract*, the preferred term of so many male political theorists. Here we will see a thoroughly different approach to that typical of mainstream, male political theory, and one with implications for the rest of the material to be discussed. There are substantial sections on government, including constitutional issues, revolution, rights and obligations, specific issues like federalism, Parliament and the public service, including practical recommendations on how to make government function better. It is remarkable that women took such interest in the workings of government when, except for a few royals, they were entirely excluded from it for most of the period in question, and only peripherally involved in the case of several of the last writers. There are themes of gender roles, but only on two topics, violence against women and the regulation of prostitution. An important theme, but one with few contributions, is *nature and society*, which shows women theorists pioneering what is now treated in environmental sociology and ethics. It, too, relates to other themes, notably violence against women and the social bond. Finally peace, war and militarism are treated as a theme, with contributions at every period of this anthology quite apart from those in the one chapter so labelled.

Women of course were not alone in protesting against war and advocating peace. Indeed most of the women whose work is reported here worked with or drew on the ideas of great men. Nonetheless the number of women and the vigour of their analyses on peace, war and militarism is remarkable, as is their refreshing tendency to de-glorify war. A distinctive women's peace movement only emerged at the beginning of the twentieth century and arguments that women had a distinctive role in the promotion of peace only emerged in World War I. Yet there is a long history of analysis, even from the first contribution in the anthology of the Renaissance. The women's work on peace, war and militarism itself reflects the tendency of women to take a different, more positive, view of basic human nature and the social bond.

For most of the themes the case to be made is that women theorists made contributions that are worthy of consideration, that should be taught, discussed and remembered, although they are not identifiably different as women's work or appropriate to be called feminist theory. In the case of the social bond and some of the work on peace, war and militarism the differences are sharp enough to warrant analysis as distinct, women's contributions. Sections in Chapters 2 to 4 accordingly give comparisons and contrasts with the work of male theorists of the same time.

Thus we will consider how women challenged the harsh depictions of the original state of nature, the war of all against all à la Hobbes and its consequence of a mighty state to which people turn to escape from a life "solitary, poor, nasty, brutish, and short."[3] From early in Chapter 2 we see Emilie du Châtelet stressing the positive, social bonds fostered by women as mothers. Du Châtelet drew on the British political theorist Bernard Mandeville as her source, one that scandalized the established religious authorities (both Catholic and Protestant), but served to make her case for positive links, notably love, rather than fear as the fundamental bond. Catharine Macaulay, similarly, expressly repudiated the Hobbesian vision of early society. Macaulay's discussion of sympathy drew on the Enlightenment moral sentiments tradition. Germaine de Staël similarly not only rejected the totalitarian version of the social contract but described research on the notion a "useless study," its results "metaphysical novels," presumably a crack at Rousseau's *Social Contract*.[4] Later still Nightingale's different approach to some military issues reveals her very positive conceptualization of basic human nature, one similar to that of other women theorists but very different from what prevailed in the War Office.

Women, as men, were excited by the French Revolution and the prospect of acquiring new political rights. The Revolution inspired declarations of rights that changed political discourse from then on although it failed to give women their rights. **Olympe de Gouges** was guillotined for demanding equal political rights. Another victim of the guillotine was Mme Roland, whose essay "On Liberty," which is reproduced here, is as stirring as any. It is unaccountably neglected in the literature on political rights, although Roland herself attained fame by dying bravely.

Gender issues have been given only limited coverage here, notably on the double sexual standard in the regulation of prostitution through the Contagious Diseases Acts. Such important subjects as suffrage, married women's property rights, and access to education and occupations, however, are not included for

---

[3] Thomas Hobbes, *Leviathan* 186.

[4] De Staël, *Circonstances actuelles*, Omacini 280.

Introduction 7

there is a strong and growing literature on them.⁵ The case to be made here rather is that women have made important contributions to the mainstream subjects of political and social theory. Many, although not all, wrote additionally on what are clearly women's issues, such as the vote, legal rights, education and participation in the labour force.

Some of the earlier writing is difficult for a contemporary reader. I have tried to make this work easier to read by updating spelling, capitalization and punctuation, breaking up overly long paragraphs and sentences and eliminating the superfluous use of "and" and "but." Spelling has been standardized to UK English. Even so the examples and style of writing may seem distant. Some readers may find it easier to skip the earlier items at first and come back to them after reading the more accessible later work. Short biographies are provided for major contributors (somewhat more extensive for the lesser-known writers than the better-known), only a brief biographical note for minor contributors. Major publications of the writers are provided in the bibliography at the end of the anthology, where also full citations are provided for all references in the text. To avoid the excessive use of footnotes, subsequent references to the same work are indicated in parentheses in the text.

To facilitate further reference page references are given both for the actual work used and recent editions, including facsimile reprints. In no case will my text be identical with any of the listed sources, for considerable editing has been done to make the work as accessible as possible to contemporary readers. As well errors in printed texts have been corrected.

A Note on Sexist versus Inclusive Language

How little the rights of man/droits de l'homme actually included rights for women can be seen in the inscription on the Panthéon in Paris, dedicated to the "Grands Hommes: la patrie reconnaissante." Indeed, until April 1995 the Panthéon honoured only male persons; the few women buried there were included only in their capacity as spouses.⁶ Realizing how little generic "man" or "l'homme" really are, those of us who agitated for the inclusion of sex in the Canadian Human Rights Code in the 1970s insisted on a genuine generic: human rights/les droits de la personne.

In *Women Social and Political Theorists* I use inclusive language and avoid the use of "man" as a generic for my own writing. But the English texts selected here frequently use "man" as a generic and the translations are all from the

---

⁵ Two excellent examples are Jane Lewis, ed., *Before the vote was won*; Susan Hamilton, ed., *Criminals, Idiots, Women and Minors*.

⁶ As one of his last acts of office, President François Mitterand attended the reburial of the ashes of Marie Curie (with those of her husband Pierre Curie) at the Panthéon.

French, where *l'homme* is the common generic.[7] *All* the contributors to this volume used man (or *l'homme*) as a generic at least some of the time; some made efforts to use "individual" and "human", et cetera, occasionally. I did not change these expressions as it seemed that this would intrude too much our sensibilities onto others' texts. In places it is not clear if "man" is a generic or refers only to males, for example in Hobbes's social contract and commentaries on it. I give what clarification I can in footnotes.

The positive presentation of this work by women is not meant to suggest that women theorists in general (or these in particular) are more virtuous, egalitarian, socially conscious, pacific or democratic than men. It is simply the case that many women theorists articulated extremely interesting and sometimes inspiring ideas, theories, analyses and claims. The influence of their writing is shown, where possible. Some of this writing is further of great contemporary interest. Women and men alike will benefit by exposure to this sometimes lost, sometimes difficult-to-find material. For women readers there is the additional benefit of enlightenment regarding one's own history and identity.

It is hoped that this anthology will prompt further work, both the publication of full texts of neglected scholars and the critical discussion of their work and its influence. I am working with a team of scholars on a collected works of Florence Nightingale. I belong to the recently formed Harriet Martineau Sociological Society and actively encourage other publishing projects. I share in the work on women theorists of the International Sociological Association, Research Group on the History of Sociology. There is more than ample material of high quality to justify a collected works of a number of the women theorists included in this anthology, notably Mary Astell, Catharine Macaulay, Harriet Martineau, Beatrice Webb and Jane Addams. An English collected works of Germaine de Staël would be a valuable addition to the political science literature, as would indeed a new French edition.

---

[7] In Greek and German there are separate terms and hence no excuse for "man" as a generic; *Menschen* and ανθροποι should be translated as "people" or "humans."

Chapter 2

Early Theorists

"Oh, you, knight who comes from such a battle, tell me, I pray you, what honour did you win there? Will they tell of your deeds to honour you more, that you were on the winning side that day?" [8]

CHRISTINE DE PISAN (C. 1364-C. 1431)

Christine de Pisan[9] is often acknowledged as the first woman professional writer (she supported herself and her family by her writing). Her father was educated in Padua and her own education reflects the progress in learning there. She lived most of her life in France where her father was employed at court. She published in French.

Peace, War and Militarism

Pisan addressed issues of war and peace in several of her numerous writings. Two are reproduced here, a lamentation on civil war and a discussion of the criteria for a "just war." Christine de Pisan lived in France at the time of the "Hundred Years' War" (1337-1453), itself a continuation of conflicts of the thirteenth century. Her "Lament on the Evils of the Civil War," written 1410, is a touching protest against the war still in course. It is not a denunciation of all war, but indeed called for the army to fight "our natural enemies," not kill one another (95). After recounting the horrors of war Pisan called on all with authority—princes, queen and clergy—to do what they could to end the war. She recalled the bravery of the Sabine women who threw themselves, with

---

[8] Pisan, "Lament on the Evils of the Civil War," *Epistle of the Prison of Human Life* 87.

[9] See Charity Cannon Willard, *Christine de Pizan. Her Life and Work* and Susan Groag Bell, "Christine de Pizan."

their children, into battle. Otherwise there is little specific to gender; war is a tragedy for all.

In an age of chivalry and knightly honour this author questioned the honourableness of doing battle. Pisan said God would be pleased if men on both sides had not the courage to bear arms (87). She would be followed by numerous women in this de-glorification of war. She warned that the outcome of all battles was unknown and even victories might be too painful, questioning the value of a "just quarrel."

Christine de Pisan's *Feats of Arms and Chivalry*, 1408-09, includes a discussion of the principles for a "just war." First published in French, it was translated into English and published by the first English printer, William Caxton, in 1489, as *The Book of Fayttes of Armes and of Chyvalrye*. It seems that no full version is available in either modern English or French.[10] The passages that are excerpted below constitute a loose "translation" into contemporary English. As an indication of its lack of accessibility consider the following example:

Thenne apperteyneth it onely vnto souerayn pryncesse tentreprise warres & bataylles / now is it for be taken hede for what causes after the lawe ought to be emprised or mayntened warres & in this wel aduysed (11).

As a result, Pisan's statement of just war theory is often referred to but seldom read.

In Book 1 of *Feats of Arms and Chivalry* Pisan explicated the strenuous requirements for a conflict to be considered a "just war." There were the usual ingredients that date back to Augustine of Hippo: that its purpose must be to sustain right and justice against serious evil and oppression, that it must be undertaken only by a sovereign prince, only after seeking impartial counsel and with significant prospect of success. Her treatment of the steps that must be taken by the sovereign before undertaking war is exceptional in its demands. The sovereign must seek the advice of wise counsellors not only from his own country but from other countries not party to the dispute. The prince must offer terms of restitution, summoning the adversary to so inform him. Only if he refuses may the war be undertaken. The text is a very free translation/updating of Caxton's edition.

---

[10] An excellent short excerpt is included in *Writings of Christine de Pizan*, ed. Charity Cannon Willard: 292-309. This partially overlaps my selection, and has the merit, which mine does not, of having been based on an original manuscript in the Bibliothèque Nationale in Paris.

Text: Pisan, "Lament on the Evils of the Civil War," *Epistle of the Prison of Human Life* 85, 87, 89, 93:

Alone, and suppressing with great difficulty the tears which blur my sight and pour down my face like a fountain, so much that I am surprised to have the time to write this weary lament, whose writing the pity for the coming disaster makes me erase with bitter tears, and I say in pain: Oh, how can it be that the human heart, as strange as Fortune is, can make man revert to the nature of a voracious and cruel beast? Where is reason which gives him the name of rational animal? How can Fortune have the power to transform man so much, that he is changed into a serpent, the enemy of humankind? Oh, alas, here is the reason why, noble French princes. With deference to you, where is now the sweet natural blood among you which has been for a long time the true summit of kindness in the world? Ancient times are full of all true stories about it and Fame used to sing its praise throughout the whole world. What became of the sharp eyes of understanding which wise men of just conscience in their counsel made you open by nature and long habit? Are the fathers of your French assembly now blind, as it seems, under whose eyes the numerous children of a land once blessed, were protected, defended and nurtured, a land now desolate, if pity does not work its influence? What wrong have those men done to you, they who, like God, loved you, and who are reputed to honour you in every land? It seems that you want to treat them, not as sons but as mortal enemies, because the discords between you—grief, war and battle—are haunting them.

For God's sake! For God's sake! high princes, let these facts open your eyes and may you see what the preparations for taking arms will achieve in the end; thus you will see ruined cities, towns and castles destroyed, and fortresses razed to the ground. And where? In the very heart of France! The noble knights and youth of France, all of one nature, one single soul and body, which used to defend the crown and the public good, are now gathered in shameful battle one against another, father against son, brother against brother, relatives against one another, with deadly swords, covering the pitiful fields with blood, dead bodies and limbs. Oh, dishonourable victory to the one who wins it! What glory will Fame give to it? Will it be crowned with laurels? Ah me, it will have to be shamefully bound with black thorns when it sees itself, not as a victor, but as the very killer of its own blood, for whom it is fit to wear black, as in the death of kin.

Oh, you, knight who comes from such a battle, tell me, I pray you, what honour did you win there? Will they tell of your deeds to honour you more, that you were on the winning side that day? May this peril, although you escaped it, be counted against your other good deeds! Because it is not proper to praise an adventure which is not blameless. Oh, would that men, since it would indeed please God, had not, on either side, the courage to bear arms!

What will follow, in God's name? Famine, because of the wasting and ruining of things that will ensue, and the lack of cultivation, from which will spring revolts by the people who have been too often robbed, deprived and oppressed, their food stolen here and there by soldiers, subversion in the towns because of outrageous taxes which will have to be levied on the citizens and dwellers to raise the needed money, and above all, the English will obtain checkmate on the side, if Fortune agrees to it. There will also be dissensions and mortal hatreds which will be rooted in many hearts...and which will engender treason.

Is it thus decided? Yes, indeed! So, cry, cry, beat your hands and cry...you ladies, damsels and women of the kingdom of France! Because the swords that will make you widows and deprive you of your children and kin have already been sharpened! Oh, ladies of the city of the Sabines, we would have needed you for this task, for the dangers and the quarrels that once were between your kin were not greater, and you, very wisely, decided to establish peace when you threw yourselves with hair dishevelled into the battlefield, your children in your arms, and in great numbers shouted: "Have pity on our dear loved ones! Make peace!"

Oh, crowned Queen of France, are you still sleeping? Who prevents you from restraining now this side of your kin and putting an end to this deadly enterprise? Do you not see the heritage of your noble children at stake? You, the mother of the noble heirs of France, revered princess, who but you can do anything, and who will disobey your sovereignty and authority if you rightly want to mediate a peace?

Come, all you wise men of this realm, come with your queen! What use are you if not for the royal council? Everyone should offer his hand. You used to concern yourselves even with small matters. How shall France be proud of so many wise men, if now they cannot see to her safety, and the fount of the clergy keep her from perishing? Where then are your plans and wise thoughts? Oh, clerics of France, will you let Fortune work its influence? Why do you not walk in processions and pray devoutly? Do you not feel the need for it? For you resemble Nineveh, which God condemned to perish, and which received His wrath because of the great sins which were many there, and because of this, the situation is very doubtful, unless the sentence is revoked by the intercession of devout prayers...

For God's sake! For God's sake! Noble Duke, please do say soon that—although it is now discussed in various tongues on each side that hopes for victory in the battle and they all say: "We will win and work for it"—they are bragging foolishly. For it must not be ignored that the outcome of all battles is strange and unknown. For although man proposed it, Fortune disposes it. What good did it do to the King of Thebes to leave as victor of the battle with only three men and no more knights, with all his kin dead on the field, lying with the multitude of his enemies killed by the swords of his parents and princes? God, this victory was too painful! Was the victory of the

King of Athens, mortally wounded in battle, of any worth to him? Is a multitude of men an advantage in such a case? Was Xerxes not defeated, although he had so many men that all vales and hills were covered with them?

Are a good reason and a just quarrel of any value? If it were so, the king Saint Louis, who won so many beautiful victories, would not have been defeated at Tunis by the infidels. What better example is it than to know that God, by marvellous disposition, lets all battles run their course, the outcome of which is certainly evil, and whose resulting good is extremely doubtful. Above all, although war and battles are in all cases very dangerous and difficult to avoid, no doubt that among such close kin, tied by nature in one bond of love, they are perverse, dishonourable and to be condemned if one cannot draw them to a good conclusion. Alas, if it has to be that wars and battles are begun for many reasons and quarrels, then they should also be avoided and shunned by better and more valid reasons, and peace should be sought.

So let virtue overcome vice now! Let one way be found to bring to peace men who are loved ones by nature, and enemies by accident. Alas! Would to God that the trouble and the mobilization that is now displayed be used to seek peace instead of the opposite! I believe the cost would be less, and that this army, by a common will and true unity, should be directed against those who are our natural enemies, and that the good and faithful French should take care of these people and not kill one another. God! What joy this would be! And what high honour would it be to the kingdom forever!

Text: Pisan, *Book of Fayttes of Armes and of Chyvalrye* 9-16:

It appears manifest that God permits wars undertaken for just cause for in Holy Scripture we find many places where our Lord himself ordained to captains of hosts what they should do against their enemies...Also Holy Scripture says that God is fierce and the governor of hosts and battles. War and battle for just cause is none other than right execution of justice. Divine law accords laws ordained by the people seemingly to repress the arrogant and malefactors...although other authors say that nothing comes of the right of war but evil of the people. It appertains to no one to undertake war or battle for any manner of cause but sovereign princes like emperors, kings and dukes...

Now we will pay heed to the causes for which wars may be undertaken or maintained...The first is to sustain right and justice, the second to withstand an evil that would defile, grieve and oppress the land, country and people, the third for recovery of lands, seigneuries or other things taken and usurped by unjust cause....

There are three principal causes by which it is lawful for a king to undertake or sustain arms, war or battles. The first is to bear and sustain the church and his patrimony against any men that would defile it....The second is for his vassal if he have a just quarrel and the said prince has to make accord between the parties, in which the adversaries will not negotiate, and third is that the prince may justly, if it please him to aid and help another prince, baron or other ally, friend or any country or land, if that the quarrel be just. In this point women, widows and orphans are included—all those who may have been wronged by another's power....It is lawful to a prince to engage war or to maintain it to recover his proper things lost...But [war is not lawful] for vengeance for some grief received...or to take foreign lands. Alexander the Great, the Romans and others are much praised in titles of chivalry and it seems that they have greatly revenged their enemies, be it well or evil...[but] I find it not in divine law nor other scripture that for these two causes...[it] is lawful to make war or battle on Christian men, but on the contrary by the law of God it does not appertain to man to take or usurp anything of others nor to covet it. Vengeance it seems has been reserved to God and not to man....

It is true that a prince may lawfully exercise for himself the same rights as for another. Yet this just prince who is wronged by others' might and power ought to obey God's law to depart and forbear and not do more to defend justice than the feat required for the trespass. For that he shall hold back, assemble great counsel of wise men in his parliament or in the council of his sovereign if he be subject. And he shall not only assemble them of his country...but to put out all suspicion of favour also of foreign countries that may be known not to adhere to either party...as well ancient nobles, jurists and others....They will report to him their determination of right....Then he shall summon his adversary to seek restitution and amends for the injuries and wrongs received. Then if the said adversary deliver defences and gainsay it he must be entirely heard without favour to himself in any wise....After all this is duly done and the said adversary be found to refuse to come to right and law the prince may justly and surely undertake war, the which ought not to be called vengeance but pure execution of rightful justice.

[While it is lawful for a prince to undertake a just war it must not be for "light motives" but for "great and powerful things" that "touch the life, blood, honour and chances" of large numbers of people.]...No prince should lightly put himself in peril of destruction of fortune which no one may know to what side it shall turn. [Plato is cited on the happiness of countries wisely governed.] There is nothing for which wisdom is more necessary than war....For there is no fault made in any matter less reparable than that which is executed by arms....[Before undertaking battle] a prince must examine and heed what power he has, as much of people as of money...And it should be much better to a prince if he feel himself not well provided of treasure or of rich subjects full of good will to aid him, to make some treaty with his enemies if he feel himself assaulted, or to depart and forbear undertaking war rather than to begin if he has not the wherewithal to continue it. For, he can be certain that if he undertakes war hoping to take more of his subjects than they may bear and against their will, the number of his enemies shall increase....

The prince captain ought not despise the power of his enemies though it seem little to him for he may not know what fortune the other shall have....Therefore to the end that he be not deceived he shall assemble to council the four estates of his country which ought to be called.

> "Upon the principles of reason, the good of *many* is preferable to the good of a *few* or of *one*, a lasting good is to be preferred before a temporary, the public before the private."[11]

MARY ASTELL (1668-1721)

Mary Astell[12] received an unusually good education for a woman of her time, thanks to a clergyman uncle. She left Newcastle, where she was born and brought up, at age twenty, after the death of her mother (her father had died earlier). With money sufficient to live on for a year she moved to London. She never married or worked for pay but was supported by wealthy women friends who shared her interests in women's education. She published four full-length books and several tracts and articles. All are witty and incisive. All but one are fierce in their claim for women's equality. This exception is *Letters concerning the Love of God*, 1695, published in the name of her male correspondent, John Norris, but including both their letters. Astell was deeply religious, a member of the Church of England who accepted its doctrines and followed even its ascetic discipline of fasting. Her religious writing shows also her fervent commitment to women's equality (especially *The Christian Religion*, 1705) and the writing on women likewise reflects its basis in Biblical revelation (both *A Serious Proposal to the Ladies*, 1694, and *Some Reflections upon Marriage*, 1700).

Astell influenced Mary Wortley Montagu with her writing. She also assisted Wortley Montagu in her project of encouraging the practice of smallpox vaccination (about which the latter learned while living in Turkey). Both women wrote popular pieces citing the available statistics to promote vaccination, at a time when the medical profession was opposed, and had every interest against the practice being taken up.

Probably on account of her loss of her own family Astell saw the need for some kind of community life for single women. She favoured a Protestant type of college, which would foster learning as well as provide a home. This,

---

[11] Astell, *Christian Religion* 200.

[12] There is an excellent biography: Ruth Perry, *The Celebrated Mary Astell*; see also Florence M. Smith, *Mary Astell*; George Ballard, *Memoirs of Several Ladies of Great Britain*; Ruth Perry, "Mary Astell's Response to the Enlightenment," in Margaret Hunt, et al., eds. *Women and the Enlightenment* 13-40; Joan K. Kinnaird, "Mary Astell and the Conservative Contribution to English Feminism," and my *Women Founders* 37-55.

however, was considered dangerously papist at the time. Astell in fact attempted to establish a college for women but the project, for which she had a donor (possibly Queen Anne) was vetoed by a bishop. Instead she founded a school for girls in Chelsea, to include well-born girls whose families could not afford to educate them. She died of breast cancer, having submitted to a mastectomy without anaesthetic.

Social Bond

Mary Astell in *Some Reflections upon Marriage* unmistakably argues the obligation of superiors to inferiors, insisting that inferiors share common principles of humanity and are as capable as their superiors of enjoying the supreme good. Conservative as she was in many respects on political theory she totally repudiated the classical justification of privilege, that since only a few could enjoy the refinements of life, the slavery or servitude of the many was acceptable. Those in authority, she held, must look on themselves as placed in that position for the good and improvement of their subjects, not themselves. As God's representatives they were obliged to imitate God's good works: meaning justice and equity in law.

Astell moved from this general discussion of superior/inferior relations to those between the sexes. She asked how a man could respect his wife if he had a contemptible opinion of her and her sex. Could he think there is any gratitude due her when he exacted the most utmost services as strict duty? Contemporary readers will note that the problem remains. Abusive husbands/partners today do not feel gratitude for the services they receive from their wives, but expect "the utmost services as strict duty," and then find grounds for complaint/abuse when there is any failure of this impossible standard.

Astell, whose writing career began at the end of John Locke's, was much influenced by Locke in epistemology and, hence, her arguments for women's education. She differed sharply from him in political theory. Astell was a conservative royalist, so that her radical claim for equality between the sexes startles. (Her pro-royalist views are not included here; the contradiction is resolved when it is realized that both positions are derived from her reading of Scripture.) In the first excerpt the point is to show the stress on responsibility and obligation in her social and political theory. And, while this writing predates utility theory, there are intimations of the principle of the greatest good or happiness for the greatest number. The pioneering work by **Francis Hutcheson (1694-1746)** on this principle appeared (posthumously) in *A System of Moral Philosophy*, 1755. **David Hume (1711-76)** published his influential *Enquiry into the Principles of Morals* in 1751. The classic formulation by **Jeremy Bentham (1748-1832)** appeared in his *Introduction to the Principles of Morals and Legislation*, 1780.

Yet Astell was using the concepts of the happiness of the whole community and the "universal and greatest good" in her *Christian Religion* of 1705. She still used the language of good and evil rather than pleasure and pain but the meaning is precisely the same: the aim of maximizing good or happiness (words used interchangeably in the moral philosophy school) and minimizing pain. There is a strong democratic theme in this formulation, no less strong for the royalist proclivities of the author. That is, the good or happiness of the whole community is the criterion for judgment, not the good or happiness of a privileged elite. It is notable that the distinction between charity and justice appears as early as Astell's *The Christian Religion*. England's "first feminist" expressly stated that it was not charity but justice that required people to give up luxuries to supply necessities for those without. Later we will see Nightingale calling philanthropy "humbug." The bonds/feelings from which moral rules develop were natural for these women theorists, but they no less led to notions of justice and obligation. Sympathy did not prompt mere good deeds but developed into rigorous notions of justice.

Bentham later went further than Astell to specify explicitly that sympathy could be as broad as the "whole sensitive creation"—meaning all species with powers of sensation, not just the human race, let alone any particular country or class. Astell's formulation of these principles drew considerably on her religious faith, as had Locke's political theory earlier.

There is an interesting mixture of deference to authority with this decidedly democratic budding utilitarianism. Astell extolled the "majesty of authority" and justified acceptance of an unjust sentence in order to avoid strife.[13] Yet she insisted on the good of the many over that of any individual. There was no "natural inequality" in "mankind in general," or an intrinsic inequality (202). Differences emerged because of differential participation in the "divine excellences" God communicated to people. This fundamental equality underlay the calculation of the greatest good, for no one had a greater claim on happiness than anyone else. Astell's formulation was clear and succinct:

> It is not reasonable, and consequently not best, that my neighbour should endure an evil to procure to me a good not equal in degree to that evil, or that I should refuse pain or loss to procure for another a good that outweighs it. Much more am I obliged to deny myself a little good in order to obtain a great one for my neighbour, and also to suffer a less evil to keep him from a greater (203).

The justification for this strict democracy was the will of God, a democrat evidently. God, who was "no respecter of persons," did not will a good to any creature that would tend to the evil of another. It was God's nature always to will "the greatest good."

---

[13] Astell, *Christian Religion* 200.

Astell used the language of rights, but always embedded in a moral community. Everyone had "a just claim to certain rights and properties from the laws of God or humanity." Hence her *appetite* had to give way to another's *rights*, for "justice is preferable to inclination" (203). Rights were based on human need and justified by Biblical ethics. Thus Astell would give priority to furnishing the *necessaries* of life to her neighbour over *conveniences* for herself. The goods that we enjoy beyond the basic requirements were "committed to our stewardship" for no other purpose than to supply our neighbour's wants. Astell here used arguments that were in the nineteenth century reworked into Christian socialism in Britain and the social gospel in the United States and Canada. They will be seen again in Elizabeth Blackwell's article on Christian socialism.

There are hints of this same line of thought in Astell's earlier *A Serious Proposal to the Ladies*, whose main object was to argue for access to education. The short excerpts here stress the goal of happiness and the necessity of considering the whole community, not just parts of it. We are so interconnected that "whenever one part suffers the rest must suffer with it" (232). This is the principle of *sympathy* later developed by the Scottish moral philosophers and which grounded Bentham's utility theory.

Astell also condemned the tendency to offer inferior things, as charity, to our neighbours, things not good enough for ourselves. This was a worse form of pride than the recipient's despising to accept such a gift. Astell's statement of the justice of the claims of the indigent evidently derives from Lockean principles. In his *Two Treatises of Government* Locke clearly stated the right of people to the products of their labour. He justified the demarcation of private property, but with limits related to the needs of others. Astell took precisely the same position in limiting possessions that were luxuries or conveniences; necessities for all took precedence. Astell's language (and du Châtelet's) may be difficult for the contemporary reader, but it is no more difficult than Locke's and other male theorists who are still read. The excerpt below is taken from an early edition; the third edition is also available in Bridget Hill's *First English Feminist* (110-12).

Text: Astell, *Some Reflections upon Marriage* 50-52:

Superiors indeed are too apt to forget the common privileges of mankind: that their inferiors share with them the greatest benefits and are as capable as themselves of enjoying the supreme good. Though the order of the world requires an *outward* respect and obedience from some to others, yet the mind is free; nothing but reason can oblige it—it is out of the reach of the most absolute tyrant. Nor will it ever be well either with those who rule or those in subjection, even from the throne to every private family, till those in authority look on themselves as placed in that station for the good and improvement of their subjects, and not for their own sakes, not as the reward of their merit, or that they may prosecute their own desires and fulfil all their pleasure. They are the representatives of God, whom they ought to imitate in the justice and equity of their laws, in doing good and communicating blessings to all beneath them by which—and not by following the imperious dictates of their own will—they become truly great and illustrious and worthily fill their place. The governed, for their part, ceasing to envy the pomp and name of authority, should respect their governors as placed in God's stead, and contribute what they can to ease them of their real cares, by a cheerful and ready compliance, with their good endeavours, and by affording them the pleasure of success in such noble and generous designs.

For, upon a due estimate, things are pretty equally divided. Those in subjection, as they have a less glorious so they have an easier task and a less account to give, whereas he who commands has in a great measure the faults of others to answer for as well as his own. It is true, he has the pleasure of doing more good than a private person can, and shall receive the reward of it when time shall be no more in compensation for the hazards he runs, the difficulties he at present encounters...

How can a man respect his wife when he has a contemptible opinion of her and her sex? When from his own elevation he looks down on them as void of understanding, full of ignorance and passion, so that folly and a woman are equivalent terms with him? Can he think there is any gratitude due to her whose utmost services he exacts as strict duty? Because she was made to be a slave to his will and has no higher end than to serve and obey him?

Text: Astell, *The Christian Religion*:

Our *neighbour* is everyone of whom we can do any manner of service, enemies as well as friends. And among all those duties we owe to God, there are not any enforced with greater earnestness than those which for his sake are due to our neighbour. They are preferred some times to those immediate acts of worship that we owe to his own majesty so little reason have we to fancy that we do God service by any rigorous usage of mankind. That we may never be at a loss in our conduct towards them, we are commanded to do to others as we, supposing we judge according to right reason, desire to be treated ourselves. But how depraved soever our judgments may be, the not doing to another that which if we were in his case, and he in ours, we would not desire he should do to us, is a rule of equity of perpetual obligation; to that a *little* share of sense, with *any* degree of honesty may direct us in this matter. Nor can we ever be absolved from any duty to our neighbour that is in our power because being due for God's sake, they must still be paid, whatever returns may be made us by our neighbour.

He who has never heard of Christianity is obliged to love his neighbours because they partake of the same nature. But Christians are under a greater and higher obligation, the duty they owe to one another being founded upon their mutual relation to Christ the head. Therefore, since everyone is, or may be, a member of Christ, he is to be treated with brotherly affection. It is as unnatural for Christians to disobey those whom Christ instituted to *have rule over them* as it is for the inferior members of the body to rebel against the superior. As well may the stomach refuse to distribute into every part of the body the nourishment it receives as Christians refuse to *do good unto all men, especially to them who are of the household of faith* (Galatians 6:10), which, by the way, instructs us to give preference to the best Christian in our acts of kindness and beneficence. Injuriousness among the members of Christ is the same thing as for one member of the body to wound and destroy another. It will be as fatal in one case as in the other for the members to transgress their several duties.

I consider myself therefore as part of one great whole, in the welfare of which my own happiness is included, and, without regarding any particular or separate interest, endeavour always to pursue that which in itself and absolutely speaking, is the most public, universal and greatest good; and to avoid that which absolutely and in itself is the greatest evil. Which principle rightly understood and strictly pursued will at once fill up all the offices of justice and charity, and every other obligation (196-98).

Upon the principles of reason, the good of *many* is preferable to the good of a *few* or of *one*; a lasting good is to be preferred before a temporary, the public before the private. Upon Christian principles...having as I think already proved the authority of holy Scripture, the good of the mind is infinitely preferable to the good of the body; spiritual advantages to temporal and temporal are to be valued among themselves in proportion as they contribute to spiritual and eternal. Christians are members one of another—therefore the good of my neighbour is not to be separated from my own good but to be estimated with it.

From all which it follows, first, in reference to superiors, it is better that I endure the unreasonableness, injustice or oppression of a parent, a master etc. than that the established rule of order and good government should be superseded on my account. It is better that my just pretensions should be thrown out, and my merit, if I have any, should be disregarded, than that I or any other private person should be our own carvers, and forced rewards from our superiors. It is better that I should submit to an unjust sentence than that there should be no end of strife; and that these private persons though ever so innocent should suffer than that the majesty of government, and herein the divine authority, should be violated and the public should be disturbed.

In regard to inferiors, I consider that since the good of many is a greater good than the good of one, it is therefore to be preferred, even though I be that one. That all authority being devolved from God's absolute dominion, such dominion in its last resort arises from the excellency of his nature, by which he is our creator, preserver and constant benefactor; consequently the person and ground of superiority is the supposed excellency of the superior because order and government must be maintained, which could not be, considering the corruption and partiality of mankind, were everyone left to be judge in this matter. Therefore we must submit to him, who by the laws and usages of the place, or by prescription when there is not a better title, has a claim to superiority, even though he be not really better than his neighbours (200-01).

As to mankind in general, among whom there is no natural inequality but what arises from their different participation of those divine excellencies which God is pleased to communicate to them, of which excellencies authority and dominion, though not being in itself, is to be most observed and respected by us because government depends upon it, and without government mankind cannot subsist, I consider that it is not only inhuman but even devilish to hurt or vex my neighbours for no other advantage to myself but the unnatural pleasure of seeing them suffer; that their greater good is preferable to my lesser good; and that a less evil suffered by me is not so bad in itself as a greater suffered by my neighbour. Therefore it is not reasonable, and consequently not best, that my neighbour should endure an evil to procure to me a good not equal in degree to that evil or that I should refuse pain or loss to procure for another a good that outweighs it. Much more am I obliged to deny myself a little good in order to obtain a great one for my neighbour and also to suffer a less evil to keep him from a greater. Nor will I in the main, and taking the *future* into computation, be a loser for giving my neighbour in these cases, and for the *present*, the preference. For the act thus is in reality to pursue my own greatest good, which they, and they only provide for, who conform themselves in all things to the will of God, who is no respecter of persons, and therefore does not, absolutely speaking, will a good to any one of his creatures that tends to the greater evil of another, but who by the prerogative of his nature always wills the greatest good.

To descend to particulars: since everyone has a just claim to certain rights and properties from the laws of God or man, it is fit that my appetite should give place to his rights, and that I should never be gratified to their prejudice. For justice is preferable to inclination, nay, even to necessities—it being better I should suffer some real wants than that, by invading my neighbour's property, the laws of society and good government should be broken. Besides, it is a fundamental rule that among corrupt mortals no man shall be his own carver, or judge in his own case, to his neighbour's damage.

It is much better that I should want some of the conveniences of life than that any of my neighbours should want the necessaries; nay, that I should abridge myself in what I may reckon necessaries, rather than that they should be driven to violent necessities and grievous wants. For unless this be the duty of everyone who loves God and hopes for his love, I know not how to make sense of that Scripture, *Whoso hath this world's good, and seeth his brother have need, and shutteth up his bowels of compassion from him, how dwelleth the love of God in him*? (1 John 3:17) Surely a well-tempered mind will make us look with greater joy on the covering we have put upon our neighbour's back than on the gaudery lavished on our own. Every morsel the hungry soul swallows so savourily will afford us a higher taste than all that cost and luxury can furnish for our own table. We shall find a much greater pleasure in making our neighbour's heart rejoice than in satisfying any of our own appetites.

Nor is it charity but justice that requires that our superfluities should be laid out upon our indigent brethren. All that which in the opinion of the soberest and wisest persons exceeds the necessities and moderate conveniences of life, according to that rank which Providence has placed us and not according to what we can compass, or to the extravagances of other people, is a superfluity in God's account, whatever it may be in ours. So that though we may not be unjust to this or that particular person, it is certainly an injustice with respect to God, to waste upon ourselves those goods of His, which he committed to our stewardship to no other end or purpose but that they should be spent in supplying our neighbour's wants.

Therefore all that which we *cannot use* is due to our neighbours; but we could never understand upon what just ground we presume to give them that which we *will not use*, because not good enough for us as we suppose; unless it is upon account of a public character, and to maintain that dignity and station the government has placed us in; splendour and show being the trappings of authority which it must put on to raise a veneration in the vulgar who won't be moved by better reasons. Or else by stipulation and agreement, since it is not unbecoming to give another that which he has sought and submitted to. Or if neither of these, then the real, not pretend, necessities that education and custom have brought upon us may be the excuse. For these do sometimes produce wants that cannot so readily be provided for as the simple and natural necessities of others whose way of living has been less delicate may. But this is far from being an advantage; it is indeed the contrary, he being farthest removed from unhappiness who has the fewest wants and such as are most easily supplied.

In the last place, we may make some allowance to ourselves to avoid singularity and affectation, and in compliance with the decent, not the extravagant customs of those among whom we live. Excepting these reasons there is no manner of ground why I, or any other person, should conclude that to be good enough for another which we do not think good enough for ourselves. It is without dispute a greater pride in us to proffer our offal to our neighbour than it can be in him to refuse or despise them (202-06).

Text: Astell, *Serious Proposal* 232-33:

When we consider that we are but several parts of one great whole, and are by nature so connected to each other that whenever one part suffers the rest must suffer with it, either by compassion or else by being punished for the want of it, we shall never be so absurd as to fancy we can do ourselves a service by anything injurious to our neighbours.

Nature and Society—Anthropocentrism

Astell, appropriately enough in *Some Reflections upon Marriage*, first published in 1700, compared the dominant male/subordinate female relationship of human society to that between humans as a species and other animals. She questioned the then scarcely challenged view that non-human species were created for human benefit. Her contemporary, **Damaris Masham**, also challenged the conventional belief in human superiority over the "brutes" by virtue of the faculty of reason.[14] The utilitarians would later be much more specific: that animals do not reason was not so relevant as the fact that they *feel*. At this time Astell (and Masham) were arguing that human superiority did not give licence to exploit or oppress, that humans had God-given responsibilities to use their superior qualities for good.

Text: Astell, *Some Reflections upon Marriage* 50-53 (Astell, *First English Feminist*, ed. Bridget Hill 111-12):

Perhaps we arrogate too much to ourselves when we say this material world was made for our sakes. That its glorious Maker has given us the use of it is certain, but when we suppose any thing to be made purely for our sakes, because we have dominion over it, we draw a false conclusion, as he who should say the people were made for the prince who is set over them would be thought to be out of his senses as well as his politics. Yet even allowing that God, who made everything in number, weight and measure, who never acts but for some great and glorious end, an end agreeable to his majesty, allowing that He created such a number of rational spirits merely to serve their fellow creatures, yet how are these lords and masters helped by the contempt they show of their poor humble vassals? Is it not rather an hindrance to that service they expect, as being an undeniable and constant proof how unworthy they are to receive it?

None of God's creatures, absolutely considered, are in their own nature contemptible; the meanest fly, the poorest insect has its use and virtue. Contempt is scarce a human passion, one may venture to say it was not in innocent man, for till sin came into the world, there was nothing in it to be condemned. But, pride, which makes everything serve its purposes, wrested this passion from its only use, so that instead of being an antidote against sin, it is become a grand promoter of it, nothing making us more worthy of that contempt we show, than when, poor, weak, dependent creatures as we are! we look down with scorn and disdain on theirs.

---

[14] Damaris Cudworth Masham, *Occasional Thoughts in reference to a vertuous or Christian Life* 66-67. Not discussed here, her epistemology is briefly related in my *Women Founders* 56-58.

"When a dog meets a dying dog he licks its blood and continues on his way, but if a human meets a dying person the first instinct will be to help. The human will surely help, having nothing to fear from this sign of compassion."[15]

EMILIE LE TONNELLIER DE BRETEUIL, MARQUISE DU CHATELET (1706-49)

Emilie du Châtelet[16] was a member of the French nobility by birth and married the Marquis du Chastellet-Lomont (the name was modernized by her friend **Voltaire**). She had three children by her husband, a French Army general, two of whom lived. At their chateau at Cirey she hired scientists to teach her mathematics and physics. Voltaire was a frequent visitor, lover for a period and intellectual collaborator. She performed in his plays and coached him on physics. Du Châtelet is known mainly for her translation of **Isaac Newton**'s *Principia Mathematica*, which she introduced to French intellectual life, and which includes discussion of **Leibniz** as well.

Social Bond

Bernard Mandeville (c. 1670-1733) scandalized society with his *Fable of the Bees* for its blatant promotion of self interest as the motive force of human morality and cynical treatment of virtue. In verse form, or even doggerel, the *Fable* was first published in 1705 as "The Grumbling Hive," and then, after several other editions, in a much expanded form in 1732. Du Châtelet's very free translation, which she did probably in 1735-38, is of the 1732 text. She not only abridged the work considerably but added her own observations and reflections so that the final form is quite different from the original.[17] In style it is much less humorous, much more staid.

The work represents an important element in the development of Enlightenment thought, the exchange of progressive views between Britain and France. Du Châtelet's friend Voltaire had already brought the British empiricists Francis Bacon and John Locke to wider knowledge in France through his *English Letters*, published in French in 1735, the year after its original English publication. Du Châtelet herself translated Newton's *Principia*

---

[15] Du Châtelet, *Fable of the Bees*, in Ira O. Wade, *Studies on Voltaire with some Unpublished Papers of Mme du Châtelet* 150.

[16] On du Châtelet see Ira O. Wade, *Voltaire and Madame du Châtelet*; Esther Ehrman, *Mme du Châtelet*; René Vaillot, *Avec Mme du Châtelet*, in René Pomeau, ed., *Voltaire en son temps*, vol. 2; Nancy Mitford, *Voltaire in Love*; Theodore Besterman, *Voltaire Essays*; Elisabeth Badinter, *Emilie, Emilie* and my *Women Founders* 73-81.

[17] Ira O. Wade, *Studies on Voltaire with some Unpublished Papers of Mme du Châtelet* 131.

Mathematica from Latin to French to make it more accessible. In translating and commenting on Mandeville's *Fable* she was bringing what can be seen in retrospect as a key component of utility theory to the French. **David Hume** and **Adam Smith** both spent significant, formative years in France where they profited from the French developments of utility theory contributed by **Claude Helvétius (1715-71)** with *On Mind*, 1758, **Paul Thiry d'Holbach (1723-89)** with *System of Nature*, 1770, and **Julien Offray de la Méttrie (1709-51)** with *Man-Machine*, 1747. Du Châtelet's work predates all of the above.

Naturally the question arises as to what influence du Châtelet's translation might have had given that she did not publish it nor was it published at all until 1947. Undoubtedly, as can be seen from his *Le Mondain*, it influenced Voltaire, perhaps the central and most influential exponent of Enlightenment thought. It seems reasonable to consider that du Châtelet's work at least contributed to the climate in which the next developments took place. That is, she helped to make known British secular, radical ideas that stimulated a rethinking of basic social institutions, even the very coherence of society.

The Mandeville/du Châtelet thesis was an early form of utility theory, that by pursuing our own narrow self interests, promoting pleasure and avoiding pain, we are all inevitably acting for the good of society. Adam Smith would later, in the *Wealth of Nations*, 1776, make essentially the same argument, but in a more polished and less provocative manner: "It is not from the benevolence of the butcher, the brewer, or the baker that we expect our dinner, but from their regard to their own self-interest" (14).

Mandeville's purpose was to explain that the bonds that hold society together were neither fear of death à la Hobbes nor the injunctions of religion à la hell, fire and brimstone. The basic elements of morality instead came from an appeal to pride and honour and aversion to shame and dishonour. There were positive incentives to act for the good of society, although for selfish motives not altruistic. Du Châtelet obviously agreed with all this, then added her own statement on love as the fundamental bond. Mandeville's treatment of human nature was cynical, du Châtelet's only slightly less so, but there is the refreshing correction of Hobbes.

The two drew their arguments from nature. Human selfishness could scarcely be avoided for it is part of our very being. Moralists made the mistake of teaching people what they should be, not what they really are. Our notions of good and evil do not, in fact, stem from any religion, the conventional explanation of the time, but from the utility principle. "Laws are to society what life is to the human body," said Mandeville in the author's preface (138). Just as the parts of the body which seem most important to us are not what conserve our life, so also it is not the amiable qualities that make people sociable but their vices. All the riches of a powerful state depend on people pursuing their selfish interest. Innocence and virtue, indeed, would be incompatible with material progress.

Mandeville/du Châtelet's purpose, as for later moral philosophers, was to show how notions of right and wrong and the moral behaviour based on them occur in spite of our relentless pursuit of self interest. In a section of her own writing du Châtelet argued that love was the beginning of society. The procreation of children makes the union of a man and woman last longer than it otherwise would. Families come together out of practical needs "and these mutual needs will give birth to society." Christine de Pisan, discussed above, similarly stressed the role of love and pity. In "Lament for the Evils of Civil War" she called for the leaders of the French nation to *love* their sons, not treat them as enemies (85). If pity did not work its influence the land would be desolate from civil war.

Mandeville and du Châtelet's version of the social contract is more benign than that of Hobbes. They recognized that people only sacrificed their personal interests for the good of society because they were convinced that they gained more in return. No one was so despicable as to be insensible to praise or to accept contempt willingly; flattery induced people "to restrain their passions" for the good of society. However outrageous their ideas, Mandeville/du Châtelet had the merit to offer their theory tentatively: "This is, or at least may be, the way in which humans were civilized" (144). Rousseau, later, was more dogmatic: "That was, or must have been, the origin of society and laws," he concluded in the "Discours Sur l'origine de l'inégalité."[18]

Mandeville/du Châtelet were particularly outrageous in claiming that the first rules of morality stemmed from the cynical use of flattery, which depended on human pride. Instead of the rules of morality being derived from religion, politicians were the inventors of moral rules. Mandeville's repudiation of traditional religion would have appealed to du Châtelet who not only rejected conventional religious belief herself but probably influenced Voltaire to a more extreme heterodoxy himself. Du Châtelet would have approved also of Mandeville's admittedly limited espousal of "natural religion," or the belief that religious and moral principles can be known through reason. Mandeville affirmed, expressly contradicting Locke, that there were "ideas of universal morality," like the golden rule, which were implanted in our hearts by the Creator.

In places du Châtelet disagreed with Mandeville. For example, when he argued that there was no merit in saving a child about to be burned in a fire, because our motive would be to save ourselves from pain, she added a corrective footnote, explaining how virtue was beneficial to society. Mandeville/du Châtelet from time to time tried to obviate criticism from the conventionally religious by pointing out how providential their theory was: that human weakness could serve for social good (150). One suspects, however, that they were deliberately being provocative.

---

[18] Rousseau, *Oeuvres complètes* 3:178.

Du Châtelet's translation and commentary disappeared for a century. It was rediscovered with some of Voltaire's letters in Leningrad and published with them. While one cannot know what her motives were for not publishing the work at the time it is easy to surmise why caution might have prevailed. Voltaire had twice been sent to prison, and went into exile the second time to avoid a prolonged stay, for publishing work less offensive. Du Châtelet was a wife and mother, not a single man. She consigned a number of essays to the bottom drawer.[19]

Some of the examples on which Mandeville and du Châtelet dwelt will seem quaint now: girls learning to curtsy and boys to doff their hat, wedding night customs and feminine modesty in blushing at explicit language. Nonetheless the point they were trying to make remains: the teaching of morals and manners to the next generation was key to the development of social bonds and civilized society.

Text: Du Châtelet, *Fable of the Bees*, in Wade, *Studies on Voltaire* [my translation]:

Author's Preface: Laws are to a society what life is to the human body. Those who understand anatomy know that the bones, nerves, skin and all other parts of the body that most affect our senses, which appear most important to us, are not what conserve our life. This depends on fine lineaments the existence of which the uneducated do not even suspect. Similarly those who study the anatomy of the human mind, if one can so describe it, and who in this research have no regard for the prejudices of education, know that it is hardly good nature, pity, nor other amiable qualities that make people sociable, but the vices which draw the preachers' bile. That is what I have attempted to develop in the following work.

This book [*Fable of the Bees*] suffered from a number of contradictions when it first appeared. Some misunderstood the author's intentions and wanted to poison him, calling the work the satyr of virtue and encouragement of vice. This calumny has made me take on the task of instructing the public of the views I held when I wrote the book. My principal goal was to show how the innocence and virtues of the so-called golden age are incompatible with the riches and power of a great state, and to show the inconsistency of those who take great pleasure in all the commodities of life and other benefits, which are only possible in a powerful state, yet who then do not cease declaiming against the disadvantages necessarily connected with them.

I wanted to show also in what I said about the different professions how the elements which comprise a powerful society are, for the most part, most

---

[19] Her "Discours sur le bonheur", written c. 1747, was first published in 1779 and republished in 1961. Her *Doutes sur les religions révélées* was published posthumously and anonymously in Paris in 1792.

detestable and vile. This analysis would make clear the wisdom and skilful management of legislators who have constructed such an admirable machine from such abject material, who found the means to serve societal good through the vices of its different members.

Having shown the drawbacks to which a nation will necessarily expose itself if its vices are unknown, and in which all individuals are full of honesty, innocence and all sorts of virtues, I show that, if these people stop being what one calls vicious—if one could cure human nature of all its faults and weaknesses—none of the great empires and polished, flourishing societies which histories relate, and which we see in our own day, ever could have existed. If you ask me why I have sought to prove all these things—what good will people obtain from my work—I reply naively that I see well enough how difficult it is to correct things, for fear that the truths contained not be unuseful. But if you asked me what fruit my work should produce I would reply very differently. I would tell you indeed that those who always find fault with others will learn on reading this book to look at their own consciences and see how they are unfair to murmur constantly against abuses which are the source and foundation of all the commodities and advantages they enjoy (138-40).

When I assert for example that vice is inseparable from the grandeur and power of a state I do not say that individuals who are vicious and trouble the order of society should not be rigorously punished. There are few people in London, especially those who go about on foot, who, having regard only for their own convenience, would not wish that the streets were cleaner than they are. But if they thought about what causes the trivial inconvenience of dirty streets, that it is the result of the large number of people who live in this immense city, the prodigious commerce they conduct and the abundance which prevails, I believe there would be few citizens who would complain of the dirtiness of the streets.

Everything depends on immense details to which few people pay attention. We look only at the surface of things. People of leisure who rise only at midday do not know the cost of the work done for their dinner—how carts, beasts and country people must enter the city so that they can be served a delicious meal when they get up. They do not see anything in all this for ease has become so ordinary as to be unremarkable. But the philosopher sees the industry of a whole people who have worked to produce these pleasures. City dwellers for their part see only the filth which spoils their shoes and do not think that cities with clean streets do not enjoy any of the commodities which London procures in abundance even for its least citizens. Surely no one who, on such reflection, would not be forced to agree that London could only be less filthy by being less flourishing and that the dirtiness of its streets is a necessary drawback, the product of the prevalent abundance. This drawback is even useful for some. It is what gives shoe cleaners, street sweepers and garbage collectors their livelihood, people who, despite the low esteem of their occupations, are members of society (140-41).

It seems to me as well that so few people know themselves because moralists have applied themselves to teach what people should be and practically never have dreamed of telling them what they are. Our mind is comprised of different passions as our body is of bone, flesh, muscles etc. These passions govern us step by step and are the source of our virtues and vices. That is what I tried to prove in the first chapter of this work. One will see from where moral good and evil are born and I hope to convince the reader that man owes none of his ideas to any religion. It is well to advise once for all that I do not intend to speak in this research either of Jews or Christians [but only humans in the state of nature and ignorance of the true Deity] (141-42).

The Origin of Moral Virtues

Every animal desires its own happiness without regard to that of others. Thus those that have the least desires would seem to be the most capable of living together. The human being is of all animals the one with the most passions and desires and, for this reason, seems to be the one least fit for society. It is, however, through the help of these same passions that the human is the only one capable of becoming social.

[The following paragraph was not in the original Mandeville]:

Love seems to have been the beginning of society. The human, like all other animals, has an invincible tendency to propagate the species. A man who falls in love with a woman will have children. The care of their family makes their union last longer than it would have from choice. Two families will have need of each other from the moment they were formed, and these mutual needs will give birth to society....Mutual needs, having brought people together, the most adroit of them realized that man was born with indomitable pride; it was from the hold this passion had on them that the first legislators drew the greatest aid to arrive at human civilization.

It would have been impossible to persuade men to sacrifice their personal interest for the good of society if one could not have shown an equivalent for the violence taken away. Pride furnished legislators this equivalent. They examined the forces and weaknesses of our nature, remarking that no one was so despicable as to tolerate contempt nor savage enough to be insensible to praise. They correctly concluded that flattery was the most powerful argument for men. Using this resource they brought praise without bounds to bear for the excellence of their nature and their pre-eminence over other animals. Having thus made themselves heard, they gave people ideas of honour and shame, painting one as the greatest good to which one can aspire and the other as the greatest of evils.

They then tried to persuade people that their understanding, the faculty that raises man over all other visible beings, must manage their senses and repress their desires; that to abandon oneself without reserve would be to act as animals, and that the difficulties we have in containing our desires must excite emulation rather than discourage us. To introduce this emulation they divided people into two classes. The first was comprised of the vulgar who, doing nothing but satisfying their desires, are incapable of sacrificing anything for the good of society, for the common good. This vile and grovelling multitude is, they said, the scum and shame of humanity, having but a human figure to distinguish themselves from animals. But the other class was formed of those who, knowing the dignity of our nature, know how to restrain their passions and subordinate them to the good of society and humanity: "He who conquers himself is stronger than one who takes the greatest fortress" (142-44).

Thus legislators, having an interest in human pride—by dividing people into two classes—it is hardly astonishing that they would have such an impact with their lessons. Even those whose hearts are the most corrupt constrain their desires and shout even louder than the others to sacrifice everything for the public good. Hence all have wanted and still want to be of the first class, even if, in the bottom of their hearts, they belong to the second.

This is, or at least may be, the way in which men were civilized, which well proves that politicians invented the first rules of morality in order to govern the multitude more securely. But the foundations of politics once in place, men inevitably were civilized, sensing that the surest means to satisfy their desires was to moderate them. Men then decided to name *vice* any action prejudicial to society and to name *virtue* all those actions that reasonable expectation of bringing good.

That is why the names *vice* and *virtue* are sometimes given to opposite actions in different countries, for the needs of society are different in different climates. But in every country what one calls *virtue* is what conforms to the established laws, and *vice* is what is opposed to them, for no society can subsist without having laws, as no one can play if there are no rules of the game. Similarly as something is an error in one game of cards but not in another, what is vice in Paris is virtue in Constantinople. But all people agree to observe their own established laws and regard acts as good or bad according to their conformity with or opposition to these laws.

There is a universal law for all that God himself engraved in people's hearts. This law is do not do to others what you would not that others do to you, and I believe that the wise Locke went too far when, after destroying all innate ideas, he proposed that there are no ideas of universal morality. There is no people, however barbarous it might be, who, from the first appearance of society, would be permitted to fail at one's word. Society requires this law as its foundation, and the needs which are different in different countries can be combined in this maxim: *do not do to others what you would not want others to do to you.* The good of society is, in truth, the sole *criterion* of vice and virtue. But this maxim is not only indispensable in our civilized society, for everyone has it imprinted on his heart. It is the necessary consequence of the natural benevolence we have for our species: goodness which the Creator has put in us and which effect we feel involuntarily, as we do hunger and thirst.

It is true that without these laws and punishments inflicted on those who harm others, personal interest would win out often over the *dictamen* of nature, for self-respect is, with reason, stronger than good will for our species. But when our interest does not suffice, there is no one at least with the sense not to assassinate his neighbour for pleasure. One will object perhaps that no society could have been formed before men agreed on some sort of religion directed to a supreme power, and consequently that our notion of good and evil, or vice and virtue, are not the work of politicians but of religion. I dare to assure you that the superstitions of the nations who do not know the true God, and the pitiful notions they have of the Supreme Being, are scarcely capable of prompting people to virtue. However history makes us see that even with such ridiculous, mistaken ideas of the divinity, human nature has furnished us with examples of all the moral virtues (144-46).

Moral virtues owe their origin then not to any religion but politicians' skilful management. The further we pursue our research on human nature the more we will be convinced that moral virtues are the political offspring that flattery engenders from pride. Anyone, however modest, can be made to appreciate artful praise. Children and fools will accept flattery in large doses but the more cunning require circumspection. The more general the praise the less suspect it is. What you say of a city's benefits will please all its inhabitants. Commend its literature and all scholars will be obliged to you. To flatter someone skillfully praise his profession or country (146-47).

This type of recompense—glory—consists of a delicious felicity a man who has performed a noble action enjoys in contemplating the applause he will win. I shall doubtless be told that, independently of the stirring actions of the ambitious and conquerors, generous acts are done in silence, for which virtue is its own reward. That those who are really good find satisfaction in the testimony of their conscience, and that among the pagans even, there are people so far from seeking praise and applause for doing good they take great pains to ensure that those who benefit from their good deeds do not know to whom they are indebted. In response I would point out that, in order to judge the merits of an action, one would have to have done it oneself, for that is the only way to understand thoroughly the motives for it. Self love is a prosthesis that takes more than one form. Pity, for example, even if it is the least dangerous of our passions and the one that most resembles virtue, has, however, like the others, its source in pride. It is one of the weaknesses of our nature, the same as anger or fear. It is what makes weak minds the most susceptible, so that no one is more compassionate than women and children.

Pity is a natural impulse that consults neither the public interest nor reason. It results equally in evil and good. It has sometimes served to destroy virgins' honour and judges' integrity, and whosoever acts by it as a principle, whatever good they accomplish cannot claim to have done anything but satisfy a passion. There is no merit in saving a child about to be devoured by fire because it is not its safety that makes us act but the desire to save ourselves from pain we would feel in seeing the child perish in flames had we not followed the natural impulse to save it.

[The following footnote by du Châtelet corrects Mandeville's argument]:

This is false even according to the principles of the author, for to save a child from fire is a very useful action for society, and in some senses is regarded as an act of virtue and not to do it would be a serious crime.

This involuntary unease we feel when we see one of our own in actual danger is a trait that the Creator himself imprinted onto his work. Man seems to be the only animal that has this benevolence towards its own species. Other animals have received an instinct for preservation and propagation from the supreme being. Several know pride and emulation, but none are marked by the love of their species that is engraved in the human heart and which appears to be one of the distinctive traits which separate different beings. When a dog meets a dying dog he licks its blood and continues on his way, but if a man meets another man his first instinct will be to help him. And he surely will help, having nothing to fear from this sign of compassion.

We extinguish this dictate of nature. People, despite their mutual good will, do not leave themselves to be eviscerated in pitched battle for mutual assassination. The bank [of the Seine] is always full of strollers who flock there for an execution, but none of the king's murderers, nor the onlookers whose curiosity seems so cruel, did not first have to overcome that natural benevolence which is never entirely erased from our soul (149-50).

A rich person who is naturally compassionate cannot brag of being virtuous (in the sense moralists attach to the word virtue) when he or she does good, for in effect this person is only satisfying his or her own passion in helping a wretch. *Gaudeant bene nati* [Those born well rejoice] is a sensible expression; its truth is recognizable in so far as one knows human nature. Those who, without any weakness or self reflection, are capable by the love of doing good alone to perform their good deeds in the shadow of silence, have no doubt purer ideas of virtue than others. I do not know, however, if one cannot perceive traces of pride even in these sorts of people (if there are any), for the most humble of all people must admit that the internal satisfaction felt on performing a good deed consists in the pleasure one feels in being well thought of. Pleasure and what prompts it are as sure signs of vanity as going pale and trembling are symptoms of fear.

If some readers condemn these ideas on the origin of moral virtue for offending Christianity I hope they will see how unfair such a suspicion is when they consider that nothing can better justify the impenetrable depths of

Providence, to show that human weaknesses can serve for social good and the good of others (151-52).

Honour and Shame

Men are so jealous of the opinion of others that soldiers who are dragged into war as punishment for crime, forced by blows into fighting, want to be esteemed for what they would have avoided if they could. Still, if men had as much reason as pride, they would blush from undeserved praise rather than seek it. *Honour* in the usual sense of the word consists in the good opinion of others, and is counted more or less substantial the more or less noise is made about it. Thus when it is said that the sovereign is the fountain of honour, this means only that he can confer distinctions on whomever he pleases, the same as he has money minted, and his power is the source of respect accorded, whether deserved or not.

The opposite to *honour* is *dishonour*, which consists in the contempt others have for us. One is the reward for virtue, the other the punishment for vice. The less public the contempt the less degraded the person. Honour and dishonour are imaginary things but ignominy, the shame we feel when we believe ourselves to be despised, is a real thing. This is a passion which has its symptoms, like other things, which often cannot be overcome by the force of reason. The power it has over us, and the part it often has in the most important actions of our life, make us conscious of its necessary causes and effects and careful research of its nature may be humanly useful (155-56).

Shame and pride—these two sources of our virtue—are not imaginary qualities but the necessary elements of our composition. Nothing proves better that the different effects these passions produce in us are the same in spite of ourselves. See how a person overcome with shame is brutalized, his blood flows out of the heart to the extremities, his face blushes, he doesn't dare lift his head, his eyes cloud over and look down, no injury can move him, his whole being becomes heavy and he will try to hide himself from others. Pride has entirely different symptoms. When this passion is aroused his blood runs faster, an extraordinary warmth strengthens and enlarges his heart...he feels light, he could walk on air, he lifts his head high, his eyes are bright, he is happy to be alive and would be glad to have all the world see his glory and satisfaction, he is easily angered and thinks everybody should yield to him.

Of all the weaknesses of our nature shame is the one we tolerate most impatiently and no one knows how to avoid or overcome it. But it would be injurious to society if we could vanquish it. No emotion is more necessary for human happiness nor has contributed more to human civilization. We seek therefore to strengthen it in children far from endeavouring to destroy it as we do other passions. We propose only to avoid the things that attract shame. But those who know human nature would be angry if humans stopped being susceptible to shame (157-58).

The difference in modesty between the two sexes is often attributed to nature but is really the result of early teaching. *Miss* is scarcely three when she is careful to cover her legs. She is scolded if she shows her leg, but her brother at the same age is taught to lift up his jacket and piss like a man. It is education which induces everything in us we call decency. Someone who told everything like it is...would be the most honest man in the world but would be regarded as the most contemptible. If there were a man gross enough to say to a woman *that he had a violent desire to take her straight away to propagate the species*, and that he was about to begin, the woman would be enraged and the man would be regarded as a brute and no one in civil society would accept him. There is nobody who, to avoid such shame, would not conquer the strongest desires. But if virtue requires us to subdue them, good breeding obliges us only to conceal them (160).

Modesty is founded on shame, a passion that makes us do either good or bad according to circumstances. Thus it takes equally the face of vice and virtue. It is shame, it is true, that prevents a courtesan from letting herself go in a public place, but it is shame also that forces a timid, well-born girl who has lost her virginity by seduction to kill her own child to avoid dishonour. Well-off people can easily conceal their pleasures and avoid awkward results but the poor cannot. An unfortunate daughter of good family is left without bread and other resources to live...She might have a good heart, religion even, and succumb however to a weakness she long fought. If this unfortunate becomes pregnant from her mistake her despair is inexpressible, the wretchedness and dishonour of her condition become clear to her in all their horror. She will lose her reputation, the only thing fortune left her. The esteem she acquired in her mistress's mind and in her house serve only to increase her sorrow. She sees the joy of her enemies, the sorrow and shame of her parents and protectors who will regard her as their disgrace. The more modest she is now the greater the fear of shame and the more trouble and despair to her soul. To avoid it there is no extremity she is not capable of—against herself and the unlucky offspring of her error.

It is commonly believed that a girl who destroys her baby, which she has carried nine months in her womb, must be a monstrous barbarian of a different nature to that of other women, but this idea is false. The same girl who kills her bastard with the most atrocious cruelty would be a tender mother with legitimate children. Self love is the centre of all our passions; it joins the tenderness of all mothers for their children and silences the voice of nature in the unlucky girls that fear of dishonour makes so barbarous. It rarely happens that common prostitutes kill their children. Women even who take part in the crimes of robbers and murderers seldom do this, not because they are less cruel or more virtuous than mothers who are guilty of it, but because they have lost their reputation. The fear of shame does not make the same impression on them.

What is not the object of our senses cannot be the object of our love. Nature says nothing to the tenderest mothers for infants who are still in the uterus "because this love is not necessary for their conservation." Love grows when these little creatures begin to express their desires and needs, and it acquires sometimes a prodigious degree of force. Maternal love has made the sex weak and timid of things that appear to surpass its force. We have seen mothers rush into the middle of danger to save their children, but the most virtuous women have nothing on the most detestable. In both tenderness is a blind instinct which takes them without regard for the good or ill it does society. And there is no merit in all that this excessive love makes them do.

[The following paragraph is not in Mandeville's original]:

It is perhaps in infancy only that nature speaks truly to mothers. It is not in what follows, that the movement of a wheel which continues to turn, though the movement of the hand that pushes it does not any more. Habit, duty and above all self-love take the place of the first dictate of nature, and it is perhaps true to say that it does not act differently between hens and women. The object for both is the preservation of the individual that it confers to their care. The hen who attaches herself to duckling chicks serves as well the veiies of nature in the conservation of these little animals as if she were raising her own.

In the same way a woman will love with the same tenderness an infant that is not hers if in fooling her one has prevented her imagination to oppose the impulse of nature. The only difference is that one can fool hens more easily than women. The excessive love of certain mothers for their children very often has been harmful to the infants, and if it was useful to them in infancy, it corrupts them often in the end. Maternal tenderness has brought more than one to the gallows.

The passions can sometimes make for good, but there is no virtue to surmount them. If modesty were a virtue by itself it would not have the same power over us that our action be unknown or known, which most assuredly is not the case. The first thing that men seek to persuade women they want to seduce is that their goodness to them will be forever unknown. There is no young woman who does not start by flattering herself and men who have a little experience know that it is fear of shame and not love of virtue they have to combat in women (162-64).

(LADY) MARY PIERREPONT WORTLEY MONTAGU (1689-1762)

Mary Wortley Montagu, whose connection with Astell has already been noted, was a brilliant writer of letters in a period in which this was a highly polished art. She also published political satire, editing an anti-government periodical, *The Nonsense of Common Sense*, 1737-38, in which she published a pro-woman essay (not included here) and a witty proposal to end corruption in politics—by abolishing Parliament. Wortley Montagu was the daughter of a duke, thus a Right Honourable Lady, wife of a titled British ambassador and mother-in-law of an earl/prime minister.[20] The body politic was a common metaphor from medieval times on. Here we see it being used for irony.

Text: Wortley Montagu, "An Expedient to Put a Stop to the Spreading Vice of Corruption":

The man that has sold his vote has taken the order of roguery upon him, solemnly renounced shame, and from that moment gives himself no farther trouble either to be or appear honest in any part of life, so far corruption influences our national morality....But how can we prevent this contagion after it has gained so strong a head that it passes among foreigners for a part of our constitution?

I humbly propose we may have no more Parliaments....I entirely agree with our patriots that Parliaments are an essential part of our body politic and I believe no man alive will deny but that legs and arms are essential and useful parts of the human body, but when a leg or an arm is so far corrupted that there appears no possibility of restoring it to its primitive soundness, all wise physicians advise the lopping it to stop the spreading corruption. No man would be thought in his senses that would choose to perish whole rather than lose a part that no longer answered the end of its being (45-46).

I here solemnly declare in the face of God and the holy angels that I nor any of my friends either enjoy or hope to enjoy any place in the government; as to my friends I think it is almost impossible, for I know none that I have; as to myself, I am sure it is impossible for a private reason that I have, which I do not think fit to show any man alive.

My proposal proceeds from a sincere love to my poor countrymen who, to preserve the shadow of a liberty which they never had, are enslaved by the worst and basest methods....Now if we good people (I now speak to real Commons of England not their pretended representatives) had the sense to make the king a present of our nominal liberty all at once...we should leave him at liberty to act the dictates of his own royal mind without constraint, and his minister would not, as the poor man is now often forced to do, advance a known blockhead or scoundrel, which even he knows to be such, to a good place because he is cousin to the wife's brother of the wife of a Parliament man, nor would a man of real merit and learning die unobserved in a little curacy or starve in a garret in Lincoln's Inn for want of such alliance. Merit would then be the road to preferment, emulation would be raised amongst the younger sort, and everyone endeavour to shine in his profession when there

---

[20] The only full, scholarly biography is Robert Halsband, *Life of Mary Wortley Montagu*; see also my *Women Founders* 62-73.

was no other way to be distinguished in it; sense, probity and courage would be recommendations at court instead of the influence over a county or the part played at the last election, and honour be no longer the jest of polite company (46-47).

I see nobody that has any reason to oppose this scheme but those who are conscious to themselves that they have nothing to recommend them but a certain profligacy of principles that renders them proper tools in a mixed government and would certainly be laid aside as useless in a plain one....The king, who is honest himself, would take pleasure in preferring an honest man, and Sir R. who went formerly to school himself, would show some value for a scholar, and at worst, if our late posterity should see on the throne a knavish king, and he should employ even a wicked minister, the greatest villain upon earth does not love another villain if they have no dirty work for them to do....

I am so well convinced of the universal benefit that would arise from this proposal I heartily pray God could open the eyes of the people to see it as plain as I do and instead of bellowing about the excise and mobbing the minister, the whole city would rise, and with a great deal of good manners surround the Parliament House the first day of their meeting, telling them plainly they are a pernicious set of people who assume to themselves a power of defrauding poor tradesmen of just debts, turn them all out of doors, distinguishing some few, by some gentle kicks, and assure them they should meet there no more, to cant liberty, promote slavery, talk pertly of the king and sell the subject (48-49).

Peace, War and Militarism

The two short excerpts that follow show an utter disdain for military institutions quite uncharacteristic of the aristocracy.

Text: Wortley Montagu, *Complete Letters* [19 July 1759]:

Algarotti is at Bologna, I believe, composing panegyrics on whoever is victor in this uncertain war;[21] and Vallisnieri[22] gone to make a tour to add to his collection. Which do you think the best employed? I confess I am woman enough to think the naturalist who searches after variegated butterflies, or even the lady who adorns her grotto with shades of shells, nay, even the devout people who spend twenty years in making a magnificent presepia at Naples, throw away time in a more rational manner than any hero, ancient or modern.

---

[21] Her friend Algarotti was supporting his former patron, Frederick II of Prussia, in the Seven Years' War.

[22] Antonio Vallisnieri, Professor of Natural History at the University of Padua, was a great collector.

The lofty Pindar who celebrated the Newmarket of those days, or the divine Homer who recorded the bloody battles the most in fashion, appear to me either to have been extremely mistaken or extremely mercenary (3:220-21).

Text: Wortley Montagu letter to her daughter, Lady Bute [September 1752]:

When I reflect on the vast increase of useful as well as speculative knowledge the last three hundred years has produced, and that the peasants of this age have more conveniences than the first emperors of Rome had any notion of, I imagine we are now arrived at that period which answers to fifteen. I cannot think we are older when I recollect the many palpable follies which are still (almost) universally persisted in. I place that of war amongst the most glaring, being full as senseless as the boxing of school boys, and whenever we come to man's estate (perhaps a thousand years hence) I do not doubt it will appear as ridiculous as the pranks of unlucky lads. Several discoveries will then be made, and several truths made clear, of which we have now [no] more idea than the ancients had of the circulation of the blood, or the optics of Sir Isaac Newton (3:17).

> "Why may not [a woman] exercise her soldiers, draw up her troops in battle array and divide her forces into battalions at land, squadrons at sea and so forth with the same pleasure she would have in...ordering it to be done?"[23]

Sophia

Peace, War and Militarism

Sophia, the Greek word for wisdom, is obviously a pseudonym; the writer of *Woman not Inferior*, 1739, from which this excerpt is taken, may have been Mary Wortley Montagu.[24] The book itself is a spirited defense of women's abilities and a claim for equal treatment. Sophia argued women's *capability* for military roles and *right* to pursue any occupation. Sophia also poked fun at the military. A woman as much as a man could read a map, charge, retreat, lay ambushes, feign and make false attacks. Differences in strength by sex might be due to differences in education or opportunity for exercise. Later in the book Sophia sought to clarify her position. By arguing women's natural abilities for military offices she did not mean that she wanted women in the military, but simply to expose the silly, masculine notion that women were naturally cowards or otherwise unfit for the army.

---

[23] Sophia, *Woman not Inferior* 49.

[24] On the authorship issue see my *Women Founders* 70-71.

Early Theorists/Sophia

Text: Sophia, "Whether Women are naturally qualified for military offices or not," *Woman not Inferior*:

I must confess I cannot find how the oddity would be greater to see a lady with a truncheon in her hand than with a crown on her head, or why it should create more surprise to see her preside in a council of war than in a council of state. Why may she not be as capable of heading an army as a parliament, or of commanding at sea as of reigning at land? What should hinder her from holding the helm of a fleet with the same safety and steadiness as that of a nation? And why may she not exercise her soldiers, draw up her troops in battle array and divide her forces into battalions at land, squadrons at sea and so forth with the same pleasure she would have in seeing or ordering it to be done?

The military art has no mystery in it beyond others which *women* cannot attain to. A *woman* is as capable as a *man* of making herself, by means of a map, acquainted with the good and bad ways, the dangerous and safe passes or the proper situations for encampment. What should hinder her from making herself mistress of all the stratagems of war, of charging, retreating, surprising, laying ambushes, counterfeiting marches, feigning flights, giving false attacks, supporting real ones, animating the soldiery and adding example to eloquence by being the first to mount a breach. Persuasion, heat and example are the soul of victory, and *women* can show as much eloquence, intrepidity and warmth, where their honour is at stake, as is requisite to attack or defend a town.

There can be no real difference pointed out between the inward or outward constitution of *men* and *women* excepting what merely tends to giving birth to posterity. The differences thence arising are no ways sufficient to argue more natural strength in the one than in the other, to qualify them more for military labours. Are not *women* of different degrees of strength like *men*? Are there not strong and weak of both sexes? *Men* educated in sloth and softness are weaker than *women* and *women*, become hardened by necessity, are often more robust than *men* (49-50).

What has greatly helped to confirm *men* in the prejudiced notion of *women's* natural weakness is the common manner of expression which this very vulgar error gave birth to. When they mean to stigmatise a man with want of courage they call him *effeminate* and when they would praise a woman for her courage they call her *manly*. But as these, and such like expressions, are merely arbitrary and but a fulsome compliment which the *men* pass on themselves, they establish no truth.

The real truth is that humanity and integrity, the characteristics of our sex, make us abhor unjust slaughter and prefer honourable peace to unjust war. Therefore, to use these expressions with propriety, when a man is possessed of our virtues he should be called *effeminate* by way of the highest praise of his good nature and justice. And a *woman* who should depart from our sex by espousing the injustice and cruelty of the *men's* nature, should be called a *man*;

that is, one whom no sacred ties can bind to the observation of just treaties and whom no bloodshed can deter from the most cruel violence and rapine.

Be this as it may, certain it is that bare strength entitles the *men* to no superiority above *us*...otherwise brutes would deserve the pre-eminence of them. Among themselves the strongest man ought to be the chief in power, whereas we plainly see that, generally speaking, the strongest are only fit to make drudges to the rest. Particularly in armies, they who have most of brutal vigour are often useful only for fascines [bundles of sticks] to men much weaker than themselves to mount a breach. On the other hand, men who have less strength have very often the most brains. The wisest *philosophers*, the ablest *poets* and the greatest *princes* have not always had the best constitutions (51-52).

It is quite idle then to insist so much on bodily strength as a necessary qualification to military employments. It is full as idle to imagine that *women* are not naturally as capable of *courage* and *resolution* as the *men*. We are indeed charged, without any exception, with being timorous and incapable of defence, frightened at our own shadows, alarmed at the cry of an infant, the bark of a dog, the whistling of the wind or a tale of hobgoblins. But is this universally true? Are there not *men* as void of courage as the most heartless of our sex? Yet it is known that the most timorous *women* often make a virtue of necessity and sacrifice their own fears for the safety of a husband, son or brother. Fearful and weak as they are, they often behave more courageously than *men* under pains, sickness, want and the terrors of death itself (52).

It is far from being true that all *women* want courage, strength or conduct to lead an army to triumph, any more than it is that all *men* are endowed with them. There are many of our sex as intrepid as the *men*, and I myself could, with more ease and less repugnance, dare the frowns and fury of an already victorious army which I had forces to resist, than I could stoop to court the smiles of a corrupt minister whom I had reason to despise (54).

There is no *science*, *office* or *dignity* which women have not an equal right to share in with the *men*. Since there can be no superiority but that of brutal strength shown in the latter to entitle them to engross all *power* and *prerogative* to themselves, nor any incapacity proved in the *former* to disqualify them of their right but what is owing to the unjust oppression of the *men*, and might be easily removed.

With regard, however, to warlike employments, it seems to be a disposition of *Providence* that custom has exempted us from them. As sailors in a storm throw overboard their more useless lumber, so it is but fit that the *men* should be exposed to the dangers and hardships of war while we remain in safety at home. They are, generally speaking, good for little else but to be our bulwarks. Our smiles are the most noble rewards which the bravest of them all ought to desire, or can deserve, for all the hazards they encounter and all the labours they go through for our defence in the most tedious campaign (55-56).

From what I said in my former treatise concerning the natural ability of *women* for military offices, no one could well be so weak as to imagine I wanted my sex to be admitted to any share in them. The contrary must appear very plain from what I there said. I neither meant nor could mean anything more than on one hand to expose the excessive silliness of the *men* who force themselves to believe from the *women's* being excluded from warlike exercises that they are naturally cowards and therefore unfit for them, and on the other hand to show that the heart of *woman* is no less capable by nature of that steady resolution which makes up virtuous courage, than her head is of that sense and discretion which is requisite to distinguish the proper occasions for exerting it. I think I have already so fully proved that the *men* have not more title to either than the *women*, that it is needless to add much more on that subject. If the *men* are more hardy than we are, that advantage...ought greatly to be attributed to their difference of education. Were both sexes equally exercised the one might possibly acquire as much vigour as the other (91-92).

Social Contract versus Social Bond

Carole Pateman's devastating critique of classical social contract theory, *The Sexual Contract*, 1988, focuses on the omission of the "sexual contract," the tacit contract between the sexes that accompanies the contract that governs the male, public domain. The case she persuasively makes is that only half the story is typically told. Yet Pateman's analysis remains a contemporary, feminist critique of earlier male theory, however right she is that:

> The original contract is merely a story, a political fiction, but the invention of the story was also a momentous intervention into the political world; the spell exerted by stories of political origins has to be broken if the fiction is to be rendered ineffective (219).

Agreed. And women centuries before us, indeed contemporaries of the male contract theorists at issue, have contested those theories and offered their quite different alternatives.

C.B. Macpherson, in his influential *Political Theory of Possessive Individualism*, 1962, argued that the roots of modern liberal democracy lie in the theory and practice of seventeenth-century England: its Parliamentary struggles, civil war, republican experiments, restoration of the monarchy and constitutional revolution. The essential ingredient was "a new belief in the value and rights of the individual" (1). The theorists on which he drew, **Hobbes**, **Locke**, **Harrington** and various Puritans and Levellers, were all men and the staunch individualism they espoused is quite different from any formulation we will see by women of the same period. The eighteenth- and nineteenth-century theorists of liberal democracy he cited were men, notably **Jeremy Bentham**, **J.S. Mill** and **T.H. Green**. Yet when we examine the work of women theorists of the same time we will see that it did not have to be thus. Accordingly we will be able to challenge Macpherson's conclusion that the later failures of liberal democracy cannot be gotten rid of by removing the utilitarian excesses, as Mill tried to do, because the central difficulty is contained in the original seventeenth-century conceptualization of the individual.[25]

The excerpts both here and in later chapters show that women's conceptualizations were not fraught with the same difficulty as those discussed by Macpherson. Thanks to their roles as child-bearers and nurturers, women theorists developed notions of responsibility, community and obligation which radically modified their views of individual rights. The excesses of possessive individualism Macpherson describes as pertaining to so many male theorists simply do not hold for theorists like Astell, du Châtelet, Macaulay, de Staël and Wollstonecraft. Macpherson argued that the conditions of the "state of nature" described in fact reflected the conditions of the theorists' own time, notably the growth of the market economy and the sense of individualism it engendered. But women were, as now, less involved in the paid economy than men. Those that were had significant roles to play also as unpaid homemakers and raisers of children. Clearly the reality for women was different from that of men. More women at all stages of this development drew on their roles as mothers, especially in theorizing on socialization and social cohesion.

Macpherson's analysis was grounded in Hobbes, notably for his discarding traditional concepts of society, justice and natural law and deducing political rights and obligation from the interest and will of dissociated individuals. Hobbes's own conclusions were, of course, not liberal, but the postulates he used to derive them were, as were later developments from them. Locke in turn modified Hobbesian theory and Bentham's utilitarianism also built on it. In Macpherson's reading, Hobbes's state of nature, the most negative of any of the social compact theorists, was the most significant for the development of the principles of liberal democracy. It is given as follows in *Leviathan*:

> It is manifest that, during the time men[26] live without a common power to keep them all in awe they are in that condition which is called war, and such a war as is of every man against every man. For war consists not in battle only or the act of fighting, but in a tract of time wherein the will to contend by battle is sufficiently known....So the nature of war consists not in actual fighting but in the known disposition thereto during all the time there is no assurance to the contrary (185-186).

---

[25] See his essays on utilitarianism (1861) and Bentham (1833) in Mill, *Collected Works* vol. 10.

[26] It is not always clear if Hobbes meant male persons only or all human beings.

Hobbes then explained that in such conditions there was no place for industry because the fruit of it was uncertain. Nor was there agriculture, navigation, trade, building, efficient transportation, arts, letters or society. "And which is worst of all, continual fear and danger of violent death and the life of man, solitary, poor, nasty, brutish and short" (186). Of course women theorists did not agree with the "solitary" portrayal of early human beings, insisting that there was always some form of community of mother/parents and children.

The corollary to this dismal portrayal of the original state of nature is a complete lack of notions of justice and right or wrong, another point which women theorists will vigorously dispute. Again, from Hobbes's *Leviathan*:

> To this war of every man against every man this also is consequent, that nothing can be unjust. The notions of right and wrong, justice and injustice have there no place. Where there is no common power there is no law, where no law no injustice. Force and fraud are in war the two cardinal virtues. Justice and injustice are none of the faculties neither of the body nor mind....They are qualities that relate to men in society not in solitude (188).

None of the women theorists included in this book ever made such a sharp break between society and a preceding state, for they imagined some form of society existing at all times and under any conditions, that based on a mother and her children. Astell, Wollstonecraft, de Staël and Macaulay, as utilitarian theorists generally, saw notions of justice and law evolving gradually through the process of sympathetic identification.

Macpherson, in *Political Theory of Possessive Individualism*, found fault with the original seventeenth-century formulation of individualism as follows:

> Its possessive quality is found in its conception of the individual as essentially the proprietor of his own person or capacities, owing nothing to society for them. The individual was seen neither as a moral whole, nor as part of a larger social whole, but as an owner of himself. The relationship of ownership, having become for more and more men the critically important relation determining their actual freedom and actual prospect of realizing their full potentialities, was read back into the nature of the individual. The individual, it was thought, is free in as much as he is proprietor of his person and capacities....Society becomes a lot of free individuals related to each other as proprietors of their own capacities and of what they have acquired by their exercise. Society consists of relations of exchange between proprietors. Political society becomes a calculated device for the protection of this property and for the maintenance of an orderly relation of exchange (3).

But this does not hold true for the women theorists. For them the prototype individual was a mother in a relationship with dependents. Some explicitly treated men/fathers in the same way. Ownership simply did not have the same significance and freedom was always qualified by the relationship of responsibility.

Hobbes's state of nature was a logical not a historical hypothesis, an inference made from the "passions" or emotions governing behaviour. His object was to describe what life would be like with no common power to fear without positing any particular, let alone necessary, phase of development. Yet this inference is precisely what women theorists repudiated, to argue instead that the passions/emotions led to positive bonds between mother and child and the teaching of moral behaviour that restrained aggression. Hobbes's view in *Leviathan* was quite different:

> The passions that incline men to peace are fear of death, desire of such things as are necessary to commodious living and a hope by their industry to obtain them (188).

Women theologians, both contemporary and earlier, have typically rejected "death-centred" religious doctrines, for the same reasons women social and political theorists have downgraded fear of death as a factor in promoting social cohesion. Fear of death simply does not figure prominently on the lists of qualities women theorists have devised as factors in promoting moral/social bonds. Perhaps their greater involvement in birth and the care of the young gave them these other ideas. As the great thinkers of the eighteenth-century Enlightenment would have it, positive bonds of sympathy were crucial, and these were based on feelings, identification with suffering and the desire to prevent or avoid it. There were direct links between this sense of sympathy and the elucidation of principles of morality. The desire for a better standard of living by co-operation and trade are also stressed by the women theorists but, while with Hobbes this *follows* fear of death, with the women theorists it *accompanies* the positive bonds from feelings.

It is no coincidence that the same women theorists preferred Locke's milder version of the state of nature in *Two Treatises of Government* to Hobbes's.[27] In Locke's state of nature people were considered to be capable of setting rules for themselves by perceiving their utility, without setting up a sovereign. Contemporary feminist critics correctly point to important anti-woman aspects of Locke's social contract.[28]

---

[27] Women theorists were attracted also to Locke's epistemology for it permitted arguments for women's education. See my *Women Founders* 56, 82, 99.

[28] For a good discussion of this point see especially Lorenne M.G. Clark, "Women and Locke," in Clark and Lynda Lange, *The Sexism of Social and Political Theory* 16-40; and

John Rawls's influential *Theory of Justice*, 1971, takes up the classical challenge of deriving obligation using a form of social contract theory. Although he devoted a whole section to "the connection between moral and natural attitudes," he paid no attention to Astell, du Châtelet, Wollstonecraft, Macaulay or indeed any of the women theorists whose work is related here. Drawing from Adam Smith's *Theory of Moral Sentiments* Rawls raised some of the same sorts of naturalistic points they did, so that one can only regret that he did not know/use their contributions. He even went so far as to the call the moral sentiments "a normal part of human life," which could not be done away with "without dismantling the natural attitudes as well." They were continuous with those attitudes in that "love of mankind and the desire to uphold the common good include the principles of right and justice" (489).

Rawls's theory of justice was constructed so as to avoid anyone being advantaged or disadvantaged by the "natural contingencies" of intelligence, strength, status, et cetera (12). This is very similar to Astell's argument for government's function as an *equalizer*, to smooth over the disparities. For Rawls inequalities in basic rights and duties could only be justified if they resulted in "compensatory benefits" for all, and in particular for the least advantaged members of society (14). Again this is very similar to Astell's treatment.

Diana Coole, *Women in Political Theory* 53-77.

Chapter 3

Theorists on Revolution

"By [Hobbes's] dogmatic assertion that the state of equality is the state of war, it is plain that the poor philosopher is ignorant of the following truth, that political equality and the laws of good government are so far from incompatible that one never can exist to perfection without the other."[29]

CATHARINE SAWBRIDGE MACAULAY (LATER GRAHAM) (1731-91)

Catharine Sawbridge[30] was given an excellent classical education at home in Norwich. All her political writing was influenced by this early exposure to Roman history, which persuaded her of the superiority of republican institutions over monarchical. On marrying a Scottish physician, George Macaulay, she settled in London. She was widowed soon after the birth of her only child, a daughter. Macaulay began publishing her eight-volume *History of England* soon after her husband's death. Her history, unlike David Hume's notoriously conservative *History of England*, was severely critical of the monarchy, and monarchical-like rulers such as **Cromwell**. It differs from Hume's also in being well documented, from her research in primary sources in the British Museum.

Macaulay's political publications excerpted below all show a fervent republicanism (her pamphlets as well as the *History* and her more philosophical *Loose Remarks on Hobbes's Philosophical Rudiments*). Her work was well received in the United States where it helped move opponents of British rule to a principled rejection of monarchy in favour of democratic

---

[29] Macaulay, *Loose Remarks on Hobbes* 12.

[30] The superb biography by Bridget Hill, *Republican Virago*, is especially good on political theory.

republicanism. The French revolutionary leader **Mirabeau** thought her *History* important enough to arrange for its translation into French during the French Revolution.

Macaulay travelled in France in the 1770s where she met leading reformers like the Intendent **Turgot** and the American **Benjamin Franklin**. Her second marriage, to a younger man of lower social rank, damaged her reputation. Yet this unconventional marriage proved to be enormously happy for both partners. Macaulay travelled with him in the United States, where they were received by **George and Martha Washington**, and which resulted in the correspondence excerpted later.

Her last book is a tour de force, *Letters on Education*, 1790, one of the great classics of feminism for its advocacy of women's education, and notable as well for its contribution to a more humane, indeed environmentally-conscious utility theory. This was the book that made Mary Wollstonecraft an advocate of women's equality. It also influenced the early American women's movement but then disappeared. It is available again in facsimile edition.

Social Bond

Macaulay's *Loose Remarks on Hobbes* was a twenty-page essay attacking his *Philosophical Elements of a True Citizen* and especially his portrayal of the state of nature—or human nature without the benefit of society—and the rights and obligations stipulated in the social contract. Her analysis was logical and legalistic. Hobbes had argued that a contract between the sovereign and the people existed; what then were the grounds for breaking it? For him a sovereign, on acquiring his immense powers from the people, had no obligation to them for they ceased to be "people" when they handed over their power. Macaulay countered that a contract had to be mutually binding. If the monarch refused to perform as contracted, the people regained the rights they had transferred to him. The sovereign himself was no more than one of the multitude. She added that there could be no lawful contract without an obligation for people could not rationally divest themselves of rights without expecting something better in return. Note how she used rational argument to defend popular rights. Macaulay similarly scorned Hobbes's rationalization that a monarch could do his subjects no harm for they had subjected their "right and will to defend themselves" to him. This was an argument Rousseau used also, although Macaulay here dealt only with Hobbes. Here we see Macaulay blending right and obligation, contrary to the possessive individualism argument discussed earlier.

Macaulay's language was lively. The essay was in effect a tract, albeit directed to refuting a work published a century earlier! Yet the substance of the work was current. Bridget Hill in *Republican Virago* (Chapter 3) pointed out that the 1760s and 1770s were a period of radical revival in England. Macaulay was directly involved herself and indirectly through her brother, **John**

Sawbridge, a well-known supporter of **John Wilkes** and the movement for a Bill of Rights. Macaulay's other writing of this period dealt with specific rights, like freedom of the press, and measures to curtail the powers of the monarch and government. Here in demolishing Hobbes she was going to the theoretical source of the sovereign-has-all-rights school. This was not an academic dispute but a matter of urgent public policy.

Text: Macaulay, *Loose Remarks on Hobbes's Philosophical Rudiments*:

Mr Hobbes, in his *Philosophical Elements of a True Citizen*, sets out with an intention to confute this received opinion, that man is a creature born fit for society. To do this he enumerates the vicious affections inherent in human nature, which affections are confined to the innate quality of selfishness. From these premises he draws this inference, that man cannot desire society from love, but through hope of gain. Therefore, says he, the origin of all great and lasting societies consisted not in the mutual good-will men had toward each other, but in the mutual fear they had of each other (1).

A monarchy, says Mr Hobbes, is derived from the power of the people transferring their right to one man. The whole right of the people conveyed on him, he can then do whatsoever the people could do before he was elected, and the people is no longer one person but a rude multitude, as being only one before by virtue of the supreme command, now conveyed from themselves on this one man. This elector monarch can do his subjects no injury because they have subjected their right and will to defend themselves to him. Neither does he oblige himself to any for the command he receives, for he receives it from the people, who cease to be a person as soon as that act is done and, the person vanishing, all obligations to the person vanish.

A contract made by two contracting parties must be equally binding; therefore Mr Hobbes's figure of the dissolution of the person does not serve his argument a whit, for if the person, namely the people, dissolves the obligation, if void of one side, is so of the other. If the person continues any breach of the contract, though it only affects an individual, disfranchises the person from the obligation of performing their part of the contract. And if a people, in transferring their right to the monarch, look upon themselves dissolved as a body and return to so many individuals, yet if that monarch refuse to perform those stipulated articles previous to his being vested with that right, that right forfeited returns again to the people and he himself is no more than one of the multitude. Farther, there can be no such contract without an obligation mentioned or supposed, for the will of the contractor is necessary to the making a lawful contract, and no rational person can will so absurdly as to give up his natural right to another, without the proposing to himself more advantages than he could otherwise have enjoyed, had he not divested himself of that right (4-6).

We know that the right of parents to expose their children has been the civil law of many countries, but that they have a natural right so to do is a bold assertion of Mr Hobbes, which nature and reason contradict. The mother's care for the preservation of her young is an invariable dictate of nature through all her works. Different animals have many qualities opposite to each other and peculiar to their different species. Yet the tenderness of maternal feeling is common to all and is a compelling force to obey this dictate. The human species are more strongly bound to this obligation than brute animals. Reason and morality strongly urge the care and preservation of an existence by themselves occasioned as a duty never to be omitted; by the law of justice, therefore, they, being thus bound to this act, cannot have it in their option whether they will do it or not. But Mr Hobbes will rather advance any absurdity than own that power has its rights from reasonable causes.

We are of Mr Hobbes's opinion that it is very absurd to derive the right of parents over their children from the act of generation; their right proceeds only from the tender feelings which are inseparable from the quality of parents. This is the first natural obligation owed by children; this makes it more advantageous for them to be under the commands of their parents than under any other government. The many benefits which a parent confers on a child in the helpless state of infancy adds to the first natural obligation. In a maturer age these obligations have force enough to make it the duty of a child to obey his parents in all things, if their commands are not opposite to the laws of his country or the dictates of reason. But, as this authority has only its right from supposed benefits bestowed, it must be greater or less in proportion to the degree of those benefits. Parents who are enemies, instead of benefactors, forfeit that right, which alone has its foundation from the obligation of received benefits.

Mr Hobbes, in his comparison of the state of nature with the civil, says that the grievance of subjects does not arise from the ill institution or ordination of the government, because in all manner of governments subjects may be oppressed, but from the ill administration of a well-established government. We agree...that the grievances and oppression of subjects arise from the ill administration of government, but...if Mr Hobbes was as well acquainted with the science of policy as he is adept in the art of confounding things, he would know that the peculiar excellence of a government, properly constituted, is to raise those to the administration whose virtues and abilities render them capable of this arduous task and to deprive those of that office, who upon trial are found at all defective. Therefore, a well-constituted government can never be so long ill administered as to become a grievance to the subject.

Mr Hobbes, in his praise of monarchy, says that the following arguments hold forth monarchy as more eminent than other governments. First, that the whole universe is governed by one God; secondly, that the ancients preferred the monarchical state beyond all others; thirdly, that the paternal government, instituted by God himself, was monarchical; and, lastly, that other governments were compacted by men on the ruins of monarchy. That the universe is governed by one God we will not dispute, and will also add that God has an undoubted right to govern what He has himself created, and that it is beneficial to the creature to be governed by the Father of all things. But that this should be an argument for a man to govern what he has not created, and with whom a nation can have no such paternal connection, is a paradox which Mr Hobbes has left unsolved. The second argument, that the ancients preferred the monarchical state before all others, is an assertion contradicted by the only civilized societies in ancient history, namely the Greeks, from whom alone we can learn ancient prudence. They disdained this government, and called all pretenders to it tyrants and usurpers.

The third argument, that the paternal government instituted by God was monarchical, is an assertion which is contradicted by many examples in the only history through which we know of this institution. The power Adam had over his children is not mentioned as of the monarchical kind. We find him nowhere exercising this power or claiming it as his due, and yet there could not have been a more equitable occasion for exercising it than the perfidious murder of Abel presented. But, if Mr Hobbes could prove that the paternal power instituted by God was monarchical, he cannot from this conclude that the monarchical government is preferable to all others, without falling into his usual absurdities, namely that a man ought to have a right of governing creatures whom He has not generated because God has given him a right of governing creatures whom he has generated (7-10).

Because, says Mr Hobbes, we have shown that the state of equality is the state of war, and that therefore inequality was introduced by a general consent. This inequality, whereby he whom we have voluntarily given more to, enjoys more, is no longer to be accounted an unreasonable thing. By this dogmatic assertion, that the state of equality is the state of war, it is plain that the poor philosopher is entirely ignorant of the following truth, that political equality and the laws of good government are so far from incompatible that one never can exist to perfection without the other (12).

Our author's next assertion is that subjects are often less undeservedly condemned under one ruler than under the people. I could wish he had taken the pains to have given us one single instance to support this assertion; I really do not know one example in settled governments where the power of the people ever, through malice, wantonness or rapaciousness, tortured or put to death one fellow-citizen. If such accidents have ever happened, it has been through mistake and these examples are so rare that, were he to produce them against the numbers of innocent, worthy people who have suffered under monarchical power, they would be found as light in the balance as his own empty arguments against proofs positive (17-18).

Mr Hobbes farther adds that the only probable security there is for safety is to dispossess yourself of everything that is desirable. This is Mr Hobbes's description of a regal government, which he has made more intolerable than his state of nature, namely every man at war with every man, for in this state strength, prudence and fortitude may support one. Flight and obscurity is the last resource, but Mr Hobbes cannot prove that even flight and obscurity will save a whole society from the evils of his regal government. There are many objections to this assertion. First, numbers of people may suffer before the disposition of a bad monarch can be known. Secondly, it is not to be supposed that such a monarch would be left alone without society, and the privilege of making use of his subjects for his state, convenience and amusement. I think Mr Hobbes cannot propose this as a means to be taken only by a few, for that would be as if he was to say that plague and famine were not evils because a small number might escape them (20).

Not only did women theorists reject the fiction of the social contract (discussed at the end of Chapter 2), they had their own more natural, less contrived alternative explanation for the development of social cohesion and morality: the bond of love, especially that between parent and child. Macaulay here joins du Châtelet, to be joined later by Sophie Grouchy de Condorcet and Germaine de Staël in using the sympathy notion of Scottish moral philosophy, usually traced from Francis Hutcheson through David Hume and Adam Smith. Each believed that the conventional male rendition of it was lacking. All three gave stronger statements, less reliant on the calculated self interest of utility theory and more confident about the good effects of positive bonds.

For Macaulay, in *Letters on Education*, sympathy was the core human affection from which all other virtues arose. Without sympathy, moreover, we probably would not have attained any ideas of equity. It was sympathy, moving us emotionally, that first inclined us to forbear our own gratifications for the sake of our "fellow creatures," including species other than the human. For Macaulay sympathy was primary, while reason followed feeling: "All human virtue must derive its source from this useful affection," sympathy. Sympathy lay dormant in every mind and had to be prompted to become active. Governments had considerable power to affect its development through enacting or promoting laws, precepts and customs. Macaulay was influenced here by Beccaria's treatise, *On Crimes and Punishments*, 1764, which she cited with approval and which gave detailed arguments for the formulation of laws that would deter bad behaviour and elicit good behaviour by the penalties and rewards attached to them.

Text: Macaulay, *Letters on Education*:

If we trace...the origin of those virtues in man which render him fit for the benign offices of life we shall find that they all centre in sympathy. For had the mind of man been totally divested of this affection, it would not in all probability have ever attained any ideas of equity. Yes, it was the movements of sympathy which first inclined man to a forbearance of his own gratifications in respect to the feelings of his fellow creatures, and his reason soon approved the dictates of his inclination. A strict adherence to the principles of equity may be said to include the perfection of moral rectitude. This being granted, all human virtue will be found to proceed from equity; consequently, if the principle of equity itself owes its source in the human mind to the feelings of sympathy, all human virtue must derive its source from this useful affection.

When this benign affection holds a superiority in the mind to other affections, inclination will lead to the performance of the duties of humanity. In those insensible minds where this affection is originally weak, or where it is extinguished by the excess of passions, equity, unsupported by benevolence, has either no place in the mind, or through the cold precept of tuition, bears a feeble sway.

We have reason to believe that all the passions which belong to humanity lie latent in every mind but we find, by experience, that they continue inactive till put in motion by the influence of some corresponding impression. Their growth and prevalence in a great measure depends on the repetition of those impressions which are in their nature adapted to affect them. Thus it will appear that, where we have power to direct the course of impression, we have power to command the state of the passions; and as laws, example, precept and custom are the prime sources of all our impressions, it must be greatly in the power of government to effect, by a proper use of these sources, that improvement on which true civilization depends.

It is known that the power of custom over the mind arises from such a repetition of the same impression as act to the weakening or destroying the force of every impression of contrary tendency. Could we therefore, by the spirit of our laws, exclude from society the operation of every impression which partook of the smallest tincture of cruelty, and did we encourage the operation of every impression which had a benevolent tendency, it appears probable that we exalt the sympathizing feeling to a degree which might act more forcibly than the coercion of rigorous laws to the restraining all acts of violence and, consequently, all acts which militate against the public peace (275-77).

Men as they gained ideas of good and evil, by experience, communicated their observations to their offspring. Domestic education, therefore, must have begun with the beginning of the life of man and, when the species formed themselves into societies, their ideas were necessarily extended from the variety of impressions and instructions which they received in such associations.

With the increase of the stock of his ideas, man increased his power of making comparisons, and consequently enlarged his knowledge of the relation of things. Some modes of conduct generally adopted, some rules and exercises fitted to a state of offence and defence, necessarily belong to all associations. Education then, in a state of the rudest society, must necessarily be more complex and more methodical than education in the natural or more solitary state of man, who, as he rises from this rude state of society, through all the degrees which form the difference between the savage and the civilized nations, must receive impressions more numerous, his motives for action must grow more complex, his duties and his obligations must enlarge, the rules for his conduct must become more nice and various, his actions be more critically observed, his offences more certainly punished, and consequently his good or ill fate must depend in a more particular manner on his education than when in a state of nature, or in a state of savage society (237-38).

Letters on Education was Macaulay's second last book (the last was a reply to Burke). In these two last works she took the opportunity of returning to the theme of her Hobbes tract, the illiberal social contract, now with the benefit of years more reading, travel and intellectual exchange. She scathingly denounced the "monstrous" notion of millions of people being made for one. She realized that even enlightened nations had adopted the theory of making a deity of their government. Another form of idolatry, almost as much against the happiness of individuals, was making a deity of "society in its aggregate," presumably Rousseau's general will. In either case, she held, a very reasonable proposition was reversed: that society was not formed "for the happiness of its citizens," but the citizen's life and happiness was to be devoted to society's glory.

As had Astell, Macaulay affirmed the obligations of governors to their subjects. People even had a right to expect *more* from their sovereign than their natural parents, for where much is given, much, "with justice," may be required. Macaulay cited the progressive, liberal Beccaria on the limits of the rights of government and its obligation to instruct rather than to punish. The office of government consisted in limiting evil as much as possible and extending good. The education of the people, broadly understood, was the most important duty of the state. Interestingly, this last point is one made much earlier by the Puritan pamphleteer, **Mary Cary Rande**, who in 1653 urged the repeal of "those great and tedious volumes of law that are either in a strange tongue or otherwise, which serve no other end but to enrich the lawyers and impoverish others." There should instead be only some plain, general rules, with which all may be acquainted.[31] It is not known if Macaulay, or Beccaria, knew this earlier work.

Text: Macaulay, *Letters on Education* 271-74:

It is well known that a great part of the ancient, and even of the modern, world have made a deity of their government, in whose high prerogatives they have buried all their natural rights. The monstrous faith of millions made for one has

---

[31] Mary Cary Rande, *Proposals to the Supreme Governours* 11.

been at different times adopted by the greater part of civilized societies, and even those enlightened nations who have been the most famed for asserting and defending their liberties ran into another species of idolatry, which is almost as much at war with the happiness of individuals. Instead of making a deity of the government, they made a deity of the society in its aggregate capacity; and to the real or imagined interests of this idol, they sacrificed the dearest interests of those individuals who formed the aggregate. Thus they reversed a very plain and reasonable proposition. Society with them was not formed for the happiness of its citizens, but the life and happiness of every citizen was to be devoted to the glory and welfare of the society.

When the happiness of an individual is properly considered, his interest will be found so intimately connected with the interests of the society of which he is a member that he cannot act in conformity to the one without having a proper consideration for the other. Reason will revolt against a service for which it finds no adequate return. When we admire the virtue of the ancients, we admire only that inflexible conduct, which carried them to sacrifice every personal interest to principle.

The moderns are grown so lax in their devotions to the shrine of patriotism as to bury in the ruins of public virtue all good faith and common honesty. A depravity in manners, which too plainly manifests that change of conduct proceeds from total want of principle, rather than from having formed just ones. We have indeed made no accurate definitions either on the duties of government or on the duties of a good citizen. And individuals, from the prevalent power of custom and precept, are content with privations which have no foundation in the common good.

Man is ever apt to run into extremes; no sooner do we discard one gross error than we deviate into another of an opposite nature. It is said that truth is always to be found in the mean. If so, those must differ widely from her who, to avoid the evil of such a power as is claimed by despots, of interfering with all private as well as public concerns, assert that the true and only office of government is to act the part of a good constable in preserving the public peace. Thus, according to the opinion of the most liberal of the moderns, governors have little else to do but to eat, drink and enjoy all the various emoluments annexed to the diadem and the purple, without disturbing their repose by fulfilling any of those parental duties which subjects, in their political connection, have a much greater right to expect from their sovereign than children have to expect from their natural parent. Where much is given much may, with justice, be required.

The marquis of Beccaria, in his excellent treatise on crimes and punishments, asserts that government has no right to punish delinquency in its subjects without having previously taken care to instruct them in the knowledge of the laws and of those duties in public and private life which are agreeable to the dictates of moral rectitude. This observation coincides with that strain of benevolence which runs through the whole of this excellent treatise. Not to dwell on the high injustice of assuming the power of punishment without fulfilling the duties of instruction, it must be obvious to enlightened reason, that the sublime office of government consists in limiting, as far as the nature of things will allow, the bounds of evil, and extending the bounds of good....Whatever be the sanguine expectations formed from some useful discoveries made in the science of physics, the conveniences and the happiness enjoyed by the generality of the world will continue to be very moderate unless the united force of society is steadily used to carry on the glorious work of improvement.

The education of the people in the most extensive sense of this word may be said to comprehend the most important duties of government. For as the education of individuals is forever going on, and consists of all the impressions received through the organs of sense from the hour of birth to the hour of death, public education, if well adapted to the improvement of man, must comprehend good laws, good examples, good customs, a proper use of the arts and wise instructions conveyed to the mind by the means of language in the way of speech and writing.

Government—France—Revolution

Macaulay on her return from a trip to the United States had planned to write a history of the American Revolution. Ill health forced her to set aside the project. When **Edmund Burke** published his attack on the French Revolution she felt she had to respond.[32] Her 95-page *Observations on the Reflections of the Rt. Hon. Edmund Burke on the Revolution in France* came out in 1790, the year before her death. Her contention that the bloodshed caused by royal despots was worse than that by the people obviously reflects the circumstances of this early period. She had herself visited France in 1777-78, and possibly also earlier in 1776. Although she had ostensibly made the trip because of ill health, she soon was ensconced in Paris society, meeting aristocrats and intellectuals and observing the great gap between rich and poor. She met the distinguished physiocrat Turgot and the widow of the materialist Helvétius. She had to avoid notorious Americans like Benjamin Franklin, however, for fear of consequences on her return to England, which had suspended the Habeas Corpus Act and was fearful of republicanism.

Macaulay was more cautious in her judgments of the French Revolution than Burke had been in his hasty denunciation. She believed it to be too early to judge whether or not truly popular government was incompatible with the

---

[32] Another woman writer sympathetic to the revolution was **Helen Maria Williams**, who lived in France many years and published some thirty volumes on French history, including eight on the revolution. Williams's *Letters written in France*, 1790, not only predates the responses to Burke but Burke's book itself. Wollstonecraft reviewed Williams's book (see *Works of Mary Wollstonecraft* 7:322-24).

human constitution, as he had maintained. A period of recovery would be required after the "convulsive struggles" to assess the situation (87). History could give no guide, for there was no example of any government in a large empire that had secured full enjoyment of its citizens' rights (87-88). While Burke had argued that the French Revolution was unnecessary, extrapolating from his interpretation of the "Glorious Revolution" of 1688-89 in England, the republican Macaulay took a totally different view. Her judicious conclusions on the French Revolution survive the test of time. She herself died before the next phase of the revolution so was unable to exercise her own judgment. The passages selected here go back to the basic issue of people's rights versus those of the sovereign, and there is explicit condemnation, again, of Hobbes.

Text: Macaulay, *Observations on Burke*:

When the succession to a crown in one family, or even the possession of private property, owes its origin to the people, most undoubtedly the authority from whence it is derived attaches itself to the gift as equally in every individual of the family through the whole line of succession, as in the first possessor. I can hardly believe that there was *one* enlightened member who composed part of that legislative body who settled the succession to the throne could possibly think that body possessed of such a plenitude of power as should give them a right, not only to *set aside* the regulations of their ancestors, but to *bind their posterity* to all succeeding generations in the permanent chains of an unalterable law. Should we once admit of a power so incompatible with the conditions of humanity, and only reserved for the dictates of divine wisdom, we have not, in these enlightened days, improved on the politics of the fanatic atheist Hobbes: *for he supposes an original right in the people to choose their governors but, in exerting this right, the citizen and his posterity forever lose their native privileges and become bound through the whole series of generations to the service of a master's will* (13-14).

The legitimate power by which governments are made or altered must either stand on the native rights of the species, or it must stand on an authority vested in an individual or in a limited number of individuals...either by the positive law of a revealed will, or by some native superiority evidently attached to their persons. That this sacred trust has never been so formally vested in *any* individual, or in *any given number* of individuals, is in a manner acknowledged by the most strenuous advocates for passive obedience, for all their arguments are built on presumptive grounds.

The contrary proposition to this, namely, *that native right in the social body to choose its own government*, which Mr Burke condemns under the description of a *metaphysical foolery*, is allowed with all its weight of authority by the greatest part of the English revolutionists, nor can any other reasonable ground of persuasion be made use of to bring the people to concur in any plan of salutary or necessary reformation (44-45).

[Burke argued:] Government is a contrivance of human wisdom, to provide for human wants. Men have a right that these wants should be provided for by this wisdom. Among these wants is...a sufficient restraint upon their passions. Society requires not only that the passions of individuals should be subjected, but even in the mass and body, as well as in individuals. The inclinations of men should frequently be thwarted, their will controlled, and their passions brought into subjection. This can only be done by a power out of themselves...

To this very ingenious reasoning...the people may possibly object that, in delivering themselves passively over to the unrestrained rule of others, on the plea of controlling their *inordinate inclinations* and *passions*, they deliver themselves over to men who, as men and partaking of the same nature as themselves, are as liable to be governed by the same principles and errors, and to men who, by the great superiority of their station, having no common interest with themselves which might lead them to preserve a salutary check over their vices, must be inclined to *abuse* in the grossest manner their trust.

To proceed with Mr Burke's argument, should the rich and opulent in the nation plead their right to the predominant sway in society, from its being a necessary circumstance to guard their wealth from the grip of poverty, men in an inferior state of fortune might argue that, should they give way to this plea in all its extent, their moderate possessions would be exposed to the burden of unequal taxes, for the rich, when possessed of the whole authority of the state, would be sure to take the first care of themselves, if they should not be tempted to secure an exoneration of all burdens, by dividing the spoils of the public....The abuse of such high trusts must necessarily arise because to act by selfish considerations is in the very constitution of our nature.

To such pleas, so plausibly urged on all sides, I know of no rational objection. Nor can I think of an expedient to remove the well-grounded apprehensions of the different interests which compose a commonwealth than a *fair* and *equal* representation of the *whole* people—a circumstance which appears very peculiarly necessary in a mixed form of government, where the democratic part of the constitution will ever be in danger of being overborne by the energy attending on its higher constituent parts (46-48).

If Mr Burke, in the management of his argument, could have descended from the lofty strain of a poetic imagination to the drudgery of close reasoning, he would have perceived the error of deviating from the line of *expediency* into the question of *right*, for when we once give up the point, that there is an inherent right attached to privileged persons to make laws for the community, we cannot fix on any other principle that will stand the test of argument but the *native* and *unalienable* rights of man. For, if we say that *lawful* governments are formed on the authority of conventions, it will be asked *who gave these conventions their authority*? If we grant that they derived their authority from the *assent of the people*, how came the people, it will be said, to exert such an authority at *one* period of society and *not at another*? If we say it was necessity that recovered to social man the full rights of his nature, it will be asked, who is to be the judge of this necessity? Why certainly the people.

Thus, in every light in which we can place the argument, in every possible mode of reasoning, we shall be driven back to elect either the first or the second of these propositions, either that an individual, or some privileged persons, have an inherent and indefeasible right to make laws for the community, or that this authority rests in the unalienable and indefeasible rights of man.

That the people have often abused their power, it must be granted, for they have often sacrificed themselves and their posterity to the wanton will of an individual, and *this* is the foundation of all the regal tyrannies which have subsisted in society, but *no abuse* of their power can take away their right, because their right *exists in the very constitution of things*. If the French people therefore should be so capricious as to fling off their new constitution, and subject themselves to more unequal forms of government, even to *tyranny*, it will be agreeable to the course of past experience, but such an exertion of power *cannot injure their right*, and whatever form or complexion any future government in France may bear, it can have no *legitimate source*, but in *the will of the people* (93-95).

Macaulay's response to Burke, as Wollstonecraft's first *Vindication*, conveys the excitement and hope prompted by the French Revolution. The revolution was so new and unique in the spirit it aroused that it naturally excited admiration among individuals and whole societies. Macaulay cited especially the relinquishment of feudal privilege to the people as a moment of "singular greatness." Yet the English who might have been expected, as more liberal, to be more careful in their criticism, were not. Macaulay doubted that the great achievement of the revolution could have occurred without bloodshed. Given the animosity between the aristocrats and the ordinary people, and the insults the people received, their moderation was more remarkable than their cruelty. Far more people suffered from the rage and pride of "kingly despots" (22-25).

Macaulay contended numerous specific points Burke had made. The excerpts here show her challenging him on the role of parliaments and the Estates-General. She described how the people came to realize that the modest concession of a vote in the Estates-General would not redress their grievances. They resolved to do the job themselves and gave up on "humble petitions." Neither the king nor Parliament could have prevented the full use of this power even if they had foreseen all the consequences.

Text: Macaulay, *Observations on Burke*:

The French Revolution was attended with something so new in the history of human affairs, there was something so singular, so unique, in that perfect unanimity in the people, in that firm spirit which baffled every hope in the interested, that they could possibly divide them into parties and render them the instruments of a re-subjection to their old bondage, that it naturally excited the surprise and the admiration of all men. It appeared as a *sudden spread of an enlightened spirit*, which promised to act as an effectual and permanent barrier to the inlet of those usurpations which from the very beginning of social life the crafty have imposed on ignorance. This was a triumph of sufficient importance to call forth the exultation of individuals and the approbation of societies (22-23).

That memorable day in which the members of the National Assembly, with a *virtuous enthusiasm*, vied with each other in the alacrity with which they surrendered to the people all their feudal privileges will forever stand in the records of time as a monument of their *singular greatness*. Such an instance of human virtue was surely a *proper subject of applause and congratulation*.

Men who have suffered in their personal interests by the new order of things in France must naturally be inclined to exaggerate every blemish which appears in the conduct of a multitude by whose spirit they have been deprived of many fond privileges. Their petulant observations, whilst their minds are beaten by imaginary wrongs and injuries, is excusable because it is a weakness almost inseparable from human frailty. It would, however, have become Englishmen, from whom might have been expected a more sympathizing indulgence towards the friends and promoters of liberty, to have been more candid in their censures. But in no part of Europe, perhaps, have the evils which must *necessarily* attend all revolutions, and especially a revolution so complete and comprehensive as that which has taken place in France, been *more exaggerated* and more affectedly lamented.

Had this great work been effected without the shedding one drop of innocent or even guilty blood, without doubt it would have better pleased the generous and benevolent mind. But, was it possible that such a pleasing circumstance could ever have had an existence? If we take into consideration that *animosity* which subsisted between the *aristocratic* and the *democratic* on the eve of revolution, an animosity which was greatly heightened by the imprudent insults which the Third Estate had received from the first mentioned body, we shall rather *wonder at the moderation* with which the people used their complete victory than lament their cruelty....

I do not indeed exactly know how much blood has been spilled in France, or how many individuals have fallen a sacrifice in the public commotions, but by all the general accounts which have been transmitted to us, the history of monarchies will point out as many sufferers who have fallen in *one hour* to the *rage* and *outrageous pride* of kingly despots (23-26).

Mr Burke, reasoning from what I regard as a groundless supposition, very pathetically laments and very severely reprehends the conduct of those who, holding out false and treacherous lures to the king, led him into concessions fatal to his personal power and the constitution of the monarchy. That the parliaments of France never intended to make any *alteration* in the old government I am thoroughly persuaded, and I am equally persuaded that they fondly imagined the people would *freely* give their money for the redress of some of the most heavy of the grievances under which they laboured. They knew, by the experience of past times, that in voting by orders, the people had never gained any *solid* advantage from an assembly of the Estates-General. Neither the court, nor the parliament of Paris who made the king so many splendid promises, were aware of the consequences which must arise from the general spread of knowledge among the people. In the event of things they were both disappointed of their purposes for the Third Estate, reflecting on the old practices which the crown, the clergy and the nobility had used against them, were determined to throw the whole weight of their natural scale into the balance and to redress their own grievances without the effect of humble petitions and discordant councils. That neither the king, nor the parliaments of France, could long have prevented the *full* exertion of this power, had they foreseen all the consequences which did arise from suffering the meeting of the Estates-General, is to me very plain (34-35).

Government—United States

The United States held enormous significance for European liberals in the eighteenth and nineteenth centuries. As it had been the land of freedom for religious expression in the seventeenth century, so it became the land looked to in the next two centuries by liberals, radicals and republicans seeking change in their own countries, normally monarchies with a well-entrenched aristocracy and few political rights for ordinary citizens.

There are two sizzling contributions on the American Revolution by Macaulay, one a pamphlet written for the British public, sympathetic to the American side, the second an exchange of correspondence with George Washington, first president of the United States. This writing, as earlier, shows her passion for democracy and abhorrence of inherited privilege. In the pamphlet, in retrospect as wise as it was vigorous, Macaulay explicitly warned that if war occurred either both sides would be ruined or the Americans would gain their independence. She foresaw no good result for Britain. Rather the British people would have to face an end of the advantages they had enjoyed by oppressive taxes and unfair trading restrictions, and which had saved them, to that point in time, from bankruptcy. America would flourish with independence, she predicted, and Britain would sink under domestic despotism or fall to a powerful European state.

Macaulay's pamphlet to her fellow citizens at home pre-dated the outbreak of the American Revolution, seeking to avoid it by urging change in policies towards the colonies. It appealed to the *people* of England, Scotland, Ireland, as opposed to their *government*, warning them of the likely dire consequences of oppressive and arbitrary government decisions, including the notorious

Stamp Act (remember "no taxation without representation"?), the closing of the Port of Boston (which led to the Boston Tea Party) and Britain's changing of the Constitution of Massachusetts against the wishes of its citizens (another of many grievances). Macaulay described the various measures the British government took against the colonies and the despair it invoked. She sought to explode the justification given by the British government for the public at home. She asked ordinary British citizens to identify with the Americans, calling on their "common interest" as subjects of a free state.

Macaulay, of course, was thoroughly correct in her unhappy predictions. Obviously she did not succeed in persuading her fellow citizens to accept greater autonomy for the colonies but the American Revolution soon broke out. It will be shown, on the other hand, that her writing had a significant impact in America, helping to shape a new spirit of republicanism among the colonists. It seems that Macaulay's trenchant criticism of monarchy convinced them that it could not be reformed.

Macaulay visited the United States in 1784-85, the first English radical to do so after the recognition of American Independence. She was by then a celebrated author, which gave her access to the highest circles. She and her husband were received for a ten-day visit at Mt. Vernon, the home of George and Martha Washington. The subsequent correspondence between Washington and Macaulay shows the familiarity of kindred spirits. Macaulay presumed to advise Washington on political institutions and democratic safeguards.

Bridget Hill's biography of Macaulay, *Republican Virago*, stresses the high esteem in which Macaulay was held. She was recognized as one of the best English friends of the Revolution, an influential figure for the generation of colonists who made the Revolution. Benjamin Franklin knew and admired her *History of England*. Thomas Jefferson not only repeatedly recommended her history to friends and colleagues, but bought a complete (eight-volume) set for the University of Virginia Library.[33] He even proposed the republication of David Hume's conservative, pro-monarchist *History of England* with Whig refutations (by Macaulay and others), to confront his "misrepresentations" with "authentic truths."[34] She was the historian Washington knew best. She exchanged information on the colonial situation with John Adams, another profound admirer of her *History of England*. Her treatment of the monarchy and the seventeenth-century English Revolution in the *History of England* helped to move American public opinion from support of the monarchy to republicanism. "An acceptance of Catharine Macaulay's evaluation of the Glorious Revolution [of 1688] had led the colonists from earlier expressions

---

[33] H. Trevor Colbourn, *The Lamp of Experience* 153.

[34] Colbourn, *Lamp of Experience* 179. On Macaulay's influence see also Pauline Maier, *From Resistance to Revolution*.

Theorists on Revolution/Macaulay

of loyalty and devotion to George III to a total rejection of monarchy."[35] Macaulay's friendship with **Mercy Otis Warren** perhaps inspired the latter to write a *History of the American Revolution*, 1805.

Text: Macaulay, "Address to the People":

It can be no secret to you, my friends and fellow citizens, that the ministry, after having exhausted all those ample sources of corruption which your own tameness under oppressive taxes have afforded, either fearing the unbiased judgement of the people, or impatient at the slow but steady progress of despotism, have attempted to wrest from our American colonists every privilege necessary to free men—privileges which they hold from the authority of their charters and the principles of the constitution.

With an entire supineness, England, Scotland and Ireland have seen the Americans, year by year, stripped of the most valuable of their rights. To the eternal shame of this country, the Stamp Act, by which they were to be taxed in an arbitrary manner, met with no opposition except from those who are particularly concerned that the commercial intercourse between Great Britain and her colonies should meet with no interruption. With the same guilty acquiescence...you have seen the last Parliament finish their venal course with passing two acts for shutting up the Port of Boston, for indemnifying the murderers of the inhabitants of Massachusetts Bay and changing their chartered constitution of government....

The anxious desire of preserving that harmony, which had so long and so happily existed between the parent state and her colonies, occasioned the Americans to bear with an almost blameable patience the innovations which were continually made on their liberty until the ministry, who imagined their moderation proceeded from ignorance and cowardice, by depriving them of almost every part of their rights which remained unviolated, have raised a spirit beyond the Atlantic, which may either recover the opportunities we have lost of restoring the breaches which for near a century have been making in our constitution or of sinking us into the lowest abyss of national misery (5-8).

There are [those] who, while they have the words "freedom," "constitution" and "privilege" continually in their mouths, are using every means in their power to render those limitations useless, which have from time to time been erected by our ancestors as mitigations of that barbarous system of despotism imposed by the Norman tyrant [William the Conqueror] on the inhabitants of this island.

These men attempt to persuade you that those who appear the most anxious for the safety of their country are the least interested in its welfare. They have had the insolence to tell you, though in contradiction to the evidence of your

---

[35] Hill, *Republican Virago* 204.

feelings, that all goes well, that your governors faithfully fulfil the duties of their office, and that there are no grievances worthy to be complained of but those which arise from that spirit of faction which, more or less, must ever exist in a limited monarchy. These men have told you that you are no judges of the state of your political happiness, that you are made of too inflammable materials to be trusted with the knowledge of your injuries, even if you have suffered any, and those who appeal to you do it only with the intention to betray you (9-10).

These men have asserted that unlimited obedience is stipulated in the acceptance of protection, and though such an assertion involves you and the subjects of every state in unlimited slavery and unlimited slavery excludes every idea of right and power, yet they have also told you that it is in vindication of your authority that your governors have exerted an arbitrary power over your brethren in America.

In order to confound your ideas on the merits of the dispute and to stifle your feelings of humanity, they have told you that the Americans, though neither adequately or inadequately represented in the case of taxation, stand on the same predicament with yourselves, and that there is no more injustice inflicting a severe punishment on the whole town of Boston for the supposed offence of a few of its inhabitants than in bombarding a town in the possession of an enemy (11-12).

To all the restrictions laid on their trade the Americans declare they will ever readily submit, on the generous consideration that they are supposed to be for the benefit and advantage of the whole empire. At the same time...the Americans declare that, if you will not concur with your own, and their, enemies, to oppress them—that is, if you will not concur with men whose every act of administration are so many evidences of a formed design to enslave the whole empire, they will ever esteem an union with you their glory and their happiness. That they will be ever ready to contribute all in their power towards the welfare of the empire, and that they will consider your enemies as their enemies, and hold your interests as dear to them as their own.

They exhort you...for the sake of that honour and justice for which this nation was once renowned, they entreat you by all those ties of common interest which are inseparable to the subjects of free states, not to suffer your enemies to effect your slavery in their ruin. They set before you in the strongest colours all those disadvantages which must attend that large independent power the sovereigns of Great Britain will gain by...taxing, in an arbitrary manner, the Americans—and they invite you, for these cogent reasons, to join with them in every legal method to disappoint the designs of our common foes.

It is not impossible...that, after having tamely suffered the government by a yearly increase of taxes, to beggar yourselves and your posterity, you may be led away with the wicked but delusive hope that the ministry, when they have the power to pick the pockets of your American brethren, will have the moderation to save those of their countrymen. If these are your thoughts...little have you studied your own natures and the experience of all ages, which must have convinced you that want of power is the only limitation to the exertion of human selfishness. Should you be contented to bid defiance to the warnings of common policy, should you be contented to be slaves on the hope that the Americans will bear the greater part of the burden of your enormous taxes, be assured that such an alternative will never be in your power.

No, if a civil war commences between Great Britain and her colonies, either the mother country, by one great exertion, may ruin both herself and America, or the Americans, by a lingering contest, will gain an independency. In this case, all those advantages which you for some time have enjoyed...which have hitherto preserved you from national bankruptcy, must forever have an end. And, while a new, flourishing and extensive empire of free men is established on the other side of the Atlantic, you, with the loss of all those blessings you have received by the unrivalled state of your commerce, will be left to the bare possession of your foggy islands, and this under the sway of a domestic despot, or you will become the provinces of some powerful European state.

If a long succession of abused prosperity should...have entirely deprived you of that virtue, the renown of which makes you even at this day respectable among all the nations of the civilized world; if neither the principles of justice or generosity have any weight with you...take into consideration the interests of your safety and preservation. Suffer me again to remind you of the imminent danger of your situation: your ministers, by attacking the rights of all America, have affected that which the malicious policy of more judicious minds would have avoided. Your colonists, convinced that their safety depends on their harmony, are now united in one strong bond of union. Nor will it be in the power of a Machiavelli to take any advantage of those feuds and jealousies which formerly subsisted among them and which exposed their liberties to more real danger than all the fleets and armies we are able to send against them.

Your ministers also, deceived by present appearances, vainly imagine, because our rivals in Europe are encouraging us to engage beyond the possibility of a retreat, that they will reject the opportunity when it offers of putting a final end to the greatness and the glory of our empire. But, if by the imprudent measures of the government, public expenses increase, or public income decreases to such a degree that the public revenue fail, and you be rendered unable to pay the interest of your debt, then will no longer be delayed the day and the hour of your destruction. Then will you become an easy prey to the courts of France and Spain who, you may depend upon it, will fall upon you as soon as they see you fairly engaged in a war with your colonists. According to what is foretold you in a late publication, that conjuncture will prove the latest and the uttermost of your prosperity, your peace and, in all probability, of your existence as an independent state and nation (23-29).

The first letter selected from the Washington-Macaulay correspondence dates from the early, optimistic period of the French Revolution, October 1789. In it Macaulay highlighted the influence of the American Revolution in prompting the outbreak. She praised **General la Fayette** for his role in the two revolutions, excepting him from her general condemnation of the holders of aristocratic privilege (he was a marquis).

Text: Macaulay in Sparks, *Correspondence of the American Revolution* 4:283-85:

It is now about a year and a half since I had the honour of receiving a letter from you, dated November 16th 1787. I do not pretend to make you any apology for not troubling you with an acknowledgment sooner, though I rather think it necessary to make one for troubling you, in the important station you now fill, with my congratulations on the event which placed you at the head of the American government. But it is not you, Sir, that I consider as benefited by the unanimous election of the Americans. Your philosophic turn of mind would have led you to the completion of human happiness in a private station; but the Americans, in their judicious choice have...secured to themselves the full and permanent enjoyment of that liberty, for which they are indebted to your persevering valour in the first instance. Your wisdom and virtue will, undoubtedly, enable you to check the progress of every opinion inimical to those rights which you have so bravely and fortunately asserted, and for which many of your countrymen have paid so dear and you will be a bright example to future Presidents of an integrity rarely to be met with in the first stations of life.

All the friends of freedom on this side the Atlantic are now rejoicing for an event which, in all probability, has been accelerated by the American Revolution. You not only possess, yourselves, the first of human blessings, but you have been the means of raising that spirit in Europe, which I sincerely hope will, in a short time, extinguish every remain of that barbarous servitude under which all the European nations, in a less or a greater degree, have so long been subject. The French have justified the nobleness of their original character and, from the immersions of luxury and frivolity, have set an example that is unique in all the histories of human society, a populous nation effecting, by the firmness of their union, the universality of their sentiments, and the energy of their actions, the entire overthrow of a despotism that had stood the test of ages. We are full of wonder, in this part of the world, and cannot conceive how such things should be. Your friend and élève, the Marquis de la Fayette, has acted a part in this revolution, which has raised him above his former exploits because his conduct has been directed to the good of his distressed countrymen, and shows him far above those base and narrow selfishnesses with which particular privileges are so apt to taint the human mind....

Mr Graham joins me in best respects to yourself and Mrs Washington. We contemplate, with no small pleasure, the advantage America will reap from that check to all the luxuries of dress which her example of an elegant simplicity in this article will undoubtedly effect.

George Washington's detailed reply expressed his frank hopes for the future of the new state: "The establishment of our new government seemed to be the last great experiment for promoting human happiness by a reasonable compact in civil society."[36] The government, "though not actually perfect," he acknowledged, was "one of the best in the world" (10:70). Washington admitted luck (a good wheat harvest and high export demand) in accounting for the government's success. He closed by noting that both he and his wife concurred with her on simplicity in dress—a point made both in her letter and in her published writing.

Macaulay had provided Washington with a copy of her Corsican paper (excerpted below), in effect an opportunity to write an "ideal" constitution. In this next letter she had to explain how she had changed her mind on some particulars. She warned that an upper house might "acquire some distinction," which could lead to political inequality. This was a circumstance that should not happen in a free society. Americans, having avoided the "evils of aristocracy," might not have the same aversion to pretensions as had the French. The letter of June 1790 has not been published anywhere in her own name. It was included as a footnote in Washington's correspondence, accompanying his letter to her.

Text: Macaulay letter, *Writings of George Washington* 10:71-72:

The present system of American government contains all those principles which have been regarded as capable of resisting every hostile influence arising either from force or seduction. I once thought that such a system of government would be invulnerable, as your Excellency must have perceived, if you have ever read a political tract of mine addressed to Paoli, the Corsican general. It is true that, in that sketch of a democratic government, I endeavoured to keep out corruption by enforcing a general rotation [of offices], but I must acknowledge to you that the corruptions, which have crept into our legislature since the revolution, with the wise caution used by the French patriots in the rules to which they have subjected their National Assembly, have led me to alter my opinion. This alteration of opinion inclines me to fear that ill consequences may arise from vesting the legislative body with the power of establishing offices, of regulating the quantum of their salaries, and

---

[36] Washington, *Writings of George Washington* 10:69.

of enjoying themselves the emoluments arising from such establishments. I should have thought it safer to have made them incapable of holding at least any civil office whilst they were members of the legislature. Those who have studied mankind with the greatest attention find that there is no depending on their virtue, except where all corrupting motives are put out of their way.

I see also that you have followed the example of the parent state in dividing your legislature into an upper and a lower house. I once thought that this was the only method of obtaining the result of deliberate counsels, but I at present am of opinion that the French have effectually secured themselves from the return of aristocracy in their government by confining the legislature to one equal assembly, committing the office of approving laws to the King and the people. May not your upper house in length of time acquire some distinction, which may lay the grounds for political inequality among you, a circumstance which never ought to take place in a society of free men. Americans, free from every part of the feudal tenure and the unjust distinctions of primogeniture, found it easy when they had shaken off the yoke of England, to form and regulate a popular government. But, from the circumstance of always having been exempt from the evils of aristocracy, they may not have the same principles of aversion to such pretensions planted in their minds as now happily exist among the French. They may also have regarded with admiration instead of disgust the splendour of European society, and mistaken the insolence and ostentation of a few citizens for national dignity.

Government—England

In her *History of England* Macaulay lambasted the House of Commons for its incompetence, negligence and corruption. New statutes were so badly drawn up that further statutes were soon required to clear up their obscurities and correct their deficiencies. Statutes were drafted by lawyers so as to keep those most interested in knowing them in the dark, while providing an "inexhaustible" supply of material for prosecutions and lawsuits. Macaulay rejected the usual provision that "ignorance of the law is no excuse," instead arguing for an obligation by government to educate and communicate. She derided the remarks of a bishop who had argued that corruption was a necessary part of (69) administration, and an independent (and hence incorruptible) Parliament inconsistent with the English constitution. The people, she sadly added, tamely suffered all these insults.

It is not known if Macaulay knew the writing of the Puritan Mary Cary Rande (cited above regarding knowledge of the law), who made precisely this point in 1653, in a pamphlet otherwise pleading the cause of the needy over the rich. She urged the repeal of "those great and tedious volumes of law that are

Theorists on Revolution/Macaulay 69

either in a strange tongue or otherwise, which serve no other end but to enrich the lawyers and impoverish others," arguing instead for "general rules."[37]

Text: Macaulay, *History of England from the Revolution* 368-72:

The Commons, instead of acting in their capacity of the grand inquisitors into public grievances, rejected petitions for these and other abuses [oppressive taxes, including a salt tax], and so little attentive were they to any of the good and useful purposes of representation, that those laws which were judged necessary to restrain the growing vices of a corrupt commercial state, were drawn up with a negligence which totally defeated all the just ends of coercion. Every new statute was followed with another to clear up its obscurities and correct its deficiencies. As the drawing up of these statutes was committed to the care of lawyers, without the attentive inspection and revision of the Commons, the ample volume of the law, instead of containing perspicuous and exact rules for the conduct of society, leaves those who are the most interested in its knowledge entirely in the dark, while it continues an inexhaustible source to supply food for the chicanery of its practitioners and the vexatious prosecutions of the quarrelsome and litigious.

Every law...relating to public or private property, and in particular penal statutes, ought to be rendered so clear and plain, and promulgated in such a manner to the public as to give a full information of its nature and contents to every citizen. Ignorance of laws, if not wilful, is a just excuse for their transgression. If the care of the government does not extend to the proper education of the subject, and to their proper information on the nature of moral turpitude and legal crimes, and to the encouragement of virtue, with what face of justice can they punish delinquency?...

While the Commons were thus careless of all the just ends for which they were entrusted with their extensive privileges, while seats in Parliament were purchased at high prices with a view to making the best penny of the public, while the members of both houses were singly engaged in the business of raising money on the people in order to exact a large share of the dividend, it is no wonder that the only laws which could possibly restrain the abuses of representation...and to restore the people to their ancient salutary privileges by shortening the duration of Parliaments, should be rejected with disdain by a venal majority.

Before I leave this subject...I must observe...that Dr Sherlock, Bishop of Bangor...made no scruple to argue avowedly in favour of that canker worm in a state, that destroyer of every political constitution, that ruin to the morals of the people, *corruption*, as a necessary part of administration. [He] declared that an independent House of Commons and an independent House of Lords were

---

[37] Mary Cary Rande, *Proposals to the Supreme Governours* 11.

as inconsistent with the English constitution as an independent or absolute king. This senseless assertion lies so open to conviction since it is plain, if an independent House of Commons is inconsistent with our constitution that a dependent one is useless, expensive, dangerous and burdensome. It is not worth the making any observation upon it, only that it proves to what a low state of depravity we were fallen, and how lost to every sense of what is just, fit, decent and expedient, when one of the heads of the English church should venture to broach doctrines which would have scandalized every pagan priest in the corruptest state of idolatry.

Suffer me to indulge my fancy for once...though I am writing on a serious subject. Methinks I hear you say, "What was become of the voice of the people?" Is it possible, that before their necks were quite bowed to the yoke by repeated ineffectual exertions, by painful executions and frightful examples of suffering patriotism, is it possible that the voice of the people, under such insulting injuries, should not have risen into a thunder which would have shaken the two houses of Parliament, and by the operation of fear have produced that reformation in the conduct of their government which neither reason nor duty could have effected?

Government—An Ideal Constitution

Macaulay's "Short Sketch of a Democratic Form of Government," 1767, is a good example of a long popular genre of political advice-giving: the formulation of an ideal constitution. For a brief period when Genoa sold its title to Corsica to the French in 1768 it seemed that Corsica would become an independent state. An independence movement, led by General **Pascal Paoli**, aided and abetted by European liberals, including Macaulay. Macaulay then took the opportunity to set out the principles necessary to ensure efficient and honest government. There was to be a bi-cameral parliament, the upper house to ensure wisdom, the lower house to protect liberty. Generals, admirals, magistrates and important officials would be selected from the fifty senators of the upper house, by the 250 (or more) representatives in the lower house. For important decisions, proposals should be promulgated before the meeting of representatives to give ordinary people time to deliberate and give their judgments to their representatives. It would seem that Macaulay intended women to have the vote and the opportunity of giving advice to representatives, for she used the term "people" for those functions, while confining office-holding to men only. She advocated strict terms of office for the various positions and a limit of one month for emergency powers. Inheritance laws at the time favoured (and some still do) inheritance by the eldest male. Macaulay rejected primogeniture for equal division of property among male heirs, with separate provision for widows and unmarried daughters and for the education of female children.

This twenty-page pamphlet was confined to only the essential points required for the functioning of government. Macaulay offered to treat next the institutions of the military, police, education and other points necessary for good government and the security of liberty. She did not, in fact, produce any further paper and the issue died with France defeating the independence forces in 1769 and assuming control of the island. That she considered her advice to be more widely useful is clear in her sending a copy of the pamphlet to George Washington. The pamphlet, as her other writing, reflects the more generous view of human nature so characteristic of women theorists. The basic material being good, Macaulay seems to be telling us that, if we could only get our social institutions right, we really could have a good society.

Text: Macaulay, "Short Sketch of a Democratic Form of Government," *Loose Remarks on Hobbes* 21-28:

Free establishments are subjects I have studied with care and the strong Rumours which prevail, that the Corsicans are going to establish a republic, makes me address you [Paoli] as if this was the determined point to which your views were turned. Of all the various models of republics which have been exhibited for the instruction of mankind, it is only the democratic system, rightly balanced, which can secure the virtue, liberty and happiness of society. In such constructions alone are to be found impassable bars to vicious preeminence and the active ambition of man will stimulate him to attain excellence where excellence can alone procure him distinction. The very nature of slavish dependence and proud superiority are equally baneful to the virtues inherent in mankind. The first, by sedulous attention and mean adulation to please its master undermines, and at last subdues, the innate generous principles of the soul, and the fond delights of superiority extinguish all the virtues which ennoble human nature, such as self-denial, general benevolence and the exalted passion of sacrificing private views to public happiness.

Having endeavoured to specify the advantages accruing from a democratic republic, I shall enter, first, into those things essential to the proper form of this species of government and, secondly, into that part of the constitution which defends it from corruption. It is necessary to the proper form of this republic that there should be two orders in the state, namely the senate and the people. The first order is necessary, because in a well-constituted senate there is wisdom and, if this order is prevented by proper restraint from invading public liberty, they will be the surest guardians of it. The second order is necessary, because [unless] the people have authority enough to be thus classed, there can be no liberty.

The form of the republic being thus established, let the debate be in the first order, namely, the senate and the result in the second order, namely the people, though with the power of debating likewise. Let not the number of men which represent the first order be above fifty, to prevent the confusion that usually springs from assemblies too numerous. Let the order of the people be represented by a certain number of men, not under 250, elected out of this order by the several districts or cities into which this island may be divided.

Let the generals, admirals, civil magistrates and officers of every important post be taken out of the senatorial order, that is, among those who have held the rank of senators, with the privilege of having a vote in the senate during the time they are in office, though not otherwise elected into that assembly. Let the power of electing these magistrates and officers be in the representative body. Let the senate, or its committee, meet thrice every week, or occasionally, as the necessity of their office requires. Let the representatives of the people meet at stated times, or occasionally, as the necessity of their office requires.

Let there be the power of appeal from every court of justice to the senate, and then to the representatives of the people. Let the affairs of commerce and all matters relative to the state and executive powers of government be determined by the representative body, after they have been first debated in the senate. But let not the representative assembly have the power of determining peace and war, imposing taxes, the making and altering of laws, till these subjects have been first debated by the senate and proposed by them to the collective body of the people. Let these proposals be promulgated one month before the meeting of the representatives towards the passing them, that the people may have time to deliberate on them and give what directions they shall judge proper to their representatives.

Having settled what relates to the form and established powers of the republic, we must consider that part which defends it from corruption....First, the rotation [of offices]: let the whole senate be changed once in three years, by a third part at a time yearly. Let the vacant posts be supplied from the body of the representatives, by the election of the people. If any of the representative members should be elected into the senate who are not by the course of the rotation to go out of the representative council, their places must be supplied from the people. Let no member of either the senatorial or the representative body be capable of re-election under the space of three years. Let the admirals, generals, civil magistrates and all the officers of important posts lay down their commission at the end of the year, nor be capable of re-election under the aforesaid time of probation.

Let the Agrarian [land tenure system] be settled in such a manner that the balance of land inclines in favour of the popular side. To prevent the alteration which time would make in this balance, let the landed and personal effects of every man be equally divided at his decease between the males, heirs of his body, in default of such heirs between his male heirs in the first and second degree of relationship, in default of these, to the third and fourth and so on, always reserving an ample provision for the widows of the deceased and the education of female children. This law, which excludes female heirship, is to prevent aristocratic accumulation of property and must be further strengthened by debarring females bringing dower in marriage. The provision for unmarried females must be made by way of annuity out of the personal estate....

If the exigencies of the republic should ever find it necessary to lodge the executive powers of government in the hands of one person, let there be a law made to limit it to one month. Let the representative assembly have the power of nominating the person and continuing this command from month to month, if the exigencies of the state demands it, but let not any one person be capable of holding this office above a year. The remedy of a dictator should never be made use of, but in the most desperate cases, and, indeed it is not probable that such a government should ever be in a situation to want it.

This is but the rough sketch of that only form of government which is capable of preserving dominion and freedom to the people. If a further correspondence...should prove agreeable to you and your illustrious countrymen, I shall in my next treat...of the militia, the police, the education of youth and other points necessary to good government and the further security of liberty.

Macaulay's description of **Queen Anne (1665-1714)** is taken from her one-volume version of the *History of England*. It is as hard hitting as one might expect from this radical republican.

Text: Macaulay, *History of England from the Revolution* 270-71:

In a history...which touches so near to the present times it is not safe for an historian to draw a very just and accurate description of the principal persons who figured on the stage of life, but...I will for once depart from the rule I have set myself in writing...and give you as just a notion as I can of the capital lines which form the character of Anne. The medium of party, which either distorts or lessens objects according to the prejudices of the observer, represents this princess as adorned with every quality which form the excellence of a Christian character and, on the other side, as a weak, superstitious bigot, divested of those principles of common reason and intellect which are absolutely necessary to give existence to any virtue either of the head or the heart.

Of all the princesses of the Stuart line, perhaps there were none whose intentions were better towards promoting the good of the society she governed than Queen Anne, but her natural capacity was narrow and her education illiberal. Far from being able to comprehend the art of government and the political happiness of society, sciences understood by very few, her natural capacity was not sufficient to direct with success...the economy of a private family. A bigot to the forms of religion, a slave to her favourites and a victim to her timidity, she was the football of all who had an opportunity of taking advantage of her weaknesses for promoting their private views. The vices of her reign were the vices of those by whom she was governed, and the virtues of her heart only rendered her a more easy dupe to the sinister schemes of her counsellors.

Nature and Society—All Species Great and Small

Macaulay, like other writers on animal welfare of her day, drew on both secular and religious sources for her arguments.[38] Like them, and practical reformers later, she took good arguments wherever she could find them, juxtaposing secular principles from the Enlightenment with references to divine will. The first excerpt puts humans in their place, as dust of the earth, on an equal footing with brute animals. Later Macaulay was clear in rejecting the common view that humans were not bound to nature and had no obligations by virtue of reason to equity or mercy. She criticized David Hume for rejecting the claim of justice for animals, although he had at least argued for their "gentle usage" in *Enquiry concerning the Principles of Morals* (190). Macaulay did not believe that the calculation of pleasures and pains of utility theory should be confined to the human species. The fact that humans abuse their powers over animals testified sadly to barbarous human sentiments for the cruelty was unprovoked. Her prescription featured giving children animals to look after, which was expected to cure their prejudices by benevolent practice.

Text: Macaulay, *Letters on Education*:

It raises in me a mixed sentiment of contempt and anger to hear the vain and contradictory creature, man, addressing the deity as the god of all perfection, yet dealing out a severe and short mortality to the various tribes of his fellow animals, assigning to himself an eternity of happiness beyond even the reach of his imagination. What was man before he was called into existence but the dust of the earth? Can the meanest insect be less; and if man and brute were upon an equal footing before the almighty *fiat* went forth, what motive, worthy of divine wisdom, could influence the deity to draw the line of separation thus wide between his creatures? (2)

Sunday shines no holiday to the miserable brutes; nor is the policy of the Jews well preserved, for the public devotion of the day always gives way to any intervening object of pleasure. Indeed, so miserably have we perverted every rational construction of the commandment, and misapplied the policy of its practice, that the sabbath day is such a day of severe labour to our horses, that many of them fall a sacrifice to the rigour of their talks (95).

Every child, from the pleasure which the exercise of power gives, is very fond of becoming the master of animals; but this inclination is often thwarted by parents, owing to prejudices arising from an undue contempt of the brutes,

---

[38] See Thomas Young, *An Essay on Humanity to Animals* and John Lawrence, "On the Rights of Beasts."

or from an apprehension of injury from them, or that they will meet with ill treatment from the caprice or injudicious fondness of children. I would therefore indulge my pupils in the keeping [of] as many animals as they can properly attend. It will give them the practice of benevolence, serve as an agreeable and innocent amusement, and by the knowledge they will thus acquire of brute nature, they will be cured of prejudices founded on ignorance, vanity and conceit of man (124-25).

We cannot help feeling a little angry with systems which confine rectitude to that mode of conduct which is the best adapted to support the happiness of man. When God subjected the far greater number of his creatures to this lord of the creation, he subjected them to a being, not bound by any tie in nature, or the reason of things, to use equity and mercy in the exercise of his power, and to whose necessary wants are added all the excitements which arise from a whimsical, depraved, and luxuriant imagination. Absurd as is this opinion...it has been supported by the great Mr Hume, who says he does not know by what principle the brutes can claim justice, which is another name for mercy, at our hands. But the difficulties which confound these reasoners lie in their founding rectitude on a principle of utility, and then in confining utility to the benefit of their own species. As utility, unless taken in a very general sense, is liable to mislead the judgment, every rule of human society, founded on partial and even mistaken views of interest, with the sentiment to which it gives rise, finds its justification on the plea of utility and Mr Hume's speculations on this subject are not free from the same errors. Thus inconsistency and mutability hang on his system in the same proportion as they hang on every system of morals founded on human sentiment. But if we take utility in a general sense, and say that virtue consists in that conduct which is of general utility, we shall come to those essential differences which regulate the divine economy, only with this distinction, that man must confine himself to what is general; it is omnipotence alone can extend to what is universal (192-93).

"No government has yet established a just system of taxation, for in every country the expenses of government have fallen unequally on the citizens."[39]

"A standing army...is incompatible with freedom because subordination and rigour are the very sinews of military discipline and despotism is necessary to give vigour to enterprises one will directs."[40]

MARY WOLLSTONECRAFT (1759-97)

Wollstonecraft is that rare exception of a woman theorist for whom there are not only good biographies and analyses[41] available but whose work is available in a full collected works, a collection of her political writing, and a critical edition of her most feminist work, references to all of which are given with the excerpts. She is considered here for her contribution to mainstream theory, on rights and obligations, social cohesion, revolution and government and human-other species relations. Her feminism comes through all those concerns but is not here the prime focus.

Social Bond

In the course of defending the French Revolution and blaming the old regime for the brutality of the ensuing Terror, the main points of *An Historical and Moral View of the Origin and Progress of the French Revolution*, 1794, Wollstonecraft also made some more general remarks on the origin and development of civil society. She mused on the original state of nature. She credited John Locke not only with advocating religious toleration but for deriving the principles of liberty that later appeared in the French Declaration of the Rights of Man. The English by her day exulted in the fact that, for them, human life and liberty never depended on the will of an individual. The English had reason to be proud of their constitution.

Wollstonecraft was critical of the period in which learning was confined to a small number of citizens, when "governments seem to have acted as if the

---

[39] Wollstonecraft, *An Historical and Moral View of the French Revolution* 390, *Works* 6:181.

[40] Wollstonecraft, *A Vindication of the Rights of Woman* 49; *Works* 5:86.

[41] See Eleanor Flexner, *Mary Wollstonecraft*; Ralph M. Wardle, *Mary Wollstonecraft*; Claire Tomalin, *Life and Death of Mary Wollstonecraft*; Emily W. Sunstein, *A Different Face*; Moïra Ferguson and Janet Todd, *Mary Wollstonecraft*; Edna Nixon, *Mary Wollstonecraft*; Emma Rauschenbushch-Clough, *A Study of Mary Wollstonecraft*; Harriet Devine Jump, *Mary Wollstonecraft Writer*; Maria J. Falco, *Feminist Interpretations of Mary Wollstonecraft* and my *Women Founders* 105-15.

people were formed only for them." She regretted that the "luxurious grandeur" those individuals enjoyed was supported by the misery of most of their fellow creatures. At no period had the scanty diffusion of knowledge permitted the great body of ordinary people to participate in discussions of political science. Yet, only by the exercise of reason, in making government a science, could usurped powers be ended. Natural inequities, far from being a justification for domination, should induce government instead to protect the weak, to destroy the inequality of nature.

Wollstonecraft seems, initially, to have accepted a negative portrayal of the state of nature. Using language reminiscent of Rousseau, whose work she knew well, she described social systems as being "founded by passion, individuals wishing to fence round their own wealth or power and make slaves of their brothers to prevent encroachment." À la Hobbes and Rousseau she referred to "men in a savage state" depending on hunting for their subsistence and making war on one another. But sympathy developed, so that in old age, after a perilous life, the same men (hunters/warriors) felt the distress of their fellow creatures, especially the aged. So bonds of friendship evolved in small communities. Wollstonecraft described the origins of society as flowing directly from these considerations, with no intermediate consignment of rights to a sovereign/Leviathan. Throughout her discussion she stressed learning, the useful arts and agriculture as means for advancement. The whole flavour of her treatment is different from that of Hobbes and Rousseau. The similarity with Macaulay is to be expected, for Wollstonecraft had read *Letters on Education* and reviewed it favourably.[42]

Text: Wollstonecraft, *French Revolution* 306-09 (*Works* 6:46-47):

Men in a savage state, without intellectual amusements or even fields or vineyards to employ them, depending for subsistence on the casual supply of the chase, seem continually to have made war one with another, or nation with nation, and the booty taken from their enemies formed the principal object of contest, because war was not, like industry, a kind of abridgement of their liberty. But the social feelings of man, after having been exercised by a perilous life, flow over in long stories when he reaches garrulous old age....His soul also warmed by sympathy, feeling for the distresses of his fellow creatures and particularly for the helpless state of decrepit age, he begins to contemplate, as desirable, associations of men to prevent the inconveniences arising from loneliness and solitude. Hence little communities living together in the bonds of friendship, securing to them the accumulated powers of man, mark the origin of society, and tribes growing into nations, spreading themselves over

---

[42] Wollstonecraft review of Macaulay, *Letters on Education*, in the *Analytical Review*, reprinted in *Works of Mary Wollstonecraft* vol. 7.

the globe, form different languages which, producing different interests and misunderstandings, excite distrust.

The invention of the arts now affords him employment and it is in proportion to their extension that he becomes domestic and attached to his home. For while they were in their infancy his restless temper and savage manners still kept alive his passion for war and plunder. We shall find, if we look back to the first improvement of man, that as his ferocity wore away, the right of property grew sacred. The prowess or abilities of the leaders of barbarians gave them likewise an ascendancy in their respective dynasties which, gaining strength in proportion to the ignorance of the age, produced the distinctions of men from which the great inequality of conditions has originated...preserved long since the necessity has ceased to exist.

During the reign of ignorance, the disagreements of states could be settled only by combats and the art of dexterously murdering seems to have decided differences where reason should have been the arbitrator. The custom then of settling disputes at the point of the bayonet, in modern Europe, has been justified by the example of barbarians. While fools continually argue from the practice of inhuman savages that wars are necessary evils, courts have found them convenient to perpetuate their power, thus slaughter has furnished a plausible pretext for peculation.

Fortunately, in spite of the various impediments that have thwarted the advancement of knowledge, the blessings of society have been sufficiently experienced to convince us that the only solid good to be expected from a government must result from the security of our persons and property. Domestic felicity has given a mild lustre to human happiness superior to the false glory of sanguinary devastation or magnificent robberies. Our fields and vineyards have thus gradually become the principal objects of our care and it is from this general sentiment governing the opinion of the civilized part of the world that we are enabled to contemplate, with some degree of certainty, the approaching age of peace.

All that could be done by a body of manners, without a soul of morals, to improve mankind had been tried in France. The result was polished slavery and such an inordinate love of pleasure as led the majority to search only for enjoyment, till the tone of nature was destroyed. Yet some few really learned the true art of living, giving that degree of elegance to domestic intercourse...whence all the social virtues spring.

Government—French Revolution

Wollstonecraft's *A Vindication of the Rights of Men* was for the most part a defence of the French Revolution and an attack on its critics, notably Edmund Burke. The first of many responses to Burke, it flowed from the pen fast and furiously. Intermixed with her analysis of French society, especially the abuses of the old regime, are remarks of a more general nature on such institutions as private property and slavery. Like so many political economists of her day, Wollstonecraft held to the labour theory of value. The only right to property authorized was that achieved by talent and industry. In a country where the oldest son inherited all the property, Wollstonecraft argued for a more equal division among the children of a family. Without it property enabled an elder son to overpower talents and depress virtue. Wollstonecraft seems thus, unlike Macaulay, to be advocating inheritance by women.

The great concern of most members of the middle class, Wollstonecraft lamented, was to live above their equals and appear richer than they were; aping the manners of the rich led to inestimable vice and misery. In all these comments she reveals herself as a liberal, progressive thinker, keen to promote both virtue and productivity, to ensure enough income and honest work for all. She blasted the idleness of the rich both as an evil in itself and as an unfortunate model for the middle class.

Text: Wollstonecraft, *A Vindication of the Rights of Men* 23-24, (in *Political Writings* 23-24 and *Works* 5:23-25):

It would be an arduous task to trace all the vice and misery that arise in society from the middle class of people aping the manners of the great. All are aiming to procure respect on account of their property, and most places are considered as sinecures that enable men to start into notice. The grand concern of three parts out of four is to contrive to live above their equals and to appear to be richer than they are. How much domestic comfort and private satisfaction is sacrificed to this irrational ambition! It is a destructive mildew that blights the fairest virtues: benevolence, friendship, generosity and all those endearing charities which bind human hearts together....

Property, I do not scruple to aver it, should be fluctuating, which would be the case if it were more equally divided among all the children of a family, else it is an everlasting rampart, in consequence of a barbarous feudal institution, that enables the elder son to overpower talents and depress virtue. Besides, an unmanly servility, most inimical to true dignity of character is, by this means, fostered in society. Men of some abilities play on the follies of the rich, and mounting to fortune as they degrade themselves, they stand in the way of men of superior talents who cannot advance in such crooked paths, or wade through the filth which *parasites* never boggle at. Pursuing their way straight forward, their spirit is either bent or broken by the rich man's contumelies, or the difficulties they have to encounter.

The only security of property that nature authorizes and reason sanctions is the right a man has to enjoy the acquisitions which his talents and industry have acquired, and to bequeath them to whom he chooses. Happy would it be for the world if there were no other road to wealth or honour, if pride, in the shape of parental affection, did not absorb the man, and prevent friendship from having the same weight as relationship. Luxury and effeminacy would not then introduce so much idiotism into the noble families which form one of the pillars of our state, the ground would not lie fallow, nor would undirected activity of mind spread the contagion of restless idleness, and its concomitant, vice, through the whole mass of society.

Instead of gaming they might nourish a virtuous ambition, and love might take place of the gallantry which you, with knightly fealty, venerate. Women would probably then act like mothers, and the fine lady, become a rational woman, might think it necessary to superintend her family and suckle her children in order to fulfil her part of the social compact. But vain is the hope while great masses of property are hedged round by hereditary honours, for numberless vices, forced in the hot-bed of wealth, assume a sightly form to dazzle the senses and cloud the understanding. The respect paid to rank and fortune damps every generous purpose of the soul, and stifles the natural affections on which human contentment ought to be built.

Burke had used custom as a defence for oppressive French institutions that Wollstonecraft condemned outright. She accordingly tried to explode custom as a legitimation. Injustices became convenient for some and consequently legal, she noted. Almost every vice had brought some benefit to society. Wollstonecraft herself believed in a conformity between reason and the laws of God. We had to go below the surface to discover the real nature of right and wrong, beyond local circumstances that confound good and evil. She commented that the rich and weak found it pleasanter to enjoy their advantages than to correct abuses. Wollstonecraft as well distinguished sharply between benevolence and the recognition of rights. For the rich and weak rights grated; they were impertinent and meddlesome. It was easier to confer benevolence than to do justice. Yet the poor were averse to accepting a favour instead of claiming a right. They might be grateful for the moment but would later consider the rich their lawful prey. Wollstonecraft was obviously sympathetic to ingratitude among the poor.

Text: Wollstonecraft, *A Vindication of the Rights of Men* 54-55 (*Political Writings* 55 and *Works* 5:52):

Right or wrong may be estimated according to the point of sight, and other adventitious circumstances but, to discover its real nature, the enquiry must go deeper than the surface, and beyond the local consequences that confound good and evil together. The rich and weak, a numerous train, will certainly applaud your system and loudly celebrate your pious reverence for authority and establishments; they find it pleasanter to enjoy than to think, to justify oppression than correct abuses. *The rights of men* are grating sounds that set their teeth on edge, the impertinent enquiry of philosophic meddling innovation. If the poor are in distress, they will make some *benevolent* exertions to assist them, they will confer obligations, but not do justice.

Benevolence is a very amiable specious quality, yet the aversion which men feel to accept a right as a favour should rather be extolled as a vestige of native dignity than stigmatized as the odious offspring of ingratitude. The poor consider the rich as their lawful prey, but we ought not too severely to animadvert on their ingratitude. When they receive an alms they are commonly grateful at the moment, but old habits quickly return, and cunning has ever been a substitute for force.

Text: Wollstonecraft, *French Revolution* 221-25 (*Works* 6:109-12):

The most high degree of civilization amongst the ancients...seems to have consisted in the perfection the arts, including language, attained while the people, only domesticated brutes, were governed and amused by religious shows that stand on record as the most egregious insult ever offered to the human understanding. Women were in a state of bondage, though the men who gave way to the most unbridled excesses, even to the outraging of nature, expected that they should be chaste and took the only method to render them so in such a depraved state of society, by ruling them with a rod of iron, making them, excepting the courtesans, merely household, breeding animals.

The state of slavery, likewise of a large proportion of men, tended probably more than any other circumstance to degrade the whole circle of society. While it gave that air of arrogance, which has falsely been called dignity, to one class, the other acquired the servile mien that fear always impresses....

In the systems of government of the ancients, in the perfection of the arts and in the ingenious conjectures which supplied the place of science, we see, however, all that the human passions can do to give grandeur to the human character, but we only see the heroism that was the effect of passion, if we except Aristides. For during this youth of the world the imagination alone was cultivated and the subordinate understanding merely exercised to regulate the taste, without extending to its grand employ the forming of principles....

Voluptuousness alone softened the character down to tenderness of heart and, as taste was cultivated, peace was sought rather because it was convenient than because it was just. But, when war could not be avoided, men were hired by the rich to secure to them the quiet enjoyment of their luxuries, so that war, become a trade, did not render ferocious all those who directly, or indirectly waged it....When we contemplate the infancy of man, his gradual advance towards maturity, his miserable weakness as a solitary being and the crudeness of his first notion respecting the nature of civil society, it will not appear extraordinary that the acquirement of political knowledge has been so extremely slow, or that public happiness has not been more rapidly and generally diffused.

The perfection attained by the ancients, it is true, has ever afforded the imagination of the poetical historian a theme to deck with the choicest flowers of rhetoric, though the cool investigation of facts seems clearly to prove that the civilization of the world, hitherto, has consisted rather in cultivating the taste than in exercising the understanding. Were not these vaunted improvements also confined to a small corner of the globe while the political view of the wisest legislators, seldom extending beyond the splendour and aggrandizement of their individual nation, they trampled with a ferocious affectation of patriotism on the most sacred rights of humanity? When the arts flourished in Greece and literature began to shed its blandishments on society the world was mostly inhabited by barbarians who waged eternal war with their more polished neighbours, the imperfection of whose government sapping its foundation, the science of politics necessarily received a check in the bud.

We have probably derived our great superiority over those nations from the discovery of the polar attraction of the needle, the perfection which astronomy and mathematics have attained and the fortunate invention of printing. For, while the revival of letters has added the collected wisdom of Antiquity to the improvements of modern research, the latter most useful art has rapidly multiplied copies of the productions of genius and compilations of learning, bringing them within the reach of all ranks of men. Scientific discoveries also have not only led us to new worlds, but, facilitating the communication between different nations, the friction of arts and commerce have given to society the transcendently pleasing polish of urbanity, and thus, by a gradual softening of manners, the complexion of social life has been completely changed. But the remains of superstition and the unnatural distinction of privileged classes, which had their origin in barbarous folly, still fettered the opinions of man and sullied his native dignity till several distinguished English writers discussed political subjects with the energy of men who began to feel their strength. While only a rumour of these sentiments roused the attention and exercised the minds of some men of letters in France, a number of staunch disputants who had more thoroughly digested them fled from oppression to put them to the test of experience in America.

Locke, following the track of these bold thinkers, recommended in a more methodical manner religious toleration, and analyzed the principles of civil liberty, for in this definition of liberty we find the elements of *The Declaration of the Rights of Man*, which in spite of the fatal errors of ignorance and the perverse obstinacy of selfishness, is now converting sublime theories in to practical truths.

The revolution, it is true, soon introduced the corruption that has ever since been corroding British freedom. Still, when the rest of Europe groaned under the weight of the most unjust and cruel laws, the life and property of Englishmen were comparatively safe. And, if an impress-warrant respected the distinction of ranks when the glory of England was at stake, splendid victories hid this flaw in the best existing constitution, and all exultingly recollected that the life or liberty of a man never depended on the will of an individual.

Englishmen were then, with reason, proud of their constitution and, if this noble pride have degenerated into arrogance, when the cause became less conspicuous, it is only a venial lapse of human nature to be lamented merely as it stops the progress of civilization and leads the people to imagine that their ancestors have done everything possible to secure the happiness of society and meliorate the condition of man, because they have done much.

When learning was confined to a small number of the citizens of a state and the investigation of its privileges was left to a number still smaller, governments seem to have acted as if the people were formed only for them and, ingeniously confounding their rights with metaphysical jargon, the luxurious grandeur of individuals has been supported by the misery of the bulk of their fellow creatures and ambition gorged by the butchery of millions of innocent victims.

The most artful chain of despotism has ever been supported by false notions of duty, enforced by those who were to profit by the cheat. Thus has the liberty of man been restrained and the spontaneous flow of his feelings, which would have fertilized his mind, being choked at the source, he is rendered in the same degree unhappy as he is made unnatural...But at no period has the scanty diffusion of knowledge permitted the body of the people to participate in the discussion of political science, and if philosophy at length have simplified the principles of social union so as to render them easy to be comprehended by every sane and thinking being, it appears to me that man may contemplate with benevolent complacency and becoming pride the approaching reign of reason and peace...

Nature having made men unequal, by giving stronger bodily and mental powers to one than to another, the end of government ought to be to destroy this inequality by protecting the weak. Instead of which it has always leaned to the opposite side, wearing itself out by disregarding the first principle of its organization. It appears to be the grand province of government, though scarcely acknowledged, so to hold the balance that the abilities or riches of individuals may not interfere with the equilibrium of the whole. For, as it is vain to expect that men should master their passions during the heat of action, legislators should have this perfection of laws ever in view when, calmly grasping the interest of humanity, reason assures them that their own is best secured by the security of the commonweal. The first social systems were certainly founded by passion, individuals wishing to fence round their own wealth or power and make slaves of their brothers to prevent encroachment. Their descendants have ever been at work to solder the chains they forged and render the usurpations of strength secure by the fraud of partial laws, laws that can be abrogated only by the exertions of reason, emancipating mankind by making government a science, instead of a craft, and civilizing the grand mass by exercising their understandings about the most important objects of inquiry.

As other defenders of the French Revolution, Wollstonecraft devoted a significant amount of space to explaining why abuses, which had become increasingly apparent by 1794, occurred. As had Macaulay and other radicals, she stressed the harshness and stupidity of the old regime. She gave examples of oppressive taxes, pointing out both how onerous they were for the poor to pay and how counter-productive they were by discouraging agriculture and industry.

In the old regime military rank was linked to a man's status in society, not his merits. The military, "a pest in every country," were leagued with the privileged, received their revenues and were a dead weight on agriculture. France had also 200,000 licentious priests to maintain, who were entitled to one-quarter of the nation's produce. In addition, propping up the priesthood, were 60,000 monks, "the leeches of the kingdom" who contributed nothing to it. Note that Wollstonecraft's position was anti-clerical but not anti-religious. She herself was a Christian believer (Protestant) and the source most cited throughout her writing was the Bible. Her language condemning the past system was strong indeed. She was no less passionate in welcoming the new. Like Macaulay, Wollstonecraft admitted to a "glow of warmth" at seeing the French exalted from their beastly degradation to where they could breathe the "invigorating air of independence" and contemplate their dawning freedom. Who could be so callow as not to see this regeneration as noble? The French were not born to be slaves.

The second selection discusses the Declaration of the Rights of Man and its principles of natural political and civil liberty. Wollstonecraft succinctly described how the declaration established equality, secured rights and derived sovereignty in the people, thus confirming the authority of the people over the king. There are remarks on the choice between one or two chambers in Parliament and concerns regarding a hereditary senate. So also are there on the difficult question of giving the executive enough power for efficiency while providing against abuse. There is much practicality, as well as passion, in Wollstonecraft's remarks here, as there is throughout the book.

Text: Wollstonecraft, *French Revolution* 75-82 (*Works* 6:49-52):

Before we enter on the grand business produced by the meeting of the Estates-General, it is necessary to take a retrospective glance over the oppression of which Frenchmen so loudly complained and, while we trace their justness, the question will only be why they did not sooner raise their shoulders to heave off the mighty load. To ascertain this truth we need not enter into deep researches, though it may be difficult to collect all the parts of the feudal chain which linked the despotism of sixty thousand nobles, who not only exercised all the tyranny that the system authorized but countenanced the still more extensive depredations of their numerous dependents. What, indeed, could equal the slavery of the poor husbandman, not only pillaged by the tithe and game laws but even obliged to let whole flocks of pigeons devour his grain without daring to destroy them because those pigeons belonged to the chateau. Afterwards forced to carry the scanty crop to be tolled at the mill of *monseigneur*, which, to follow a Frenchman's staff of life through all its stages of taxation, must then be baked at the privileged oven?

It would be captious, perhaps, to dwell on some of the abominable tenures of personal servitude which, though grown obsolete, were not abrogated, especially as more specious, if not less grinding, not less debasing, exactions were in force, to deprave every moral feeling of the two divisions of society: the governing and governed. When chased from the country of which the chief charm is independence by such worrying restraints, a man wished to pursue any occupation in a town, he must previously purchase a patent of some privileged person to whom this tax had been sold by a farmer-general or the parasite of a minister. All lived by plunder and its universality gave it a sanction that took off the odium, though nothing could varnish the injustice. Yet, such was the insensibility of the great, the pleasures these extortions procured were not less grateful to the senses because paid by the sweat of industry. No...money was money, and who cared on what it was levied? Thus the rich necessarily became robbers and the poor thieves. Talking of honour, honesty was overlooked and, custom giving a soft name to different atrocities, few thought it a duty to investigate disregarded principles or to relinquish their share of the plunder to satisfy a romantic singularity of opinion which excited ridicule rather than imitation.

The military, a pest in every country, were here also all noble and leagued with a hundred thousand privileged persons of different descriptions, to support their prerogative of receiving a revenue, which was a dead weight on agriculture, while they were not obliged in a direct way to advance anything towards defraying the public expenditure. The gabelle [salt tax], the corvee [forced labour], the obligation to supply horses to transport the troops from one part of the kingdom to another, even when most necessary at the farm, clogs on husbandry, equally unjust and vexatious, were riveted only on the ankles of labour. Activity then being continually damped by such various restrictions, instead of being braced by encouragement an invincible impediment was thrown in the way of agricultural improvements....

Beside which France maintained two hundred thousand priests, united in the same spirit of licentiousness, who indulged themselves in all the depraved pleasures of cloaked immorality. At the same time they brutalized the people by sanctifying the most diabolical prejudices to whose empire every consideration of justice and political improvement was sacrificed. Added to evils of this magnitude, there were the canker-worms that lurked behind monastic walls. For sixty thousand persons, who by renouncing the world cut the thread of nature, served as a prop to the priesthood that enjoyed more than a fourth of the produce of all France, independent of the estates it possessed, which were immense. This body of men, the leeches of the kingdom, the idols of the ignorant...contributed not a farthing to the support of the hydra, whom they were anxious to protect as a guard to themselves. Ostentatiously boasting of their charity, while revelling on the spoil of fraud, by a sacrilege the most nefarious, their whole lives were a mockery of the doctrines which they taught and pretended to reverence....

There were also the Farmers-General with their army of fifty thousand collectors who, by their manner of levying and amassing the revenue, gave an additional gripe to an oppression, the most wringing that could be invented, because its very principles led to the exercise of the vilest peculation and impunity was secured by a coalition of robbers, that multitude of men in office whose families and flatterers all...fattened on the spoils of their continual war with justice. And, while the interest of the people was continually sacrificed by parliaments, the inferior courts of law were still more venal, because composed of those litigious practitioners, who thicken like spawn on putrid bodies, when a state is become corrupt. Such were the grievances!...

Who is so callous to the interest of humanity as to say it was not a noble regeneration? Who is so benumbed by selfish fears as not to feel a glow of warmth at seeing the inhabitants of a vast empire exalted from the lowest state of beastly degradation to a summit where, contemplating the dawn of freedom, they may breath the invigorating air of independence, which will give them a new constitution of mind? Who is so much under the influence of prejudice as to insist that Frenchmen are a distinct race, formed by nature or habit to be slaves, incapable of ever attaining those noble sentiments which characterize a free people?

Text: Wollstonecraft, *French Revolution* 345-47 (*Works* 6:162-63):

The foundation of liberty was laid in the declaration of rights, the first three articles of which contain the great principles of natural, political and civil liberty. First, that men are born and always continue, free and equal in respect to their rights; civil distinctions, therefore, can be founded only on public utility. Secondly, the end of all political associations is the preservation of the natural and imprescriptible rights of man, which rights are liberty, property, security and resistance of oppression. Thirdly, the nation is the source of all sovereignty; no body of men, no individual, can then be entitled to any authority which is not derived from it.

The first article, establishing the equality of man, strikes at the root of all useless distinctions; the second, securing his rights against oppression, maintains his dignity; and the third, acknowledging the sovereignty of the nation, confirms the authority of the people. These are the essential points of a good government and it is only necessary, when these points are ascertained by a nation and solemnly ratified in the hearts of its citizens, to take care in the formation of a political system to provide against the abuse of the executive part while equal caution should be observed not to destroy its efficiency, as on that depend its justice, vigour and promptitude....

While defining the authority of the king, or rather determining that he should have not authority unless the option of disturbing the legislation deserve that name, they debated the question of two chambers with equal inconsideration and all the puerile self-sufficiency of ignorance. The opposers of two chambers ...ridiculed the idea of a balance of power and instanced the abuses of the English government to give force to their objections. At the same time, fearing that the nobles of the court would contend for an hereditary senate similar to the British House of Peers or, at least, for a seat during life, paramount to the representatives who they determined should be elected every two years, they sought to bring the business to a speedy issue. The very division of the nobility served to hasten it, and strengthened the arguments of the popular members, who finding that they could rely on the concurrence of the parish priests, whose wishes in favour of the unity of the assembly were quickly betrayed by the opinions of their leading orator, demanded the decision of a question that had been agitated in the most tumultuous manner.

Wollstonecraft's denunciation of slavery was brief but passionate. Liberty was a birthright of all, to be denied only for such abuses as the commission of serious crimes. Yet slavery was justified by "timid or interested politicians" on the basis of property rights. Slavery had been abolished in Britain in effect by the courts ruling it to be illegal. The slave trade itself was abolished only in 1807 after a 35-year campaign led by William Wilberforce. Wollstonecraft challenged the legislators to let their natural feelings of humanity silence their timidity and wipe out slavery. She remarked that the caste system in India could be equally well justified by its usefulness or custom.

Text: Wollstonecraft, *A Vindication of the Rights of Men* (*Political Writings* 53-55 and *Works* 5:50-52):

You find it very difficult to separate policy from justice; in the political world they have frequently been separated with shameful dexterity. To mention a recent instance: according to the limited views of timid, or interested, politicians an abolition of the infernal slave trade would not only be unsound policy, but a flagrant infringement of the laws (which are allowed to have been infamous) that induce the planters to purchase their estates. But is it not consonant with justice, with the common principles of humanity, not to mention Christianity, to abolish this abominable mischief?....

The same arguments might be used in India if any attempt were made to bring back things to nature, to prove that man ought never to quit the caste that confined him to the profession of his lineal forefathers. The Brahmins would doubtless find many ingenious reasons to justify this debasing, though venerable prejudice, and would not, it is to be supposed, forget to observe that time, by interweaving the oppressive law with many useful customs, had rendered it for the present very convenient and consequently legal. Almost every vice that has degraded our nature might be justified by showing that it had been productive of *some* benefit to society.

Wollstonecraft's chief work on the French Revolution argued for "gradual" revolution in government, for during violent changes measures were adopted for their popularity, not their wisdom. The great majority would choose an abstract sketch of a perfect system of government without reference to practical questions as to the readiness of the people to implement it. Governments that have the happiness of their people as their object must then make the power of peaceable alteration of their constitutions a fundamental principle. Wollstonecraft warned also about being too cautious. The slow improvements made in the British Constitution were condemned as impractical by even the most enlightened minds. She reflected Enlightenment optimism also in referring to the "science of government."

Wollstonecraft's advice on taxes is still timely. She asserted the universality of tax unfairness. Governments should be regular in their demands, anticipate their wants and avoid running a deficit. Increasing the debt by recourse to paper notes only extended the evil. She suggested that a tax on land might be the fairest, the approach of the eighteenth-century French physiocrats and nineteenth-century progressives like the American Henry George—for land was the "mother of every production."

Text: Wollstonecraft, *French Revolution* 355-58 (*Works* 6:166-67):

The revolution of states ought to be gradual for, during violent or material changes, it is not so much the wisdom of measures as the popularity they acquire by being adapted to the foibles of the great body of the community which gives them success. Men are most easily led away by the ingenious arguments that dwell on the equality of man, and these are always employed by the different leaders of popular governments.

While the most ingenious theorists or desperate partisans of the people take advantage of this infirmity of our nature, the consequences must sometimes prove destructive to society if they do not end in the most dreadful anarchy. For when the members of a state are not directed by practical knowledge everyone produces a plan of polity, till the confusion becomes general and the nation plunges into wretchedness—pursuing the schemes of those philosophers of genius who, advancing before their age, have sketched the model of a perfect system of government. Thus it happened in France, that Hume's idea of a perfect commonwealth, the adoption of which would be eligible only when civilization has arrived at a much greater degree of perfection and knowledge is more generally diffused than at the present period, was nevertheless chosen as the model of their new government, with a few exceptions, by the Constituent Assembly, which choice doubtless proceeded from members not having had an opportunity to acquire a knowledge of practical liberty.

Some of the members, it is true, alluded to the improvements made by the Americans on the plan of the English constitution, but the great majority, despising experience, were for forming, at once, a system much more perfect.

This self-sufficiency has produced those dreadful outrages and attacks made by the anarchists of that country on personal liberty, property and whatever else society holds sacred. These melancholy considerations seem to me to afford irrefragable arguments, to prove that it is necessary for all governments which have for their object the happiness of the people, to make the power of altering peaceably a fundamental principle of their constitution.

Still, if the attempt to carry prematurely into execution the sublime theory, which has occupied some of the best heads to form, have afforded an opportunity to superficial politicians to condemn it as absurd and chimerical because it has not been attended with immediate success, the advocates for the extension of truth and reason ought not to despair. For when we contemplate the slow improvement that has been made in the science of government and that even the system of the British constitution was considered, by some of the most enlightened ancients, as the sublimest theory the human mind was able to conceive, though not reducible to practice, they should not relax in their endeavours to bring to maturity a polity more simple, which promises more equal freedom and general happiness to mankind.

Text: Wollstonecraft, *French Revolution* 302-04 (*Works* 6:302):

Every great reform requires systematic management and, however lightly weak daring heads may treat the gravity of such a remark, the pacific progress of every revolution will depend in a very material degree on the moderation and reciprocity of concessions made by the acting parties. It is true that in a nation chiefly celebrated for wit so much prudence could scarcely be expected, yet that is not a sufficient reason for condemning all the principles that produced the revolution, for liberty cannot be considered as belonging exclusively to any particular climate or temper of mind as a physical effect. It was peculiarly urgent, indeed, to form such a coalition to counteract the dangerous consequences of old prejudices....

Had the conduct of men been sincere and had they really pursued the fraternity about which they so continually declaimed, they might, in consolidating the rights of French citizens, have established every political advantage which the then state of reason was capable of adopting for the immediate benefit of society. But resentment bursting forth, which had long lain concealed (the effect of servitude and contumely), joined with the vanity of excelling all other nations in the science of government to produce an insolent audacity of conduct which, aiming at overturning everything, discouraged the wavering and frightened the timid.

Text: Wollstonecraft, *French Revolution* 390-93 (*Works* 6:180-82):

Governments which ought to protect and not oppress mankind cannot be too regular in their demands, for the manner of levying taxes is of the highest importance to political economy and the happiness of individuals. No government has yet established a just system of taxation, for in every country the expenses of government have fallen unequally on the citizens. Perhaps it is not possible to render them perfectly equal but by laying all the taxes on land, the mother of every production.

In this posture of affairs, the enthusiasm of the French in the cause of liberty might have been turned to the advantage of a new and permanent system of finance. An able, bold minister who possessed the confidence of the nation might have recommended with success the taking of the national property under the direct management of the Assembly, and then endeavouring to raise a loan on that property he would have given respectability to the new government by immediately procuring the supplies indispensably necessary not only to keep it but to put it in motion.

The immediate and incessant wants of a state must always be supplied; prudence therefore requires that the directors of the finances should rather provide by anticipation for its wants than suffer a *deficit*. The government being once in arrears, additional taxes become indispensable to bring forward the balance, or the nation must have recourse to paper notes and expedient as experience has shown, always to be dreaded because by increasing the debt it only extends the evil. This increasing debt, like a ball of snow, gathering as it rolls, soon attains a wonderful magnitude. Every state which has unavoidably accumulated its debt ought, provided those at the helm wish to preserve the government and extend the security and comforts of its citizens, to take every just measure to render the interest secure and to fund the principal.

Peace, War and Militarism—and Gender

Excerpts from Wollstonecraft's *A Vindication of the Rights of Woman* show both a contempt for military virtues and an incipient understanding that military institutions are antithetical to a free society. The gallantry and polished manners of officers were positively dangerous in a country town because they concealed "vice and folly." Wollstonecraft even compared soldiers to uneducated women. Both had the misfortune to acquire "manners" before "morals"—the external behaviour before the inward conviction. Yet Wollstonecraft assured her readers that she was not going to advise women "to turn their distaff into a musket." She wished indeed, using the prophetic words of Isaiah, to turn swords into pruning-hooks.

Text: Wollstonecraft, *A Vindication of the Rights of Woman* 235-36 (*Works* 5:216):

I know that, as a proof of the inferiority of the sex, Rousseau has exultingly exclaimed, "How can they leave the nursery for the [military] camp!"[43] And the camp has by some moralists been termed the school of the most heroic virtues, though I think it would puzzle a keen casuist to prove the reasonableness of the greater number of wars that have dubbed heroes. I do not mean to consider this question critically because, having frequently viewed these freaks of ambition as the first natural mode of civilization, when the ground must be torn up and the woods cleared by fire and sword, I do not choose to call them pests. But surely the present system of war has little connection with virtue of any denomination, being rather the school of *finesse* and effeminacy than of fortitude.

Yet, if defensive war, the only justifiable war, in the present advanced state of society, where virtue can show its face and ripen amidst the rigours which purify the air on the mountain's top, were alone to be adopted as just and glorious, the true heroism of Antiquity might again animate female bosoms. But...gentle reader, male or female, do not alarm thyself, for though I have compared the character of a modern soldier with that of a civilized woman, I am not going to advise them to turn their distaff into a musket, though I sincerely wish to see the bayonet converted into a pruning-hook.

Text: Wollstonecraft, *A Vindication of the Rights of Woman* 84-86 (*Works* 5:86-93):

After attacking the sacred majesty of kings, I shall scarcely excite surprise by adding my firm persuasion that every profession in which great subordination of rank constitutes its power is highly injurious to morality. A standing army, for instance, is incompatible with freedom because subordination and rigour are the very sinews of military discipline and despotism is necessary to give vigour to enterprises that one will directs. A spirit inspired by romantic notions of honour, a kind of morality founded on the fashion of the age, can only be felt by a few officers, while the main body must be moved by command, like the waves of the sea, for the strong wind of authority pushes the crowd of subalterns forward, they scarcely know or care why, with headlong fury.

Nothing can be so prejudicial to the morals of the inhabitants of country towns as the occasional residence of a set of idle superficial young men, whose only occupation is gallantry, whose polished manners render vice more dangerous by concealing its deformity under gay ornamental drapery....Every

---

[43] Rousseau's *Emile* is cited: "Can a woman be one day a nurse, and the next a soldier?" (4:13).

corps is a chain of despots who, submitting and tyrannizing without exercising their reason, become dead weights of vice and folly on the community.

[Wollstonecraft observed that military men, like women, were sent into the world before their minds had been stored with knowledge or fortified by principles.] Standing armies can never consist of resolute, robust men; they may be well disciplined machines, but they will seldom contain men under the influence of strong passions, or with very vigorous faculties. As for any depth of understanding, I will venture to affirm that it is as rarely to be found in the army as amongst women, and the cause, I maintain, is the same. It may be further observed that officers are also particularly attentive to their persons, fond of dancing, crowded rooms, adventures and ridicule. Like the *fair* sex, the business of their lives is gallantry. They were taught to please, and they only live to please. Yet they do not lose their rank in the distinction of sexes, for they are still reckoned superior to women, though in what their superiority consists, beyond what I have just mentioned, it is difficult to discover.

The great misfortune is this, that they both acquire manners before morals, and a knowledge of life before they have, from reflection, any acquaintance with the grand ideal outline of human nature. The consequence is natural. Satisfied with common nature, they become a prey to prejudices and, taking all their opinions on credit, they blindly submit to authority.

Nature and Society—Animal Welfare

Wollstonecraft's "Moral Conversations and Stories" was written for the moral edification of children. The moral lessons are clearly set out and there is no bothering with subtlety. As well as the need for kind treatment of animals there were lessons on anger, lying, goodness, honour, truth, duties, folly, immoderate indulgence, idleness and misery. This sort of literature was popular in England for a long time. The stories, written in 1788, were republished several times in Wollstonecraft's lifetime. They are flagged here, but not excerpted, for the sympathy shown non-human species in a period still of considerable everyday cruelty and no protection in law against it. Bear-baiting and cock fighting were entertainment; birds were killed in vast numbers for sport. Wollstonecraft tried to impart her own delight in nature to children. God is described as "the Father of all creatures" and his benevolent intentions for all creatures insisted on. God cares even for worms, giving them "everything necessary for a comfortable existence." Reminding the children that they were often troublesome and she was stronger than they: "Yet I do not kill you."[44]

The arguments on cruelty to animals in *A Vindication of the Rights of Woman* seem to take up Macaulay's points from *Letters on Education* about the need to teach kindness to children. Wollstonecraft now argued that cruelty

---

[44] Wollstonecraft, *Original Stories* 2 and *Works* 4:367-73.

to animals would lead to tyrannical treatment of wives, children and servants, a point that is still frequently made in pleas for humane treatment of animals.

Text: Wollstonecraft, *A Vindication of the Rights of Woman* 268 (*Works* 5:243-244):

Humanity to animals should be particularly inculcated as a part of national education, for it is not at present one of our national virtues. Tenderness for their humble dumb domestics, among the lower class, is oftener to be found in a savage than a civilized state. For civilization prevents that intercourse which creates affection in the rude hut or mud hovel and leads uncultivated minds who are only depraved by the refinements which prevail in the society...to domineer over them to revenge the insults that they are obliged to bear from their superiors.

This habitual cruelty is first caught at school where it is one of the rare sports of the boys to torment the miserable brutes that fall in their way. The transition, as they grow up, from barbarity to brutes to domestic tyranny over wives, children and servants, is very easy. Justice, or even benevolence, will not be a powerful spring of action unless it [extend] to the whole creation. Nay, I believe that it may be delivered as an axiom that those who can see pain, unmoved, will soon learn to inflict it.

> "A race of men 'born only to consume the fruits of the earth' and set on high for others to maintain by the sweat of their brow must necessarily be corrupt, for idleness engenders every evil."[45]

MARY HAYS (1760-1843)

Hays,[46] an essayist and novelist, was born to a middle-class nonconformist family in London. She joined a radical group associated with the (radical) publisher Joseph Johnson. Her feminism was influenced by Mary Wollstonecraft, whose work she continued on Wollstonecraft's death. Hays published a six-volume collection of biographies of women, two feminist novels and *Letters and Essays*, her most theoretical work.

---

[45] Hays, "Thoughts on Civil Liberty," *Letters and Essays* 15.

[46] On Hays see the introductions to her *Letters and Essays* and her novel, *Memoirs of Emma Courtney* and my *Women Founders* 115-23.

Government—Civil Liberties

Mary Hays's essay on civil liberty is filled with apt observations on civil liberties, gender and the French Revolution. It upsets numerous items of the conventional wisdom on political liberty. That the "tyranny of custom" is sometimes worse than the "tyranny of government" we must still agree. So also must we agree with her statement that governments were not impartial and indeed are more injurious to women than to men. Since women are excluded from high places and pensions and are less in the "vortex of influence," they could examine subjects without prejudice. Hays is remarkable also in her citation of a Greek philosopher that the "most necessary part of learning is to unlearn our errors."

Another of the many fine turns of phrase in the essay is the statement that monarchical and aristocratic governments "carry within themselves the seeds of their dissolution." Corruption and oppression necessarily led to revolt. The "body politic," a common medieval metaphor, was like a natural body, liable to dangerous convulsions when struggling to expel "morbid humours." The remedy, she warned, might kill the patient.

The tone of "Thoughts on Civil Liberty" is sensible and moderate. Hays admitted that she herself shrank from revolution, hoping that change would be made by legislation keeping pace with enlightened thought. She did not doubt that posterity would reap the benefit of the "present struggles" in France, but they were ruinous to those engaged in them. Hays was unusual for a defender of the French Revolution to offer grounds for sympathy with the royal family. Allowances had to be made for the prejudices with which they had been raised. As would de Staël in her more extensive *Circonstances actuelles*, Hays cautioned against blaming the disorders, which would be transient, on the principles of the revolution.

Text: Hays, "Thoughts on Civil Liberty," *Letters and Essays* 10-19:

The ingenious author of "An Enquiry into the Nature of Subscription" has observed in a note affixed to his elegant address to freedom "that the most sensible females when they turn their attention to political subjects, are more uniformly on the side of liberty than the other sex." In proof of which he celebrates the respectable names of Macaulay, Wollstonecraft, Barbauld, Jebb, Williams and Smith. This predilection, he says, "may be accounted for without adopting the sentiments or the language of gallantry. The truth is the modes of education and the customs of society are degrading to the female character and the tyranny of custom is sometimes worse than the tyranny of government. When a sensible woman rises above the tyranny of custom she feels a generous indignation, which when turned against the exclusive claims of the other sex is favourable to female pretensions, when turned against the tyranny of government, it is commonly favourable to the rights of both sexes. Most governments are partial and more injurious to women than to men."

It may likewise be added that as women have no claims to expect either pension or place they are less in the vortex of influence; they are also more unsophisticated by education, having neither system, test or subscription imposed upon them, and some subjects require only to be examined with an impartial and unprejudiced eye to ensure conviction.

Without pretending to any profound knowledge of the arcana of politics, every thinking mind must be struck with the exorbitant taxation which is thought necessary to defray the expenses of certain establishments both in church and state. By what infatuation and magic so many hug their chains and bow down before the idol in power at first view appears inconceivable, but when the progress of corruption is traced and the force of habit acknowledged our wonder ceases. "The most necessary part of learning, said one of the Grecian philosophers, is to unlearn our errors," and a conviction of the truth of the doctrine of association compels us to add, it is also the most difficult. Novel truths, or rather truths represented in a new point of view, operate most forcibly on the rising generation where the memory is not preoccupied.

It needs little of the spirit of prophecy to predict that the present just and liberal notions on the subject of civil government, which like a flood of light irradiate Europe, will in future periods produce certain though slow effects, the feeble efforts of prejudice and interest must in the end give way to truth, however gradual may be their declining struggles.

Look back through the history of the world from its golden days of infancy and innocence to the maturity of the present times and you will discern various truths first dawning like the sun through a misty horizon. After encountering many dark clouds of error and opposition, at length beaming forth in meridian brightness, thus gently and gradually diffusing light and happiness....Our nature is progressive and everything around us is the same. Wise and benevolent plan! for "happiness," truly observes Epicurus, "resembles neither a standing pool nor a rapid torrent but is like a gentle stream that glides smoothly and silently along." Surely legislation in which the peace and virtue of millions are concerned cannot be the only subject that admits of no improvement. "In different communities different laws are instituted according to the circumstances of the people who enact them. Whatever is thus prescribed should be a rule of justice so long as the society shall judge the observance of it to be for the benefit of the whole, but when this is found upon experience not to be the case, being no longer useful, it should be no longer prescribed."

I love peace, and am one of those who "faint when they do look on blood," and most devoutly do I pray that a wise and peaceful reformation of the gross corruptions and abuses which deform the present system of government in this country may preclude all dreadful extremities. To say nothing of the justice of such measures, sound policy requires them, for the historic page has invariably attested the vanity of fines, proscriptions, proclamations and prohibitions, to arrest the progress of the human mind....

A race of men "born only to consume the fruits of the earth" and set on high for others to maintain by the sweat of their brow, must necessarily be corrupt, for idleness engenders every evil, and how few comparatively are there who know how to spend leisure well! "The ranks of society arose from the vices and follies of mankind and are therefore to be despised," said an ancient sage. And they are most certainly calculated to perpetuate the crimes and frivolity from whence they sprung....

I should shrink from the idea of a revolution, for I want sufficient courage to claim the crown of martyrdom, and those who suffer in endeavouring to benefit others, whatever be the cause, are unquestionably martyrs. I again earnestly repeat the wish that the wisdom of the legislature may keep pace with the national light. The emancipated mind is impatient of imposition, nor can it, in a retrograde course, unlearn what it has learned or unknow what it has known.

It appears to me that all monarchical and aristocratic governments carry within themselves the seeds of their dissolution, for when they become corrupt and oppressive to a certain degree, the effects must necessarily be murmurs, remonstrances and revolt. I almost shudder at the present general diffusion of political knowledge for, however I approve the principles, the desolations in a neighbouring country make me tremble at the very idea of the dangers (from the opposition of jarring interests) attending the practice. Posterity will, I have no doubt, reap the benefit of the present struggles in France, but they are ruinous and dreadful to those actually engaged in them. How will the page of history (while it records the noble efforts "inspiring glory through remotest time") be clouded and stained with sanguinary details, and how complicated, how affecting, must be the scenes of private calamity!...

The above observations were written while the public mind was agitated with the account of the massacres and popular insurrections in Paris, the mere temporary effervescence of spirits heated by the enthusiasm of the moment, and irritated by treachery and cruelty. In a generous and enlightened nation, such disorders must necessarily be transient, and it would be equally as absurd as unjust to charge them upon principles to which they are utterly repugnant.

Though very far from being a well-wisher to their cause yet, as individuals, I must commiserate the sufferings of the late reigning family. Great allowances ought to be made for early prejudices and associations and for the peculiar temptations attending peculiar situations, neither can their former luxury and security by any means have fitted their minds to encounter with firmness the terrible reverse, the flattery and prosperity attendant upon high stations, enervate the mind and deprive it of its natural strength, steadiness and fortitude are the hardy offspring of adversity. A little reflection on the structure of the human understanding, on the force of habit, the allurements of power and the influence of external circumstances would tend to mitigate the severity of our censures and soften the stern inflexibility of justice with the tear of sympathy.

The body politic of Europe in general seems at present like the body natural; when struggling to expel offensive and morbid humours the convulsive efforts threaten more immediate danger than even the lurking mischief, and there is reason to dread lest the patient expire under the operation of the powerful remedy.

Peace, War and Militarism—and Gender

The short excerpt from Hays's *Appeal to the Men of Great Britain*, 1798, shows a similar approach to Sophia's. Both made a case for women's equality. Hays's discussion of military education focused on the practical advantages that that training gave. Yet she disdained "masculine ideas" and "boldness of manner." She was raising the dilemma contemporary feminists still face: whether to claim equality of access to all institutions, including military colleges and combat roles in the Army, Navy, Air Force and Marines, or to reject certain roles as wrong for women/humankind. Hays of course was only musing about possibilities at this time; later feminists have had to confront the dilemma and take sides.

Text: Hays, *Appeal to the Men of Great Britain* 188-89:

Last in the list of masculine accomplishments...we shall take a little notice of a certain portion of military education which is not denied to women in this liberal age. A drill sergeant is a man of no small consequence in many families and is looked up to even by the fathers as to him who is to give the last, finest polish to their darlings, if by a kind of insulting prudence and foresight, highly dishonourable to the sex, they do not give them this striking advantage at an earlier period.

Though I have too good an opinion of women to be very uneasy about their conduct in consequence of this strange mode of commencing or finishing their education, and though it may not injure their morals and may very much improve their paces, and though it may make them look fierce enough to frighten the French in case of an invasion...Yet after all, who can deny this we have been speaking of to be a masculine attainment and likely to produce masculine ideas, masculine attitudes and upon the whole masculine boldness of manner?

"I know that the austere language of truth is rarely welcome at the throne; I know also that revolutions become necessary because it is hardly ever heard."[47]

Political liberty "is the power of being happy without doing harm to anyone."[48]

MARIE-JEANNE PHLIPON ROLAND DE LA PLATIÈRE (1754-93)

Roland[49] was Paris born, the daughter of an engraver, educated in Latin and English as well as French. She married an older man, a progressive administrator whom she assisted in his duties. They had one daughter. The two were active in the (moderate) Girondin movement in the French Revolution. Both were named in warrants but he escaped; she was jailed, released, but then re-arrested and executed on the guillotine. She went to her death with heroic dignity. Her posthumously published letters and memoirs, in both a French edition and English translation, are the source of the following excerpts.

Government—Political Liberty

Roland's essay "On Liberty," written just before the outbreak of the French Revolution, is a short, polished work on a theme much in the air. Its ideas are not original but reflect the views of France's enlightened, educated elite. They are similar to those of the philosophe, feminist Condorcet. They would soon appear in the Declaration of the Rights of Man. **J.S. Mill** and **Harriet Taylor Mill**, in their famous essay "On Liberty," 1859, would take up the same themes in greater elaboration.

Roland held that slavery and virtue were incompatible, for slavery broke social ties and destroyed the self-esteem essential for the development of our faculties. Only the free person could be courageous. Tyranny, she affirmed, degraded equally the oppressor and victim. The text that follows is an adaptation of the English translation in the *Works*, 1800. Not only have the spelling and grammar been updated, but awkward sections have been re-translated from the original *Oeuvres* and errors corrected.

---

[47] Lettre de M Roland 45.

[48] "On Liberty," *Works* 132.

[49] Biographies are: Gita May, *Madame Roland and the Age of Revolution*; Mary Patricia Willcocks, *Madame Roland*; Madeleine Clémenceau-Jacquemarie, *Life of Madame Roland*; see also my *Women Founders* 123-31.

Text: Roland, "On Liberty," *Works* 132-38:

What is liberty? I cannot consider it generally but distinguish liberty of the will from that of actions and of the mind. I doubt whether the first exists; the second appears to me very uncommon, and the third belongs but to sages. Metaphysical liberty is a problem on which I seek to exercise my ideas; political liberty is a blessing the image and utility of which I love to recall to mind; philosophical liberty, the only liberty, perhaps, that it is my province to know, is a treasure I wish to acquire.

Political liberty, for each individual of a society, consists in doing everything that he judges proper for his own happiness but which does not injure others. It is the power of being happy without doing harm to anyone. Is there an advantage that can be compared to it? Nothing in the world can take its place; delicious fruit of laws, it gives the human soul all the energy it can use.

The reign of the general will is the only one that maintains public happiness; from the moment when power secures independence to some parts of the state, corruption appears and soon manifests itself in the misery of the oppressed. Slavery and virtue are incompatible. Slavery breaks all the ties that connect man with his fellow creature. It releases and destroys the two springs that contribute most to the development of our faculties: self-esteem and glory, which is the result of public esteem. It lets nothing subsist but odious force and degrading fear.

Tyranny degrades equally the one who exercises it and the one who is enslaved by it; by it all lose the sentiment of truth, the idea of justice and the taste of good. We can look to the one who knows the extent and limits of his or her rights for respect for those of others, a generous intrepidity to defend them and the noble care to preserve them. True courage belongs only to the free man. What can those be capable of who are nothing except by the will of the master? To what obligations would he believe himself limited, the one who must imagine himself to be of a superior nature to that of the people he commands?

The essence of liberty consists in the enjoyment of and the inviolability of the first rights of social man: personal security and property, with the power to claim them in case of an accidental injury. This is the masterpiece of legislation, but so many things prevent it from being carried out or oppose its full realization and concur in its ruin that very rarely can one see it subsist unaltered even for a short time.

Not all peoples are capable of enjoying liberty; the same nation cannot sustain it equally at all times. Climate, soil, the nature of production, the situation of the land, its extent etc. either prepare the way for or distance it from its inhabitants, according to the mind, needs and resources given to them. Companion to poverty ordinarily, liberty is stifled by riches; the fertility of an abundant land makes it superfluous. It is also generally true that the most refined countries have the worst government. Bare subsistence or ease through labour make people honest and the state happy. Here, for the nation as for individuals, too many wants incite greed and cause corruption.

It is said that the English are free, and I believe that they are more than their neighbours, more than most of the peoples of Europe, except for the Swiss. But commerce and the love of gain, riches and luxury have weakened their morals and sapped their constitution....

Liberty suits none but simple people with few wants. When we consider the infinite care, continual vigilance required to maintain law in a free state, the time taken for sovereign acts for each of the citizens, one sees how little is left for other occupations. If we consider, besides, that industry and the arts open the first door to inequality, isolate those who profess to them by giving them extraordinary means to acquire property and offering resources independent of the common good, we will perceive how great was the wisdom of the legislators who banished them from their states.

The Lacedemonians were nothing but agriculturists and soldiers but they had serfs. It would be astonishing if in the same government the slavery of one part of the species were absolutely necessary for the perfect happiness of the other. This idea makes me shudder; I dare not pursue it. I hasten to arrive at what suits me much better. I leave metaphysical dreams and political speculations to the clever; I prefer what pertains to action and I believe that this is my element. I understand by liberty of mind not only the healthy view of an enlightened judgment not disturbed by prejudice or passion, but also that firm and quiet position of a strong soul, superior to events. I call it philosophical because it is the product of wisdom and one of its most unequivocal signs....

We must love people enough to concern ourselves with their welfare, and esteem them little enough as not to expect any return on their part. Judgment appears to me to consist in discovering that we can achieve our own happiness only in working for that of others; reason seems to me to be the firm resolution to act always agreeably to this principle. The highest degree of virtue is to do good with enthusiasm because it is honourable and delightful...Exact calculation and cold reasoning never make us capable of it; feeling alone inspires us.

Roland is believed to have drafted the letter which follows for her husband after his dismissal as Minister of the Interior by **Louis XVI**. The letter was read out loud to the National Assembly, then still a talking shop with no legislative or executive powers. Members showed their agreement with frequent applause. In 1792, the "fourth year of liberty" in revolutionary language, the king still ran the government. The crux of the Rolands' message was to persuade him to accede voluntarily to the demands of the nation, both to a new Constitution and to specific decrees. The arguments stress the changes already accomplished among the people. In four years they had seen hereditary privileges abolished; they yearned for even more benefits from a new constitution. They were confident that their Constitution *could* function, if only the king would give needed executive powers to the legislative body of the people. By the king's openly siding with the people he would end the malcontents' hope of a return to the old regime. The Rolands warned the king explicitly about the provocative conduct on the part of the nobility.

The letter is prescient in many respects. It warned clearly that there could be no more temporizing. It warned that the fate of the king and Constitution were "intimately linked," that misfortune would follow if he would not support the new Constitution. The letter begged Louis to distance himself from the nobility and clergy and ally himself with the people instead of mistrusting them. Poignant also was the Rolands' plea to the king to obey the law.

Text: Roland letter June 10 1792, *Histoire parlementaire* 39-45 [my translation]:

The hope of coming to the aid of the state has been the sole motive to persuade patriotic citizens to accept the burden of a ministry in these tempestuous times. This hope was founded on the conformity of principles which seemed to animate equally all the members of the council. Unreservedly devoted to the public good, I tried to fulfil the honourable task which was imposed on me. I have only this moment received the king's order to give up the portfolio of the Interior to M Mourgues. I retire with tranquillity and good conscience. But I owe to the assembly and to public opinion the communication of a letter which I had the honour to address to the king last Monday. The truth, which I do myself the honour to believe has characterized all my actions, dictated this letter; it again is the truth which requires me to share it with the assembly. (Applause)

Sire: The present state of France cannot long continue; we are at a state of crisis with violence reaching the highest degree. It must end with an outbreak that will concern your majesty as much as the entire empire. Honoured by your confidence and placed in a position where I owe you the truth, I venture to tell you the whole truth; it is an obligation you yourself imposed on me.

The French now have a Constitution. This has made for discontents and rebels but the majority of the nation want to maintain it. They have sworn to defend it at the cost of their blood and they regard with joy the war that gives them the means to assure its continuation. The hopeful minority, however, has mustered all its efforts to win. Hence this civil war against law, this anarchy which good citizens bewail and which the malevolent have taken advantage of to slander the new regime. Hence division spreading everywhere, everywhere excited, for nowhere is there indifference. People want either the triumph or the amendment of the Constitution; they act to support it or alter it....

Your majesty enjoys great prerogatives which you believe pertain to royalty. Raised with the idea of conserving them, you could not enjoy seeing them removed; the desire to take them away is as natural as the regret to see them abolished. These feelings, natural to the human heart, had to enter into the calculations of the revolution's enemies. They have then counted on secret favour up to circumstances permitting a declared protection. These dispositions could not escape the notice of the nation itself, and it has been defiant. Your majesty has accordingly alternated between ceding to your earliest habits and particular feelings and making the sacrifices dictated by philosophy, required by necessity—as a result hardening the rebels in disturbing the nation—or to joining it. Everything comes to its end, and that of uncertainty has finally arrived.

Can your majesty today ally yourself openly with those who claim to reform the Constitution, or generously give yourself without reserve to make it triumph? That is the real question made inevitable by the present state of things. As to the metaphysical question: whether or not the French are mature enough for liberty is not for discussion here for it would be useless to judge what we will become in a century. The point is to see what the present generation is capable of.

What has come of the agitation we have lived in for four years now? Privileges onerous to the people have been abolished; ideas of justice and equality have become universal, penetrating everywhere. The yearning for rights has become justified in opinion; the solemn recognition of rights has become a sacred doctrine. Hatred of the feudal nobility has taken deep root, exacerbated by the manifest opposition of the majority of nobles to the Constitution which destroyed them. In the first year of the revolution the people saw in these nobles men made odious by the oppressive privileges which they enjoyed. But they would have stopped hating them if, on the ending of these privileges, the nobles had conducted themselves so as not to cause dread and make the people want to combat them as an irreconcilable enemy.

Attachment to the Constitution grew in the same proportion. Not only did the people owe concrete benefits to it, but they judged that it would produce even greater because those who habitually made them bear all the burdens sought so powerfully to destroy or at least weaken the Constitution. The Declaration of Rights became a political gospel and the French Constitution a religion for which the people were prepared to die. Zeal as well sometimes made up for what was lacking in the law. And when the law was not sufficiently repressive to contain the upstarts, the citizens took it upon themselves to punish them themselves. Thus it was that the property of émigrés or persons recognized as such were exposed to ravages of vengeance. That is why so many *departements* were forced to deal severely with the priests which opinion had proscribed and which made them its victims.

In this clash of interests, all feelings gained in passion. *La patrie* is hardly a word for the imagination to embellish; it is a being for which people have made sacrifices and to which they are every day more attached by the anxieties it causes. It was created by great effort, rising in the middle of anxieties and loved as much by what it cost as by what was hoped from it. All the attacks on it inflamed enthusiasm for it.

At what point will this enthusiasm rise when enemy forces from outside join together with those from within, to strike the most deadly blows? Fermentation is extreme in all parts of the empire; it will burst out in a terrible manner, at least unless a reasoned confidence in your majesty's intentions can calm it. But this confidence will not be established by protestation; it must have its basis in fact. The French nation knows that its Constitution can function, that the government will have all the force it needs the moment your majesty, desiring the victory of this Constitution, will support the legislative body with executive powers, thus removing all pretext for the people's anxiety and all hope to the malcontents.

For example, two important decrees have been rendered; both profoundly concern public tranquillity and state security. Delay in sanctioning them inspires defiance. If that is prolonged it will produce discontent and—I must say it—in the present turbulence of spirits discontent can lead to anything. The time to draw back is over and there are no means to temporize. The revolution exists in people's minds; it will be completed with the price of blood...if wisdom does not prevent the misfortunes that it is still possible to escape.

I know that extreme measures can be imagined that will do anything and contain everything. But when force is deployed to constrain the assembly, when terror is spread in Paris, division and stupor in the suburbs, all of France will rise in indignation. Tearing itself apart in the horrors of civil war, it will develop this sombre energy, mother of virtues and of crimes, always deadly to those who provoke it. The safety of the state and the happiness of your majesty are intimately linked; no power can separate them. If you do not yourself rest your throne on the base of the Constitution and consolidate it in the peace which its maintenance must procure us, cruel agonies and certain misfortunes will surround it.

Thus the disposition of minds, the course of events, the reasons of politics, the interest of your majesty make for an indispensable obligation to join with the legislative body and to respond to the wishes of the nation. They make necessary that which principles present as duty, but natural sense for this affectionate people is ready to find a motive for recognition. They have cruelly misled you, Sire, when they inspired you to distance yourself and mistrust a people easy to touch; on disturbing you perpetually they brought you to an alarming conduct. If they see that you will put into operation this Constitution to which their happiness is attached you will soon become the subject of their gracious actions.

The conduct of priests in many places, the priests who furnish fanaticism to the malcontents, has made for a wise law against the disturbers. Your majesty should give it your sanction; public tranquillity demands it and the people's safety earnestly requires it. If this law is not put into practice, the *departements* will be forced to substitute violent measures, as they have in all areas, and an irritated people will go to excess.

The machinations of our enemies, the agitations manifest in the capital, the extreme anxiety which prompted the removal of your guard and which further foster acknowledgement of the satisfactions made by your majesty by a very impolitic proclamation in the circumstances of the situation in Paris, its proximity to the borders, have made evident the need of a camp in the neighbourhood. This measure, the wisdom and urgency of which have struck all good minds, awaits but your majesty's sanction. Delay gives an air of regret when speed would win everyone's heart! Already the attempts of the general staff of the Paris National Guard against this measure have made for suspicions that it acts by a superior inspiration. Already the declarations of some extreme demagogues awake suspicion of their relations with those interested in overturning the Constitution. Already opinion compromises the intentions of your majesty in further delay, and the grieving people will see in their king the friend and collaborator of conspirators.

Heavenly justice! Would you strike the powers of the earth from their blindness, and would they never have advice which brings them to their ruin! I know that the austere language of truth is rarely welcomed at the throne; I know also that revolutions become necessary because it is hardly ever heard. I know above all that I owe to your majesty, not only as a citizen submitting to law, but as a minister honoured by your confidence, clothed in an office which supposes it, I know nothing that can stop me from fulfilling a duty I feel in conscience.

It is in the same spirit that I reiterate my representations to your majesty on the obligation and usefulness of putting into place the *law* that requires a secretary at the council. The very existence of the *law* speaks so powerfully that it would seem that its execution should follow without delay. It is important to use all means to conserve the gravity of deliberations, the wisdom and maturity necessary. And a means for ascertaining the opinions of responsible ministers is necessary. If that had existed I would not be writing at this moment to your majesty. Life is nothing for the man who considers his duty above all. After the joy of having fulfilled them, the only good to which he remains sensitive is that of proving that he has done so faithfully, and that is indeed an obligation for the public man.
(signed) Roland

Opinions were sharply divided in eighteenth-century France as to the relative importance of primary industry (agriculture, forestry, mining and fishing) and secondary manufacturing. The physiocrats, led by **Quesnai** and **Turgot**,[50] held

---

[50] François Quesnai, *Quesnay's tableau économique* and *Oeuvres économiques et philosophiques*; A.R.J. Turgot, *Oeuvres de Turgot*.

Theorists on Revolution/Roland

that all value came ultimately from the "land," broadly conceived as all natural resources or primary industry. The progressive "single tax" movement in the United States derives from this theory; logically, if all value comes from the land (the resource base) that is where taxes should be levied. Mme Roland briefly noted a couple of practical implications from the position taken in this land/industry dispute. A minister, **Colbert**, who favoured industry kept agricultural prices low to support the artisans, thereby crushing the farmers. Ministers of the physiocrat persuasion let the price of provisions rise to make farmers rich, but the poor suffered because they could not pay.

Roland was astute in discussing the relationship between the amount of taxes a people would bear and the kind of government it has. Effectively taxes would and must be heavier in a democratic republic than in an absolute monarchy; when people are taxing themselves they will pay more. They see the merit of the taxes, for their private interests are in fact bound up in the public. Roland's analysis here is similar to Rousseau's treatment of taxes in the *Social Contract* (in Book 3, Chapter 8). She knew Rousseau's work well and presumably was influenced by it. Her version of the argument, however, is more moderate than Rousseau's and leaves out some of his more questionable, and extreme, points. Her final words consist of a sad forecast of the next stage of the French Revolution. The text below combines some passages from the English *Works* with a new translation from the *Oeuvres*.

Text: Roland, "Political Reverie," *Works* 107-09 (*Oeuvres* 1:138-41):

The great Colbert has been reproached with having favoured industry at the expense of agriculture. It is said that he considered artisans as the only valuable subjects of the state. As a result, he lowered the price of provisions as much as he could and farmers were crushed. It appears that, at this day, we have adopted a very different system. A young studious prince devotes himself to agricultural details and seems not much to befriend the arts. Ministers consider agriculture alone as the sole basis of the state's wealth and use every method to encourage it. Accordingly provisions have risen to a price which makes the farmer rich, no doubt, but which the poor cannot pay. M Turgot is represented to us as a man who combines knowledge with good intentions. I hope that is the case and I even believe it for his conduct as Intendant at Limoges speaks greatly in his favour; an intendant who leaves office beloved and far from rich is quite a phenomenon.

But there are some very healthy views which are not only thwarted but even made dangerous by circumstances. In a free state the people accept indigence without sorrow. If they lead a hard and painful life they are and see themselves to be compensated for this by their participation in government. The taxes they pay they themselves impose and on that account seem less odious. Besides, they see their advantage, for private and general good are so connected that they do nothing for the latter without themselves reaping some benefit. But in every government in which the state and the people seem to be two separate bodies, the people do not give their labour, sweat and trouble without murmuring. They are not willing to pay for their livelihood twice: by paying a high price for necessities after they have already paid for them by their labour and taxes. Experience confirms all this.

Taxes are and must be much heavier in republics than in absolute governments. Accordingly I would ask what is the sort of government under which we live at present? It is monarchical, I shall be told, and intermediate bodies counterbalance the royal authority. The equilibrium, if I am not mistaken, is not maintained. Parliaments and the clergy are these intermediate bodies, but, in their reciprocal opposition they give the monarch an opportunity to humble them, the one by the other, and thus he remains master. There are fundamental laws, but those who are their guardians scarcely preserve the right of speaking of them sometimes.

Since the last revolutions Parliaments have become nothing more than courts of justice and officers of the crown. The people's representatives have vanished. Where are the organs of the public's voice? A confused murmur may be heard, which produces a few storms, but these storms burst again where they were formed, without reaching the region where the tranquil prince remains surrounded by courtiers and cheats.

Vile spying and frightful informing extended their degrading sway over the close of the last reign. These horrors seem to have been softened and to disappear, but since want has cried *I am hungry*, troops are marched from one end of the kingdom to the other, and make it appear like a plain bristling with bayonets. Here then a reign of terror is established, the resort of a despotic government. Did it ever produce any good? Alas! it can only nourish animosity, lead to despair or bury every virtue. It is too much to lose our liberty and the means of living at the same time. Slaves should not have to pay for their bread; they purchase it with their slavery. The French may be sufficiently debased not to care much for political liberty, but on that very account they are more alive to evils which are of a personal nature.

If this system lasts, if food and rent remain expensive, and if the people continue to suffer, either a violent crisis which could overturn the throne and give us another form of government will happen, or a lethargy like death. How sad it is to foresee such a future!

"The military mind hates reason as the beginning of indiscipline ...Anger is often a heroic principle in a warrior; in government it produces nothing but injustice and tyranny."[51]

GERMAINE NECKER DE STAËL HOLSTEIN (1766-1817)

Born in Geneva, Germaine Necker[52] was the only child of **Jacques Necker**, a wealthy banker and later Minister of Finance to **Louis XVI**, and his wife, a former school teacher and *salonière*. The family was Protestant and liberal so that it is fitting that Mme de Staël's chateau outside Geneva now houses the World Council of Churches. Germaine Necker met the great *philosophes* at her mother's salon. She was given a good, literary education at home and early began to write. In 1786 she entered an arranged marriage with a Swedish Protestant, Baron de Staël, a political liberal and then ambassador to France. Their one child was followed by four others by other partners. Mme de Staël had obtained a legal separation from her husband (there was then no divorce) when he was found to have spent her dowry rather speedily.

De Staël's first important book, the *Treatise on the Influence of the Passions*, appeared in 1786. She then began her *Literature and Social Institutions*, published in 1800. She also wrote several novels, which were widely translated and re-published. They have acquired some new interest for their sensitivity to women.[53] De Staël also translated books and plays and wrote poetry. She certainly has every right to be treated as a woman of letters, although it is her political writing that is of interest here.

De Staël played only a marginal role in the French Revolution but she knew the main players. She assisted in the attempted escape of the royal family and published a defence of the queen. She was more successful in helping a number of members of the nobility to escape. She spent the worst years of the Terror in England and Switzerland. **Napoleon** later banned her from France. Her *Ten Years of Exile* reports on this period of enforced travel. Also at this time she learned German and travelled in Germany. Her *On Germany* contains both extensive literary commentary and political and social observations.

---

[51] De Staël, *Circonstances actuelles*, Omacini 290, Viénot 203-04.

[52] The best biography is Simone Balayé, *Madame de Staël*; see also Ghislain de Diesbach, *Madame de Staël*; in English see J. Christopher Herold, *Mistress to an Age*; David Glass Larg, *Madame de Staël*; there are several editions of de Staël's works, a 17-volume *Oeuvres complètes*, several shorter collections: *Madame de Staël on Politics, Literature, and National Character*, ed. Morroe Berger and *Major Writings of Germaine de Staël*, ed. Vivian Folkenflik; six volumes of published correspondence and see my *Women Founders* 134-50.

[53] See especially Gretchen Rous Besser, *Germaine de Staël Revisited* and Madelyn Gutwirth, *Germaine de Staël: Crossing the Borders*.

Neither of de Staël's two books on the French Revolution was published in her lifetime. She wrote *Circonstances actuelles* probably in 1796-98 but it was initially too risky to publish, while, later, events had passed it by. Her lengthy history of the French Revolution was published soon after her death.

A committed opponent of the slave trade, de Staël had met William Wilberforce in England and helped to disseminate his anti-slavery writing in France. During the peace negotiations after the Napoleonic Wars de Staël urged the victor nations to show their gratitude for deliverance from Napoleon by abolishing the slave trade. She wrote the **Duke of Wellington**, both on the slave trade and to urge an early end to the occupation of France and non-punitive terms in the peace treaty.

Social Bond

The Influence of the Passions is the book that first made de Staël's reputation as a serious writer. It was widely praised and promptly translated into German and English. With the great interest of current psychologists and philosophers in women's different approaches to ethics it is astonishing that this work is not more used. It is a major, early example of Carol Gilligan's argument in *In a Different Voice*. *The Influence of the Passions* plainly states de Staël's association of passion and virtue. While her contemporary **Immanuel Kant**, and a host of male philosophers, denigrated passion and related morality to reason, de Staël believed that "deep rooted passion" would not "mislead us from the path of virtue." Passions themselves were "that impulsive force which domineers over the will of man" (5). Without their interference, she acknowledged, the operations of government would be as simple as machines.

> In whatever situation we may be placed by a deep-rooted passion, I can never believe that it misleads us from the path of virtue. Everything is sacrifice, everything is indifference to our own gratifications in the exalted attachment of love; selfishness alone degrades (133).

Here also is de Staël's unequivocal statement about the fundamental tie being that between parents and their children:

> The most sacred of the moral elements of the world are the ties that bind together parents and their children. On this holy duty is equally poised the basis of nature and society, and nothing short of extreme depravity can make us spurn at this involuntary instinct which...prompts us to everything which virtue can impose (233).

De Staël used Adam Smith's *Theory of Moral Sentiments*, 1759, but was critical of its element of self-centredness. That we are able to feel like another person in distress was one cause of pity but not the only one. Smith's definition was too narrow.

Text: de Staël, *Influence of the Passions*:

Smith, in his excellent work, *The Theory of Moral Sentiments*, makes pity consist in that sympathy which places us in the situation of another and renders us sensible to all the feelings which such a situation may impress. That most undoubtedly is one of the causes of pity, but there is this inconvenience in that definition, which, indeed, attends almost every other: it narrows the thought to which the word to be defined gave rise. That word was clothed with a number of accessory ideas of impressions wholly peculiar to each individual that heard it, and you restrict its signification by attempting an analysis which always proves incomplete when a sentiment is the object to be defined. For a sentiment is a compound of sensations and thoughts which you can never cause to be understood without the united help of judgment and emotion....In a word, the spectacle of misfortune must move and melt mankind by means of commotion or, as it were, by a talisman, and not by examination or combination (331).

It is almost always the interest of wise policy to listen to the voice of pity....In fine, in whatever point of view we contemplate the sentiment of pity, it will be found wonderfully fertile in the production of beneficial consequences both to individuals and to nations. Nor shall we feel reluctant to persuade ourselves that it is the only primitive idea that is implanted in the nature of man, for it is the only one that is necessary to the culture of every virtue and to the enjoyment of every blessing (334-35).

De Staël's optimistic view of human nature appears also in her *Circonstances actuelles* with a brief, caustic comment on contract theory. She not only had little herself to say about the original state of nature, she denigrated the very endeavour to describe it. Rather than accepting any theory on the origins, de Staël insisted that "society is formed in a thousand ways." Our knowledge must depend on facts, and these could only be relied on after the invention of printing, which provided for their preservation.

> If history, before the discovery of printing, cannot serve to make known the progress the human mind is capable of, there is even more reason to consider research on the origin of society useless. These sorts of metaphysical novels have neither the interest of invention nor the precision of truth. One stumbles about by chance, as the imagination, but one loses oneself in a desert and chimerical abstraction is as much arid as it is futile. Society was formed in a thousand different ways. We know nothing except what we have gained from facts, and that only after

printing, so that achievements already made can be used to predict subsequent ones (Viénot 193, Omacini 280 [my translation]).

Rousseau, incidentally, was the subject of de Staël's first published essay, *Letters on the Works and the Character of J.J. Rousseau*, 1788, when she was aged twenty-two.

Women theorists generally condemned Rousseau's sharp juncture between human nature in the state of nature and in civil society, for reasons similar to those discussed in Chapter 2 regarding their rejection of Hobbes. In his chapter on civil society in the *Social Contract* Rousseau described passing from the state of nature to civil society as changing "man" (again it is not clear if men only or all humans are included).

> It puts justice as a rule of conduct in the place of instinct and gives his actions the moral quality they previously lacked. It is only then, when the voice of duty has taken the place of physical impulse...that man, who has hitherto thought only of himself, finds himself compelled to act on other principles and to consult his reason rather than...his inclinations (64).

But neither for de Staël, nor du Châtelet, nor Grouchy de Condorcet shortly, did human beings ever think only of themselves. Unlike the women theorists, Rousseau's own experience of natural instincts for children was egregiously suspect. He fathered five children by **Thérèse Levasseur** when she was his common-law wife (they married later), all taken to a foundling hospital.[54] Most of the women theorists had children of their own and those who did not taught children and had responsibilities for them (Nightingale identified as mother to her soldiers).

Rousseau argued that "man" acquired moral freedom with civil society, "which alone makes man the master of himself, for to be governed by appetite alone is slavery while obedience to a law one prescribes to oneself is freedom" (65). But this distinction between appetite/slavery on the one hand, and law/freedom on the other, made no sense for de Staël or any of the other women theorists. Appetite, emotion and passion were not necessarily bad things at all for them, nor are they for contemporary women theorists. Nor did they consider that self "mastery" was a product of civil society only but women, as mothers, had long moderated their selfish desires in their children's interests. Instead of the sharp juncture between a selfish state of nature and a moral, civil society the women theorists understood a gradual development of positive bonds, based on feeling, especially maternal feeling, that led to the enunciation

---

[54] Charly Guyot, *Plaidoyer pour Thérèse Levasseur*.

of moral rules and positive laws. Some of the women (notably Macaulay) noted how women shared the maternal instinct with other animals.

Government—French Revolution

Germaine de Staël wrote two full books and numerous shorter pieces on the French Revolution, beginning with a defence of **Marie Antoinette**.[55] *Circonstances actuelles* is both the most analytical and most practical of all these works. Its object was to determine the social and political institutions necessary to end the civil war unleashed by the revolution. *Circonstances actuelles* was first published only in 1906; an excellent critical edition appeared in 1979. The book has yet to be translated into English or any other language. *The Influence of the Passions on the Happiness of Individuals and Nations*, 1796, also contains some sections on the French Revolution. De Staël had evidently projected a two-volume work, the second of which would deal with nations, the first with individuals. She did, however, sketch out her position on nations in the first volume, and some of that material is excerpted here. It seems she wrote *Circonstances actuelles* instead of proceeding to volume two.

Circonstances actuelles is remarkable for its cogent, lucid institutional analysis. De Staël was a skilled political observer who personally knew the major leaders. From her own (private) education in Enlightenment thought she thoroughly understood the principles and concepts at issue. She sought to explain the abuses of the revolution without impugning its basic principle of sovereignty in the people. Like Macaulay and Wollstonecraft she laid the blame on the core institutions and practices of the old regime. De Staël, however, went much further than either of the two English women in speculating about different possible scenarios. She argued that a republic would have been reached by consensus if only there had been time—say ten years—of constitutional monarchy to prepare for it.

De Staël sought reconciliation between the factions of her country. She was firmly committed to the new republic but insisted that a place must be made for any royalist who would accept it. She even argued (elsewhere in the book) that the new government could learn from the nobility who, after all, had had centuries of experience of staying in power. Yet she would not give comfort to the royalists, insisting just as strenuously on the faults of the old system and the need for profound, systemic change.

A liberal Protestant, de Staël detested fanaticism in any form. Doubtless her comparison of the fanaticism of the French Terrorists with that of the Catholic Church would have offended both. Here de Staël stressed the key role of sympathy in the development of morality, a point dealt with at length in the earlier *Influence of the Passions*. In *Circonstances actuelles* she held that

---

[55] De Staël, *Oeuvres complètes* vol. 2.

fanaticism kills sympathy, "the only guarantee of human virtue." "Human pity" was replaced by a "philosophical system" and individuals tortured for the good of the species.

De Staël's advice was eminently practical: people had to be attracted to the new regime; punishment and the threat of it would not suffice. "Moral force" was needed. If people could not be positively drawn to the new government they might not revolt, but they would not obey, and passive resistance would disorganize the new republic. People needed an economic stake in the system to be loyal to it, a point expanded on in her discussion of property institutions. "Prosperity is the price of republicanism," she argued. (Mme Roland had argued the opposite, that people would bear a greater burden in a republic, seeing it as self-imposed.) De Staël's concern was that people had to be motivated to switch their allegiance, hence the onus was on the new regime to produce concrete results.

Text: de Staël, *Circonstances actuelles* [my translation]:

The horrors of the French Revolution can be attributed to several principles. The chief ones are the obstacles the revolution had to overturn: the character of the people formed by the abuses of the old regime, the absolute lack of public morality and finally the false application of the sovereignty principle in representative government. None of these causes came from the political theory of enlightened republicans. Thus in adopting a theory of sovereignty of the people, far from perpetuating the horrors of the Revolution, brings the only efficacious remedy, born of the principle even and the object of the revolution.

Let us develop these observations. The horrors of the revolution were the product of the obstacles it met. The republic was established in France before the enlightenment which should have prepared it. The nation in 1789 was at the stage of a tempered monarchy, but its writers, under a legally absolute monarchy and with no time to prepare for the republic, the institution came into being before the general spirit that should have brought it....

A revolution which has changing a dynasty as its object, the repulsing of foreigners, is a sort of event for which one battle victory decides everything. It is a question of power; the dynasty changes hands by the lot of arms, then the revolution in popular opinion occurs. A change in religion, in convictions of people's minds, makes the revolution more bloody and more internal....A revolution purely of political reason needs the general accord of enlightenment to function without shocks. Everyone believes themselves judge of all that is done for the good of all, and successes do not reassure the conquerors because they cannot found their institution according to the mind, that is to let it go by itself without being at all assured of public opinion.

If the constitutional monarchy could have lasted ten years in France the republic would have arrived by consent, but because there was revolutionary agitation in these ten years many republicans in opinion distanced themselves agitation in these ten years many republicans in opinion distanced themselves from the means to force the republic. Bolder men who wanted the revolution before its time found themselves abandoned by many of the pure friends of equality and liberty and, to defend themselves, had recourse to criminals, who in turn assassinated them. These ferocious men, far from raising the nation to the republic, made the public mind draw back instead of progressing, and in time the reaction of the Terror was such that the considered writings under the old monarchy were taken for revolutionary under the new republic (Viénot 32-35, Omacini 33-35).

Put emulation in the place of fear; prosperity is the price of republicanism. Instead of endlessly offering the machinery of penalties, remove hell and leave a paradise. There is no splendour in negativity: to have no place, no fortune, to be worthy of no glory but always to have to brave the dangers of the unknown. I would say to the aristocrats: "The government refuses you honours and dangers equally. In so far as you maintain your prejudices you will be subjects of a free state [and punished if you conspire] but you will be subjects. When you have broken with your prejudices, when you have given real evidence of republican opinions, you will be enfranchised. As long ago the slaves were released from their servitude you will become Roman citizens. Until that day you will be every way reduced to inutility. No persecution will touch you, no power [nor place] will be left you and, as the ancients combed limbo where the souls sojourned before existence, you will wait, without fear or hope, that reason will give you life."

I believe that a larger, more generous system is also much more politic. The reaction will not end in France so long as persecution and misfortune exist. Men do not believe the end has come until there is justice; they do not envisage peace without a measure of the happiness the government owes them. They do not ever believe in the perpetuity of an intolerable existence, and this consoling hope is itself a means of realizing what they hope for. The words "it will not last" is the instinct of the unfortunate and soon becomes a sort of contagious opinion which inspires insubordination among the governed and false measures to the governors. Stability is justice, peace and happiness.

The small number of physical laws, so to speak, which exist in the social world cannot ever be reversed. Injustice comes to its end as a rock falls by its own weight. In seeking, as one must, models among the old republican institutions, it would be very useful also to acknowledge the spirit of grandeur, which tames the republic's enemies with means other than punishment and terror.

Without doubt the methods of punishment and terror alone will not suffice in France, because the republic's adversaries have in their power a sort of partisan opinion which keeps them from being influenced by republican blame. But it is very certain that the moment has come to add moral force to physical might. In a country like France not every desire can be satiated—even terror. And if this mind gains everywhere people will not revolt but they will not obey, and a passive resistance will disorganize both the republic and the republican spirit.

Now it is necessary to think to administer. For a long time the art of governing the republic was a military science. But today we must consider opinion and, so long as it is not too agitated in France to be reversed, to know that it is always enough to prevent it from being established: protect commerce, respect what remains in the public debt, choose enlightened men, give back their fatherland to those unjustly forced to emigrate, take advantage of the moment to accord anything that does not compromise the security of the republic, leave no justice to be achieved by enemies so that they will not increase.

We do not know enough how equity, in a period of force, has a lasting effect. There are so many people who are disposed to rally to the powers-that-be if they are solaced by being permitted to set a value on what they fear (Viénot 113-16, Omacini 133-35).

Can...the majority impose highly despotic laws on the minority? With the furor of parties the majority and the minority have become...two different nations or, rather, the slaves and the oppressors. As soon as you suppose certain established, immutable principles of justice there will still be differences of opinion, but there will be neither despotism nor tyranny. In a country where justice reigns there is neither majority nor minority, neither one nor several, but all will be equally subject to universal morality and the particular laws of the country. It suffices for these particular laws to be legitimate that they not contradict morality and that they be made according to the legislative and judicial forms which ground free government (Viénot 240-41, Omacini 252-53).

Mme de Staël's observations on fanaticism and "party spirit," both from *Circonstances actuelles* and the *Influence of the Passions* have practical lessons for us yet. Note how she showed how fanaticism destroyed the power of pity, the key force for virtuous conduct.

Text: de Staël, *Influence of the Passions*:

If there be any passion destructive to the happiness, and even the existence of free countries, it is revenge....Surely France, then, might display the fairest example which can be conceived of foregoing revenge, if animosity would cease to renew revolutions, in the French name, from pride and patriotism, would rally all those who are not too criminal to permit their own hearts to form the idea of pardon. Surely this would be a heroic oblivion, but it is so extremely necessary that though aware of its astonishing difficulty, we are compelled to hope that it will succeed. France can only be saved by means of this mutual forgiveness (172-73).

In the spirit of party, however, men prefer falling, if they can involve their enemies in their overthrow, to a triumph in conjunction with any of them...The purity of a dogma is deemed of more importance than the success of its cause. The more sincere the spirit, the less disposed it is to admit of conciliation or compromise of any kind (180-81).

There is no passion which must tend more to hurry men into every species of crimes than party spirit, for this very reason that he who is under its influence is really intoxicated and the end of this passion, not being personal to the individual whom it governs, he conceives that, even in doing wrong, he devotes himself meritoriously. In committing crimes he preserves the sentiment of virtue, and experiences neither the fear nor the remorse inseparable from selfish passions, passions culpable even in the estimation of him who acts under their influence. The spirit of party has no remorse; its first character is that it considers its object so superior to everything that exists that it can repent of no sacrifice when so great an end is to be obtained.

The spirit of party is exempt from fear, not only on account of the extravagant courage which it can inspire, but also by the security which it produces. The Jacobins [extreme revolutionaries] and the aristocrats, since the commencement of the revolution, have never for a moment despaired of the triumph of their opinion (183-84).

The spirit of party is the only passion which erects the destruction of all the virtues into a virtue, which lays claim to glory from all those actions which men would labour to conceal if they were performed from motives of personal interest...Pity, that divine sentiment which renders sorrow a bond of union among mankind, pity, that virtue of instinct which preserves the human species by preserving individuals from the effects of their own madness...the spirit of party effaces the feelings of sympathy in order to substitute the ties of opinion, and represents actual sufferings as the means, as the pledge of an immortal futurity, of a political happiness beyond all the sacrifices that may be required for its attainment (191-92).

Text: de Staël, *Circonstances actuelles*, Viénot 243-47, Omacini 255-57 [my translation]:

Fanaticism, the most deadly of emotions, is nothing but the despotism of a single idea on the mind of man. It is always a vague principle, and, consequently, of infinite extension. Catholics long ago found in the words of the gospel, "Make them come in," the doctrine that outside the church there is no salvation, the pretext for the most dreadful persecutions. French terrorists have found in the same way the pretext for their barbarism in this maxim: the safety of the people is the first law. Religion, says the Catholic, is the first good of man. The Catholic religion is the only true one, thus we must force all people to be Catholics. Fanatical revolutionaries in France, who must be well distinguished from enlightened republicans, have said: political liberty and equality are the first goods; there must be certain laws which will assure them. Thus we must take all measures to force people to want these laws. And if you follow next the progress, character and conduct of all these fanatics, you will see that nothing is so similar whatever may be the differences in motivation. Religious fanatics, as political fanatics, base themselves on a primitive truth but they draw diametrically opposed consequences from it as to its essence. The fanatics of religion are first of all cruel and then despotic while the fanatics of liberty are despots first and then cruel, because religion is what is most human and liberty what is most tolerant....

There is not, otherwise, and this is a truth of which political fanatics must convince themselves—there is no more capacity in their heads than in those of religious fanatics. The thought from which they derive all their errors is in itself more philosophical than that of the religious fanatics, but it is by the same weakness of mind, the same anger of character, that they see but one idea, that they attach everything to it, take it out of context, separate it from its connections and make thus, always, an error of a good idea. But nothing in the moral [social] world is true but relatively, to a degree, in its place, with its neighbours, each idea related to all the others.

When fanatics see a duty which they separate from all others they are much more dangerous to society than the ambitious who admit to themselves that they sacrifice morality to their interests. Do you know anything more redoubtable than a man who unites intrepidity of crime with inflexibility of virtue, in whom human pity is replaced by a philanthropic system and who tortures the individual for the good of the species? He destroys in his heart the only guarantee of human virtue—sympathy—to substitute for it a feeling of universal goodwill with no relation to the nature of man (255-57).

De Staël's advice for France to remain a republic, while other countries of Europe should not, again shows her practicality and moderation. She did not believe in the export of revolution. Yet her insistence that France stick with her decision—or the horrors of the revolution would have been in vain—offended the royalists hoping for a return to the old ways.

Text: de Staël, *Influence of the Passions*:

Every consideration invites France to remain a republic. Every consideration imperiously prohibits Europe to follow her example....Can the people of France wish to undergo the miseries of a new revolution in order to supersede that which establishes the republic? Is the courage of so many armies and the blood of so many heroes to be lavished in the name of a chimera, which should leave nothing behind it but the memory of the crimes which it has cost?

France ought to persevere in that grand experiment the calamities of which are passed, the hopes of which are in futurity. But can Europe be inspired with sufficient horror for revolutions?...No monarchical government, at present, contains such inveterate abuses but that a single day of revolution would extort more tears than all the miseries it was intended to remedy. To wish for revolution is to consign to death the innocent and guilty alike; it is perhaps to condemn to destruction the object we hold most dear!...No man can flatter himself with the hope that he shall be able to regulate an impulse of which the nature of things necessarily assumes the guidance.

Permit us in France to fight and conquer, let us submit to torture and to death in the sacrifice of our warmest affections, our dearest attachments, destined, perhaps, one day to revive for the astonishment and admiration of the world. At least, however, allow an age to pass over our destinies and then you will know whether we have acquired the true science of the happiness of mankind...Is it not fortunate for you that a whole nation has thus placed itself as the vanguard of the human species, to brave all prejudices, to try all principles? (28-30)

Crimes of every description, crimes wholly useless to the success of the cause, are dictated by the ferocious enthusiasm of the populace. They dread pity, whatever be the degree of its force. It is in fury, not in clemency, that they are sensible of their power. A people who govern never cease to be under the influence of fear; they imagine themselves every moment on the point of losing their authority and prove, from their situation, to the emotions of envy, they never feel for the vanquished that interest which oppressed weakness is calculated to inspire. They view the fallen still as objects of alarm.

Your judges, your assassins, are in the crowd that surrounds you, and the transport that raises you to distinction becomes the very impulse which precipitates your overthrow....The people, when they abandon the ambitious man, for the first time recognize the crimes which they have forced him to commit, and reproach him with the guilt in order to absolve themselves from the charge.

When the cause of revolutions...is the extravagant excess of all ideas of liberty, it is impossible that the first leaders of the insurrection should preserve their power. They are doomed to excite the movement by which they are to be the first overwhelmed. They are fated to develop the principles by which they are to be condemned. In a word, they may gratify their opinion, but never their interest and, in a revolution, fanaticism is even more sober than ambition (94-97).

At the time Mme de Staël wrote her appeal to the sovereigns of Europe, in 1814, slavery had been abolished throughout Europe but the slave trade not everywhere. Britain's legislation ending the slave trade was passed only in 1807. Entrepreneurs made large sums of money from transporting slaves from Africa to the West Indies and United States. Ports servicing the ships also profited, hence many Europeans had an economic stake in continuing the trade. Mme de Staël had met **William Wilberforce**, the leader of the anti-slavery movement in Britain, while she was living there in exile. She wrote a preface also in 1814 for a translation of an anti-slavery book of Wilberforce's.[56]

In the "Appeal" which follows de Staël challenged the sovereigns of Europe meeting to negotiate the terms of peace after the (second) defeat of Napoleon. Just as medieval crusaders took vows before their departure for the Holy Land, so now should Europe's sovereigns "promise the happiness of Africa" in gratitude for deliverance from Napoleon's tyranny. What more fitting monument could there be to remember the oppressor's fall? De Staël cited Europe's debt to England especially, for her consistent resistance to Napoleon, often alone. The appeal both described the cruelty of the slave trade and argued "how can anyone call themselves Christian if they are cruel?" She appealed to the highest instincts of each country's national tradition, particularly crediting the tsar of Russia, an absolute ruler, with equitable, lawful rule. The appeal ended with a classic, universalistic Enlightenment assertion: "There is no country on earth which is not worthy of justice."

Text: de Staël, "Appel aux souverains," *Oeuvres complètes* 17:376-82 [my translation]:

In spite of the violent crisis England endured for twenty-five years, she did not use these dangers as a pretext for neglecting the good she could do. She was steadfastly concerned with humanity and the general good even in the midst of war and the threat to her political existence....The parties opposed to the slave trade among the English were united in a goal as much moral as religious. Mr Pitt and Mr Fox[57] competed with equal ardour. Mr Wilberforce, a Christian orator, gave to this great work a perseverance ordinarily seen only for personal interests.

The abolition of the slave trade, which took place seven years ago, has had no effect on the prosperity of the English colonies. The blacks have multiplied sufficiently to do the necessary work. As it always happens when a matter of justice is concerned, alarmists did not cease to speak of the disadvantages that this measure could bring. But, when the deed was done, we never heard again of these so-called disadvantages. Thus millions of people and whole nations have been saved from all manner of wrongs, without commerce suffering financial losses.

Since this time England, on signing a peace treaty with Denmark, made abolition of the slave trade one of the articles of the treaty. The same condition was requested of Portugal who, to now, has only restricted the trade. But today the confederation of sovereigns now gathered to strengthen with peace the

---

[56] De Staël, *Oeuvres complètes* 17:369-75.

[57] Charles James Fox (1749-1806), a radical MP and minister, moved the abolition of the slave trade shortly before his death.

truce won by arms, it seems that nothing could be more worthy of the august congress about to open than to consecrate the triumph of Europe by an act of benevolence. The crusaders in the Middle Ages did not leave for the Holy Land without binding themselves with vows for their return. The sovereigns now assembled in France should promise the happiness of Africa to a propitious heaven by which they have obtained Europe's deliverance.

Many political interests will be discussed, but some hours given to such a great religious interest would not seem unuseful for the affairs of this world. From now on it would be said that it was by the peace of Paris that all Europe abolished the slave trade; this peace must then be sacred because such an act of grace proceeded from it to the God of armies. It has been suggested that a monument should be raised to consecrate the fall of the oppressor who oppressed the human species. Here it is—this monument which requires but a word to raise: the slave trade is abolished by the kings who overturned the tyranny of Europe's conquest.

The suffering the unfortunate slaves were forced to endure in transportation from their homes to the colonies almost made their destined slavery a relief. War was provoked in their own country to make some people betray others; to be sold as a slave is the accepted punishment for all sorts of faults on the coasts of Africa. Black chiefs who permit this infamous traffic excite the blacks to crime by drunkenness, or by other means, so as to have the right to export them to America. Often, under the ridiculous pretext of sorcery, these unfortunates were exiled forever from the shores which saw them born...."Long caskets," to use the expression of a French writer, transported them on the seas. They were packed in vessels in less space than if they were dead, because their bodies would at least have been laid out on the miserable planks.

Mr Pitt, in his speech against the slave trade, said: "I know of no evil that has ever existed and I cannot imagine one which would be worse than 80,000 people yearly being torn from their countries of birth by the combined efforts of the most civilized nations of Europe." We know what were Mr Pitt's principles and the part he played by his unshakable belief in the eventual victory of the allies. Should not his authority be recognized, and that of the three powers of England: the House of Commons, the House of Lords and the king, to dedicate the truth of the facts and principles now submitted to the attention of the monarchs?

Finally...Europe owes much to England which often resisted alone in the course of these twenty-five years; there was no combat not supported by her soldiers or her assistance. We do not know how to recompense the richest and happiest country in the universe. A soldier receives an award of honour from his sovereign, but what can we do for a nation which has acted like a soldier? We must adopt the great act of humanity she recommended to all the governments of Europe....

The same advocate for humanity, Mr Wilberforce, heads an establishment of missionaries in England to carry the light of Christianity to Asia and Africa.

But how can anyone call themselves Christian if they are cruel? Can we not ask of the king of France, this pious descendent of Saint Louis and of Louis XVI, to accede to the abolition of the slave trade, so that this act of humanity can persuade the hearts of those to whom the gospel is preached? Can we not ask also the accession of Spain...Portugal...Austria...Prussia....The emperor of Russia...reigns over the confines of Asia, peoples of diverse degrees of civilization. He allows all religions and customs and his reign is as equitable as the law; Asia and Europe bless the name of Alexander. That this name should ring out further on the shores of Africa! There is no country on earth which is not worthy of justice.

One of the chief theses of Germaine de Staël's *Circonstances actuelles* was the ending of inherited privileges. In the excerpt here she took care to distinguish between the abolition of those privileges, which she so heartily desired, and the institution of property, the continuation of which she considered to be vital. She stated, moreover, that she would not believe in the abolition of inheritance if she could not have confidence in the institution of property serving as the base of society. Property institutions benefited both owners and non-owners alike by encouraging industry. Hereditary privileges, to the contrary, closed off careers before they started and stifled innovation.

Text: de Staël, *Circonstances actuelles*, Viénot 44-47, Omacini 45-46 [my translation]:

A Note on Property

The very small number of Babouvist democrats, the very large number of political thieves, the aristocrats who flatter themselves to have wiped out the principle of equality on forcing its consequences, want only that the destruction of property be founded on the same reasons that upset slavery, feudalism and inheritance. Nothing in the world is more absurd. All truths have two distinct powers, as does nature, from which they emanate: a destructive force and a creative force. The one acts contrary to prejudices, the other replaces them with principles. You have done nothing, neither in the human heart nor for social institutions, if you destroy without putting something in its place....

Without the institution of property to serve as the base of society I would not believe in the abolition of inheritance. A war can be nothing but the destruction of men; a revolution in political systems is a replacement of ideas. Nature takes care of the re-creation of men, but whatever pertains to moral truths must be renewed by the human spirit....

How can one prove that the maintenance of property is not an error of the same nature as that of inherited privileges? Because the same principle that destroys these privileges conserves property, for the cause and object of the two institutions are opposed. Let us develop this assertion. What is the object of all society? The happiness of the greatest number. Hereditary privileges (if, as I believe, they are not necessary for public order) are for the advantage of some at the expense of others. But property is useful to non-owners as well as to owners....

The security and certainty of property and, consequently, the encouragement of industry are in the true interests of the majority of generations. Hereditary privileges, on the contrary, weigh on the future; they close off careers to those not yet born; life deprives them, death endows them. Property is an object of emulation for all; inherited privilege discourages emulation by giving an advantage to some that nothing can help others acquire. Property multiples for everybody all sorts of enjoyments through all kinds of discoveries; inheritance hoards known goods and opposes innovation. Property is open to all; inheritance isolates. Property is the origin, the base and the bond of the social compact; inherited privilege comes from conquest and is maintained by servitude. Nothing voluntary has ever existed in its essence...Property and society are one and the same thing. Inherited privilege and society are almost always at war because the one favours rules the other exceptions (45-48).

Germaine de Staël and **Thomas Jefferson** knew each other from Jefferson's stays in Paris before the French Revolution; Jacques Necker, de Staël's father and Minister of Finance to Louis XVI, had received and entertained him cordially. Some of the correspondence is on such practical matters as the possible visit, or emigration, of de Staël's son to the United States. De Staël and Jefferson were kindred spirits in that each loved and respected the other's country. The liberal and republican Jefferson had been in Paris at the outbreak of the French Revolution and knew many of the leading *philosophes*. De Staël's liberal republicanism gave her a fondness for the United States although she never visited it. She also approved of federal institutions and the United States was then the leading example.

By the time of their correspondence the urgent issue was Napoleon's domination of Europe; Germany, Italy, Holland and Denmark had been made "provinces" of France. De Staël was herself forced into exile by Napoleon, who detested both her liberal principles and her ability to articulate them. The object being the downfall of Napoleon, de Staël had to support England, the nation fighting him. Hence she reproached Jefferson for American opposition to England and indirect, at least, support for Napoleon. She appealed to Jefferson's reputation as a liberal. She could understand German princes being listed with the "allies of despotism," but Jefferson?

Jefferson did not agree, as his letter of May 1813 (not included here) most decidedly shows. For him England was not the defender of liberty but the "enemy of all maritime nations" just as Napoleon was the enemy of all continental nations. England's object was the "permanent dominion of the ocean" and "monopoly" of world trade. Moreover, the harm done would be lasting; Napoleon would die but a nation did not. The enemy was not the king, "poor maniac George," but his government and nation, a tyrant as unprincipled and overwhelming as Napoleon. Jefferson did, however, give de Staël comfort in predicting the overthrow of Napoleon, likening it to Robespierre's meeting his fate and his memory being justly execrated. The day would come when Napoleon would be known for the "only pre-eminence he has earned, that of having been the greatest of the destroyers of the human race" (67).

De Staël was again out of the country thanks to Napoleon when she wrote Jefferson in 1816; she had fled to Italy on Napoleon's escape from Elba and landing in France. "The greatest evil which Bonaparte inflicted on the world was so to have confused tyranny with liberty that people profess to be liberal while re-establishing the old despotism," she wrote (69). Both *Circonstances actuelles* and her history of the French Revolution eloquently testify to her ardent opposition to the old regime. She sought a third way, a constitutional, liberal republic, like the United States, rejecting both the old regime and Napoleon.

De Staël recognized the great lapse in America's commitment to liberty: slavery. In this last letter she boldly stated to Jefferson, a slave owner, "If you should succeed in destroying slavery in the South there would be at least one government in the world as perfect as the human mind can conceive" (70).

Text: de Staël, "Unpublished Correspondence...with Thomas Jefferson" 65-67:

November 10 1812/Stockholm
I have finally escaped, my dear Sir, from the yoke which weighs so heavily upon half of Europe and I can reply freely to the letter which you did me the honour of sending....Present events induce me to write you my thoughts and I hope you will receive them with a friendliness as great as the sincerity which inspires them. I do not profess to be acquainted with the circumstances which have given rise to the differences between America and England; I make bold to present the question to you in a broader way. You witnessed the first days of the French Revolution and I recall that, at my father's house, you told the exaggerated radicals that their demagogic principles would lead to despotism in France. Your predictions have been fulfilled. Europe and the human race are bent under the will of a single man who wished to establish a universal monarchy. Already Germany, Italy, Holland and Denmark are provinces of France. Free governments are what Emperor Napoleon hates especially. He makes use of you now against England, but when he hoped to conclude a treacherous peace with England you surely know that he proposed to aid her in making the United States an appanage of an English prince, a plan which she rejected with the greatest disdain.

If by a misfortune which would plunge all the world into mourning, England were to be subjected and her navy were to fall into the hands of the conqueror of the earth, it is against you that he would turn, for your principles are most in the world opposed to his and he would wish to efface from the very pages of history the time when men were not subjected to the despotism of one man. Your old friends M de la Fayette[58] and M de Sully would speak just as I do were they once more permitted to break silence.

You tell me that America has nothing to do with the continent of Europe. Has she nothing to do with the human race? Can you be indifferent to the cause of free nations, you the most republican of all? Are you indifferent to the cause of thinking men, you, my dear Sir, who are placed in the very first rank of them? If you were to pass three months in France your generous blood would boil in your veins and you could not bear to serve Napoleon's projects, even though believing it for the good of your country.

For ten years England has been the sole barrier against this singular despotism which unites all the means barbarism and civilization can furnish to debase humanity. When a nation of twelve million souls is obliged to struggle against one hundred million coerced by one man, is it astonishing that certain abuses creep into the means it is obliged to employ in order to resist?

All your old friends in Europe, all those who thought as you did when you upheld the independence of America, expect you to put an end to a war which seems to them a civil war, for free people are all of the same family. Yes, the greatest misfortune which could come to the American people in the present war would be to do real damage to their enemies, for then the English would no longer be in a condition to serve you as a bulwark against the despotism of the emperor of France, or rather of Europe. When he shall have overthrown the liberty of England it will be yours that he will next attack. The emperor, so versed in the art of dissimulation, does not even conceal his resolution of destroying every nation which desires to be independent. It is thus impossible to be in doubt as to the intention of this man who is even more remarkable as a system than as a character, and this system is made up of all the most unphilosophical ideas which have ever oppressed the world.

Pardon me...for having ventured to speak to you with so much frankness. I can view without suffering the names of German princes on the lists of the allies of despotism, but the name of Jefferson in such company—it is this which troubles the friends of liberty, and you will perhaps end by yourself discouraging the political belief which you have all your life so bravely professed. Reply to me...in care of your consul in Sweden...and tell me above all that you are not displeased with me for having presumed to address you as you would have addressed my father were he, whose spirit was as devoted to order as to liberty, still on this earth.

Adieu, Adieu...God bless you and deliver Europe.

Farewell [in English]

Necker de Staël Holstein

---

[58] The French marquis de la Fayette fought with the Americans in the Revolution against Britain.

Text: de Staël's letter to Jefferson January 6 1816, from Pisa:

I do not know whether the papers have told you that I had upheld the cause of your America against a very noble adversary, the Duke of Wellington. If you should succeed in destroying slavery in the South there would be at least one government in the world as perfect as the human mind can conceive.

I was in Italy when your letter of July reached me. I fled France the moment Bonaparte disembarked there. Nothing could induce me to have dealings with him. I cannot yet make up my mind to return to France while foreigners are masters of it (70).

Peace, War and Militarism—Military Institutions

Composed 1796-98, *Circonstances actuelles* reflects the conditions of the Terror and ensuing civil war, but not yet the extensive Napoleonic campaigns. The focus is on conflict between different social institutions, and notably how the institutions of the military are not conducive to free institutions, ordinary constitutional government and the rule of law. The military mind was willing to sacrifice people but liberty increased the ties that hold people together. For de Staël, France needed learning to promote the qualities needed for peaceful, orderly government, but the military hated reason as inimical to discipline.

Other contributions on peace by de Staël include an essay, "Reflections on Peace addressed to Mr Pitt and French Citizens," 1794 (not included here). In it she astutely observed the implications for political advantage of different policies on war: "War keeps Pitt in government; peace would bring back Mr Fox."[59] She urged practical measures to incorporate discharged soldiers back into civilian life, by encouraging agriculture, restoring freedom to commerce and establishing "large and useful public works" (2:82). During the peace conference after the Napoleonic Wars, in 1815, she wrote to the Duke of Wellington, the British general who defeated Napoleon, urging generous terms to be reached by conciliation not suppression.[60]

Text: de Staël, *Circonstances actuelles* 289-90 [my translation]:

Nothing is more worthy of admiration than success in arms, the invincible valour of generals and soldiers, but nothing is more contrary to liberty than the military mind. A long and violent war is scarcely compatible with the maintenance of any constitution and everything that assures triumph in war is subversive of the reign of law. Revolutionary enthusiasm without doubt adds

---

[59] De Staël, *Oeuvres complètes* 2:76. A further essay (2:95-172), "Reflections on Internal Peace," 1795, was printed but not distributed.

[60] De Staël, *Unpublished Correspondance of Madame de Staël and the Duke of Wellington*.

greatly to soldierly gallantry. Liberty succeeds the war sustained for it but never accompanies it.

The military mind is for conquest, liberty is for conservation. The military mind explains everything, functions in everything by force; liberty does not exist except with the support of learning. The military mind sacrifices men; liberty multiples the ties between them; the military mind hates reason as the beginning of indiscipline; liberty bases its authority on conviction. Finally, armies, even if comprised of citizens, in the long run take on the corporate spirit which makes them like all the armies of the world. In effect interest unites men. In every century in every country a confederation of priests has had the same results. In every century in every country armies will have the same mind, though their goals differ. The armies of France will never serve the cause of tyranny, but they always like the means, and the army which fights for liberty must have, to triumph, despotic mores and ideas.

Anger is often a heroic principle in a warrior; in government anger produces nothing but injustice and tyranny, and all governments which win by arms end up by being resentful. All associations, except those of enlightened men, have an "esprit de corps." Learning excludes prejudices by its nature...[Army men] will tell you incessantly, "as an individual I have my own opinions, but as a soldier I must obey." But, when a man is other than a citizen the state loses in liberty all his influence. To strengthen the principles of the French Revolution France must promote the rise of learning.

Sophie Grouchy (Marquise) de Condorcet (1764-1822)

Sophie Grouchy was the wife of the great feminist *philosophe* **Condorcet**. Both were supporters of the revolution, she being more radical than he. She translated Adam Smith's *Theory of Moral Sentiments* and wrote a commentary on it, in the form of letters, in 1793, when her husband was in hiding under sentence of death. (Condorcet died, either from exposure or suicide, in 1794, the night he was captured.) Both husband and wife were faithful to their Enlightenment ideals under the most difficult of circumstances. She did this hopeful work while surrounded by hate; the aristocrats considered her a traitor to her class which, ardent supporter of the revolution, she was. Grouchy de Condorcet also translated Thomas Paine's appeal for the republic and put it up on the walls of Paris, July 1 1791. The letters are addressed to "C," her husband—she used this designation in correspondence, while "GC" for herself. Grouchy de Condorcet published her husband's last historical work, *Sketch of the Progress of the Human Mind*, with its optimistic projection into the future, in 1795, after his death. She published another edition in 1822, the year of her death. She supported her husband's anti-slavery work as well; he was president of the Société des Amis des Noirs.

Social Bond

In his introduction to the 1994 edition of her *Huit Lettres sur la sympathie*, Jean-Paul de Lagrave aptly affirmed the importance of the concept of sympathy, without which we cannot be happy ourselves unless working for the happiness of others: "All the morality of the Enlightenment is contained in this affirmation" (9). Grouchy de Condorcet seems to have gone further than Smith in stressing the positive force of sympathy, as a human sentiment deposited in the human heart, developed by reflection. The first tie comes from the child's dependence on the mother in the cradle. Grouchy de Condorcet also believed that the pleasure we receive on fulfilling an obligation is independent of the opinion of others; it is not mere utility that motivates us (460). Moreover we sympathize with moral pleasures and pains as well as physical (423).

Grouchy de Condorcet was critical of Smith who, while he recognized that reason was the source of general rules of morality, found it impossible to deduce our first ideas of the just and unjust from reason. He then manufactured a sentiment from which our knowledge of the just and unjust, virtue and vice, was derived. He "supposed without defining" this fictitious sentiment. For her this intimate sense was not one of the first causes but itself the effect of sympathy. The original edition of the letters has been excerpted here but Lagrave's 1994 edition is also available (and is recommended for its introduction).

Text: Grouchy de Condorcet, *Théorie des sentimens moraux et huit lettres sur la sympathie* [my translation]:

The pleasure we find on fulfilling an obligation holds more urgently than security, and the comfort of feeling safe from resentment, vengeance and hatred, the particular satisfaction of having avoided the regret which would otherwise have followed us, is increased by the hope of never experiencing remorse. This is a delectable hope because it banishes any idea of an internal obstacle to our happiness.

Here then we have the motives, not only of doing good to others, but of preferring good to bad, and even the just to the unjust, motives based on our natural sympathy, which is itself a consequence of our sensitivity....The morality of our actions, the idea of justice, the desire to follow it, are the necessary work of sensibility and reason; every reasonable and sensitive being will have the same ideas; the limits to these ideas will be the same. They can then become the object of certain science because they are invariable objects. One can in effect express by the word *just* whatever idea one wants, but everyone who reasons well will have a common notion of justice. Moral ideas are not arbitrary....

It is necessary to establish this first as a base; we must then show in the natural and direct sympathy for the physical pains of others the origin of our moral sentiments, in reflection the origin of our moral ideas. We must above all make it recognized that assent to a moral truth differs from assent to a mathematical or physical truth, in that it is naturally joined to an intimate desire to conform one's conduct to it, to see others submit their own, fear from not so conforming and regret at having not. We cannot say, however, that morality is founded uniquely on sentiment for it is reason that shows us what is just and unjust. But there is less support for the notion that morality is founded uniquely on reason because the judgment of reason is almost always preceded and followed by a sentiment which announces it and confirms it (2:462-64).

We must guard against the dangerous tendency to suppose a sense or faculty every time we meet a fact the explanation for which escapes us. Whosoever imagines when he should but observe invents causes which he cannot discover, and which not only distance him from the true ones but weaken their discernment. This is how systems are created that are insufficient or false in their principles....

It is not necessary to look for motives to be good outside of and distant from nature...Man is by his constitution neither evil and corrupt nor indifferent to good, for carries in himself a general motive to be good and there is no one by nature evil (2:465-66).

Grouchy de Condorcet differed from Smith also in finding much wrong with inequality. [Text resumes:]

The extreme inequality in wealth which exists between one class and another makes people strangers to each other. Virtues, to be recognized and communicated, must be in some fashion at the same level. The powerful man and the worker he employs are too far apart to judge each other and in this distance their respective duties seem to disappear. The one can oppress the other almost without remorse, and the one who is wronged think he does justice by returning the wrong (2:501).

Laws which favour inequality in fortune apart from [inspiring hatred] multiply the number of people who have nothing to lose. The man who owns a piece of property not only feels more strongly that it is right to respect that of others, but is restrained by the fear of losing his own (2:493-94).

Chapter 4

Theorists on Social Reform

"When the division of labour is carried to extreme, industry makes enormous progress, but it dispenses with man's intelligence and reduces him to the function of a mere cog in the machine."[61]

"The average citizen of the middle or upper class takes for granted the constantly recurring destitution among wage-earning families due to unemployment as part of the natural order of things, as no more to be combated than the east wind."[62]

FLORA TRISTAN (1803-44)

Flora Tristan[63] published her *London Journal* in 1840 in French as *Promenades dans Londres*, a sociological report on her four trips to England between 1826 and 1839. The two excerpts here are thus part of an old tradition of "travel literature" from the period preceding more academic treatments of other societies. The work appeared just after Martineau's *Society in America* and *How to Observe Morals and Manners*, but Tristan seems not to have been familiar with either work. The *London Journal* is also part of the pre-Marxist revolutionary literature. It contains not only a description of appalling social conditions but class analysis and stern denunciations. There are chapters on the

---

[61] Tristan, *London Journal* 67.

[62] Webb, "Public Organization of the Labour Market" 323.

[63] Good biographies of Tristan in English are Laura S. Strumingher, *Odyssey of Flora Tristan*; Dominique Desanti, *A Woman in Revolt*; a chapter in Margaret Goldsmith, *Seven Women Against the World*; and see my *Women Founders* 177-83. In French see her *Lettres*, ed. Stéphane Michaud; Dominique Desanti, ed., *Flora Tristan oeuvres et vie mêlées*; Stéphane Michaud, ed., *Un fabuleux destin*; Pierre Leprohon, Flora Tristan; Gerhard Lee, *Flora Tristan*.

situation of women, prostitution, the causes of crime, treatment of criminals and ethnicity as well as the two excerpted here on the Chartists and factory workers. Tristan visited prisons, factories and workhouses; she witnessed a public execution. When women were not permitted even in the visitors' gallery of the House of Commons, she managed a visit with the help of a Turkish diplomat, who took her disguised as a man.

Tristan then went on, after returning to France and the publication of the *Promenades*, to organizing French workers into a Union Ouvrière. The third selection comes from her last book, which reports on her organizing tour. Tristan died in Bordeaux while still on that trip. The book was published in French in 1844 and in English in 1983.

"The Chartists" chapter contains both description and analysis, a report on the most concerted efforts to date in Britain for workers to obtain political rights. It is not a manifesto but is enthusiastically supportive of the workers' cause.[64] While she devoted more space to the condition of the urban than the rural poor, she did not neglect "the impoverishment of the rural working class." Since the landowners controlled the administration of justice and the police as well as economic conditions, their workers sank to the status of slaves. Like **Karl Marx** later, Tristan saw changes in the manufacturing process leading to changes in the division of labour and in turn the political organization of society.

The Chartist movement was the most formidable association that had arisen in Britain, a working-class movement seeking to use the political process to end aristocratic privilege in favour of equal political rights. For Tristan, as other believers in the labour theory of value, the wealth of the country had been produced by labour, so that shopkeepers, bankers, businessmen and landowners were all pariahs (39). With the Chartists, and suffragists a generation later, she believed that universal suffrage would end the injustices described. Her points on the differential treatment of the rich and poor in the criminal justice system are the same as those still raised by conflict theorists.

Government—Pre-Marxist Socialism

Tristan's observations of British society occurred at a time of very great misery. Wages were miserable, working conditions unsafe, accidents frequent, disease rampant: no "social safety net" of unemployment insurance, workers' compensation, disability benefits or public health care. Unemployed workers in extreme cases actually starved to death; many went hungry and succumbed to disease. The only welfare available was "indoor relief," meaning that a family had to enter the workhouse to be given any subsistence. Unions were "illegal combinations" and workers liable to fines and imprisonment for

---

[64] On the movement itself, especially the participation of women, see Dorothy Thompson, *The Chartists*, chapter 7.

Theorists on Reform/Tristan

attempting to organize or negotiate wages collectively. There was no legal framework to permit producers' co-operatives.

Tristan's *London Journal* preceded Friedrich Engels's *Condition of the Working Class in England in 1844*, published in 1845, and Henry Mayhew's *London Labour and the London Poor*, 1861, a massive, four-volume work. It preceded also the French Moreau-Christophe's substantial two-volume *Du problème de la misère et de sa solution*. Statistical studies of crime, especially its relation with poverty, had only begun in the late 1820s and 1830s.[65]

Tristan was convinced that conditions for workers were worse in England than in France; indeed England's industrial and rural workers were both worse off than slaves in America. She movingly described working conditions in the factories of Victorian/Dickensian England: cramped space, dirt, stench. She noted places where the machines were kept meticulously clean but the floors were dirty and the yards squalid with pools of stagnant water. She gave a graphic description of a visit to the gasworks which lit the lamps of London's great shopping centre, Oxford Street.

If it was humiliating to see human life brought so low, Tristan was quick to appreciate the benefits of applying scientific discoveries in industry: brute force banished, less time required for physical labour and more leisure with which to cultivate the mind. To realize these benefits, however, would require a social revolution (71). That such would come was for her a matter of faith, for "God has not revealed such admirable inventions to men only to have them remain the slaves of a handful of manufacturers and landed proprietors" (71-72).

Text: Tristan, "The Chartists," *London Journal*:

My readers will all have heard of Whigs and Tories, Reformers and Conservatives, Radicals and Chartists. All these parties are at war among themselves, but the great struggle, the struggle which is destined to transform the social order, is between landowners and capitalists on the one hand, and urban and rural workers on the other, that is, between men who possess both wealth and power, and for whose profit the land is governed, and men who possess nothing: no land, capital or political power, yet pay two-thirds of the taxes, provide recruits for the army and navy and are starved by the rich whenever it suits their interests to make them work for less pay.

In the three kingdoms a very small number of families owns all the land, the result of feudal laws which control inheritance. Large farms predominate;

---

[65] See Edouard Ducpétiaux, *Statistique comparée de la criminalité en France, en Belgique, en Angleterre et en Allemagne*; L.A.J. Quetelet, *Traité sur l'homme et le développement de ses facultés* and "Du Nombre des Crimes et des Délits dans les provinces," A.M. Guerry, *Essai sur la statistique morale de la France*; W. Rawson, "An Inquiry into the statistics of crime in England and Wales," Mary Carpenter, *Juvenile Delinquents*.

arable land has reverted to pasture and common land has been distributed exclusively among the landed proprietors. The inevitable consequence of these measures has been the complete impoverishment of the rural working class. And, as the administration, the police, civil and criminal justice are all in the hands of the landlord class, it follows that the worker has sunk to being the landlord's slave, even worse off than the Negro or the serf, because *their* masters would never leave them to die of hunger or rot in prison for having killed a partridge or a hare.

There have been three great revolutions in the manufacturing process. The division of labour has been carried to its utmost limit; machines have taken over every stage of production; the capitalist has the unlimited resources of the steam engine at his command. These three will bring about equally important revolutions in the political organization of society. Isolated industries are gradually disappearing; there is hardly anything man uses that cannot be made by machines in large factories. The work left for the worker to do demands so little skill that virtually anyone can do it.

At first the workers benefited from these advances in industry. The high quality and low price of goods increased the number of consumers and wages rose. But, when peace came [after the Napoleonic wars], competition from the Continent began to develop. The English manufacturer fought it with the help of the vast capital he had amassed. He built up enormous stocks in his warehouses at home and in the trading posts the English had set up all over the world, and he successively reduced the worker's wages. In this situation the English worker is entirely at the mercy of the capitalist manufacturer, who can continue to meet demand for a long time without needing to spare a thought for his workers. He takes every penny of the profits and the worker has nothing to show for his fourteen hours of toil except his daily bread.

The Radicals demand the abolition of the corn laws, but what the workers want is universal suffrage, because they know full well that if they had any hand in law-making they would very soon obtain the abolition of all duties affecting grain and every other kind of food, as well as the right to form unions to fight against the capitalists.

So far the Chartists constitute the most formidable association that has arisen in the three kingdoms....The Chartists are not to be fobbed off with half measures; they will never trust a party whose object is to transfer the privileges of the aristocracy to the middle class, for this would only lead to more oppression. The workers, who have raised the fortunes of England to such heights, to whom shopkeepers, bankers, businessmen and landowners all owe their wealth, are the pariahs of society; their name is never mentioned in Parliament unless it be to propose laws to restrict their freedom. It is therefore their unshakable conviction that any measure which is not based on the equality of political rights can be only an illusory gain.

If there were universal suffrage would a government propose to raise the price of bread so high that the workers starve? Would there be a ban on importing almost every kind of foodstuff? Would the basic necessities of the poor be taxed three times more heavily than the luxuries of the rich? If all men could elect their representatives would the administration of justice be so odious? Would the nobleman's son be fined a derisory sum for violating a woman or beating a subordinate almost to death, while the poor worker is mercilessly punished for some petty offence, sent to languish in prison and leave his family to die of hunger because he is unable to provide bail? Would fines be fixed in such a way that the *minimum* was equal to several weeks' wages for a worker, and the *maximum* half the daily expenditure of a rich man? Would there be more people in prison for infringing the game laws than for all the felonies and misdemeanours put together? Would the military be sent out to do battle with poachers to avenge the death of a few pheasants? Would the Court of King's Bench decree that when common land was enclosed or expropriated, only the landowner was entitled to compensation, while the poor folk who had built dwellings on the land could be evicted together with the cow or pig they had raised? If the people who form the bulk of the army and navy were represented in Parliament, would soldiers and sailors still be beaten and flogged, would army commissions be sold, would a sailor be pressed into the service of the state, only to be paid less than he could earn ashore?...

At the first sign of organized activity in the working classes the aristocracy sounded the alarm and declared that the workers were bent on destruction. Now the Chartists look forward to the reign of justice, so they must appear vandals in the eyes of those who owe their wealth to privilege, and it is the virulence of this class which accounts for the repugnance and terror—whether real or feigned—that the Chartists inspire. But the workers who take an active part in the movement are the elite of their class....The lords of industry understand the implications of these new ideas only too well, which is why they have misrepresented the intentions of any workers who plan to set up in competition with them....

In the national petition presented to Parliament on June 14 1839, the workers and the more enlightened among the manufacturers exposed their grievances. They attributed the cause to the massive taxation which weighed so heavily upon the people and to the squandering of public resources. They declared that electoral reform [1832] was a derisory measure which no longer deceived anybody and had done nothing but transfer power from one faction to another, leaving the people as wretched as before; that the capital of the master could no longer be deprived of its rightful interest or the worker's labour of its due reward; that the laws which made food dear, money scarce and labour cheap must be abolished; that as the good of the greatest number was the only legitimate goal, it should also be the chief study of government; that the present state of affairs could not continue much longer without serious danger to the stability of the throne and the peace of the kingdom; and that if legal means proved of no avail they were resolved to take action themselves. As an indispensable preliminary to the changes which the welfare of the people required, they demanded universal suffrage, the secret ballot, annual Parliaments, the abolition of all voting qualifications and the payment of members of Parliament (36-42) [Tristan next related the more detailed, tougher petition of 1842].

As may be seen, the conclusions of the two petitions are the same, but what a world of difference lies between them! In 1839 men, who were still prepared to *reason* with their rulers, soberly pointed out the inevitable consequences of the existing state of affairs; they demanded that all should share the same political rights because the corruption, greed, plundering and oppression of the aristocracy reduced them to the most appalling poverty, destroyed public prosperity and threatened the peace of the realm by driving people to despair.

Today it is 3,317,702 individuals, nearly one half of the male population of the three kingdoms over the age of twenty-one who inform the House that it has no authority to enact laws and demand obedience to them, that the people will *resist* Parliament because they have not appointed it. They are no longer begging for concessions, they *demand their rights* and will seize them *by force* if they continue to be withheld. They protest against Parliament for using the powers it has *usurped* to rob and plunder the people, against the scandalous rapacity of the clergy imposed on them against their will, against organized tyranny with its police, its soldiers, its arbitrary imprisonment and the iniquitous partiality of its law courts. They contrast the income of eminent sinecurists from the Queen downwards with the wages of productive workers, and consider the comparative usefulness to society of each.

This petition is nothing less than the English people's declaration of war against the aristocracy, and now we wait to see if words will be followed by deeds, if our brothers in Great Britain will imitate the example we have set them since 1789, if they will engage in battle, burn down castles and resolve never to lay down their arms until they have won back their rights!...

Just now England presents a bizarre anomaly. Among the workers prejudice is gradually dying out and religious and national hatreds are on the wane, whereas in the upper ranks of society the aristocracy, terrified by the spread of enlightenment, withdraws into impenetrable darkness, buries itself in the obscurity of the Middle Ages...At a time when the people are dying of hunger the aristocracy seeks to embroil them in religious controversy and longs to return to the benighted days when men would cut one another's throats over a theological quibble. And these are the men who claim the right to lead the nation!

As for the Whigs, they still live in the century of Louis XIV. Look how important they think it is that one royal family should govern a country rather than another! They imagine that in Europe it is kings who decide what people think and that rulers may act as they please without the assent of their subjects. Poor creatures! They do not see that national prejudice is declining, that every day the people are becoming more closely united, that the interests of the masses dominate every issue on the Continent as well as in England, and that an unpopular war could no longer succeed in any country in Europe, but would spell eternal ruin for the aristocracy which provoked it! (45-57)

Text: Tristan, "Factory Workers," *London Journal*:

In the beginning all societies go through a period of slavery, but the evils it produces make it essentially transitory, and its duration is in inverse ratio to its harshness. If our [French] fathers had not treated their serfs with more humanity than English industrialists treat their workers, servitude would never have lasted all through the Middle Ages. The existence of the English worker, whatever his occupation, is so appalling that the Negroes who left the sugar plantations of Guadeloupe and Martinique to enjoy English "freedom" in Dominica and St Lucia are glad to return, when they can, to their former masters. But do not think for a moment that I should want to commit the sacrilege of condoning any form of slavery! I only want to show that English law treats the workers more harshly than the autocratic French master treats his Negroes, and that the slave of English capitalism has a far heavier task to earn his daily bread and pay his taxes....

When the division of labour is carried to extremes, industry makes enormous progress, but it dispenses with man's intelligence and reduces him to the function of a mere cog in the machine. If the worker were still capable of performing more than one stage in the manufacturing process, he would enjoy more independence and his greedy employer would have fewer opportunities to torment him...If the worker were engaged in various stages of production he would not feel crushed by a sense of his utter insignificance, nor would his intelligence become dulled through constant repetition of the same actions....

Most workers lack clothing, bed, furniture, fuel, wholesome food—even potatoes! They spend from twelve to fourteen hours each day shut up in low-ceilinged rooms where with every breath of foul air they absorb fibres of cotton, wool or flax, or particles of copper, lead or iron. They live suspended between an insufficiency of food and an excess of strong drink; they are all wizened, sickly and emaciated; their bodies are thin and frail, their limbs feeble, their complexions pale, their eyes dead. They look as if they all suffer from consumption. It is painful to see the expression on their faces....

In my eyes slavery is no longer the greatest human misfortune since I have become acquainted with the English proletariat, for the slave knows he will get his daily bread all his life and be cared for when he falls ill, but there is no bond between the English worker and his master. If the employer has no work to offer the worker dies of hunger; if he falls ill he dies on his wretched straw pallet, unless when he is on the point of death he has the good fortune to be taken into hospital, for it is a special favour even to be admitted. If he is old or crippled in an accident he is dismissed and has to resort to begging, but then he has to be careful not to be arrested for vagrancy. All in all, his position is so appalling that you feel he must be possessed of either superhuman courage or total apathy to endure it.

Cramped conditions are commonplace in English factories. The space allowed each worker is calculated with a careful eye. The yards are small, the staircases narrow; the worker is obliged to move around his machine or loom *sideways*. If you visit a factory it is easy to see that the comfort and welfare, even the health, of the men destined to spend their lives within its walls have never entered the builder's head. Cleanliness, one of the surest roads to health, is sadly neglected. The more meticulously the machines are painted, varnished, cleaned and polished, the dirtier are the floors, the dustier the windows, the more squalid the yards with their pools of stagnant water (66-70).

If at first I felt humiliated to see man brought so low, his functions reduced to those of a machine, I was quick to realize the immense advances which all these scientific discoveries would bring: brute force banished, less time expended on physical labour, more leisure for man to cultivate his intelligence. But if these great benefits are to be realized there must be a social revolution, and that revolution will come, for God has not revealed such admirable inventions...only to have them remain the slaves of a handful of manufacturers and landed proprietors (71-72).

Tristan's "How to Consolidate the Working Class" marks an odd phase in the history of socialism. She distinguished the organization she sought to build from the "aid" societies intended to "alleviate misery" or "relieve individual suffering" (49). Yet she did not advocate public ownership of the means of production, distribution and exchange as **Marx and Engels** soon would.[66] The Workers' Union she sought would provide for the education of working class children, build up capital through voluntary contributions and remunerate labour generously and fairly. Yet in places it seems that Tristan had nothing more in mind than a political organization able to support a paid spokesperson. As an example she cited the Irish Association of Daniel O'Connell.

Tristan noted the weakness of mere political rights, which the French enjoyed from the Declaration of the Rights of Man, 1791, and the Charter of 1831. Before citizenship rights could be meaningful, she asserted, economic rights were required: "the right to live," which meant the right to work and

---

[66] On Tristan's socialism see G.D.H. Cole, *History of Socialist Thought* 1:187. On her feminism and socialism see: Susan K. Grogan, "Flora Tristan and the Moral Superiority of Women," *French Socialism and Social Difference*; S. Joan Moon, "Feminism and Socialism: The Utopian Synthesis of Flora Tristan," in Marilyn J. Boxer and Jean H. Quataert, eds., *Socialist Women*; Daniel Armogathe, "Flora Tristan, féministe et socialiste," in *Fini le féminisme? Compte rendu du colloque international féminisme et socialismes*, 58-73; Marie Cross and Tim Gray, *The Feminism of Flora Tristan*; Johanna Busmann, *Feminismus and Sozialismus in den Schriften Flora Tristan*.

organize.[67] Before Marx, Tristan described how the bourgeoisie had successfully established itself, through the French Revolution of 1789, and consolidated its hold in 1830 by bringing down the king. It accomplished this by being more numerous and useful than the nobility. On unification the working class would be strong and able to make itself heard, to demand the right to work and organize.

Text: Tristan, "How to Consolidate the Working Class," *Workers' Union* 49 and *Union ouvrière* 14 [my translation, and use of English text]:

It is very important for workers to distinguish between the Workers' Union as I conceive of the idea and what exists today under the titles of guild associations, unions, mutual aid societies etc. The goal of all these various private groups is simply to give aid, mutually and individually....Thus they were set up to provide in case of sickness, accidents and long periods of unemployment. Given the working class's current state of isolation, desertion and misery, these sorts of societies are useful, for their aim is to give a bit of aid to the most needy, thereby mitigating personal suffering....But alleviating misery does not *destroy* it; mitigating the evil is not the same as *eradicating* it. If one really wants to attack the root of evil, obviously one needs something other than private societies.

Tristan rued the fact that societies "acting in the name of the individual" offered the same thing and were able to create nothing good. Workers "since the time of Solomon" fifty centuries ago were still in "poverty, ignorance and slavery, the only change being the types and names of slaves."

> Workers, you must leave behind this division and isolation as quickly as possible and march courageously and fraternally down the only appropriate path: *unity*. My union plan rests upon a broad base and its spirit is capable of fully satisfying the moral [social] and material needs of a great people...Its goals are: (1) To establish the solid, indissoluble unity of the working class; (2) To provide the Workers' Union with enormous capital through the voluntary subscription of every worker; (3) To acquire a real power backed by this capital; (4) By means of this power to prevent poverty and eradicate abuse by giving working-class children a solid, rational education which will make them educated, reasonable, intelligent and able men and women in their work; (5) To remunerate labour as it ought to be, generously and fairly.[68]

---

[67] Tristan, *Workers' Union* 54.

[68] *Workers' Union* 49-51, *Union Ouvrière* 17-18 [my translation and use of English text].

Tristan urged workers not suppress their feelings and imagination with the "icy words" that it was *impossible*. France had between seven and eight million workers, some well-off and many with "generous souls," able to give two, four...or twenty francs. Through voluntary contributions they could collect up to 50 million francs a year, hardly anything for "a huge machine" like the government. Used carefully and economically toward a specific object this was "enormous wealth" sufficient to give the Workers' Union the sort of power money could.

She next set out the argument of the labour theory of value, the single point on which Marx and Engels referred to Tristan's work. Engels's short note on the *Union ouvrière* was complimentary, defending her from attack by "a critical critic," who had referred to it as an example of "feminine dogmatism."[69] Tristan explained that the working class's own property and the only one it could ever possess was its hands: "That is its patrimony, its sole wealth... For if the earth produces it is thanks to manual labour."[70]

Tristan next made the analogy with the bourgeoisie's gain of independence in 1789 with the capture of the Bastille:

Workers, for more than 200 years the bourgeois have fought courageously and ardently against the privileges of the nobility and for the victory of their rights. When the day of victory came...they seized all the gains and advantages of the conquest *for themselves alone*...The advantage all large constitutional bodies enjoy is the power to count for something in the state, and in this way be represented.

Tristan noted that the royalists and colonialists were represented in the chamber, why not the working class—to defend its interests? "Indeed, in number and importance it equals at least the royalist group and the body of colonial landowners. Workers, think about this: the first thing you have to do is to get yourselves represented before the nation."[71]

HARRIET MARTINEAU (1802-76)

Harriet Martineau[72] was born in Norwich to a politically liberal, Unitarian, family of Huguenot origin. She was educated at home with her brothers, whereupon they went to university where she of course could not go. (Her

---

[69] Marx and Engels, *Holy Family* 31.

[70] *Workers' Union* 52-55.

[71] *Workers' Union* 57-59, *Union ouvrière* 27-28 [my translation and use of English text].

[72] Biographies are Susan Hoecker-Drysdale, *Harriet Martineau*; John Cranstoun Nevill, *Harriet Martineau*; Valerie Kossew Pichanick, *Harriet Martineau*; R.K. Webb, *Harriet Martineau*; Vera Wheatley, *Life and Work of Harriet Martineau. A Selected Letters* is available and see my *Women Founders* 164-75 and 206-11.

brother **James** was a much respected Unitarian minister and author.) Martineau became deaf at a young age but was able to hear fairly well with the use of an ear trumpet. She also used a travelling companion/research assistant on her American trip to conduct observations in crowded situations where she herself could not hear adequately. She never married, but it seems that she had a romance with a cousin of Charles Darwin.

Martineau had to earn her own living from the age of twenty-four, when her father died. She had already begun to publish articles; now her writing career began in earnest. She published more than 1600 leading articles for the *Daily News* and some fifty books (some of which are only reprints of her articles). She also published in leading academic and progressive journals, both British and American. Her first great success occurred in 1832 with *Illustrations of Political Economy*, a popular presentation of the principles of laissez-faire economics. This harsh philosophy gave her an entrée to high society. (Later she modified her views considerably.) The proceeds from sales funded her trip to the United States, where she travelled 1834-36. She published *Society in America* in 1837. Further material appeared in *Retrospect of Western Travel*.

Martineau's best methodological work is *How to Observe Morals and Manners*, which Seymour Martin Lipset described as "perhaps the first book on the methodology of social research."[73] She did the first draft en route to the United States by sailing ship. She produced books from her travels in the Middle East, and two books on India, although she never visited it. She published a popular *History of the Thirty Years' Peace*, 1849. She published several novels which were well received at the time; the Brontë sisters and **George Eliot** liked her work. In 1853 she published a greatly condensed English translation of **Auguste Comte's** *Cours de philosophie positive*, the only work with which she is credited in most textbooks on sociology.

Martineau wrote a three-volume autobiography in 1855 when she was expecting to die. She survived many more years, however, so that the work was only published in 1876, on her death, without any material on the last, and very productive, period of her life (which includes her collaboration with Nightingale). Her literary earnings were sufficient for her to buy a house and live comfortably in the Lake District in the last two decades of her life.

Martineau's early and severe conservatism mellowed in time. Her later journalism shows her advocating government intervention where practical. She gave many years of her life to advocacy of the equality of women (notably suffrage, education, occupations and legal rights) and the abolition of slavery. Nightingale recruited her to promote sanitary reform on numerous fronts, to fight the Contagious Diseases Acts and to reform British rule in India.

---

[73] Lipset, Introduction, *Society in America* 7.

Government—Abolition of Slavery

Martineau's excellent *Society in America* is available in a good edited version by Seymour Martin Lipset, 1962, and accordingly is not excerpted here. It includes substantial treatment of the issue of slavery, and the movement to abolish it which was then in its early stages. Martineau continued to write on slavery, both in scholarly journals and, more often, in the popular press. Two of her numerous unsigned "leaders" for the *Daily News* are excerpted here, along with parts of two journal articles, one early and one late. All of these build on the information she obtained first hand, from visiting plantations and slave auctions, and by keeping in touch with abolitionists.[74]

Martineau's "The Martyr Age of the United States" was published in 1838 in the liberal *London and Westminster Review*, ostensibly as a review article on three issues of an anti-slavery publication, *Right and Wrong in Boston*. The martyrs were the pioneer workers in the anti-slavery cause. They suffered loss of jobs and business, the derision and contempt of their neighbours, and, for some, beatings by mobs, arson and even murder. Martineau was keen to show her British readership the heroism of the early abolitionists. The short excerpts (from a 59-page article) highlight a range of people and events, beginning with **William Lloyd Garrison**, the abolition leader most known in Europe. One excerpt focused on the links between the anti-slavery cause and women's rights, another favourite Martineau subject. She also reported a speech of **John Quincy Adams** favourable to women's rights. Alongside the exemplary conduct of the anti-slavery leaders Martineau described the venality of Congress, then showing little sign of concern. The last selection relates the speech by **Angelina Grimké**, a leading Quaker abolitionist, to a committee of the Massachusetts Legislature.

Text: Martineau, "Martyr Age of the United States":

There is a remarkable set of people now living and vigorously acting in the world, with a consonance of will and understanding which has perhaps never before been witnessed among so large a number of individuals of such diversified powers, habits, opinions, tastes and circumstances. The body comprehends men and women of every shade of colour, of every degree of education, of every variety of religious opinion, of every gradation of rank, bound together by no vow, no pledge, no stipulation but of each preserving his individual liberty. Yet they act as if they were of one heart and one soul. Such union could be secured by no principle of worldly interest, nor, for a term of years, by the most stringent fanaticism. A well-grounded faith, directed towards a noble object, is the only principle which can account for such a

---

[74] See also Lydia Maria Child, *An Appeal in favor of Americans called Africans*, 1833, which Martineau cited with favour.

spectacle as the world is now waking up to contemplate in the abolitionists of the United States.

Before we fix our attention on the history of the body it may be remarked that it is a totally different thing to be an abolitionist on a soil actually trodden by slaves and in a far-off country where opinion is already on the side of emancipation or ready to be converted, where only a fraction of society, instead of the whole, has to be convicted of guilt, and where no interests are put in jeopardy but pecuniary ones, and those limited and remote. Great honour is due to the first movers in the anti-slavery cause in every land, but those of European countries may take rank with the philanthropists of America who may espouse the cause of the aborigines, while the primary abolitionists of the United States have encountered, with steady purpose, such opposition as might here await assailants of the whole set of aristocratic institutions at once, from the throne to pauper apprenticeship.

Slavery is as thoroughly interwoven with American institutions, ramifies as extensively through American society, as the aristocratic spirit pervades Great Britain. The fate of reformers whose lives are devoted to making war upon either the one or the other must be remarkable (1-2) [Martineau then recounted numerous examples of violence].

The most melancholy feature of the struggle, more so than even the conduct of the clergy...is the degeneracy of Congress. The right of petition has been virtually annihilated for these three years past and the nation has been left unrepresented on the most important question which has been occupying the nation's mind. The people hold their remedy in the ballot box (53).

During the last year several halls of state legislatures have been granted to the abolitionists for their meetings while the churches have remained closed against them. The aspect of these assemblages has been very remarkable from the union of religious and political action witnessed there. But the most extraordinary spectacle of all, a spectacle perhaps unrivalled in the history of the world, was the address of Angelina Grimké before a committee of the Legislature of Massachusetts. Some have likened it to the appeal of Hortensia to the Roman Senate, but others have truly observed that the address of Angelina Grimké was far the nobler of the two, as she complained not as the voice of a party remonstrating against injuries done to itself but as the advocate of a class too degraded and helpless to move or speak on its own behalf....

The history of this struggle seems to yield a few inferences which must, we think, be evident to all impartial minds....One is that this is a struggle which cannot subside till it has prevailed. If this be true, the consequence of yielding to it would be the saving of a world of guilt and woe. Another is that other sorts of freedom, besides emancipation from slavery, will come in with it, that the aristocratic spirit in all its manifestations is being purged out of the community, that with every black slave a white will be also freed. Another is that republicanism is in no degree answerable for the want of freedom and of the turbulence and tyranny are the immediate and visible offspring of the old-world, feudal, European spirit which still lives in the institution assailed, and in the bosoms of the aristocracy of the country, while the bulwarks of the Constitution, the true republicans, are the "peacemen," the sufferers, the moral soldiers, who have gone out armed only with faith, hope and charity. Another is that the coloured people have a promising *morale* on which to ground their civilization. Their whole conduct affords evidences of generosity, patience and hopefulness from which fine results of character may be anticipated whenever this unfortunate race shall have leave to exert its unfettered energies under circumstances of average fairness (57-58).

If it is true that **Abraham Lincoln** was the president who freed the slaves, it is also true that he took a long time in coming to it. Martineau shared the frustration of abolitionists over the timidity of his initial position (on election he was committed only to opposing the extension of slavery), and prevarication in the early years of his presidency. This can be seen in many of her *Daily News* leaders. In the first one below Martineau argued that Washington had to make a choice. She reiterated the position she had taken from the time of her first writing on the subject in *Society in America*, 1837, as to the inevitability of slavery's end. She pointed out that there were areas in the South ready to exchange slave for free labour. Yet the Northern position was not yet clear. Lincoln was still declaring his intention of "upholding the Constitution in its entirety," though slavery was *the* great issue.

In the second selection Martineau was trying to make federalist attitudes and prospects clear to European readers. The critical period of abolition, foreseen for thirty years, had now arrived. Martineau lamented the "degrading complicity" of the North with the South in maintaining slavery. This leader is a good source also on the (futile) steps Lincoln went through before he reached a decisive policy of full-scale abolition. She related the changes that had occurred among the blacks that made the re-establishment of slavery impossible; they would not permit it. Black soldiers and sailors were able to keep the ground they had won and proven their capacity to work in freedom.

Text: Martineau, *Daily News* March 1 1862:4:

There can be no doubt that the time has arrived when we must form a judgment for ourselves, independent of American guidance, about the course and probabilities of political affairs at Washington. There is naturally a strong desire on all hands to guide European opinion, and we are presented with the sanguine views and pet projects of every section which has a plan to propose....It is a clear duty now for us to take whatever pains are requisite to understand the position of affairs at the moment when a choice must be made at Washington of one course among several.

Of the South there is little to be said except that the despondent tone of the Richmond papers, and other utterances in the Border states, is no longer met and corrected by the jubilant manifestoes of the Southern cities. On the contrary, the more thoroughgoing Confederates seem to have passed into the other extreme, and to be addressing their fellow-citizens in a tone of despair. If this sort of appeal is really suitable to the situation it will soon be seen whether there is or is not any considerable portion of the population disposed for continued union on the simple terms of giving up slavery and the political privileges it carried with it. The evidence seems to us just what it always was, that the Confederacy must collapse whenever attacked with energy, and that there are districts where the inhabitants would be glad to exchange slave for free labour, and to have Washington for their metropolis rather than Montgomery or Richmond. The military and civil action of the Northern government will soon disclose what remains to be known of the condition of the South....

A bill is to be brought before Congress which will provide for the abolition of slavery in the District of Columbia, the district over which Congress has unrestricted power. Well! This move has been made often before....The federal soldiery declare, almost to a man, that they will not be employed as slave catchers, nor as escort to Negroes delivered up to their owners. This is an interesting manifestation of opinion and feeling in an important class of society, but, as regards action at Washington, it indicates only that there may be antagonism between the army and the government.

The abolitionists have for months been circulating a form of memorial to government by which they propose, and petition for, a freeing of the slaves wherever the federal flag advances, in accordance with interpretations of the Constitution by very high authorities, and moreover pledge themselves to contribute all they have, if necessary, to start and sustain a sound organization of labour on the Southern plantations, under federal officials. The answer to this is Lincoln's demonstration that he abides by the existing Constitution....

There is the great Union party of the North, which would perpetuate slavery with all its heart to get the union back again. This party will support Mr Lincoln, and strive to prevent that abdication which is now so strongly and widely rumoured. The slave traders in the Atlantic ports, the Mammon worshippers of all sorts, and the Union worshippers and the quiet Tories who are disturbed by the restless spirit of the time, are now in great complacency about Mr Lincoln's decision, and will support him to the utmost. There is another large section of the people who are for sustaining the Constitution till the South is subdued and amending it afterwards. Then there is the great Republican Party, which has become much more anti-slavery than Mr Lincoln since it elected him.

The numbers, strength and reputation of this party increase daily and on it rests the hope of the country. Through it we see that public speech has become free at Washington and in churches and lecture rooms where no anti-slavery doctrine could have been uttered a year ago. Through it we see the Northern people becoming hourly more worthy of the great strife, as well as more awake to its nature and bearings....On this party rests the hope of the republic. It can save the republic easily enough if aware of its duty....A frank and sound emancipation policy is the only safe and expedient one for the North....It is too late now to pretend that the promoters and opponents of that policy, and the waiters upon Providence in regard to it, do or ever can again work together as if united by a common patriotic enthusiasm.

Text: Martineau, *Daily News* August 13 1862:4:

It is not at all surprising that many European observers, journalists as well as others, should fail to understand the conditions of the American quarrel as far as the Negro element is concerned....The hour is critical precisely for the reason which has been foreshown for thirty years....The old methods of appeal are done with and it is as the decisive element of the political quarrel, and not as "a man and a brother" that the "inevitable Negro" is now implicated in the conflict.

For a long course of years the North exhibited a lamentable and degrading complicity with the South in the maintenance of slavery. We need not relate how citizen pride in their republic, and Southern ties of blood and commerce, corrupted the principles, tempers and manners of society, leaving room for slave traders to ply their traffic and affording encouragement to bullies, both in rags and in broadcloth, to break any and all laws in their attacks on the best citizens in the republic....The government and the people were united in their determination to put down rebellion, but it was always doubtful whether this could be accomplished otherwise than by destroying the barbarism which bred the tyranny first, and the rebellion afterwards....

As the war proceeded it became necessary for the government to inaugurate a more decisive policy on the subject of slavery. At length the president opened his lips on emancipation, but it was at first only to propose a practically futile scheme of slave deportation. It was generally said, and probably with truth, that this was a device to gain time, for the president's own mind and for the people to decide upon and declare their will. No great deal of time has been lost, for such a series of vital reforms has seldom or never been wrought in so few weeks as those which have freed the District of Columbia, secured the territories from the curse of slavery, doomed the African slave trade in American waters and gone forth vigorously against it on the African coasts. It is not loss of time that is so much to be lamented as the sacrifice of life and treasure incident to the continuance of the war....

In regard to the Negroes, man may propose from day to day, but God has disposed...The plain truth is that it is now too late to re-establish slavery because the Negroes do not choose it and they have friends enough to let the world know that they need not submit to slavery and will not....Their regiments are as promising as those of any other young soldiers....As naval gunners they are actually preferred to the whites who have practised with them....They work exactly as other men work, badly without inducement and to any extent for natural rewards. The earthworks, the clearings, the building, the tillage, the journeying and the voyaging that hundreds, thousands and tens of thousands of them have accomplished since last winter prove their capacity to work in freedom. As for the rest, it is not true that...they are willing to abide in slavery in the Gulf states. They do not rise upon old men, boys and women on the plantations, but they join the Federals as opportunity offers....There is, at least, concert among them. In their own way they have leaders, deputies and a registration. If they can remain where they are in freedom they will stay, but they will not stay as slaves. This is so far understood in the Border states that the peculiar anti-slavery party belonging to such societies as that of Maryland is growing and becoming more active every day. There is no such unreason in the Border states as the notion that by joining the South they could sustain slavery...they are aware that the Confederates are bound to slavery and that slavery is bound to destruction.

The federal Constitution will no longer be the shield and support of slavery. Whatever might have been thought possible before the liberation of the Negroes began, it can never be possible to remand them to bondage, practised in arms, accustomed to wages, introduced to letters, awakened in mind, cheered in heart and encouraged by the sympathy of all good citizens....Wherever the armies go the Negroes are free henceforth. The outcry in England about fire and slaughter will soon cease, for it needs no more than average English wit to see that the risk of fire and slaughter is not when an oppressed people obtain what they want, but when they are disappointed of it....Every step towards avowed emancipation is a saving of life, as every appearance of vacillation has wasted much. The crisis is passing; every moment makes new abolitionists, and when there are enough to satisfy the president he will speak the word and make the sign which will save the republic.

Martineau's "Negro Race in America" dates from 1864, or just after the Civil War. Black slavery had by then received its "death sentence" and abolitionists were looking forward to a new age of emancipation. Martineau examined the process of education for freedom that had taken place in the preceding two generations. In *Society in America* she discussed the situation of freed black slaves in the North as well as that of slaves in the South. She was well aware that the problems of racism, although the term was not then used, were quite different from those of slavery. With legal emancipation, important as it was, there would still be serious problems.

Martineau described the success of the first racial integration of schools in the United States, in Massachusetts seven years earlier. She also cited the successful opening of universities and colleges to blacks. She related census and other statistical data showing that the free blacks of the North had lower rates of crime, pauperism and mortality than any other class of people (238). She made the case for the readiness of free blacks for full integration (again, the term was not then used). The article ended with the assertion that the establishment of slavery as a dominant institution was now inconceivable. Slave owners had, ironically, precipitated the very revolution they hoped to prevent.

Text: Martineau, "The Negro Race in America":

If it is talking politics to assume that slavery is drawing to an end in the United States then we must be political to that extent. But, as there is probably no one in Europe, and as there are certainly few in America, who believe that "the peculiar institution" can ever be again what it was in the slave states before the war, we incur no charge of political partisanship in assuming that Negro slavery in America has received its death sentence. Of the disclosures here referred to the greatest and most interesting is that of the effective education the Negroes have been receiving, for a long course of years, for the new destiny which is opening before them. Where the speculations of their friends or of their enemies are now found to be wide of the mark, it is because they were unaware to what extent the process of training for freedom had already advanced, and that it was becoming accelerated from day to day. By looking over the facts of the life of one or two generations of American slaves, we shall learn how the process went on....

So far as it is true that the first emancipation of a slave on the ground of personal or political right is a pledge of ultimate release for all, the doom of American slavery was passed before the Declaration of Independence. A Negro woman was born in slavery in 1742 who obtained her own freedom on that ground, and thus brought about the abolition of slavery in Massachusetts first, and afterwards in the other Northern states (203-04).

Seven years ago the free coloured people of New England had to make an important decision. The Legislature of Massachusetts declared the common schools open unconditionally to all the children in the state. There were anxious consultations among the people of colour in Boston whether to accept this concession, implying as it did the closing of their own schools. They made the venture and have rejoiced ever since....The opening of colleges in the same spirit—so that Negro students have been and are now seen even at Harvard University—had by this time caused the free people of colour to have educated men and women of their own race. There was wealth among them before and now they had physicians, clergymen, tutors and schoolmasters, engineers and men of business, and of the other sex a considerable number of well-cultivated school mistresses, governesses, music teachers and artists (218).

The free blacks in the Northern states are shown by the Census and other returns to yield fewer criminals and fewer paupers, and to exhibit a lower mortality in proportion to their numbers than any other class in the republic. The love of a warm climate and the attachment of the people to the soil on which they have lived from birth afford the best promise that Negroes will not desert the territory where their labour is needed and to which it is adapted. At the same time it is plain to all eyes that slavery can never exist again where the labouring class has tasted freedom and shown itself worthy of the free man's privileges and adequate to the free man's duties. The territory which is now practically exempted from slavery is so large and so rapidly augmenting that it is already inconceivable that any remnant of it can preserve its "peculiar institution" after the close of the war, whatever the issue may be.

The depressed race may be regarded now as having received an authorization to try what it can do to obtain a free social position, after having gone through the discipline and training by which it can be raised. It has made a better beginning that could have been hoped, and its own manifestation of high qualities of mind and conscience has had a larger share than any working of events in releasing it from the contempt and dislike under which it has hitherto suffered in the freest states of the American union. That species of oppression can never be renewed when colour ceases to be a badge of slavery, a consummation which we may now regard as nearly attained (237-38).

We thus see how inconceivable it is that slavery can ever again be an established and supreme institution in the Southern states and, unless supreme, slavery cannot exist. The Confederacy, aware of this, but apparently unaware of the certainty of failure in the condition of their own fortunes and of their Negroes, struck a bold stroke for their social system, putting everything to hazard for assurance on this one point. Nothing better could have been desired by the friends of liberty and the deliverers of the Negro than that the end of the oppression should be brought about by the oppressors themselves.

Slavery would soon have become impossible except by a fearful social retrogression, an extension of its bounds and a reopening of the Negro trade. Such a retrogression has been rendered impossible and the slave holders have sought to avert the gradual disintegration of their system by a sharp and perilous effort at isolation from outward influences. The result proves that they have miscalculated their chances, and have precipitated the revolution in their labour system which they intended to prevent....

If it be true that the object of secession was to extend and perpetuate slavery, that object has signally failed; nay more, emancipation has been its direct consequence. If, on the other hand, we are to believe that the seceding states are fighting not for slavery but for their own independence, then it becomes their first interest to accept and complete the abolition of slavery, for it is that which cuts them off from the sympathy of mankind....Whatever be the political result of the war, President Lincoln declares...that he abides by the policy of emancipation. One million of the four millions of men [and women] of colour who were slaves two years since are now free under express federal protection; many more have found their own way to liberty and now the distinct purpose of the federal government is to emancipate the rest as far as its power extends (241-42).

Martineau, thanks to her work with Nightingale, had another cause to serve apart from the abolition of slavery in her writing on the Civil War. From her years of promoting Nightingale's principles of preventive medicine she wanted also to minimize deaths from illness and wounds; the lessons learned in the Crimean War only a few years earlier (1854-56) ought to be applied in the United States (especially the anti-slavery North). Martineau's characterization of the Southern troops is quite rude. There was only the most perfunctory desire for keeping "them" alive, too, and almost relief that she had no access to the Southern government to help to do so. Martineau took the initiative here in promoting what she rightly called their joint work. Her reference to *England and her Soldiers* as "our" book is apt. Although Martineau wrote it and it was published with her name only on it, the material was all supplied by Nightingale, up to the provision of printers' plates for the charts.[75] Nightingale was pleased to co-operate, preparing bundles of forms as well as the background documents themselves, to facilitate the adoption of the new sanitary measures. The brief excerpted correspondence that follows relates these initiatives. The articles in the *Atlantic Monthly* to which Martineau referred were popularizations of the sanitary principles intended to drum up support among the citizenry.

Text: Martineau letter September 20 1861, Add Mss 45788 folios 125-26:

No answer needed
Dear Miss Nightingale,
The reason of my writing now is that I have just heard something that I think will gratify you. *Our* book, *England and her Soldiers*, is at present quoted largely and incessantly in American medical journals, as a guide in the newness of military management in the Northern states. Before I knew this, I had sent one of two articles (the second goes today) on "Health in the Camp," and "Health in the Hospital," to the *Atlantic Monthly*. I don't like magazines, or writing for them, but that very good one has such an enormous circulation that I now and then say "yes" when the proprietors ask me to write. In spite of the war, they have again asked me now and I thought it a good opportunity to interest their public in saving their citizen-soldiers' lives and health. It is more to the purpose that the medical journals are learning from us; and I am sure you will be glad to hear it.

---

[75] On the Nightingale-Martineau collaboration see my *Women Founders* 206-11. Original sources are in the Nightingale Collection, British Library.

Theorists on Reform/Martineau   149

Text: Nightingale reply September 24 1861, Add Mss 45788 folios 127-30:

I am really grateful to you for what you tell me about the Northern states. When you speak of their "newness of military management" it occurs to me, would you like to send them a collection of what might be useful "as a guide" in the Sanitary Service? If so, I should recommend (and would gladly send to you for transmission....Dr Edward Jarvis (U.S.) president of the American Statistical Association, who was in London last year for the International Statistical Congress, but of whom I know nothing but that he was sent to me to obtain information, was very anxious to get all our War Office Regulations and blue books. I gave him what were out then. This year he has written for more, and those issued this year were sent. But I fancy they will be used more for a scientific than a practical purpose.

Should there really be an opening for practically helping the Northern states in their military organization, I could recommend many other books, as for example our forms and returns for keeping the Army Health Statistics, as at present in use, which would be the more easily adopted in the U.S. as they have already adopted our civil Registrar General's nomenclature which is the one used in these our returns and reports.

September 25 1861
Dear Miss Nightingale,
Your offered documents will be received with fervent gratitude at Washington, I am very sure. I write to accept them and to say that we will write again in a few posts to say where the parcel had better be sent to in London. I have no means of forwarding anything bulky from this place, but one of the American publishers in London will no doubt undertake it. Meantime, I will write by next mail to the Secretary at War at Washington to prepare him for what is coming. I know nothing can exceed the anxiety of officials there to do right by the soldiery and their welcome of what you offer will be hearty accordingly. I'm sure I wish we could help the Southern leaders to keep *their* men alive too. But, even if I had access to them (which I have not) the case really seems desperate. That soldiery is at once barbaric and corrupt. Their bodily condition is shocking—from drink, tobacco-chewing and the vice which always rages where slavery is. Those "mean whites" are the very lowest specimen of the white race—almost of the human race. They are dying off fast now in cholera, fever and so on. They ordinarily live in a state compounded of apathy and mad excitement, from drink and passion. Such material for troops! And a very large proportion is of that sort (folios 146-47).

Government—India

Martineau began publishing (unsigned) leaders on India in the *Daily News* as early as 1853, before the collaboration with Nightingale. She took up the subject in earnest in 1857,[76] with the Bengali mutiny/First War of Independence, and from then until 1861 published nine or ten leaders each year. Her focus was primarily economic: finance, taxes, tariffs, manufacturing and currency reform, with some leaders on education and women. When the report of the Royal Commission on the Sanitary Condition of the Army in India came out in 1863 she gave it considerable attention (sixteen leaders in 1862, seventeen in 1863, ten in 1864, eight in 1865, and two in 1866, in which year she published only fifteen articles. Martineau also published an article in *Macmillan's Magazine* in 1863 to publicize the royal commission report, "Death or Life in India," a reversal of the title Nightingale often used. Martineau and Nightingale complemented each other in their interests, Martineau supporting sanitary reform measures while highlighting economics, Nightingale stressing the issues of disease and famine, fully understanding that remedy could only be achieved by social and political change.[77]

The first of the two leaders reprinted below deals with economics. Martineau explained that three-fifths of existing revenues came from the land. Land once fertile became barren because the public works to carry products to market were absent, or because the occupiers of the land were not allowed to earn enough from production to make it worthwhile. She proposed reversion to the ancient, collective, system of Indian land tenure given the impossibility of raising sufficient taxes. Martineau questioned why so much territory was alienated in gifts or sold. The purchaser of land paid only so many years' value for a commodity certain to increase in value "and to sell the very source of wealth does seem to be an insanity in a state which can retain possession of it." This preference for public ownership over private comes from a devoted follower of the laissez-faire school of political economy!

A commission was then studying the conditions under which lands had been granted, in order to enforce those conditions or take back territories where the conditions were extinct. Martineau asked what hindered the restoration of these territories, mentioning no less than stolen territories, forged titles and neglected obligations. She blamed ignorance of Indian institutions on the part of Members of Parliament and their constituencies.

Text: Martineau, *Daily News* August 16 1859:

The more we hear of the proposed retrenchments by which it is imagined that India can be made to live upon her income, the more convinced we are that

---

[76] Martineau's two books on India are more favourable to British rule than these articles: the descriptive *British Rule in India* and the more prescriptive *Suggestions Towards the Future Government of India*.

[77] There are extracts from Martineau, Nightingale and Butler on India in Penelope Tuson, ed., *Queen's Daughters*.

retrenchment is not the source to which we can reasonably look for the retrieval of our great dependency....Every thousand pounds that can be saved without injury is of importance, but that object should never be allowed to divert attention from the more vast, effectual and beneficial aim of developing the natural resources of the richest country in the world....Other retrenchments may be pointed out and put into action but still such debts as those of India cannot be paid, nor such deficits filled up, otherwise than by a vastly increased revenue. As three-fifths of the existing revenue are derived from the land, and as the prosperity of the land uniformly leads to more cultivation, more prosperity and more revenue, we are always brought round to the consideration of extending and deepening the sources of wealth from the land. It is true the process is actively going on, while the great debt is increasing, but this does not prove that the one is not the cure for the other. The income of the state went on increasing before the mutiny, during the mutiny, and after the mutiny, in places and in ways which showed that the increase was not, in the main, due to the expenditure caused by the mutiny. It was traceable to improved tillage, which was followed, as it always is, by commerce and new stretches of tillage. The whole history of improved revenue in India is just this, and the origin of the improvement has always been the limitation of the tax or rent to a point which leaves a surplus to the occupier sufficient to encourage industry.

We have over and over again adverted to the enormous quantity of land lying at our disposal in India. If it was once fertile and is now barren, it is either because the public works which would educe its fertility or carry its produce to market are absent, or because the occupier was not allowed to retain enough of the produce to make it answer for him to stay. No land in India ever lies barren for want of hands to till it. As sure as ever the terms are favourable the soil is taken up. We ought to be quite familiar with this fact, for the experiment of reducing government demand has been continuous for a long course of years and the response, in the form of extended tillage and augmented revenue, has been too clear to be mistaken.

Where the state is the landlord, and the rent supersedes taxation, a large and fertile territory is so inexhaustibly rich that debt is a sign of ignorance and folly, except in rare cases in which a sudden, unforeseen and profuse expenditure is necessary. When the land is all sold away into private hands the only resource of government is taxation on commodities, or on persons and their acts. The difficulty of inventing and raising revenue being considerable, loans are resorted to, and the interest of a permanent debt is added to the annual charge. The occupiers of the land have to pay their rent on the one hand and their taxes on the other. Yet they are able to support their burdens while facilities are afforded for industrial development and the workers are left in possession of a surplus on which they can live. The case of the inhabitants of India might be, and ought to be, more favourable than this. They are scarcely taxed at all, and if the whole instead of a part of the soil belonged to the state, their rent might be much less than the rent and taxes together of other countries, while the government would be much more rapidly enriched. All experience, and all philosophy derived from experience, indicate this, and the way to retrieve India is by putting the lesson in practice.

How is this to be done? By making it the steady aim of government to restore the proprietorship of land to the state wherever an opportunity can be found. In all countries there was a time when private proprietorship of land was unknown; in India that time was not very long ago and it is consonant with the fundamental ideas of society in India that the occupier of land should be its hereditary tenant, and not its proprietor in fee-simple. When a continuance of that tenure would satisfy the inhabitants, secure cultivation of the soil, maintain the government and provide an ever increasing fund of wealth, it appears strange that so many efforts have been made in an opposite direction—so much territory alienated in gifts and sold off where a purchaser could be found.

A purchaser pays only so many years' value for a commodity which is certain to increase in value through all time, and to sell the very source of wealth does seem to be insanity in a state which can retain possession of it. Even at this day, however, we see efforts made to incite the Government of India to attract colonists from Europe by selling them lands which may tempt them with the prospect of grand family estates hereafter. Whereas it ought to be perceived that such sales would be, in fact, agreements to tax the rest of society for the benefit of the purchaser, to the amount of the whole future value of his estate over and above its original price and the interest upon that sum....It would be a blessed sight to see every possible opportunity embraced of inducing an occupation of waste lands by tenants, who should be encouraged by the goodness of the conditions—of roads, water supply etc.—to see every effort made to recover by negotiation, by enforcement of sound claims and by re-purchase, the lands that have been alienated up to this day. The best benefactors of India have prepared the way for the enterprise in parts of the country. Sir Charles Napier did not restore unconditionally the territories which had been granted away before the conquest. He established the principle that the estates belonged to the state—to the whole community—and that they could be held by individuals only on conditions—rent, in one form or another, whether of service, public improvement or money.

Sir C. Trevelyan is now contemplating the enforcement of the same principle by his Enam commission, the business of which is to ascertain the conditions under which lands have been granted away, in order to the enforcement of those conditions, or of forfeiture or the resumption of the territory where the conditions are extinct. The same inquiry carried throughout the length and the breadth of India would restore a great deal of territory to the state, or a part of its value in the fulfillment of conditions....What then hinders the introduction of a system by which all honest and simple people would benefit, and which would inflict no further evil than a natural retribution on people who steal territory, forge titles and neglect obligations? Merely the ignorance of Parliament and of their constituencies.

Our legislators are not learned on the subject of Indian land questions either as to philosophy or fact. Their views of debt and taxation are formed on the circumstances of their own country and its neighbours. The best thing they can do is to look for men who have studied India from the true point of view—as a sort of new country to us (however old in itself), and as peculiarly fitted for development under the principles of political economy, on the basis of the indigenous institutions of the country. Then let such men be made the rulers of India on the understanding that due support will be granted to their policy from home. For instance, provision must be made, under their guidance, for such public works as are necessary to give the land its full value and, if such works can be executed only under the security of the imperial guarantee, that guarantee must be given. Under such a method as this every year would carry us on with accelerated rapidity towards total emancipation from the great Indian debt, and the command of a growing surplus, for the perpetual development of new wealth in the vast empire where now the few rich hoard their treasures and the multitude of ordinary inhabitants are miserably poor. Before that surplus is attained from the land, however, there will be a great accession of income from other sources. But we have no room now to enter upon the vast subject of the commercial capabilities and tendencies of India.

Martineau's next leader praised the royal commission report, looking forward to its saving more lives than the worst wars ever lost. The report's recommendations, however, were fought by the India Office and were only implemented partially, and then after decades of pressure.

Text: Martineau, *Daily News* July 16 1863:2:

At last we have the long-promised sanitary report about military life in India, which if wisely and boldly used will save more lives than the most fatal of Indian wars has ever extinguished and preclude more sickness than will remain to be treated. The commission, appointed in May 1859, chiefly through the influence of Lord Herbert and Miss Nightingale, was charged to make inquiries under eight heads. It was to ascertain the amount of mortality and sickness in the European and native forces in India, and the main causes of both, to point out what military stations are unhealthy and why, to recommend wholesome sites for new stations and indicate whether good positions can be found within easy reach of those unhealthy ones which, for military reasons, cannot be given up, to afford guidance as to the best construction of barracks, huts, hospitals and tents, to inquire into the regulations and practice for preserving the health of the troops, and enforcing care by an effective medical and sanitary police, to ascertain what is the present organization of the Army Medical and Sanitary Service, to point out how a system of medical statistics may be established throughout India, and how the facts may be brought into comparison with those of the diseases and mortality of the rest of the population, native and

European and, finally, to recommend such a procedure as may best preclude the causes of death and sickness.

The results of these inquiries are now presented in two large volumes, of which the Report occupies 84 pages, while the evidence is of a character truly extraordinary, for importance, variety and interest....No other book exists which affords such a disclosure of the character and details of life in India, so that it is as interesting to the general reader who cares for pictures of life in a tropical country as to the medical profession and military authorities who are responsible for the use of this mass of knowledge.

The facts relating to times past...are appalling. The only compensation is in the conviction that the production of the evidence must form a turning point into a better course. We have seen at home what may be done to raise the life of the soldier from being a sort of doom to premature decay, if not early death, to being as vigorous and hopeful as that of the young manhood of the country in the most favorable circumstances, and we see in this evidence how the liabilities of Indian life may be got rid of like those of barrack life in England. Meantime, the truth about those special liabilities is more fearful than even the popular imagination had conceived.

Four regiments out of eleven of our whole army are usually on service in India, so that if all took their turn equally, our soldiery would be in India ten years in twenty-seven and a half. Many never go there, so that the risks are much heavier than this for those who bear the larger share of the service. Owing to the establishment of funds for the purpose of insurance we have hitherto had the means of knowing some leading facts about the length of life of civil servants in India, and of widows and orphans. Till now we have had no information about the chances of life and health for the soldier. They are abundantly grave now that they are disclosed. The case, we find, is not one of adverse climate, or only in a slight degree. It is a case of poisoning—like that of residents in unwholesome places at home. Among young men of the age and standing from which our soldiers are selected at home, eight in one thousand of those who live in healthy spots die each year, in less favourable circumstances, nine in one thousand....It has been diminishing year by year under the partial reforms which have been instituted, and no time is to be lost in setting similar reforms on foot in India, for the mortality there, excluding the casualties of war, has been sixty in one thousand. For those casualties only ten have to be added, bringing up the amount to seventy per thousand.

This average embraces the years from 1817 to 1855. Our present knowledge authorizes us to call this mortality of sixty in one thousand needless. We have considered it (without knowing its precise extent) the price we have paid for our possession of India. We now learn that it is a gratuitous sacrifice, which may cease whenever we choose to take measures to extinguish it. Meantime those whom we send on that service, men in the prime of life, waste and perish, in the proportion of a company in each regiment every twenty months, and we send out recruits, to cost us annually £100 per man—a large proportion of whom will decline and die in like manner....

Are these evils really needless? The evidence before us leaves no doubt of it. The four kinds of disease which carry off or disable nearly all these victims arise from well understood and preventible causes. They are fevers, which carry off 23 1/2 per 100 of those who die (taking the Presidency of Bombay during a period of 16 years); dysentery and diarrhoea which kill 32 1/2; liver complaints, fatal to more than 9 1/2; and cholera, fatal to 10 1/4 [Statistics of other regions follow]. The sick part of the army costs the country as much as the effective part and the effective part is less vigorous and reliable than if there were no sick and thus, by allowing the causes of these preventible diseases to prevail, we directly waste nearly £400,000 a year in India, and bury or send home as invalids thousands of men in the vigour of their years who ought to have become veterans such as their country is wont to be proud of. Such a state of things warrants and demands courageous treatment, a liberal disposition in Parliament and people to do what can be done in the way of remedy now and prevention for the future. The recommendations of the commission seem to be adequate to the occasion. We shall bring them forward another day.

Nature and Society—Species Protection

In her early *Illustrations of Political Economy* Martineau took the classical political economy approach to the environment, as an inexhaustible resource, value coming wholly from labour. Yet in her decades of journalism later she showed considerable sensitivity to many issues. Martineau's leaders for the *Daily News* covered numerous aspects of "scientific agriculture" and rural life, food and nutrition, irrigation and water quality. She seems to have been as interested in agricultural drainage as Nightingale was in sewers. The article that follows here is unusual in dealing with the killing of birds. It dates from 1862, when there was no law against the killing of any species in any number or way. (Legislation prohibiting cruelty to farm animals dates from 1822.) Massive numbers of birds were killed for plumage for women's hats. "Sportsmen" killed birds by the hundred, not for food use. In rural areas prizes were given for large kills. Martineau had an understanding of what would now be called the "web" of life, in her terms "the wonderful machine of Nature." She warned that killing birds also meant reduced crops, for birds ate planteating insects.

Agitation for the protection of birds began in 1867 with a petition to the House of Commons. The first bird protection society was formed in 1868 in Bridlington, Yorkshire, a coastal area of abundant bird life, then at risk from increased access thanks to steamboat excursions. This local group was soon expanded to become a national society, later the Royal Society for the Protection of Birds, Britain's largest environmental organization. The first legislation, limited to the protection of sea birds, was passed in 1868 as a result of its agitation. It is instructive to compare Martineau's arguments with those of activists on the subject, for example the 1867 petition by **H.J. Barnes**, rector of Nunbarnholme, Yorkshire, and leader of the local conservation group:

> That birds perform a most useful part in the economy of Nature; that if they are unduly destroyed insects increase in similar proportion and do vast damage to the produce of both farms and gardens; that birds are ornamental as well as useful, and give great pleasure and instruction to naturalists and others that observe their habits; that, owing to the indiscriminate and untaxed use of guns, they are recklessly destroyed in great numbers every year; and that many important species have in this way already become extinct in Great Britain, and that others have become more or less rare, and will in like manner be exterminated if some means for their protection and preservation be not adopted.[78]

Environmentalist arguments, then and now, are a combination of appeals to reason, compassion and human self-interest.

Text: Martineau, *Daily News* June 3 1862:5:

What can be done to stop the madness of destroying birds? When the potato famine comes we speak of fortitude and patience and try to keep up one another's cheerfulness and resignation, but how will it be with us when we have brought on ourselves a worse dearth than the potato failure by this folly of destroying the creatures which preserve our crops from insect plagues? If we choose to draw out a pin from the wonderful machine of Nature, so that an important movement is set wrong, we can hardly presume to derive comfort from patience and resignation....What are we to say to sufferers to whom the dearness of the loaf is a grave calamity? After killing off the guardians of our crops, how can we preach patience to hungering people? We should remember this now when we are hearing every day of the plague of insects on the one hand, and of the destruction of small birds on the other....

In the early spring boys were bird nesting all over the country. In a multitude of townships there is a standing offer of rewards for birds' eggs, and thousands of dozens of eggs have this spring been paid for within an area of two or three parishes. Where no such inducement exists there has been the same plunder. Long rows of speckled eggs are hung in cottage windows and over the fireplaces, under the approving eye of the farmer, if not of the curate and the squire. As the season advanced and the bloom of our fruit-trees afforded as fine a promise of fruit as ever was seen in this country, the war

---

[78] M.C.F. Morris, *Francis Orpen Morris* 136.

against the small birds became very animated. They were accused of having sometimes, after very severe winters, eaten out the heart of fruit buds, and if they were left alive they would eat the juicy shoots of the young peas, and hereafter some of the peas themselves, cherries and black currants.

Not only have guns been heard popping in many country parishes but men have shown themselves in markets and fairs, all hung over with strings of dead finches, robins, thrushes and sparrows, as an advertisement in their line of business. Members of sparrow clubs have met, awarded prizes, dined and drunk destruction to the order of birds. One prize winner the other day boasted of having killed 1,860 sparrows in the course of the year. A lady, meantime, had at one stroke killed with strychnine 800 small birds in her own garden. And if one owner of a garden has done such a thing, how many more may have lessened the number of our winged friends? The discovery of the efficacy of poisoned grain in killing off the birds has wrought prodigiously. One rookery after another has gone to destruction, the birds dropping in their flight and lying dead all over the lawns and fields, while their young are starving in the nests. There has been silence in many lanes and copses formerly all alive with songsters. Travelled men have observed in some parts of the country that it was becoming almost like France for the scarcity of birds....We shall have to pay, very soon, if we allow ignorant men, ladies and boys to destroy the natural check upon insect ravages. Most of the birds that we are hunting out of life eat both insects and grain and some take to fruit, but their attacks upon the fruit are more useful in destroying the insects that were there already than mischievous for their own sakes. These birds eat more seeds of weeds than of corn, so that we have a plague of weeds as well as insects when the birds are destroyed....

We are proud, pleased and happy to see the progress made in agriculture by science and art, which enables us to form a perfect seed-bed, and to administer the proper elements to the growth of the plant. But all the benefits of our knowledge, and our care and our expenditure of money and of thought, will be lost if we permit poisoned grain to be strewn so as to depopulate our rookeries, and the nests in our woodlands and our hedges, and the eaves of the house and the furrows of the field. It would lead us too far to show how our timber is suffering from the same fatal mistake and how rats and mice are gaining upon us in our drains, our granaries, our outhouses, gardens and stockyards....If we are to hope for the natural produce we must put an end to the destruction of the natural safeguard against insect ravage.

In France, the government commends the case, with all seriousness, to the clergy and the school-masters. We may appeal to them, and to every man who has influence in the rural districts, to get an end put to sparrow-clubs and rewards for bird-nesting and especially to the new and fatal practice of strewing poisoned grain....It is a disgrace to us that not only cottage children and raw rustics should make war against any order in nature (fools rushing in where angels fear to tread), but that ladies should spread strychnine and farmers take prizes for such ignorant destruction....Children may be taught at school to preserve birds instead of destroying them but the worst of it is that the peril is already upon us. We are subject to a plague of insects at this moment and there is not a day to lose in taking measures against it. Man is not made to catch worms and flies; he is made able to see how Nature deals with worms and flies and how it is his best wisdom to let her alone to do her own work, while he profits by it.

Gender—Regulation of Prostitution

While it was Nightingale who led the early struggle against the institution of repressive legislation to attempt to control syphilis through the Contagious Diseases Acts, Martineau played not only her usual role as publicist but went on to give leadership to the intermediate stage. Repeal of the legislation was finally achieved after a long battle led by Josephine Butler. Unlike Nightingale, Martineau both joined and publicly supported Butler's association for repeal when it was formed in 1869. There is material on this campaign in the sections of Nightingale and Butler to follow. This introduction will serve to give historical context for all three.

Britain was the last country of Europe to adopt the "continental" or French system (it had been initiated by France) for the "regulation of vice," that is the compulsory examination and treatment of women prostitutes as the means to reduce sexually-transmitted diseases, especially syphilis. The first of the Contagious Diseases Acts, 1864, was confined to garrison towns and naval ports. Subsequent amendments in 1866 and 1868 extended their coverage to other garrison towns and ports and to the London metropolitan area, thus including more and more of the civilian population.[79] The legislation required a prostitute so identified by a police officer to submit to a painful, internal physical examination, which some women called a form of rape. If found to be diseased treatment in a "lock hospital" was compulsory. Nowhere were men targeted either for examination or treatment. The acts reflect the utter powerlessness of women who then had no vote or voice on public policy. Custom required that respectable women not even discuss such unsavoury matters as prostitution and venereal disease. When women began to organize for repeal they had enormous difficulty in getting any press coverage of their views.

Legislation to "regulate vice" was first proposed for Britain shortly before **Queen Victoria** came to the throne, but it was apparently considered unseemly for the young, unmarried Queen Victoria to have to read and sign such a bill.[80]

---

[79] For a comprehensive analysis of the legislation at its different stages see Sheldon Amos, *Comparative Survey of Laws in Force for the Prohibition, Regulation, and Licensing of Vice*; see also Judith R. Walkowitz, *Prostitution and Victorian Society*; F.B. Smith, "Ethics and Disease in the Later Nineteenth Century;" Keith Nield, *Prostitution in the Victorian Age*.

[80] Martineau, letter from "an Englishwoman," *Daily News* Dec. 28 1869.

Theorists on Reform/Martineau 159

Prince Albert is credited with stopping the second attempt at legislation.[81] British women were thus spared until 1864 when a bill was pushed swiftly through Parliament. The timing is perhaps noteworthy; Queen Victoria had only recently been widowed. The British establishment (Parliament, the Home and War Offices, the established church, the mainstream press, the universities and medical profession) solidly supported the acts. Opponents accordingly had to seek other alliances. The women found sympathizers among trade-union men, radical Quakers and some other dissenters. The repeal movement in Britain itself involved more people than the movement for women's suffrage. There were national associations, separate ladies' associations and a network of local groups. Tactics included intervention in election campaigns, with notable success in two by-elections.

The Contagious Diseases Acts raised a number of philosophical issues regarding the nature of sex differences. The women who fought against the acts adamantly rejected the whole premise of the double standard: that men could not be chaste. The first corollary of this was that prostitutes had to be provided for soldiers and sailors without wives or stationed away from them. The women opposing the Contagious Diseases Acts forcefully argued the opposite, making practical suggestions for work and leisure activities that would keep the men from "vice." They insisted on a common moral nature shared by men and women. For those who were religious—and many in the movement were—the double standard was particularly offensive as contrary to Christian teaching of a common morality for all. The second corollary was that a "fallen woman" was worse than her male partner. This conveniently excused the brutality of the measures used in the forcible examination and treatment of women.

The women argued also against the purported necessity of sacrificing their interests, notably the loss of liberty, for the sake of army policy. They recognized the seriousness of sexually-transmitted diseases but argued for voluntary treatment of infected women. The notion of compulsory treatment for men seems to have been too extreme for anyone to raise. Some women did propose, or at least entertained the idea of, the eradication of prostitution as the better solution. They believed that prostitution was degrading in and of itself, not just on account of its link with disease. They had a keen sense of women prostitutes as victims of male-dominated society and were incensed that society would punish the victims and not the perpetrators of "vice."

Martineau managed to get several leaders published in the *Daily News* arguing for positive measures to prevent "vice" rather than the punitive measures for control of the act. Her leader of May 10 1864 ended with a plea for positive measures of prevention before undertaking the perilous step of

---

[81] A.S.G. Butler, *Portrait of Josephine Butler* 69.

legislation. A similar leader, June 3 1864, argued for the merits of gymnasia, reading rooms, workshops, cricket clubs, et cetera:

> We have created the evil by subjecting our soldiers to unnatural restraints and to temptations which are therefore irresistible, and there are some among us who propose to meet the mischief by arrangements which, however legalized, must ever be morally illicit.

The leader excerpted below is the only one, in this round, that dealt directly with the proposed legislation.

Text: Martineau, *Daily News* July 2 1864:

It is an awkward and difficult state of things when legislation is necessary, or is sought without being necessary, on matters unfit to be brought under the eye of a great part of the public. The awkwardness and difficulty, however, are no justification to journalists for permitting the slightest risk of bad legislation which they may preclude by timely warning. The bill brought in by Lord Clarence Paget, called the "Contagious Diseases Bill," is of this nature. If this bill had a fair chance of careful examination by persons of an accurate habit of mind, it would be speedily prevented doing further mischief than the proposal of it has done already. If it was seriously considered by persons who understand the dangers to which it relates, persons whose duty compels them to know the character and workings of the places of evil resort in which many of our soldiers and sailors lose their health and self-respect, the bill would be condemned at once as unsuited to its object, while affording openings for worse mischiefs than it will ever cure. The fear is that such an examination is not likely to be obtained. The object of the proposer is to get the bill passed with as little noise and as few words as possible, and his plan is but too likely to succeed, unless Members of Parliament will take the trouble to learn for themselves those faults of the measure which it is scarcely possible to point out with any clearness in the columns of a newspaper.

In the position of the mover it is very natural that he should do as he is doing: endeavour to obtain a committee so large that, when the bill has passed it, the House will accept the measure without discussion, but a responsibility is thus thrown on the committee which no man of them all can take to heart too seriously. If they will accept a hint, there is an obvious one which all impartial and well-informed thinkers on the subject would agree in giving them on the present occasion, to see that the terms describing offenders and offences are so definite as to be of practical use and not liable to involve innocent persons, and further to see whether the proposed remedy can be applied with any certainty of involving the right persons, or whether those persons may not evade every provision of the bill, leaving it to do mischief or to do nothing....In plain word, here is a bill which promises to secure soldiers and sailors from the consequences of illicit pleasures. It invariably happens that such protection creates a false security, however careful the legislature may be.

This bill is our first step...which can never be retracted...it must lead us on to attempt a similar protection on behalf of civil society. Yet all important as such an initiatory measure must be, the one before the House is full of ill-defined or undefined terms, provisions for punishing unproved and unprovable offences and for remedying evils which cannot be ascertained to exist. It is not conceivable that the House will pass such a bill if its members will but compel their attention to it. If it was framed by a faultless intelligence it would be a fearful venture, but vague, ineffective and delusive as it is in it whole fabric its passage would be a national calamity.

It may be pleaded that some of its shortcomings may be supplied in committee, that, for instance, some precision may be given to the term "solicitation," some definition afforded for the term "prostitute," and that inducements yet absent may be provided for hospitals to undertake the work laid out for them, but there are deficiencies which can in no such way be supplied. The very commonest and most fatal mischiefs are in a no way touched by this bill. For instance, it does not, and cannot be made to, reach the case of the beer shop inhabited by the female servants of the proprietor, where the soldier or sailor pays high for his beer, and with his entertainers remains beyond the reach of the law and police supervision....

We trust that our representatives...will surely not forget that to pass such a measure as this is to enter on a new and fearful province of legislation, from which we can never withdraw to the previous moral position, and that it is proposed to us to do this while existing laws against brothels and violations of decency in our streets remain unenforced, and while there is evidence in existence of the operation in other countries of laws for the protection of men from the consequences of their own passions which would make it a less evil to any conscientious member to quit public life than to have the smallest share in bringing down such a curse on this nation and on the moral repute and prospects of his country.

Martineau's four letters from "an Englishwoman" were strong and well-argued pleas for repeal of the legislation, giving more attention to civil liberties for women than before. Here we see her handing over the leadership to Butler, although she continued to play a supportive role in the ongoing campaign. This last letter ended with a petition, signed initially by 128 women, later 2000.

Text: "The Ladies' National Association for the Repeal of the Contagious Diseases Acts," *Daily News* December 31 1869:

The law is ostensibly framed for a certain class of women, but in order to reach these, all the women residing within the districts where it is in force are brought under the provisions of the acts. Any woman can be dragged into court and required to prove that she is not a common prostitute....When condemned, the sentence is...to have her person outraged by the periodical inspection of a surgeon, through a period of twelve months, or, resisting that, to be imprisoned with or without hard labour—first for a month, next for three months—such imprisonment to be continuously renewed through her whole life unless she submit periodically to the brutal requirements of this law....

We, the undersigned, enter our solemn protest against these acts:
1. Because, involving as they do such a momentous change in the legal safeguards hitherto enjoyed by women in common with men, they have been passed, not only without the knowledge of the country, but unknown to Parliament itself, and we hold that neither the representatives of the people nor the press fulfil the duties which are expected of them when they allow such legislation to take place without the fullest discussion.
2. Because, so far as women are concerned, they remove every guarantee of personal security which the law has established and held sacred, and put their reputation, their freedom and their persons absolutely in the power of the police.
3. Because the law is bound, in any country professing to give civil liberty to its subjects, to define clearly an offence which it punishes.
4. Because it is unjust to punish the sex who are the victims of a vice, and leave unpunished the sex who are the main cause, both of the vice and its dreaded consequences; and we consider that liability to arrest, forced surgical examination and, where this is resisted, imprisonment with hard labour, to which these acts subject women, are punishments of the most degrading kind.
5. Because, by such a system, the path of evil is made more easy to our sons, and to the whole of the youth of England, inasmuch as a moral restraint is withdrawn the moment the state recognizes and provides convenience for the practice of a vice which it thereby declares to be necessary and venial.
6. Because these measures are cruel to the women who come under their action—violating the feelings of those whose sense of shame is not wholly lost, and further brutalizing even the most abandoned.
7. Because the disease which these acts seek to remove has never been removed by any such legislation. The advocates of the system have utterly failed to show, by statistics or otherwise, that these regulations have in any case, after several years' trial and when applied to one sex only, diminished disease, reclaimed the fallen or improved the general morality of the country. We have, on the contrary, the strongest evidence to show that in Paris and other continental cities where women have long been outraged by this forced inspection, public health and morals are worse than at home.
8. Because the conditions of this disease in the first instance are moral, not physical. The moral evil through which the disease makes its way separates the case entirely from that of plague or other scourges which have been placed under police control or sanitary care. We hold that we are bound, before rushing into the experiment of legalizing a revolting vice, to try to deal with

the causes of the evil, and we dare to believe that with wiser teaching and more capable legislation those causes would not be beyond control.

A Ladies Association has been formed for the purpose of obtaining the repeal of these obnoxious acts. The necessity for such an association becomes more urgent from the fact that a society is already in existence for procuring their extension to the women of the whole kingdom. We earnestly entreat our country women, of every class and party, to help us in the difficult and painful task which only a deep sense of duty could have forced us to undertake. We have not entered lightly upon it, nor shall we lightly abandon it, because we believe that in its attainment are involved not only the personal rights of our sex but the morality of the nation.

As a journalist Martineau was greatly sensitive to the press's treatment of the repeal campaign: indifference largely, ridicule and hostility otherwise for their cause, active support for the acts. She protested the unfairness of the press when the *Pall Mall Gazette* published a long article in favour of the acts by Elizabeth Garrett, but refused a joint letter from her and Butler on the other side. The movement's own organ published the protest against the "conspiracy of silence" practised among leading journalists.[82] The editorship of the *Daily News* changed hands after the publication of Martineau's four letters from "an Englishwoman" and she lost her opportunity to publish leaders for the campaign. Her last agitation for repeal was a letter to a friend in 1871, copied to a Member of Parliament.

Text: Martineau letter to Isabella Spring Brown, copy to Rt Hon W.E. Forster July 16 1871, National Library of Scotland:

It is said—I don't know how truly—that members of the government of the day usually know everything that is said and thought within the bounds of Parliament, and very little of what is going on outside. In my time I have seen reason to believe that there is, at least occasionally, a good deal of truth in this....I am aware that Mr Gladstone and some of his colleagues have for many weeks had some idea (through the Post Office and otherwise) of the agitation which spreads and deepens in the country about the Contagious Diseases Acts, but I strongly doubt, as many others do, how far ministers are aware of the extreme importance, to themselves and to the state, of the next step they take.

We, opponents of such legislation, were abundantly disgusted at being saddled with a royal commission on a subject to which such a method of inquiry is entirely inapplicable, except in matters of detail of administration. We never acknowledged that jurisdiction in such a case, and we saw that, as long as the commission was used as the government reply to our

---

[82] *The Shield* February 16 1870.

remonstrances, we were either trickily used, or our complaints were not in the least understood. Both suppositions turn out to be true. The audacity of the false dealing with facts by official agents and other advocates of the acts has been beyond all our expectation.

But I, for one, have been much more struck by the other phenomenon—the innocent wickedness—educational and conventional—of the upper and middle classes—men who go to church on Sundays and call themselves Christians, who set out from the supposition that men's passions must be gratified, and that, if women are ruined in that process it is simply necessary and a matter of course. There is something amazing to people more naturally trained in the annoyance manifested even by virtuous and domestic men at all endeavours to question this necessity, and all resentment at the intrusion of the profligacy of the country into the domain of our laws. The immense question of today is whether our law makers and members are sufficiently aware of the state of the public mind to deal with the opposition of the profligacy and the conventionalism of English society of that part of society which upholds the doomed system, and whether the existing government has the courage to avow its mistake in proposing the Act of 1869, and sufficient political faith to change its course on behalf of the great moral and domestic interests of the nation.

The singular issue of the Inquiry of the Commission affords a capital opportunity for retreat....The demand for the abolition of the whole scheme of these acts will never be surrendered nor moderated till we have blotted out of our law books the most detestable enactments that ever cursed our country and people.

Mr Gladstone knows, I believe, a good deal more than some of his colleagues of the certain consequences of any attempt to preserve a particle of this legislation, and indeed his habits of thought and feeling enable and compel him to understand the popular mind in these matters....The question is how far the country is likely to benefit by his higher quality and how boldly he will proceed to act on the plain fact of the unconstitutional character of the acts, and in rebuke of the audacious sacrifice of virtue to passion, and of the defenceless to the strong and self-seeking half of society....

Stormy as is the prospect for the minister in any case, there is, in our view, no doubt as to the direction in which the sky will clear first, and permanently. On his action this week, it seems to me, depends much of the future of his country (the most essential part of it) and all his own. We count the days and hours till we see how he deals with the gravest crisis witnessed in England for centuries. A short time will show us now whether a total repeal of the acts will be wisely proposed at once, or whether there will be a suspension of them till the repeal can be accomplished or whether that resistance will be adventured which neither laws nor governments can survive.

Theorists on Reform/Nightingale 165

> "I have been nine years in the War Office this very week, in which I started for the Crimea in 1854 and I have still something to learn every day of the invincible strength of inertia."[83]

> "We do *not* want a great arithmetical law; we want to know *what* we are doing in things which must be tested by results....We legislate *without knowing* what we are doing."[84]

> "Has any effort been made not to prevent deaths from famine, but to *prevent famine itself?*...How can we realise what the misery is of everyone of those figures [5-6 million people]—a living soul, slowly starving to death?"[85]

FLORENCE NIGHTINGALE (1820-1910)

Florence Nightingale[86] was born in Florence to wealthy English parents travelling on the Continent. Her father educated her at home in the classics. She acquired fluency in French, Italian and German as well as Greek and Latin. At age sixteen Nightingale received a "call to service," although she did not understand for some years precisely what she should do. Her family vehemently opposed her becoming a nurse, then an occupation akin to that of kitchen maid. It was not until age thirty that Nightingale was able to begin nursing, after a short stay at a Protestant deaconess institute in Kaiserswerth, Germany, and visits to various European hospitals to obtain information. In the meantime she was permitted to travel and made extensive trips to Italy, France, Egypt and Greece. Her journals and letters from these years show a keen and observant mind and a well-worked out philosophy, some years before her heroic work in the Crimean War. Her only nursing position before Crimea was as head of a small institution on Harley Street for the care of ill "distressed gentlewomen."

On her return from Crimea in 1856 (after two exhausting years, illness and near death) Nightingale immediately set to work to reform medical/nursing

---

[83] Nightingale letter to Martineau, October 27 1863, Martineau Manuscripts No. 703.

[84] Nightingale letter to Jowett January 3 1891, Add Mss 45784 folio 144.

[85] Nightingale, "The People of India" 195.

[86] The best biography is still Edward T. Cook, *The Life of Florence Nightingale*; see also Cecil Woodham-Smith, *Florence Nightingale* and my *Women Founders* 183-211. There are five books of published correspondence, the most useful of which is *Ever Yours, Florence Nightingale*, eds. Martha Vicinus and Bea Nergaard.

services in the British Army. She had vowed that the appalling mortality then taken for granted—by the army, not her—would never recur. She succeeded not only in getting a royal commission established to investigate conditions, but she saw to the implementation of most its recommendations. She worked indeed at every stage of the process from the appointment of members through the preparation of witnesses to the graphical presentation of the data. Her second royal commission, on the British Army in India, was similar in the comprehensiveness of its analysis and recommendations, but implementation was resisted by the India Office and British officials running the government in India. Nightingale was to work forty years to improve the living conditions of—and prevent famine among—ordinary Indian people. She became an expert on issues of municipal government, taxation, irrigation, transportation, and the culture and religion of India.

Nightingale established the first secular school for nurses in the world, using the funds raised to honour her for her work in the Crimea. (She had had enough of sectarian ploys in the Crimea—nurses keener to convert their patients than treat them.) She established an institution to train mid-wives, then closed it when she discovered that its mortality rate was unacceptably high. In the course of investigating mortality in childbirth Nightingale herself sent out questionnaires to collect data. Her publication, *Introductory Notes on Lying-in Institutions*, is a classic in applied statistics.

As a woman Nightingale did not have the vote and, as a person with high connections, did not feel she needed it. She continued for years to work for the War Office as an unpaid adviser. She made her advice available on how to save lives to any who would use it. She was thus honoured for her services to both belligerents in the Franco-Prussian War.

Nightingale never identified with the suffrage movement, considering that economic equality was more important. She was keener to get women into nursing than medicine largely because she disapproved of too much medical practice, and sought an expanded role for nurses as midwives. She was the first person to oppose the Contagious Diseases Acts and worked assiduously, first to prevent their being adopted by Parliament and, later and more peripherally, for their repeal.

Nightingale spent years of her post-Crimean life as an invalid (she nearly died there). She managed to accomplish an enormous amount of writing and planning by harbouring her resources, seeing visitors only one at a time and by appointment. While some biographers have charged her with malingering, or a neurotic complaint, recent information suggests that she suffered from brucellosis, a seriously debilitating disease in which there can also be significant periods of remission.[87] Nightingale died at age ninety. She was the first woman to receive the Order of Merit, in 1907.

---

[87] D.A.B. Young, "Florence Nightingale's fever."

Government—Foundations of Public Health Care

It is not well known that Florence Nightingale formulated some of the key principles of the welfare state, notably on the provision of public health care, indeed as early as the 1860s.[88] The three items that follow will show her significant contribution to the basic ideas of public responsibility for health care, based on a notion of "brotherhood" (which of course included women), coupled with a public system of financing, complete with accountability back to the public's elected representatives in Parliament.

The key element was Nightingale's understanding of "brotherhood," which for her stemmed from religious faith. In a letter to her father she explained that, from the moment a poor pauper becomes sick "he ceases to be a pauper and becomes brother to the best of us and as a brother he should be cared for. I would make this a cardinal principle in Poor Law relief." This entailed quality care for the sick regardless of their poverty. Sickness and disability, mental and physical, were "general afflictions" affecting the entire community, to be treated differently from pauperism. The community at large should be financially responsible for the care of the "fellow-creature in suffering." Nightingale utterly rejected the two-tier system for health care, of high quality for those who could pay for it, and whatever charity would provide for those who could not. She consistently rejected the conventional practice of giving what is second best to the poor: "philanthropy is humbug." She sought systemic change based on a radical principle: "love to mankind ought to be our one principle in the Poor Law."[89]

Nightingale's draft note "East End Distress" was first of all a devastating critique of the existing Poor Law, even calling the workhouse test a "torture test." This referred to the requirement that a destitute person enter the workhouse to receive any assistance, a practice intended to be, and which was in fact, a deterrent to asking for financial help. The note also speculated about the possibility of the state providing jobs directly, "at least in exceptional times of distress." Nightingale was critical of unions for some of their protective practices but clearly in favour of the right of workers to organize and bargain collectively.

This excerpt was taken from a long draft note which also attacked J.S. Mill's focus on the vote and political remedies for women's poor situation. Nightingale's argument will be familiar to contemporary feminists, the priority of economic rights: "I want my bread first and then you may give me my votes."[90] It seems, however, that Nightingale never sent Mill either these or

---

[88] See Brian Abel-Smith, *The Hospitals 1800-1948*, chapter 5.

[89] Nightingale, draft letter October 1867, Add Mss 45790 folio 358.

[90] Add Mss 47753 folio 50.

other somewhat rude remarks she made about his feminist thought. Nightingale greatly respected him and even joined his suffrage society at his request although she was never active in it.

Nightingale's letter of December 30 1864, to the president of the Poor Law Board, **C.P. Villiers**, MP, was step one of a concerted campaign for Poor Law reform. Here she used a specific, scandalous case that was much in the newspapers, a man who died in a workhouse for lack of nursing care. The Nightingale method always included both carrot and stick. There was the allusion to an impending investigation and the laying of blame, but much more she appealed to principle and reason. Nightingale invited Villiers to work with her, even offering her own efforts "as far as my strength will permit." Who would not have been flattered by this appeal from the legendary Nightingale: "Could you help in this great improvement by having a searching enquiry made into the nursing system in all workhouses?" Villiers did then work with her, and got his deputy Farnall, who was much more committed, onto the issue. But Nightingale's aspirations for reform went far beyond Villiers, and even Farnall.

Frances Power Cobbe also wrote a pamphlet, not included in this anthology, on the reform of workhouse infirmaries, 1861. It described the poor conditions of care, even the failure to provide the legal minimum of "necessaries."[91] Cobbe was aware of systemic problems, including the conflict of interest in doctor's roles, but her remedy, the appointment of workhouse visitors, did not go nearly as far as Nightingale's. Workhouse visiting itself was pioneered by a great woman philanthropist, **Louisa Twining.**

Fundamental to the proposed reform was the separation and classification of the inmates of workhouses according to the causes of their destitution. People went into workhouses for different reasons and required different types of help. The sick required treatment and needed to be separated from the healthy unemployed, "paupers." The infirm, aged, insane and imbeciles all, too, had different needs, requiring long-term care in "asylums." Children were different again. For Nightingale—a point she insisted on time and again—children should not be in workhouses at all but in schools. The only people who would be left in the traditional workhouse would be the "able-bodied lazy," paupers who chose not to work. These numbers, too, would diminish as the state took on more of a role in providing work. The whole approach stems directly from Nightingale's understanding of the universe being regulated by law. It was our duty to study to ascertain the causes of social problems, and then to intervene appropriately to remedy them. Nightingale's religious faith grounded both her scholarship and her political activism.

---

[91] Cobbe, "Workhouse as an Hospital" 3.

Nightingale stressed the social and economic causes of ill health in this analysis. The deplorable state of housing and unsanitary conditions were major causes of ill health of all kinds, not just epidemics of typhus and cholera. She also repudiated the usual objection to reform from her own social class: higher taxes. Instead she pointed to the higher costs of inaction.

Text: Nightingale draft letter or copy to the governor of Liverpool Workhouse January 31 1864, Add Mss 47753 folios 50-53:

East-End Distress

Poor Law completely broken down; private charity completely broken down and worse, for it has increased the evil. "Workhouse test" completely broken down; labour test ditto. Not only are they torturing these poor fellows with unproductive labour at unremunerative prices, but the torture-test is of no avail, for the workhouses are overflowing and the people are starving. And *the least harm* of the overflowing workhouse is the burden of the rates (9 shillings on the pound). The harm is the withdrawing all these heads and arms from *production.* The "workhouse test" has saddled the country with pauperism—more perhaps than anything else except the want of education.

Yet the remedy, Mr Mill says, is *more* political liberties. It is not political liberties we want, it is legislative honesties. Give us honesties first—and then you may offer us liberties. I want my bread first and then you may give me my votes.

Is it really possible to believe that these legislators could not, if they laid their heads together, frame an act by which the workman might make his own bargain as to wages with his employer, with an appeal to courts of justice or other authorities? As long as you steal from a man his own labour, his power of production, where and how he likes, you can't call him a free man. All your political liberties are a farce. As long as your legislator can find no legislative remedy against the tyranny of trades' unions, who decree work to be judged by quantity, not quality, who decree that superior quality of work shall not be paid for—the first element of liberty is wanting. For this is not to steal from me my power of production. Who steals my purse steals trash, but who steals my power of production steals all I have. I was interfered with in my power of production when I was a girl—so are all women.

Is it possible to believe that at least in exceptional times of distress the state could not give productive work at remunerative prices, as in Lancashire—not on the principle of ateliers nationaux [national workshops]? The unproductive work seem to me as great a blunder as the trades' unions ever made.

Text: Nightingale draft letter or copy to C.P. Villiers, December 1864, Add Mss 47753 folios 54-55:

I need not tell you how much I have been shocked, as who has not been shocked by the dreadful death of poor Daly from injuries inflicted...in the Holborn Union Workhouse. I feel the case to be to a certain extent my case, because I have been put in trust by my fellow countrymen with the means of training nurses, whose duty it is to nurse, not to seem to nurse, and although the subject of nursing the sick has been discussed earnestly ever since the beginning of the Crimean War, we have here ten years afterwards a case such as we saw when we began in the hospitals of the East, but not after.

I am emboldened to address *you* on the subject because I see by today's *Times* that the Holborn Guardians have referred the case to the Poor Law Board. You will no doubt examine into it thoroughly and find out who is to blame. I have no desire in the slightest degree to influence your decision. My object in writing is quite different, to bring before you the whole question of hospital nursing in workhouses. I would be the last person to add to the difficulties of Poor Law Guardians by declaiming against their inhumanity. They have a difficult task enough to perform in steering their way between pauperism and real want, but fortunately there is no such difficulty when the poor pauper becomes sick. From that moment he ceases to be a pauper and becomes brother to the best of us and as a brother he should be cared for. I would make this a cardinal distinction in Poor Law relief. It is in some sense admitted already. Workhouse sick wards are generally better than the others; they are more comfortable; [there] is better diet. I happen to know that in many instances everything but one that money can get is supplied, but that one may at any time lead to great suffering or, as in this Holborn case, to death. That want is efficient nursing.

On reading the evidence before the coroner it is impossible not to see that there was no nursing in the case worthy of the name. I am afraid that nearly every workhouse in England could tell a similar tale. If you could only get to know how many poor have died because they were not nursed you would be shocked. You are perhaps aware that at Liverpool the evil of this system of pauper nursing is now working its cure. One noble man there [William Rathbone] has devoted £1200 a year for three years to introduce trained nurses into the large workhouse infirmary simply with the view of giving a blow to the old system and to show these unions what is possible in the way of improvements. Manchester it is expected will soon follow.

So far as our opportunities of training nurses under the "Fund"[92] will enable us to help in such a work, we are ready. We have supplied all the head nurses and the matrons in Liverpool and they will begin on Sunday or Monday. The

---

[92] The Nightingale Fund, established by public subscription on her return from Crimea, was used to pay for the training of nurses and midwives.

Theorists on Reform/Nightingale

improved nursing system is thus about to be instituted in one of the largest establishments in the kingdom and there is no reason why it should not in time be introduced in every workhouse. Could you help in this great improvement by having a searching enquiry made into the nursing system in all workhouses? The occasion appears to be a suitable one, and if you can see your way to undertake so good a work I will be most happy to help so far as my strength will permit. [The draft ends abruptly.]

Nightingale's correspondent replied the very next day, New Year's Eve. He defended the system but left the door open. "I shall do my utmost, while I am at this Board, to favour the extension of that system of sanitary improvement to which you have devoted your time and energies with such signal success," he promised.[93] A postscript added his willingness to communicate with Nightingale at any convenient time as to her proposal of an inquiry into the general system of nursing in workhouses. The two met and worked together closely for the next few years on Poor Law reform.

A draft letter of July 1865 brought together Nightingale's next phase of formulation of systemic reform. She realized that her scheme for providing good nursing care for the sick poor had to be part of a broader system. Environmental conditions, unsanitary housing, unsafe water and poor nutrition, had all to be addressed.

Text: Nightingale draft note [after July 1 1865] Add Mss 47753 folios 61-65:

A. To insist on the great principle of separating the sick, insane, incurable (how many of those called incurable are *not* incurable a life's hospital experience has taught me; old age is, of course, incurable—I mean to return to this) and children from the usual pauper population of the metropolis;
B. To advocate a general metropolitan rate for this purpose and a central administration;
C. To leave the pauper and casual population and the rating for them under the Boards of Guardians, as at present; these are the A.B.C. of the reform required. Centralize all the sanitary powers at present exercised by the Guardians; release them from these duties entirely. Provide a scheme of suburban hospitals and asylums:
    1. for sick,
    2. for infirm, aged and invalids,
    3. for insane and imbeciles,
    4. industrial schools for children.

---

[93] Add Mss 47753 folio 57.

Pay for them by a general school and hospital rate. I am well aware how much has been done already for the children and how admirably it has answered. Is not that a reason for doing it entirely?—for completing the work? There are children still in the London workhouses. Children should all belong to the central authority from the moment they enter school until they are provided for; they should never enter the workhouse after entering school....

All those classes which suffer from any disease, bodily or mental, should be placed under a district responsible administration amenable directly to Parliament. Uniformity of system in this matter is absolutely necessary in order that the suffering poor should be properly cared for, and in order that vacant beds and places may be filled up, wherever space exists. These infirmaries and asylums are of course to admit of separation of classes and sexes, so that sick, insane, imbeciles, aged infirm, and above all children, may not be mixed up in the same wards or under the same roof.

All the officers of these infirmaries and asylums should be appointed by and should be responsible to the central authority which is responsible to Parliament. Sickness, madness, imbecility and permanent infirmity are general afflictions affecting the entire community and are not (like pauperism) to be kept down by local knowledge or by hard usage. The sick, infirm or mad pauper ceases to be a pauper when so afflicted and should be chargeable to the community at large, as a fellow-creature in suffering. Hence there should be a general rate for this purpose to be levied over the whole metropolitan area, to be administered by the central authority.

May I make here two remarks by the way?

1. The state of the dwellings of the poor, the sanitary or rather un-sanitary state of London in general, is not often taken into account in the ill health it produces, e.g. consumption, weakness of intellect, rheumatism. We only think of the "violent" and "sudden" deaths of typhus and cholera. Yet the poor cannot drain their own streets, nor reform their own dwellings. Is it not hard to visit our shortcomings (in making London unhealthy) upon the disease they engender by calling it pauperism, by treating the sick or imbecile like the able-bodied lazy, immoral paupers and tramps, living on other people's labour?

2. What might be done in the way of cure, I say nothing of prevention, must be at present quite unknown....

Query—is it cheaper to have poor sick people recovering in good suburban hospitals, or becoming paupers for life in London workhouses, the ground of which, besides, would sell for far more than the workhouses are worth? But, if none but the casual tramps are left under the London Guardians will London workhouses be necessary at all?...

Sick infirm, idiots and mad persons require special construction arrangements, special medical care and nursing and special dieting. Of all these they have little or none that is worthy the name in the present London workhouses. They are not "paupers," they are "poor and in affliction." Society certainly owes them, if it owes anything, every necessary care for recovery. In practice, there should be consolidated and uniform administrative arrangements. Sickness is not parochial; it is general and human and its cost should be borne by all.

N.B. Those who come from the worst dwellings are always the most sickly. For sick you want hospitals as good as the best civil hospitals. You want the best nurses you can find. You want efficient sufficient medical attendance. You want an energetic and wise administration.

J.S. Mill supported the legislation that eventually was presented to Parliament in 1867. It had been watered down when the more radical Whigs were replaced by a Conservative government but activists have often had to take half a loaf rather than none at all. Nightingale had Mill briefed on the bill by the great sanitary leader Edwin Chadwick. Speaking in the House of Commons Mill regretted that the reforms did not go further. He took up Nightingale's argument for a national system. For future legislation on the sick poor of London "central instead of local management" should be considered.[94]

Government—Health Care for the Army

Nightingale's first action on return from the Crimean War was to press for what became the Royal Commission on the Sanitary Condition of the British Army. She succeeded mightily in getting a set of strong, comprehensive recommendations brought forward in the final report. Nightingale was fully aware that their application in practice would require broad public support, so she launched a media campaign. For this she enlisted the help of Harriet Martineau, who wrote a popular version of the royal commission report, *England and her Soldiers*, 1859, and numerous *Daily News* leaders urging implementation. The item below is interesting in showing how far Nightingale pressed her campaign: she actually drafted a leader ready for the printers! Alas, Nightingale's scathing invective was never published, although whether it was because Martineau did not pass it on to her editor, or the latter found it too hot to handle, is not known. Certainly Nightingale's would-be leader was much more sarcastic in style than anything Martineau wrote.

Text: Nightingale draft leader for the *Daily News*, with letter January 23 1859, Add Mss 45788 folios 23-28:

The Royal Commission on the Sanitary State of the Army, while exposing defects in present sanitary arrangements and their results to soldiers, appears to have carefully considered the means of remedy. Two plans come out in the evidence. One, to place the whole Sanitary Administration under an officer

---

[94] Mill, *Collected Works* 28:138.

quite unconnected with Army Medical Department. The other, to use the department and its officers for preserving health as well as curing disease.

There are strong arguments for both methods. Hygiene is a specialty and like other specialties requires undivided attention. Treating disease is also a specialty, requiring a man's whole thoughts and it is doubtful whether the train of thought, which makes a good physician does not make a bad sanitarian. Some of the evidence tends this way. Other witnesses consider that as the public pays a large staff of educated medical officers, these ought to be employed for sanitary service. Against this proposal stands the fact that, under the present system, the army has suffered so vast a rate of preventible disease and mortality. Can we hope to redress this by employing the same machinery under which it has occurred? The royal commission appears to have considered that the machinery might be improved, and rendered efficient by two measures: (1) educating every medical officer in the specialties of hygiene; (2) creating a council to be attached to the Army Medical Department of three members, one for hygiene, one for hospitals, one for statistics....

In considering our progress in army reform we ask what has become of this council? Are the deliberate recommendations of a royal commission of "experts" to be adopted and future armies saved or has the whole plan so carefully considered and so intelligently framed been shelved by the genius of dulness and stupidity in the War Office to which Great Britain from time immemorial has committed the destinies of her soldiers, in peace and in war? Why all this delay? Or rather has not the time arrived when the nation should call for a Royal Commission of Inquiry into the manner in which the interests of the army are neglected through the ignorance of a set of obscure paid officials who in all probability would never have been able to earn their salt in any other walk of life?

The House of Commons last session decreed barrack reform by an unanimous vote sanctioning by the national voice one recommendation of the royal commission. Our columns show from time to time the progress which is made. Let them also tell the War Office that unless other equally necessary reforms are carried out it is quite possible that better men may be found to attend to the health and efficiency of the army.

N.B. I don't think, (this is between ourselves), that hardly anyone is awake to this fact. The House of Commons thinks it has done great things when it has turned out one minister and put in another. It has done nothing at all. At least I can answer for the War Office, which is the only public department I know well enough to make any assertion about. I always thought John Bull hated a bureaucracy but the War Office is the veriest bureaucracy I know. The War Secretary of State is entirely in the hands of his permanent subordinates and a change in the Cabinet makes no change whatever in the administration of the War Office. Also these permanent subordinates are certainly men very much beneath par—you will understand that this is by no means for the *Daily News* but only for yourself.

Government—Social Statistics and their Application

Nightingale devoted decades of her life to the reform of government, national, imperial and, later, also local government, both for her own country and India. Politically she was a pragmatic, left-leaning liberal (a "tax and spend Democrat" in contemporary American terms). At a time when laissez-faire principles had much credence she advocated an extensive role for government. At the national level she sought to improve the calibre of the civil service by dramatically changing the university education future civil servants would receive, at least at Oxford University, the main training ground for the senior administration. The correspondence with **Francis Galton** excerpted below relates her attempt to have a statistical chair or readership in applied statistics established, for which she was prepared to give some of her own money. Galton, alas, did not share her vision. He went along at first, but it became clear that he would be content with the provision of essay prizes instead of her proposal. Nightingale dropped the project. The letter to her friend Benjamin Jowett, as Master of Balliol College a person who educated future civil servants, explains the crux of Nightingale's proposal.

Text: Nightingale letter to Jowett January 3 1891, Add Mss 45785 folios 144-45:

Our chief point was that the enormous amount of statistics at this moment available at their disposal (or in their pigeon holes which means *not* at their disposal) is almost absolutely useless. Why? Because the cabinet ministers... their subordinates, the large majority of whom have received a university education, have received no education whatever on the point upon which all legislation and all administration must—to be progressive and not *vibratory*—ultimately be based. We do *not* want a *great arithmetical law*—we want to know *what we are doing* in things which must be tested by results. We want experience and not experiment. We legislate *without knowing* what we are doing.

The War Office has on some subjects some of the finest statistics in the world. What comes of them? Little or nothing. Why? Because the heads don't know how to make anything of them (with the two exceptions of Sidney Herbert and W.H. Smith). Our Indian statistics are really better on some subjects than those of England. Of these *nothing* is made in administration....What we want first is not so much an accumulation of facts...but to teach them to the men who are to govern the country.

Text: Nightingale letter to Francis Galton, in Karl Pearson, ed., *Life and Letters of Francis Galton* February 7 1891 2:416-24 (original manuscript in University College Archives, Galton Papers 290 folios 1-17):

Sir Douglas Galton has given me your most kind message saying that if I will explain in writing to you what I think needs doing, you will be so good as to give it the experienced attention without which it would be worthless. By your kind leave, it is this: a scheme from someone of high authority as to what should be *the work and subjects in teaching social physics and their practical application* in the event of our being able to obtain a statistical professorship or readership at the University of Oxford. I am not thinking so much of hygiene and sanitary work because these and their statistics have been more closely studied in England than probably any other branch of statistics, though much remains to be desired, as for example the result of the food and cooking of the poor as seen in the children of the infant schools and those of somewhat higher ages. But I would—subject always to your criticism and only for the sake of illustration—mention a few of the other branches in which we appear hardly to know anything, for example:

A. The results of Forster's [Education] Act, now twenty years old. We sweep annually into our elementary schools hundreds of thousands of children, spending millions of money. Do we know for example:

(1) What proportion of children forget their whole education after leaving school; whether all they have been taught is wasted? (The almost accidental statistics of Guards recruits would point to a large proportion);

(2) What are the results upon the lives and conduct of children in after life who don't forget all they have been taught?

(3) What are the methods and what are the results, for example in night schools and secondary schools, in preventing primary education from being a waste? If we know not what are the effects upon our national life of Forster's Act is not this strange gap in reasonable England's knowledge?

B (1) The results of legal punishments—e.g. the deterrent or encouraging effects upon crime of being in gaol. Some excellent and hardworking reformers tell us: whatever you do keep a boy out of gaol...once in gaol, always in gaol; gaol is the cradle of crime. Other equally zealous and active reformers say a boy must be in gaol once at least to learn its hardships before he can be rescued. Is it again not strange in practical England that we know no more about this?

B (2) Is the career of a criminal from his first committal—and for what action—to his last, whether to the gallows, or to rehabilitation, recorded? It is stated by trustworthy persons that no such statistics exist, and that we can only learn the criminal's career from himself in friendly confidence—what it has been from being in gaol, say for stealing a turnip for a boys' feast, or for breaking his schoolroom window in a temper because he has been turned out of school for making a noise—to murder or to morality. In many cases all our legislation must be experiment, not experience. Any experience must be thrown away.

B (3) What effect has education on crime? Some people answer unhesitatingly: as education increases crime decreases, others as unhesitatingly: education only teaches to escape conviction, or to steal better when released. Others again: education has nothing to do with it either way.

C. We spend millions in rates [local taxes] in putting people into workhouses and millions in charity in taking them out. What is the proportion of names which from generation to generation appear the same in workhouse records? What is the proportion of children de-pauperized or pauperized by the workhouse? Do the large union schools, or the small, or "boarding out" return more pauper children to honest independent life? On girls what is the result of the training of the large union schools in fitting them for honest...domestic places—and what proportion of them falling into vice have to return to the workhouse? Upon all such subjects how could the use of statistics be taught?

D. India with its 250 millions—200 millions being our fellow subjects, I suppose—enters so little into practical English public life that many scarcely know where this small country is. It forms scarcely an element in our calculation, though we have piles of Indian statistics.

(i) Whether the peoples there are growing richer or poorer, better or worse fed and clothed?

(ii) Whether their physical powers are deteriorating or not?

(iii) Whether fever not only kills less or more, but whether it incapacitates from labour for fewer or more months in the year?

(iv) What are the native manufactures and productions, needed by the greatest customer in the world, the Government of India, which could be had as good and cheap in India, as those to be had from England?

(v) Whether the native trades and handicrafts are being ruined or being encouraged under our rule?

(vi) What is the result of Sir C. Wood's (1853) Education Act in India?

These are but a very few of the Indian things, which I will not say are hotly contested, for few care either in the House of Commons or out, but have their opposites asserted with equal positiveness....What is wanted is that so high an authority as Mr Francis Galton should jot down other great branches upon which he would wish for statistics, and for *the teaching how to use these statistics in order to legislate for and to administer our national life* with more precision and experience.

One authority was consulted and he answered that we have statistics and that government "must do it." Surely the answering question is: the government does not use the statistics which it has in administering and legislating—except indeed to "deal damnation" across the floor of the House of Commons at the Opposition and vice versa. Why? Because though of cabinet ministers, of the army, of the executive, of both Houses of Parliament the great majority have received a university education, what has the university education taught them of the practical application of statistics? Many of the government offices have splendid statistics. What use do they make of them? One of the last words Dr Farr of the General Register Office said to me was: "Yes, you must get an Oxford Professorship; don't let it drop."

M Quetelet gave me his *Physique sociale* and his *Anthropométrie*. He said almost like Sir Isaac Newton: "These are only a few pebbles picked up on the vast seashore of the ocean to be explored. Let the explorations be carried out." You know how Quetelet reduced the most (apparently) accidental carelessness to ever-recurring facts, so that as long as the same conditions exist, the same "accidents" will recur with absolutely unfailing regularity. You remember what Quetelet wrote—and Sir J. Herschel enforced the advice—'Put down what you expect from such and such legislation; after —— years, see where it has given you what you expected and where it has failed. But you change your laws and your administering of them so fast, and without inquiry after results past or present, that it is all experiment, see-saw, doctrinaire, a shuttlecock between two battledores."

Comment by Karl Pearson (2:424):
One can but regret this conclusion to what might have been a great success, the realization of an ideal common to two of the most remarkable minds of the nineteenth century. They were both "passionate statisticians," themselves capable of carrying great enterprises to successful conclusions. Yet somehow Francis Galton seemed to overlook the very kernel of Florence Nightingale's scheme, and the whole vanished in a trivial essay project. Yet the correspondence was, I believe, not without influence on Galton himself, and probably contributed not a little to guide him consciously or unconsciously when he came to make his own foundation in linking it up with a school of statistical training.

Government intervention had to be at the right level. Thus Nightingale wanted national data on illness in the census,[95] and standardized forms for hospitals to ensure that an accurate estimate of national trends would be available. Yet there was also a role for county and local endeavours at health promotion.

An International Statistical Congress was held in London in 1860, opened by Prince Albert, the Prince Consort and former pupil in probability and statistics of the Belgian statistician, **L.A.J. Quetelet**, Nightingale's mentor. Quetelet himself was a main organizer and president of the Congress. Nightingale did not attend public events of any kind by this stage but she keenly supported the congress. She invited Quetelet to bring colleagues to her home for breakfast (and strategy). She sent a short paper and a letter with precise recommendations for the reform of hospital statistics. Her letter to the congress was read by a fellow supporter of reform causes, Lord Shaftesbury, who had first earned Nightingale's gratitude by supporting investigation into conditions in the Crimean War.

---

[95] For an account of Nightingale's attempts to get a question added to the census in 1860 see my *Women Founders* 190.

The proposal now was to take better advantage of information routinely available. Governments collect a large amount of statistical information on the prevalence of disease. The delegates were urged to bring to the next statistical congress reports showing examples of diminished mortality and disease and the cost savings achieved. Politically it was important to show the cost of not acting, for it was cost that frightened communities from carrying out works necessary for public health improvements. Advocates of reform still typically urge the cost of not adopting their proposals.

Text: Nightingale letter to the International Statistical Congress, July 19 1860:

My lord, Pardon me for suggesting to you, first, that there must be a large amount of statistical information bearing on the prevention of disease in possession of the governments of different countries and, secondly, that it would be of great importance at the next meeting of this congress if each delegate would include, in any report to be presented, any marked examples of diminution of mortality and disease, together with the saving of cost consequent on the carrying out of sanitary improvements in towns, in dwellings of the labouring classes, in schools, in hospitals and in armies. For example, it is stated to be a fact, demonstrated by statistics, that in improved dwellings the mortality has fallen in certain cases from 25 and 24 to 14 per 1000, and that in common lodging-houses, which have been hotbeds of epidemics, such diseases have almost disappeared as heads of statistics, through the adoption of sanitary measures. As no one has been more instrumental than your lordship in bringing about these happy results, so no one is better acquainted than yourself with these facts.

It is also stated that in the British Army large bodies of men, living under certain improved sanitary conditions, have presented a death-rate about one-third only of what the army has suffered in past years.[96] Would not your lordship consider it as of great importance that the statistics of these and similar cases should be carefully collected and presented for comparison with the statistics of ordinary mortality?

Again it is stated that in our colonial schools for aborigines we have in many instances exposed the children to the risk of scrofula and consumption, while christianizing and civilizing them. Might not this be avoided by sanitary arrangements? Again, to take a different case from the experience of schools, it is stated as statistically true of some industrial and half-time schools for orphan and destitute children, that whereas formerly two-thirds of the pupils became sacrifices to vice and crime (as indeed is stated to be still the case in some instances), the failures on account of misconduct among the pupils have been reduced to less than two per cent. Might it not be well to consider whether

---

[96] Edwin Chadwick had provided that figure to the congress.

these statistical results do not exemplify what may be done by application of like means?

I am encouraged to make these suggestions by the following words from the statesman Guizot: "Valuable reports, replete with facts and suggestions drawn up by committees, inspectors, directors and prefects remain unknown to the public. Government ought to take care to make itself acquainted with and promote the diffusion of all good methods, to watch all endeavours, to encourage every improvement. With our habits and institutions there is but one instrument endowed with energy and power sufficient to secure this salutary influence, that instrument is the press."

If facts already existing regarding the points I have mentioned above were carefully abstracted and made accessible to the public, through the medium of the congress, there cannot be a doubt of the great benefits which would accrue to science and humanity. If, as it is the cost which frightens communities from executing the works necessary to carry out sanitary improvements, it could be shown that the cost of crime, disease and excess of mortality is actually greater, it would remove one of the most legitimate objections in the minds of governments and nations against such measures.

Nightingale's short paper on hospital statistics for the congress (not included here) proposed a uniform plan for the keeping of hospital statistics so that comparisons could be made on relative mortality and the frequency of diseases and injury by class, country and district. With these data it would be possible to ascertain what diseases "wasted" people's lives, and at what ages. The value of the different methods of treatment used could be ascertained by examining data on mortality and duration of the disease. Trustworthy data could be obtained "to guide future experience." Nightingale was showing how to implement one of the key themes of her philosophy: the routine evaluation of programs of intervention. Scientific study was required to ascertain the right method and place of intervention to effect desirable change. Application of the results was the next step. But Nightingale had a healthy scepticism about any projected reform thanks to her regard for the power of unintended consequences. Hence the need for routine data collection and monitoring.

Quetelet and a colleague who were official delegates to the congress formally proposed the ratification on Nightingale's proposals. **Edwin Chadwick**, a leading British sanitarian and close collaborator with Nightingale, gave his support. The proceedings report enthusiastic and unanimous approval by the delegates.[97]

Buckinghamshire was the county seat and constituency of **Harry Verney**, husband of Florence Nightingale's sister **Parthenope**. Nightingale had worked

---

[97] International Statistical Congress, *Proceedings* 181.

with her brother-in-law behind the scenes on various national concerns like the Contagious Diseases Acts and reform of the civil service. She continued to work with his sons on matters of mutual concern. As a frequent guest in the Verney home (a magnificent property now part of the National Trust) Nightingale knew the local area well. In 1892 she sent a letter to the *Times* to give public support to local efforts to institute a sanitary committee. A similar short paper, "Health and Local Government," 1894, not excerpted here, is one of the last pieces of her writing, and vibrant with good advice and trenchant observations. Money would be better spent on maintaining health in infancy and childhood than in building hospitals to alleviate or cure disease later.

Text: "Miss F. Nightingale on Local Sanitation," letter read by F.W. Verney to the Buckinghamshire County Council, (*Times* November 25 1892):

We must create a public opinion which must drive the government, instead of the government having to drive us—an enlightened public opinion, wise in principles, wise in details. We hail the county council as being or becoming one of the strongest engines in our favour, at once fathering and obeying the great impulse for national health against national and local disease. For we have learnt that we have national health in our own hands—local sanitation, national health. But we have to contend against centuries of superstition and generations of indifference. Let the county council take the lead. Let it represent us, command us, instruct us by a sanitary committee in our struggle for health. We do not ask at present for county council executive power. But what a moving power would such a sanitary committee, if wisely conducted, be, gathering experience every day, encouraging the true reports of able medical officers of health instead of quashing them, saying, "We will not have cholera, we will not have fever, nor infantile complaints, the true test of what is sanitary or insanitary—sickly children growing into sickly parents. We will have good water supply, good drainage, no overcrowding, pure air, pure water, pure earth; for disease is more expensive than sanitation. We will be able to say to cholera, if it comes—there is no room for you here, there is no place for you to plant your foot. Scarlet fever, typhoid, cannot come here. Buckinghamshire shall be a county of healthy villages." Sanitary reform must be a work of years, not of a day. Other counties have undertaken it, but there must not be a day lost in beginning it. Cholera may be upon us next summer; disease is always with us. Give us our sanitary committee. Good speed to you. God speed you.

Government—India

Florence Nightingale's interest in India was prompted by the mutiny of 1857/First War of Independence from the Indian perspective, when she offered to go out to nurse the victims. Her first writing on India also dates from 1857, a brief addition to *Notes on the Army* urging the adoption of sanitary measures in spite of the fact that there was no precedent to do so.[98] In 1858, when her royal commission on the army in the Crimea was finished she began pressing for a royal commission on India. India was taken under British government rule from the East India Company in 1858, to become the "jewel of the crown" of British possessions. Queen Victoria was proclaimed Empress of India in 1876.

When the commission Nightingale sought was officially proclaimed she clipped the announcement and added it to the following:

June 1 1859
Parable—The unjust judge & the importunate widow
Dramatis Personae—
Ld. Stanley—Unjust Judge[99]
F.N. Importunate widow
Result of 8 months' importunacy—as below

From the *London Gazette* of Tuesday, May 31, India Office:

The Queen has been pleased to issue a commission under Her Royal sign manual, appointing...to be Her Majesty's Commissioners to inquire into, and report upon, the measures which it may be expedient to take for maintaining and improving the health of all ranks of Her Majesty's army serving in India.

Nightingale realized that soldiers could not be kept healthy if the civilian population among whom they lived were not. For decades she devoted herself to raising the standard of living, assuring adequate food supplies, clean water and healthy living conditions for the vast mass of ordinary Indian peasants and workers. Similarly she had a clear understanding of the civilian death toll from war. In the mutiny of 1857 she noted that sixty-four wives and 166 children (out of 554 wives and 770 children respectively) had been killed by dysentery at a military station, for a "massacre" as great as that by the mutineers.[100] Her royal commission was always concerned with public health more broadly. She did an enormous amount of the work of the commission itself, sending out questionnaires to the stations, analyzing and summarizing the results. The recommendations of the final report in 1863 were for massive, systemic

---

[98] Cook, *Life of Florence Nightingale* 1:371 and 2:20. See also Penelope Tuson, ed., *Queen's Daughters* on Nightingale's work in India.

[99] Lord Stanley was not an unjust judge but a long-time ally on reform issues.

[100] "Observations by Miss Nightingale" 368.

reform.[101] Nightingale related her happiness to Martineau when the work was done:

> I cannot help telling you, in the joy of my heart, that the final meeting of the India Sanitary Commission was held today—that the report was signed—and that after a very tough battle, lasting over three days, to convince these people that a report was not self-executive, our working commission was carried, not quite in the original form proposed, but in what may prove even a better working form because grafted on what exists. This is the dawn of a new day for India in sanitary things, not only as regards our army, but as regards the native population.[102]

Nightingale made concerted efforts, with little success, to get the royal commission reforms implemented.[103] Bureaucratic in-fighting—the India Office was jealous of the War Office—and the disdain of the senior Imperial Civil Service for ordinary Indian nationals together sufficed to prevent change. The failure of her modus operandi of reform from on high convinced Nightingale of the need for a new strategy: change from below. She had welcomed Queen Victoria's proclamation, 1858, admitting Indian nationals into the Civil Service. She thought that western-educated Indian nationals should, and would, increasingly run the government of India. What was needed was an amalgamation of the traditional Indian principles of local self-government with modern western education. The old panchayat council system was key to India's future. By the mid-1860s Nightingale became aware that British administration of India was actually worsening the situation for ordinary people. Irrigation systems and railroad construction, essential improvements, were carried out in such a way as to worsen public health and increase mortality. British economic policies increased the debt and insecurity of ordinary agriculturists. She published a number of papers on the subject and wrote even more.[104] She wrote letters to the editor and feature articles for the popular press in England, sometimes clipping and circulating them to influential people, with a flattering covering letter. She wrote articles and manifestos and sent encouragement to Indian public health organizations and their journals.

---

[101] United Kingdom, *Report of the Royal Commission on the Sanitary State of the Army in India*.

[102] Letter to Martineau May 19 1863, Add Mss 45788 folio 184.

[103] Marc Jason Gilbert, "An Eminent Victorian as Outsider," on Nightingale's influence on Indian nationalism.

[104] Nightingale, *How People may Live and not Die in India*; printed but not published was *Life or Death in India under the Zemindary System* c. 1874.

Interspersed with her efforts for systemic reform Nightingale rallied to help with immediate emergencies. The south Indian famine of 1877 prompted a donation to the Lord Mayor's Fund and a letter to the *Times*. The famine was "worse than a battlefield" and the Indian ryot (peasant farmer) the most "industrious being on the face of the earth," deserving of all that we can give to "our own starving fellow-subjects."[105]

Nightingale met with and encouraged the first generation of Indian nationalists, who used her ideas and publicly cited them. She supported Indian nationals seeking election to the British Parliament. She promoted publication in the English press of pro-reform articles by Indians. As late as 1897 when she was very weak, she opened her home for meetings and strategizing to a nationalist delegation to a British royal commission, led by **Gopale Krishna Ghokale**. Too feeble to gather data herself, she helped analyze what data were available for presentation.

Unpublished material shows Nightingale's yearning for new leadership to emerge among Indian nationals. When an Indian newspaper editorialized: "What we want from Sir Richard Temple," who had been appointed to head a commission to revise Bengal's rent laws, Nightingale rephrased the question: "What India 'wants' not from Sir Richard Temple she 'wants' it from herself."[106] She was acutely aware of the obstacles to reform imposed by the caste system but remained hopeful that between economic incentives and deeply implanted "pity and charity" these would be overcome (folios 261-62). "Alas, civilization brings with it the vices of civilization," she observed. Brahmins ceased to have Brahmin virtues without adopting western (folio 257). She described both Hindus and Muslims as being superior in supporting their sick, aged and infirm than the British—and they did it without a Poor Law (folio 262). Institutional reform was required, of the legal profession, newspaper publishing and local politics. The struggle required steady, persevering, dogged work, for a lifetime. Examples given were the leader of Irish Home Rule, Daniel O'Connell, the anti-slavery leaders Wilberforce and Clarkson (Nightingale noting that her own grandfather had worked for Wilberforce in the abolition movement), and even Christ and Buddha (folio 256).

The major paper reproduced here began with Nightingale's damning conclusion on British policy: "We do not care for the people of India." It is not clear if she approved in principle of imperialism; it was a fact that Britain governed India. Hence it had a responsibility to govern wisely and well, for the benefit of the people of the country. The reality was otherwise, and this Nightingale condemned clearly, concisely and repeatedly. One-quarter of the population in some areas had died from famine, an estimated six million

---

[105] Letter to the *Times*, August 20 1877.

[106] Add Mss 45834 folio 254.

people died in South India. She wondered what would be said of a war that killed that many in a year in a region half the size of France. In London one death from starvation prompted an inquest and numerous newspaper reports. Public opinion ought to hold a gigantic inquest on the six million bodies, she argued (195). Britain boasted about her system of justice; she had abolished the slave trade. But poverty in India led to virtual slavery, indeed as a consequence of British laws (201). She condemned the salt tax for strangling manufacturing and hindering agriculture and animal husbandry. She understood and condemned its regressive features; salt was an essential food purchase for all people and poor people paid a higher portion of their low incomes in the tax.

Text: Nightingale, "The People of India":

We do not care for the people of India. This is a heavy indictment, but how else account for the facts about to be given? Do we even care enough to know about their daily lives of lingering death from causes which we could so well remove? We have taken their lands and their rule and their rulers into our charge for state reasons of our own. Nay, the hour is coming, and even now is, when for "state reasons" we are annexing, or preparing to annex or to reorganize or to "protect"—by whatever name we call it—huge and immeasurable territories because they lie between us and them. But for them themselves, these patient, silent, toiling millions of India, who scarcely but for suffering know their right hand from their left and yet who are so teachable, so ready to abide by law instead of resisting "their enemy the Law," for their daily lives and deaths, we do *not* as a nation practically care. Or should we not as a nation practically rise en masse to see that the remediable things to which good public servants have so often vainly called attention *shall* be remedied? Have we no voice for these voiceless millions?

What is the saddest sight to be seen in the East, nay probably in the world? The saddest sight to be seen is the peasant in our own Eastern Empire, but we do not look at this sight, no, not even those few who travel in India....The bulk of the people of India are paupers; they can just pay their cesses in a good year, and fail altogether when the season is bad. Remissions have to be made perhaps every third year in most districts. There is a bad year in some one district or group of districts every year. Whose striking words are these? Not those of a Member of Parliament or advocate making a case, or historian or gazetteer writing in his closet. They are those of one of our great English proconsuls ruling in India over a population nearly twice as large as that of France, second only to a viceroy and who has done perhaps more than any in raising the Indian peasant, in giving him a kind of representation, a voice to rate himself, in giving him education, roads and a sort of independence or power to hold his own.

Let us try to take a glimpse of one or two of the various provinces in regard principally to material prosperity or rather adversity, first of Madras because the famine, not yet over, and the help given by England have tended to fix our eyes just half an hour more than usual upon this presidency as upon India in general....

What we engaged to do was to prevent any from dying of famine. What have we done? In many parts one-fourth have died....We have lost in one year not less than three millions out of the twenty millions more especially under the famine scourge in Madras....In southern India, that is in Mysore, Bombay and Madras our loss in one year's famine has not been far short of 6,000,000 souls; this had been our care of the bodies....

What should we say of a war which had killed 6,000,000 in one year in a region not much more than half the size of France, or indeed in all the wars in all Europe of the greatest of conquerors? It has not entered into the imagination of man to conceive of such a destruction. One death from starvation in London fills all the newspapers with reports of the inquest upon the body. There is a machinery which costs us seven millions of money a year to prevent it [Poor Law relief]. Public opinion is now holding, holding did I say? It is not holding—it ought to hold a gigantic inquest upon 6,000,000 bodies, dead less indeed by our fault in sparing effort than in spite of every effort, to save them from dying of famine, to save them, *not to prevent famine*. Has any effort been made not to prevent deaths from famine, but *to prevent famine itself*? (193-95)

Manufactures are strangled by the tax on salt....The food of the poor requires more salt than the better diet of the rich, but no man could live without nine pounds of salt per annum....The French gabelle [salt tax] was "a law of conscription against the well-being of man, a law entailing misery on unborn generations." Can India become prosperous under it?...

The chief object of this attempt is to ask as well as I can, in so brief a space where only a few questions can be asked...how it is that whole peoples among the most industrious in the world, on perhaps the most fertile soils in the world, are the poorest in the world. How it is that whole peoples always in a state of semi-starvation are from time to time on the brink of famine?...Is there any fatal necessity for this? Is it not due to two or three causes, not only preventible, but which we, their rulers, having ourselves induced, either by doing or by not doing, can ourselves gradually remove. [Nightingale next discussed money lending]....

Is it not strange that, under a country boasting herself the justest in the world, and the abolisher of the slave trade, a poverty, an impecuniosity, an "impropertyness" leading to virtual slavery, should be growing up, actually the *consequence* of our own laws, which outstrips in its miserable results, because it enslaves and renders destitute a land-possessing peasantry....One thing has been much urged: a system of small loans from government at moderate interest to the country ryot [peasant farmer]...to be extended to meet the need and supported by British capital (199-201).

Were it possible that England should reconquer India by enabling the indebted country ryot to redeem his lands and pay off his debts...by introducing factories, perhaps the co-operative store, for which the village community of India would seem the very soil; by opening cheap village courts, enough to place one within easy reach of every village, so that litigants may be able to go to the court in the morning and return home at night...by restoring courts of conciliation, for which also India is the soil, for the settlement of class disputes, as well as courts of arbitration for the cheap and ready disposal of individual suits—panchayats...if England could thus reconquer India from the money lender what a glorious conquest that would be (204).

We are told that the ryot has the remedy of English justice...our courts and the rest. He has not. A man has not that which he can't use....Hear what the government itself says but does not do. Once when a Revenue Commissioner brought the matter before the Governor-in-Council the Governor-in-Council recorded the following resolution: He "entertains no doubt of the fact that the labouring classes of the native community suffer enormous injustice from the want of protection by law from the extortionate practice of money lenders. He believes that our civil courts have become *hateful*...to the masses of our Indian subjects from being made the instruments of the almost *incredible* rapacity of usurious capitalists. Nothing can be more calculated to give rise to wide-spread discontent and disaffection to the British government than the practical working of the present law" (218-19).

Peace, War and Militarism—the Franco-Prussian War

Henri Dunant, founder of the Red Cross,[107] credited Florence Nightingale with the key principle of the Geneva Convention, the neutralization of the war wounded, that is, that injured soldiers should be treated without regard to their nationality. This convention, first signed in 1864, has been amended many times since, always to limit the ravages of war by imposing specific obligations on signatory powers. (Further conventions have dealt with biological and germ warfare; there are proposals now to limit environmental destruction from war and outlaw rape in war.)

Nightingale's involvement was complicated. The War Office asked her to help prepare a briefing document on the British position, but she profoundly disagreed with the government's whole approach. Her objection was the focus on voluntary efforts for treatment of the sick and injured, not the neutralization principle itself, whose merits were obvious to her. She insisted on government's responsibility to look after, and plan for, their own sick and wounded. Moreover she believed that the availability of voluntary measures would weaken governmental responsibility. As well she was sceptical of the

---

[107] Dunant was responding to the carnage of the Battle of Solferino in the Italian Wars of Independence, 1859, just after Crimea; Cook, *Life of Florence Nightingale* 2:205 and John Hutchinson, *Champions of Charity*.

value of mere declarations of principle. Nightingale's two letters to Professor Longmore below show her thoroughly negative, even bellicose, views.

Text: Nightingale letter July 23 1864, Wellcome Trust, Contemporary Medical Archives RAMC/1139/LP54/7 (photocopy of unsigned handscript); typescript British Library Add Mss 45773 folios 168-69:

I am afraid you will be rather surprised at me writing to you on the following subject but not so much surprised as I am at being desired to do so. Lord de Grey is about to request you and Dr Rutherford to represent the War Office at the Geneva Conference in August and wishes you to have an authorized War Office account with you as to our provision for sick and wounded in the British Army.

The conference has, as you know, advocated a voluntary international system of purveying and nursing. I need hardly say that I think its views most absurd—just such as would originate in a little state, like Geneva or Baden, which never can see war. They tend to remove responsibility from governments. They are *practically impracticable*. Voluntary effort is desirable just in so far as it can be incorporated into military system.

Our present system (military) is the result of voluntary additions to the service made during the Crimean War, but was prepared to obviate the necessity of future voluntary efforts as far as possible. If the present regulations are not sufficient to provide for wounded, they should be made so. It would be an error to revert to a voluntary system or to weaken the military character of the present system by introducing voluntary effort, unless such effort were to become military in its organization.

The War Office proposes to draw up such a statement of our present arrangements as will satisfy the Geneva folk that every precaution has been taken and can be taken and make it as strong and as complete as possible—then return it to me. I will send it to the War Office and they will make an authoritative document out of it. The matter rather presses as the conference meets early in August.

Text: Nightingale letter to Longmore, August 31 1864, Add Mss 45773 folios 173-74, and in *News Review of British Red Cross Society* April 1959:

I have to thank you very much for taking the trouble to send me M Dunant's pamphlet. The War Office sent me the manuscript copy of the printed article with other papers furnished by you. I agree with you that it will be quite harmless for our government to sign the convention as it now stands. It amounts to nothing more than the declaration that humanity to the wounded is a good thing. It is like an opera chorus, and if the principal European characters sing "We never will be cruel more," I am sure if England likes to sing too "I never will be cruel more," I see no objection. But it is like vows: people who keep a vow would do the same without the vow, and if people will not do it *without* the vow, they will not do it with. England and France will not be more humane to the enemy's wounded for having signed the convention, and the convention will not keep semi-barbarous nations like Russia from being *inhuman*. Besides which though I do not reckon myself an inhuman person I can conceive of circumstances of force majeure in war when the more people are killed, the better.

Professor Longmore wrote Nightingale in 1869 at the next stage of deliberations on the Geneva Convention. He understood the interest of people on the Continent for "popular aid" to the sick and wounded, but considered that the schemes were "visionary." He had recently participated in a conference on the subject in Berlin, where war was expected to break out at any time.[108] This as well as other correspondence show how much Longmore shared both Nightingale's pragmatism and scepticism.

When the Franco-Prussian War broke out in 1870 Nightingale again sprang into action. If she could have, she would have gone to the front herself to nurse. Instead she worked night and day, for both sides, answering queries, providing plans, finding supplies and personnel and advising on all kinds of technical problems. A long letter to her brother-in-law Harry Verney below set out the situation in detail. She recognized that the British Red Cross had done nothing to prepare for any role in providing aid in war. Nightingale then reviewed the practical issues regarding nurses, supplies, transport, hospitals and finance. In between she expressed her horror of this war and all war. The toll on ordinary people moved her. Should we not, she asked, go to the relief of such suffering, on whichever side, in whichever race we find it?

Text: Nightingale letter to Harry Verney, Wellcome Trust, August 2 1870:

Anniversary of Sidney Herbert's death 9 years ago
In answer to your twice urged enquiry, respecting the "Society" forming for "Help to the Sick and Wounded" in this awful war—may God's best blessing go with it—as must the sympathy of all who have a heart in their bodies! What strikes me is this: this lamentable, this deadly war, has found us without any organization wherewith to proceed at once to the assistance of our suffering brothers and sisters across the channel. There is nevertheless an organization in existence having branches, among other places, in Berlin and Paris. There is, I believe, a common code of regulations pointing out the kind of supplies which ought to be sent to the field hospitals, together with the steps to be taken to ensure their neutralization and distribution. Had we in this country proceeded with the same activity as has been shown by both sides in this war,

---

[108] Add Mss 47753 folios 189-90.

we should not now be calling meetings to enquire what ought to be done and where the funds ought to come from.

We have no practical knowledge of how to go about the work ourselves, but we can assist those who are engaged in it. I would venture to suggest, if this has not been done already, which probably it has, that an active business committee be at once formed. Funds must of course in the first instance be obtained, and while this preliminary and most necessary work is being done, the proposed committee should communicate with the branch organizations in Paris and Berlin and obtain from them the requisite information....

If supplies in kind are sent from this country to the seat of war, it would be necessary to obtain their neutralization until they arrived at their destination. Persons in charge of them would probably need safe conducts. If the two (French and German) branch organizations require only money, this whole work would be simplified by sending money only and allowing the respective branches to expend it. I need hardly suggest because Englishmen will always see fair play done, that the most rigid impartiality should be observed in the division of funds.

It is not unlikely that, besides supplies in money and kind, personal service in field hospitals might be asked for. I have myself received an application, or rather an offer of acceptance of war nurses, should such volunteer, from one whom we all love and revere [the crown princess of Prussia, daughter of Queen Victoria], and who is now in the thick of the dreadful turmoil. There will probably be a demand for efficient nurses, both men and women.

If I could rise from my bed of illness, so as to be of any use, I should, before now, have been off to wherever the authorities would accept my services as most wanted. If *I* cannot, there are better than me, who will be able and willing to go under this awful emergency which has come over Europe. Those who are bone of our bone and flesh of our flesh, our brothers, our fellow Christians (oh that I should have to say it!) are met face to face in the deadliest struggle of our time, armed with every instrument of destruction which the latest science has placed in human hands. Can we stand idly by or take a sentimental part either on one side or the other in the face of all this suffering? Ought we not rather to think only of one thing—the suffering incalculably greater than anything that *our* eyes have seen, or *our* ears heard, or that it has entered into *our* imaginations to conceive. When we think of the peasants taken from their harvestings to fight, the whole organization of labour broken up, the women and children starving and helpless, we see the misery of war doubled and tripled, ten folded by want and scarcity, ought we not to go to the relief of such suffering on whichever side, in whichever race we find it, wherever we are allowed to go to it?

I have put down, because you asked me, the very most elementary considerations, certain that these of a great many others and much further steps will have been taken by the able and earnest men who, I rejoice to see, form the Committee of Aid. May God bless them.

Theorists on Reform/Nightingale

Another letter to Harry Verney is more political, blaming **Bismarck** in no uncertain terms for the war. Dedicated as Nightingale was to the neutralization principle, she had no reluctance to take sides on various aspects of the war. She was appalled by Prussian militarism and carefully distinguished "Prussian" from "German" in her comments. So, of course, did Bismarck, bragging about making Germany Prussian. Her sympathies were overwhelmingly with the invaded and occupied French. (She herself had lived in Paris briefly.) In a letter not included here Nightingale related the seige of Paris to Christ's weeping over Jerusalem.[109] She pointed out the hypocrisy of blaming **Louis Napoleon** for declaring war.

Text: Nightingale letter to Harry Verney, Wellcome Trust, August 25 1870 7:00 a.m:

Let us not forget that, at the time of or soon after the coup d'état Lord John Russell (the prime minister of England) declared in the House of Commons what he knew what we knew that he knew was untrue—mainly that the coup d'état was a great act of patriotism or of good government or some stuff of that sort. *This* to secure a strong ally. We have perpetrated enough baseness in kicking Louis Napoleon now he is down and a weak ally. If the government had...declared openly their disapproval of him now, that *would* have been capping all baseness.

We have our reward. The Prussian papers, so far from being satisfied with our licking Bismarck's shoes, are clamouring that we ought not so much as to think of mediating a peace till they have conquered France. If Prussia next turns her victorious arms against us (by sea) what a reaction there will be. O then Napoleon will indeed be the whiter devil. Only that the Crown Princess is very spontaneous though ambitious, and that she would not think it worth while to *make* friendship to me, I could almost think her letters meant "*we* have no part in all this Prussian newspaper bluster."

But, that we have not seen the end of the blacker devil, Bismarck, I suppose every one feels convinced, first—and that, secondly, had he died in his cradle, Europe would not now have been deluged with blood. I think it is so like "straining at a gnat and swallowing a camel" to dwell upon *Napoleon* having sent the Declaration of War!

A third letter, of November 11 1870 to Harry Verney pointed out that the problems with the Red Cross approach she had predicted as early as 1864 had in fact occurred. Voluntary efforts were, in effect, subsidizing war, making war "cheap." The Prussians were avoiding their responsibilities for their sick by relying on the Red Cross so that "*we* are *in fact* paying a large quota to the expenses of the Prussians making war." The Prussian medical services were

---

[109] Nightingale, unpublished note, 1870, Add Mss 45845 folio 31.

not as good as the French; their death rates were demonstrably higher. Though the Prussians were beating the French in battle their hospitals were of the order of Louis XIV or Frederick II of the previous century. Nightingale blamed French administration for their albeit lower losses: "pillage and dishonesty has been quite beyond belief." Stores, ammunition, clothing, guns, everything was in short supply.[110]

Harry Verney's daughter Emily, from a previous marriage, worked with Nightingale throughout the war on the full range of practical matters. Nightingale's letter to her, below, argued the need to learn from past mistakes, ask the right questions and devise a better system.

Text: Nightingale letter October 22 1870, Add Mss 45802 folios 188-89:

Dearest Emily:
It is of vital importance now that we should be collecting and learning from all the experience we can get. Solferino abolished in part or greatly modified the experience of the Crimea. Sadowa did the same by Solferino. Now Metz and Sedan have done the same by Sadowa. And Paris threatens to be the most tremendous crisis of all. All this ought to be woven up in a tradition of experience by us....

There are four practical questions, the very first which present themselves to the nakedest eye, upon which we ought by this time to have some sort of experience...for example (1) Should each nation have its own complete ambulances or help the ambulances of belligerents with matériel and personnel? (2) Should women be sent as nurses? And if so *how* to ensure their services being used, whether with their own special ambulance or to be attached, one here one there, to others? (3) Same question as to infirmiers [male nurses] or orderlies. (4) If complete ambulances are to be sent by each nation, what are their best sizes? These questions, which are of the very simplest and which leave out all the great questions of the organization of Red Cross societies—their relations to local committees and agents; their relations to governments can only be decided by practical working....

Nightingale helped raise money for the million and a half French refugees from the war. The Lord Mayor of London established a fund for British contributions. Nightingale sent in her "mite" with a moving letter to the *Times*, reproduced below. Note how this short letter flags three of her greatest preoccupations: the neutralization principle, respect for the working class and the need to learn for systemic change. Even though the object was to raise money for French refugees Nightingale mentioned the working people of France and Germany.

---

[110] Unpublished note, Add Mss 45845 folio 32.

Text: Nightingale, "Distress in and About Paris" *Times* February 1 1871:6:

May I be permitted to contribute through your hands my mite—£5 a week for four weeks—to the most appalling distress this country has seen—that of the starving population in Paris, where, on the opening of the gates, a million and a half of non-combatants, principally women and children, will have to be fed like babies?

But the charity of England will be equal, under your auspices, to the emergency. For this terrible new year what can one wish but that there never may be such another to the end of the world? Still, England's "generosity and magnificent charity"...has risen equal to the wants. I do not believe there is one man, woman or child above pauperism who has not given...far above their means, for Germans and French who can never give again to them; "and all for love and nothing for reward."

I should like the working people of England to know that the working people of France and of Germany feel this. One expression of it—it was from a German—struck me particularly; it was to the effect that Prussian elementary education was far superior to the English—let the London School Board show that that this shall not be the case long; but for the "education of the heart," continued my correspondent, give me the English working people. I fully endorse this.

Nightingale, like de Staël before her, saw the threat of militarism to democratic institutions at home. She cited with approval a French article on the defeat of Italy at the battles of Custoza (in the Italian Wars of Independence) and Lipa: "how happy to have achieved her independence and not been victorious. Had she won those battles she would have fallen under military dictatorship; now she can turn her attention to internal reform and improvement." Germany was never farther "from free representative institutions than at this moment," in the Franco-Prussian War.[111] The annexation of Alsace and Lorraine by Germany was a mistake which would weaken Germany. Nevertheless she doubted "whether any statesman, whether even the emperor, is strong enough to march the German Army out of Strasburg" without risk to the throne.[112] To her friend **Benjamin Jowett**, Master of Balliol College, she asked if even "the ruin of poor, torn and trampled France" was as bad as the effect Bismarck had had in besotting a "whole central continent of the most philosophical and civilized peoples of the earth."[113] The "tyranny" possessed her more than the "actual sufferings, frightful, ghastly as they are" (folio 224). The contrast in philosophy with

---

[111] Unpublished note, Add Mss 45845 folios 34-35.

[112] Unpublished note February 7 1871, Add Mss 45845 folio 89.

[113] Add Mss 45783 folio 226.

Bismarck, who dominated European politics 1860-90, is stark. Bismarck considered that war was the "natural condition of mankind," specifically using the language of social Darwinism on struggle and survival to justify war.[114] Nightingale's conceptualization of human nature was much more benign; she rejected the views of **Charles Darwin** as well as his more extreme followers as unscientific.[115] Three other unpublished notes of 1871 give similar views:

> As for German unity, if Prussians (of all ranks) are now in the process of developing into Germans, who are, as a body, civilized and human beings—then even this great earthquake and hurricane of misery may have been worthwhile (though I myself should prefer annihilation). But, if German unity means Germany (of all ranks) developing into Prussia, upon my honour I think I had rather be...lying 200 fathoms deep off the coast of Spain....Lord have mercy upon us his poor children, who have all turned out murderers and robbers and villains![116]

> The danger of German militarism is not so much the danger of war, though that is not small, as the danger to its own institutions, to its own national progress. All representative rights and liberties, all freedom of the press, such as they were, are not only declining but absolutely annihilating, if not annihilated, under the present régime. A military dictatorship seems all that is before them—absorbing all the better tendencies not only of Prussia but the tendencies far nobler and better than Prussian of all that is not Prussia into Prussia. I have just been declaiming against Mr Gladstone with his Parliament. But only imagine Mr Gladstone without a Parliament![117]

> The powers that have been set loose are now beyond all control—they are irrational, inaccessible to reason. Nations, like engines, are under control up to a certain point but if that point is once past all becomes hopeless. Germany will not listen to any argument now, and good advice will only make her more angry and unreasonable. Success intoxicates a nation and no one can fail to see that the nation at large is not in its right mind. The king and his daily companions are soldiers by profession; they look at everything from a military point of view. They despise moral forces; they want material guarantees. If men like the crown

---

[114] Sybil Oldfield, *Women against the Iron Fist* 6.

[115] Add Mss 45842 folio 17.

[116] Undated note probably to Harry Verney, 1871, Woodward Biomedical Library A46.

[117] Unpublished note, 1871, Add Mss 45845 folio 34.

Theorists on Reform/Nightingale 195

prince are powerless and think it wise to be silent, whose voice is likely to do any good?[118]

Gender/Regulation of Prostitution

Nightingale led the battle to prevent legislation of the Contagious Diseases Acts. She was aware of the serious problem syphilis posed; it accounted for an enormous proportion of hospital admissions among troops, both in Britain and in stations abroad.[119] A letter to Harriet Martineau September 24 1861, otherwise on the subject of assisting the United States government in the Civil War, noted the problem and the fear of legislation as the government's remedy.

> We find that the disease of vice is daily increasing in the army so that fully one half of all the sickness *at home* is owing to that. And that the *absolute inability* of the magistrates even to enforce the existing law...at all our garrison towns makes the public houses nothing but bad houses, where prostitutes are openly kept by the beerhouse keepers for their customers. It is to be feared that the present War Secretary, who is totally ignorant of his business, considers that there is no remedy for this but the French plan (of inspection and breveting of the women a plan invented expressly to degrade the national character.[120]

Nightingale went on to propose alternative means of combatting vice, the provision of day rooms or clubs for healthy leisure time pursuits, pointing out that in fact soldiers did use such facilities when provided, as she had found out in the Crimean War. She, as numerous other women, contested the prevailing War Office opinion of ordinary soldiers as brutes from whom little could be expected. Nightingale had dealt with the issue briefly in commenting on reports for her second royal commission, on India. She referred to statistics showing for Seconderabad that 20 per cent of hospital admissions of British troops were for the "disease engendered by vice," while only 4 per cent were for native troops.[121] But general statistics were lacking. Nightingale here also took the view that regulation was ineffective as well as wrong. Compulsory treatment in "lock hospitals" was incompatible with morality and utterly useless in practice.

---

[118] Unpublished note, February 7 1871, Add Mss 45845 folio 89.

[119] Admissions for all forms of venereal disease in the Army in Britain averaged 369 per 1000 soldiers in 1860 (as high as 503 at Portsmouth, a major naval base), for a loss to the army at home of 8.7 days of service every year per soldier (UK Army Medical Department, *Statistical, Sanitary, and Medical Reports*).

[120] Add Mss 45788 folio 128.

[121] "Observations by Miss Nightingale 370.

In 1862 Nightingale prepared, at the request of the War Minister, a seven-page briefing paper on the subject. Only twenty copies were printed and it nowhere bears her name. The title itself makes clear her opposition: "Note on the Supposed Protection afforded against venereal disease by recognizing prostitution and putting it under Police Regulation." Nightingale opposed both the recognition of prostitution as acceptable so long as disease did not ensue, and the contention that compulsory examination and treatment would serve to reduce the incidence of syphilis. At the time she did not accept the then new-fangled "germ theory," which specified that certain diseases were caused by specific germs. Instead she held that generalized filth and immorality were the causal factors for contagious diseases. Apart from her insistence that contagion was "pure assertion" her analysis stands the test of time. She provided data collected by the War Office (only one table of which is reproduced below), to show that there was considerable variation in rates of syphilis and no tendency for it to be reduced where police regulation was in force. She argued for the suppression of prostitution as a better solution, for the consequences of these diseases went on for generations. There was more reason to legislate against prostitution than theft.

Text: Nightingale, " Note on the Supposed Protection":

There is absolutely no evidence that there is less syphilis among populations under police restrictions and certificates of health than among populations under none. It is pure assertion. The first step, therefore, requisite before the protective power of regulation can be admitted, is to discard mere opinion and to obtain correct statistics of syphilis in England to contrast with those of parts of France and Belgium where the police arrangements in this particular are supposed to be most complete....

Still, if it can be proved that syphilis has been suppressed by police regulation, the question should be studied as a branch of sanitary medicine....As regards civil populations, the proof of protection from syphilis by police regulation is *absent*. Yet any repressive measures for protecting the army must include repressive measures for the whole civil population among whom the army is placed, so that we are asked to recognize vice on hypothetical grounds in order that we may hypothetically diminish its consequences after recognition....

As regards stations *under* police regulation: Gibraltar, Malta and the Ionian Islands have been for years under what is considered as rigid a police system as can be carried out. All infected women are at once sent to hospital. We should naturally expect a very marked effect in these garrisons. The following are the results of this police inspection of prostitutes on bodies of men living among small fixed groups of population....

	Admissions per 1000			
	1817-36	1837-46	1859	1860
Malta	180	99	149	148
Gibraltar	57	78	259	171
Ionian Islands	66	85	31	117

This disease appears to care little for the police and to be guided by other laws entirely....The assumed protection of the troops at Malta, Gibraltar and Corfu is simply a myth. When we compare the results there with those among bodies of troops similarly situated at other warm climate stations, the balance is rather the other way, i.e. it is in favour of non-protection in the proportion of 9 to 12. If indeed the figures prove anything, they prove that restriction by police inspection of these unfortunate women (climatic conditions being similar) tends rather to increase the disease.

The only way of dealing with the question, so far as present experience enables us to judge, is: first, as one of nuisance. The number of women can be reduced by suppressing brothels and punishing with the utmost rigour their keepers. This principle is recognized in matters of less importance, e.g. thieving. Thieving cannot be suppressed, and yet thieves, their trainers and resetters, are punished, although thieving is a much less injury to society than prostitution. The consequences of prostitution pass into the blood of generations. The sin of the father is visited on the child literally to the third and fourth generation. The evil is *irremediable* as regards health....

It has been stated on good authority that army medical officers are wanting in knowledge of the treatment of this disease, and that this accounts for the high percentage of constantly sick in military hospitals and the extent of invaliding from syphilis. The remedy is to give more attention to the study of the disease at the Army Medical School.

To sum up—up to the present time we have arrived at these conclusions: There is no proof that legal recognition of prostitution and police regulation are protective of the soldier's health. The most likely means of diminishing the disease (*not* the evil) are an extension of voluntary dispensary relief for the poor women to these as well as to other cases of disease, but, above all, the soldiers should be provided with every means of occupation and amusement to keep them out of mischief, the only rational remedy for *the evil*....No sanitary improvement will prevent syphilis. The sanitary improvement for syphilis is moral reform, not police regulation, while police regulation would involve authoritative recognition of prostitution, an evil greater than the thing itself.

Nightingale attempted to enlist the then Member of Parliament, later Prime Minister, **William Gladstone** as a supporter (he was a progressive generally and had helped in "rescue work," the attempt to rehabilitate prostitutes). In April 1862 she sent him a copy of the briefing paper with the following letter.

Here Nightingale evidently felt that she had to explain how she, a respectable woman, was conversant with the subject. Gladstone, however, did not help on this issue, although he would be appealed to from time to time by the organized forces for abolition. Martineau as late as 1871 considered that he was at least with their movement in spirit (see her letter above). Perhaps he was. He was also a cautious politician well aware of how contentious the issue was, and that there were far more votes to be lost on it than gained. Gladstone also resisted appeals to give leadership to the anti-vivisection campaign.

Text: Nightingale letter April 26 1862, Gladstone Papers Add Mss 44398 folios 213-16:

There is a strong influence at work to introduce into our army the French system of police regulations and lock hospitals [places of compulsory treatment] in order to prevent the disease caused by vice. The enclosed paper I prepared at the request of the War Office. In India, it is wished to do the same thing for our troops. And in our Indian Sanitary Report (that Commission of which Lord Stanley is now chairman) I mean to reproduce the same figures—with this addition which I find in the "Replies" from the Indian stations. Those stations which were most eager to introduce lock hospitals, and which have done so, give in evidence that the number of cases is *not* diminished, although their severity appears to be so, by these measures.

You will be much surprised at my writing to you on this subject. You are known to have seriously considered the growing evil in civil life. And I have been told that you would not throw aside any evidence (on either side) which could be offered you. Unfortunately it is impossible for a life spent (as mine) in foreign and in English armies, in foreign and in English hospitals, for this subject *not* to have been forced upon it as a duty. Most unhesitatingly do I wish that the French police system of preventing unnecessary temptations to young persons, held out in the streets, could be introduced here. Most unhesitatingly do I say, "better 1000 times our hideous exposure of vice than the French, legalized, protected vice holding out the promise of protection where God has said that none is possible—*if* it is proposed to introduce the *whole* French system in this particular here."

The enclosed paper refers solely to that army. But much might be done in civil life to prevent vice. The French do not succeed even in preventing disease, while pretending to do so encourages vice. Pardon me for writing to you on such a subject. Perhaps you will be so good as to return my paper to me as I am not able to reproduce it.

The following letter, to Martineau, resulted in Martineau's active involvement on the issue, related above.

Text: Nightingale letter July 11 1863, Add Mss 45788 folios 208-11:

I forget whether I have ever mentioned this disagreeable subject to you before.[122] You perhaps know that for the last two years great efforts have been made by the War Office to see if the country would bear (that is, if the House of Commons was likely to listen to) any measure which would enable the system of French Medical Police to be introduced among the prostitutes of Aldershot and the other camps. Sir George Lewis was decidedly in its favour. Mr Higgins of the India Office proposed (or was proposed to) to "sound" the country by means of the *Times*. The enclosed paper was drawn up, at Sir George Lewis's own request, by me. But, if he was converted from that it was only by death. Since this death, Mr Higgins applied at the War Office to know what he was to do and this paper was shown him. But Dr Sutherland's name[123] was put to it. An extremely abusive correspondence followed, between him and Dr Sutherland, which I did not see.

I have corresponded with Lord de Grey [War Secretary] and Mr Gladstone (at their own request) about it. Mr Higgins, however, intends to pursue his purpose of "sounding" the world in the *Times*. There was a leader, vague and foolish, in the *Times* of the 19th (Wednesday) And since that there has been the enclosed letter in the issue of 22nd (Saturday) and another leader today, 25th, all three I believe by the same hand, and a letter by another hand today 25th. I am sorry to say that our director-general, a very silly fellow, is decidedly in favour.

I received a threatening (anonymous) letter from the Army Medical Department, Whitehall Yard—no need to trouble you with telling you how I knew its origin in case I continued my opposition. I have no idea (not that it much matters how they knew that I prompted the "opposition," or how they knew that paper was mine. Sir G. Lewis himself volunteered secrecy.) Of course, if I thought it right, I should go on all the more, for their threatening letters. But I don't. It is not a subject on which I *can* have much official knowledge as to head an opposition of this kind, with my name. However I may choose to go on working.

I have been asked to ask you to put the *Daily News* to watch the *Times*, and if necessary, to answer it. The enemy has not one tittle of evidence as to the success (in abating disease) in favour of the French Medical Police system, which would be admitted for one moment in a scientific enquiry or in a court of law.

---

[122] Nightingale had raised it in a letter of 1861 on sanitary measures for the United States Army.

[123] John Sutherland was a sanitary expert and close collaborator with Nightingale from Crimea onwards.

[PS] You know Captain Pilkington Jackson I reckon. He became aware at Aldershot of what was going on and said, "to make the plan complete, the prostitutes who survive five years of this life should have Good Service Pensions." And my brother-in-law, Sir [Harry] Verney said, "And Jackson should award them!" Certainly, this is logical.

Nightingale was concerned that her friend, Sidney Herbert, Secretary for War, had been taken in by the data provided him by his officials. "His figures are extravagantly wrong," she told Martineau. "The *Daily News* should certainly enlighten the public with a better principle."[124] The next attack, though, came from the *Saturday Review* and again Nightingale appealed to Martineau for help in countering it.

Text resumes: September 17 1963, folios 224-25:

I saw the *Saturday Review* and was amazed at its audacity, unless it is simple stupidity. The Malta case, as reported there, contains a statement said to be by the "Deputy Inspector General of Hospitals" leaving one to suppose that this refers to the army. It refers to the Navy, and is consequently a misquotation as you will see at p. 19 of the report I enclose. Therefore it does not touch the army question.

At p. 25 n, look at the table for troops. It contains eight years of inspection, during which the average admissions were 12.52 per cent. It contains one year—of inspection six months, of non inspection six months. For the six months inspection the average was 15.71 per cent per annum. For the six months of *non-inspection* the proportion fell to 11.02. And the next year of non-inspection it was 13.13.

This is the latest published information. This gives a very different account from the *Saturday Review*. I have marked in blue on the margin the most important passages. Please show up the *Saturday Review*. Please use the facts in the report and return it to me.

Another Nightingale letter to Martineau, with a report on syphilis in the army in India, gives her considered remarks on the medical aspects of the matter.

Text: Nightingale letter March 14 1864, Add Mss 45788 folios 253-56:

There is little literature on the subject. What there is relates solely to the *disease*, the mode of treatment. The present movement should be discussed under the head of public morality, public policy, public utility. Proof of all

---

[124] Add Mss 45788 folio 218.

three—overwhelming proof—ought to be produced. Medical *opinion* is absolutely worthless except as to the treatment. As to prevention, that is another thing. About that, they have given us no evidence at all. My evidence is (but all Paris police papers are kept so secret that I cannot produce any) that the Paris police, the only people who know anything about it, state that there the disease among the prostitutes is very small, among the men is very much *increasing*; that, in thousands of cases among *men* examined and traced at great expense, *not one* was traced to a diseased woman. The act of vice between a man and a prostitute, even not diseased, seems to produce the disease, but not invariably (no more that everybody catches smallpox under bad sanitary conditions) in the man.

Oh that a medical man would observe, as I have observed, in Paris! There, where the perfection of medical police exists, are the worst forms of disease among men—married men—! If Paris civil life were to be sent to hospital as our soldiers are, half Paris would be in hospital. The reason is that vice has been made prevalent there by the fancied immunity from disease, to a degree we have no idea of.

The *Times* letters are not worthy of notice. They are merely medical opinion. If, after careful *statistical* enquiry, there were proof to show benefit, there would still be left the questions of policy and morality. As regards soldiers, until we have provided men with rational means of work and recreation for their spare time what can we expect but dissipation and disease?

I am afraid there is too much reason to fear what the government may do. I understand Mr Robert Lowe has told the Cabinet he would willingly propose (in Parliament) an Act for a Medical Police *for the whole country* after the Paris fashion. We are not idle—I sent all your former *Daily News* articles (cut out and pasted) to Lord de Grey.

In April 1864 Nightingale learned of the preparation of a bill for Parliament. She was then carrying out an enquiry "by which I hope at least to procure a clause punishing all procurers and solicitors and also to call the attention of the House of Commons to the fact that justices won't convict even on the existing law against 'bawdy houses.'"[125] Late in May she advised Martineau of the content of the second draft of the bill. At this point she still thought that the legislation would not go through: "I don't believe any House of Commons will pass this bill. Any honest girl might be locked up all night by mistake by it."[126]

The bill was introduced in June, 1864 and passed in July with scarcely any debate. The correspondence shows that Nightingale was active behind the scenes criticizing provisions, pointing out loopholes and arguing forcefully

---

[125] Add Mss 45788 folio 163.

[126] Add Mss 45788 folio 269.

against the government's approach. A letter to her MP brother-in-law, Sir Harry Verney, a loyal ally in many political struggles, is indicative:

> No copy of the amended "Contagious Diseases" bill has been sent me. But a copy, left for a few minutes at the War Office, shows that they have avoided our original strictures but by placing the whole female population of the towns (in the act) at the mercy of the Inspector of Police—and with nothing but a pecuniary compensation for mistake!!!![127]

It seems that Nightingale was successful in mitigating the legislation. A comparison of the original bill and the act as passed shows a significant limiting of police powers.[128] Harry Verney had earlier suggested a royal commission on prostitution but Nightingale thought it would not help and the idea was dropped. Nightingale continued to argue that the proposed legislation would not do what it was intended—reduce disease—and that it would, for the first time, legitimate prostitution in England. She was all too aware that the existing legislation on prostitution was not enforced, and that the proposed legislation had the same loopholes with regard to prostitution organized through beerhouses.

When the women opposing the acts were unable to get press coverage for their side of the issue, Nightingale helped. For example the *Pall Mall Gazette* published a letter (January 25 1870) by Elizabeth Garrett supporting the acts but declined a response by Josephine Butler and Elizabeth Blackwell—the "conspiracy of silence." Nightingale succeeded in getting two letters, by "Justina," into the same journal (March 3 and 18 1870), both with vigorous refutations of Garrett's arguments and data showing no good effect from the acts medically. Both letters show Nightingale had lost none of her commitment to the cause.

> "That you could write such a letter shows how this electioneering, hurry and excitement unfits you for writing." Helen Taylor to John Stuart Mill[129]

HELEN TAYLOR (1831-1907)

Helen Taylor was born, in London, just before her mother, **Harriet Hardy Taylor**, met John Stuart Mill, with whom she became a close friend and

---

[127] Nightingale copy of letter, July 1864, Wellcome Institute.

[128] Amos, *Comparative Survey* 423-35. Amos gave no credit to Nightingale or any of the women opponents of the legislation in this long work, although his position was similar.

[129] Taylor letter November 12 1868 item 53 folio 149.

collaborator, and whom she married a respectable two years after her husband's death. Helen Taylor and her two brothers thus grew up in a household in which the forms of marriage were observed, but her mother's soul-mate and intellectual co-worker was Mill. As a young woman Taylor pursued a career as an actress, using a stage name, Miss Trevor. She won serious parts in provincial companies and toured in the north of England, but never won critical success or a living from it. Her mother supported her financially.

On her mother's death in 1858 Helen Taylor took on many of the duties as research assistant and secretary to Mill, especially on the suffrage cause. She drafted much of his correspondence.[130] She published essays herself and edited his famous "Subjection of Women" essay. Helen Taylor shared Mill's concern for land reform. She was an organizer and frequent speaker for the English branch of the Irish Ladies' Land League as well as being a leading member of the Land Reform Union. Later in life she took up the "social purity" cause, including abolition of the Contagious Diseases Acts.

Helen Taylor shared her mother and Mill's fondness for the south of France. Taylor, who inherited the Mill house in Avignon, used it as a summer residence and spent many of her retirement years there. She followed French politics and wrote on French social and political issues. Mill entrusted Taylor with his literary legacy. She edited his *Autobiography* and his essays on nature and religion. She was evidently difficult to deal with as literary executrix and Mill's correspondents or their literary executors had to press for the return of letters they wanted to publish. It seems that Taylor suppressed at least four of Mill's letters to her. These are missing from the correspondence held at the British Library of Political and Economic Science and hence the Mill *Collected Works*, but are referred to in her letters to him that are extant. The four letters concern an incident in Mill's second election campaign, 1868. The reason why is evident in her letter below, castigating Mill unmercifully for, she thought, giving way on the issue of freedom of religion. He protested and she had to admit that she had over-reacted.

Taylor served for many years on the London School Board. She was first elected in 1876, leading the polls, after a stormy campaign. She was triumphantly re-elected in 1879 and 1882. She worked for the abolition of school fees and corporal punishment, for the provision of school meals and shoes for needy children, for smaller classes and better equipment. An able public speaker, in 1885 she audaciously ran for Parliament, at a time women did not even have the vote! She put on a lively campaign as a radical candidate, but the returning officer refused her nomination papers on election day. Her platform included such feminist demands as the repeal of the Contagious Diseases Acts, custody rights for mothers and the prevention of war. One example of her campaign literature is excerpted below.

---

[130] See Mill, *Collected Works* vol. 33 for a list.

Although her mother and step-father got no closer to socialism than some sympathy for some aspects of it (notably Mill's concern for land reform) Taylor actually joined a socialist party. She became a member of the executive of the Democratic Federation, forerunner of the Social Democratic Federation and in turn a forerunner of the British Labour Party.

Taylor published numerous articles in progressive journals and edited the posthumous works of **H.T. Buckle**. She was generous in her support of many causes. Her tombstone, in the cemetery in Torquay, is appropriately engraved "She fought for the people." There has yet to be a full-length biography although considerable material is available both on her life and of her writing.[131]

Government—Extension of Suffrage

Taylor's "Personal Representation" was an unsigned review article in the liberal journal, *Westminster Review*, founded by **James Mill**, J.S. Mill's father. As was the custom at the time, the article gave ample scope for the reviewer's own views; there is actually little on the ostensible subject, Thomas Hare's *The Election of Representatives*, 1865. Britain's "great reform bill" had been passed in 1832. The country by early 1867 was in full debate about the next extension of the franchise, to the working class, which was achieved later in the year. Taylor's article then was an ardent plea for the extension. She would devote years of her life to the next great extension: the vote for women. This article shows how Taylor first developed her arguments for a group to which she did not belong, the working class, before applying the same principles to the one to which she did, women. This echoes the experience of an earlier generation of anti-slavery activists, who later transferred their militancy, and skills, to equality rights for women. The article rehearses arguments that would be used for decades hence in the debate on the vote for women, which of course was not achieved in Britain until 1917, and then only partially.

A major argument against extension of the franchise had to be demolished, namely the danger of "class legislation," that the interests of the numerical majority, the working class, might overpower the interests of the nation as a whole (146). Taylor took her refutation of this argument the next step to a positive statement that "the interest of the majority of the nation must surely be the interest of the nation itself" (148). She supported the system of representation advocated by Hare because it would secure the representation of the largest possible majority. In this article she argued, reasonably enough, but contrary to most of her class, that if the great mass of the English nation believed that current property institutions were unjust that would constitute strong evidence that change was needed for the public good (149).

---

[131] See the entry in the *Dictionary of National Biography* 483-85. Her papers are in the Mill-Taylor Collection at the British Library of Political and Economic Science); journal publications are listed in *The Wellesley Index to Victorian Periodicals 1824-1900* 5:765.

Text: Taylor, "Personal Representation":

In spite of some few well-paid and prosperous optimists who assert that we are all so well off already that none of us could possibly be better off under any other than our present system, there is a widely-spread impression in all ranks and in every part of the country that some change in our political system is imminent and that it must be in the direction of democracy....We have but to glance at the events of the last forty years to see that everything at the present time conduces towards a general feeling in favour of political reform and against mere conservatism as such. Thirty years ago an important measure was carried through [the Great Reform Act of 1832], which was only an instalment of the reform that had long been thought necessary by the most enlightened politicians. This measure succeeded perfectly so far as it went, its working was thought satisfactory by those who had most opposed it at first, and it only fell short of the wishes of those who at the time it was passed would have desired something more....

Each class in England as it has, by the natural progress of civilization...advanced to a consciousness of its own condition and a comparison between itself and others has in turn demanded to be admitted to a share in the government. Each in turn has been admitted and the country has grown more powerful and the population more contented as the basis of freedom has gone down lower and spread out wider....The fact that [universal, male suffrage] exists in the only countries that rival us in power, wealth and general prosperity, or the fact that these nations are, since its adoption, rapidly equalling and in some points outstripping us in the advance we had gained during centuries of superior civilization and freedom, does not seem so sure to be taken into account in our speculations....

In all discussions on the probable effects, either of universal suffrage or of a very wide extension of the franchise, the point upon which most attention has been fixed is the danger of class legislation, legislation, that is, in favour of the real or supposed class interests of the most numerous class in the country. Great importance is attached to the danger that class interests may overpower in the minds of the numerical majority of the nation the united interests of the nation as a whole, and even those of the most numerous class itself if considered, not in antagonism to some other class or classes, but with due regard to its share in the interests of humanity in general. It is argued against any thorough political representation of the whole people that in the present state of England the population is divided by so sharply-defined a line between employers and employed that the feelings and interests created by the distinction may be expected to surpass all others in force, while the division is so numerically unequal that, if political power is distributed according to numbers, one side will be able to oppress the other....On some of these questions the interests of the working classes are supposed to be at least apparently antagonistic to those of the employers, and it is presumed that the working classes are, and are likely to remain, too ignorant to know their own real interests or to be capable of understanding the laws of supply and demand, or the importance of encouraging the accumulation of capital 145-47).

It may well be doubted whether the dreaded omnipotence of the working classes would be more fatal to the future prosperity of the country than the continued preponderance in our government of the idle and frivolous men whom our present system has a tendency to bring to the top, who, while their character and position generally preclude them from either knowing the wants or caring for the fate of the great mass of suffering humanity that constitutes their fellow countrymen, are too prejudiced to look at any subject from a philosophical point of view and too indolent to examine into any in all its bearings.

Such men as these, who have constituted the majority of the House of Commons (and a still larger majority of the House of Lords), are utterly ignorant of the very grounds on which political science must be built. Too limited in their mental powers to grasp effectually even any ready-made theory, they also have not present to their observation the realities of human life. Shut up within those barriers of comfort and luxury by which our well-to-do classes screen off the real facts of life, possessed of that sort of education...[in which] their knowledge of the world is confined to one very limited class of one nation and of one period, if they do not care for the interests of any other their best excuse is that they are not, properly speaking, aware of the existence of any other. Foreigners, or the working classes, are to them like women, not exactly fellow creatures but a kind of animal whom they have never dreamt of considering as on a level with themselves, nor, therefore, as altogether human. Hence such monstrous anomalies as our game laws and marriage legislation and the fatuous exhibitions of unconscious want of principle which often take place in discussions of the House of Commons on foreign policy. If one class must legislate for another, it is not the mere gentlemen class that should legislate for the workers, since neither by numbers nor utility have they so good a claim to be considered first....

It is usual for admirers of things as they are in this country to appeal to results, to say how rich, how powerful, how prosperous England has grown to be under the government of these mere gentlemen! Nothing could better show how limited is their knowledge of the world and of history....The paternal despotism of Austria can point to the population of a large part of its dominions happier, more moral, more intelligent than any we can show in the most favoured districts of England, and we should seek in vain under its government for misery and demoralization greater than is to be found in our large cities. The democratic government of the free states of America has bestowed upon the people an amount of education which makes them the most economically productive people in the world, and therefore must make them, even without other advantages, the richest. The mixed and incessantly changing government of France has not prevented that nation from being at least as powerful as our own....

When we look closely into the theory that the government of the nation cannot be safely given to the whole nation because it will then be governed according to the interests or wishes of the majority, the first objection that strikes us is that the interest of the majority of the nation must surely be the interest of the nation itself....When once the wishes of the largest possible proportion of the population are known, on what grounds can it be maintained that it will not be for their good to carry them out?...Would not the fact that the great majority of a civilized people agree in desiring some particular measure afford in itself a strong presumption that that measure would be desirable for them?

Let us suppose, for example, that the great mass of the English nation had arrived at the opinion that the present foundations of property are injurious to the welfare of the greater part of the community. We take it that this fact would be in itself strong evidence that there was something amiss in the laws of property as at present existing and that some alterations in them...would be for the public good....We know it will be at once answered that any attempt to meddle with the laws of property would be, in the supremest degree, an instance of mischievous class legislation. We shall be told that in such a case all who have property would be on one side and all who have none on the other, and that therefore...for those who have no property to legislate for their own interests instead of allowing those who have property to legislate for theirs, would be gross partiality and utterly ruinous to the general interests....

[Yet] it is not true that opinion would always follow external circumstances, for there are and always have been...many rich people whose sympathies are with the poor and poor people who sympathize with the rich. But putting this aside and supposing...that people would be guided in their judgment of institutions solely by their own experience of them, does it not appear that that which is condemned by the unanimous experience of the great majority is not likely to conduce to their happiness? Is it not by uneasiness in their present circumstances that people are led to seek for better, and if we eliminate the action of discontent from political life do we not shut out the very means through which by the laws of human nature, if not of animal life, all amelioration is procured, either individual or social?...

If we believe that the laws of human nature tend towards progress, or at least that mankind will do well to act on that hypothesis till they have exhausted every possible experiment that can establish its truth, we can scarcely avoid the conclusion that the voice of the majority will most effectually secure the main object of government, the comfort of the governed, if only because each individual knows best what he himself likes....If the object of government is the happiness of the largest possible number of those governed, and if people generally know their own business best, it follows that the ends of government will be most effectually carried out where the largest number can be got to concur in it (147-50).

Government—Land Ownership

Helen Taylor was evidently a more lively and gifted speaker than her illustrious, earnest step-father John Stuart Mill. Newspaper accounts typically record that her speeches were well received and the selection that follows is no exception. Taylor shared the cause of land reform with Mill and had worked on it with him as she had the status of women. Mill continued to work, write and speak on both causes to his death in 1873. Taylor was a disciple continuing the work and giving full credit to her predecessor. Neither Mill nor Taylor accepted such key socialist objectives as public ownership of industry. Yet both held strong views on public ownership of land. Taylor knew and corresponded with the American progressive Henry George, advocate of the single tax on land as the most equitable and efficient form of taxation. Her discussion of the fundamental importance of land for all production is reminiscent both of the pre-revolutionary physiocrats of France and her American contemporary.

Taylor's speech set out the problem of gross inequalities in land ownership in England, yet the absolute dependence of all on the land for the necessities of life. The issue, as well, was a good one for women. Taylor adduced numerous arguments and examples to make the case for the people's right to land. What Parliament had improperly taken from the people it could in turn restore, although here, with the Land Nationalization Society, she advocated full compensation to the current owners. The text is a consolidation of two newspaper accounts.

Text: Taylor, "Land for the People," *Darwen News* November 6 1886 and *Northern Daily Telegraph* November 4 1886:

This question of the right of the nation to own the land upon which it dwelt is no new question. Like all such questions it has long been before the thinkers and readers of the nation. It has not been fifty years since my dear step-father, in one of his earliest writings, published words which they might accept as the charter of the land question. He said, "that the land which no man made, no man had a right to own," and that "the land which was necessary for the existence of all could not be justly monopolized by the few." It might interest some...to know that these were the opinions of Coleridge, and that it was in his article on Coleridge[132] that John Stuart Mill laid down those two principles.

Mr Mill did not vary in the course of his life from those two principles, for the last time he appeared in public was at a meeting in St James's Hall, in

---

[132] Mill, *Collected Works* vol. 10.

favour of asking that the state should have the unearned increase in the value of the land. At that time that opinion was held to be extremely revolutionary; to-day it was upheld as quite a mild measure by those who would not go so far as the nationalization of land....In another thirty years we should find our Prime Minister thinking nationalization quite a mild measure.

The land which was necessary for all could not justly be monopolized by a few. We must consider how literally and practically true it is that the land is necessary for all. Is there anything that passes our lips as food, is there any article of clothing that we put on, is there anything we need to cover us as a home or house which does not come from the land? There is no article of food, drink or clothing, from the apparel of the humblest to the much more useless robes of state and of the House of Peers—all come from the land. That being so, is it not plain enough that if all those things upon which life depend come from the land, and it alone, those who own the land are practically masters of the people, and the latter are their slaves? We are practically as dependent upon the earth for our existence as the new-born babe is upon its mother.

There are 30,000,000 inhabitants in the United Kingdom, and the landowners are much fewer than 30,000. What 30,000,000 people have to live upon to-day is practically owned by less than 30,000 people. We have got so used to this state of things now in England that we have come to regard it as the natural order of things. It is neither natural nor right and is only peculiar to England. More than that, it is illegal and unconstitutional. In feudal times, when William the Conqueror distributed land he did not vest it in his followers.

Lawyers used to deny it, but I do not think there is a lawyer left in England so ignorant as to venture to deny it to-day. They have found in indubitable language that it is the law of England that no man can own the soil of England. Own any absolute property! How came it about? They venture to claim a right which does not belong to them. Sir Henry Maine asked in one of his most valuable books, "How comes it that while it is indisputable that the land of England under the feudal system was entrusted to landowners for the purposes of enabling them to fulfil public duties, and was entrusted to them to help the king as the representative of the state, how came it that the idea of private property had grown up?" That great eminent Conservative lawyer told them that change had probably come about by the mistakes of lawyers. Another sort of confiscation of the land of England took place at the time of Reformation....

Up to that time the land had been held by the old Church, and it was understood that one-third of the value of the land was devoted to the relief of the poor. The inhabitants of the property in Covent Garden and the surrounding district, which formerly was the site of a convent, would be very glad if the Duke of Bedford, who owned it, would give one-third for the relief of the poor. When King Henry wanted the lands of the church to distribute among his courtiers, he got them by law. He confiscated them by law but the landlords, who took the land, never took over also the duty of paying one-third of the rents to the poor.

Others had been perpetrated by fencing in of common land by the landowners, leaving them who thought their right was being infringed to resort to the law, a very expensive process for a poor man. I am conservative enough to wish that, as far as the land goes, we could go back to the old days. Those common lands should have been paid for to the poor people. The inhabitants round the common did not have a moral right to sell it, but they might have had a legal one. The commons were for the use of them and their descendants, and it was not fair for one generation to sell what was for the use of following generations....

Even in these days it was universally held that those to whom the king gave the land of England he gave it to them in trust....The whole of the landowners were entrusted with the care of the land which they held, but which they did not own...on condition of furnishing out of the rents the whole of the cost of the government and the defence of the nation. To-day they find them in the position in which they sometimes find fraudulent trustees; they have taken for their own property that with which they were entrusted as the property of others. They have done even more...for while they have taken as private property the public property of the nation, they have left the nation to pay the taxes for the payment of which they had formerly been entrusted with the land. How had all that come about?...By what the great poet called:

> The good old rule, the simple plan,
> That they shall take who have the power,
> And they shall keep who can.

Within the last few centuries, millions of acres of common lands have been enclosed without the shadow or pretext of law. The last...piece of common land in Yorkshire, the greater part of which was enclosed forty years ago, was enclosed only last year. Remember the last acre of the hereditary right of the people who lived there enclosed—stolen from them in 1885. There does not exist a landowner, great or small, in England who can give such clear historical evidence of legal right as the owners of those common lands could give. Therefore, when they were enclosed an act of theft was perpetrated as clear and distinct as if anybody were to take a handkerchief or purse out of my pocket.

We are the richest nation on the face of the earth...and the condemnation of our system of distributing those riches was that being the richest, our people suffered the most of any people. Members of Parliament and writers in newspapers would say that our system of common lands was a very good one for old times. It was suitable where the community was widespread, where the population was small and there was no stress of commerce, but it would not suit modern times....

In conclusion, what has been taken from the people by Act of Parliament can be restored to them by similar means; and while, in accordance with the principles of the Land Nationalization Society, they would treat the owners justly, compensating them for the land they held at its present value. We must take back the land which belonged to us and use it not for the caprice and profit of the few, but for the health and happiness of the whole people. It should not be done by any illegal or violent means, for no such means ever prospered. We have learned a lesson how the landlords did it, and we are not to do it as they have often done it—by theft. God forbid that the workers of England should ever descend to the morals of the aristocracy! Do it by law...take it legally back again....If the House of Commons could take from the people their clear rights ...the House of Commons could again take back the land and restore it to its proper owners.

Government—the Constitution of France

Taylor's concern in this article, which was published in a progressive journal, *Fortnightly Review*, was to deal not with the recent Franco-Prussian War and the suffering it caused, but with the underlying political situation that had led to it. The "political restlessness" of France she saw as being due to the incompatibility between town and country, effectively Paris and the provinces. The result was that no political system was given enough time for a fair trial. The French oscillated between wild revolution and apathetic submission to despotism. This instability made it vulnerable to attack.

So much of Taylor's description of the differences between Paris and the provinces will still seem pertinent. The political system should permit diversity, she argued, yet its rulers were passionate centralizers. Nor had centralism been in place long, for the despotism of the old regime was not systematic and had not lasted long enough to mould the people. Mme de Staël had recommended federal institutions for France in her *Circonstances actuelles*. Taylor here did also, either a federation of republics or even "free cities" as an experiment, a recommendation more recently of urban expert **Jane Jacobs** in *Cities and the Wealth of Nations*. Taylor acknowledged that the trend elsewhere in Europe, notably Italy and Germany, was for unity. But there was no reason why European politics should not run in opposite currents. A free nation like France could retrace steps taken in the wrong direction.

Text: Taylor, "Paris and France," 451-58:

The obvious cause of the political restlessness of France, which denies to any political system time enough for a fair trial is the incompatibility between town and country, and pre-eminently between Paris and the provinces. This is the reason why France oscillates between the wildest experiments of revolution and apathetic submission to despotic authority. At one time it is Paris which, urged on to desperation by the desire to make the most of its opportunities, strives during the few days at its command to commit the nation to principles and ideas utterly strange and repugnant to it. At another time it is provincial

France which, trembling lest Paris should be able to stir hand or foot, suffers itself to be bound in company with her by bonds infinitely tighter than it would think it necessary to endure were itself only in question.

On the one hand, a very large, and certainly the most energetic, portion of the Parisians are ardently desirous of trying the experiment of some socialist form of government. They cannot be brought into willing obedience to any other form, however mild and enlightened it may be. Nay, mildness and enlightenment are probably a positive disadvantage in their eyes, since such qualities may give a government a better chance of permanence. They wish as an ultimate object to abolish the institution of private property altogether. And this idea is no passing whim; it has grown with the growth of Paris. It is far more widely spread now than it was twenty years ago; under the Empire it spread and ramified in all directions. However chimerical it may seem to the majority of modern minds it has the sanction of many great thinkers of the past and it is in entire accord with many of the most intelligent and disinterested political men of modern France.

Socialism has, moreover, the power to arouse an amount of enthusiasm which nothing else appears able to call forth from Frenchmen of the present day, and it is extremely doubtful whether it will die out until it has been allowed a fair trial. The attempt to keep it down by physical force must be an ever-recurring cause of bloodshed and disorder. The provinces, on the other hand, are as ardently attached to the institution of private property as Paris is to socialist ideas. Cautious and patient, the country people of France would easily bear with almost any government rather than run the risk of war or revolution, but it is probable they would prefer a moderate republic or a monarchy to a "brilliant" empire, because they are shrewd enough to know that it is they who must pay the cost of the brilliancy....

Now in this apparent political deadlock between Paris and the provinces it is encouraging to those who look to human nature for the signs of the elements out of which future progress must be evolved to see how much more far-sighted are the people, and the representatives of universal suffrage, than the writers and politicians of France, for statesmen she has none. It is an encouraging evidence of the true value of a widely-extended suffrage that the majority of the men sent by the people to represent them in the National Assembly are strongly in favour of removing the seat of government from Paris.

Paris, in truth, however much to the holiday-making foreigner it seems to constitute France itself, does not in any sense whatever represent the France of the French. Paris is the great meeting place of foreigners in search of amusement; the French have the least sympathy with foreigners of any civilized people and are probably content with as little amusement as any people in the world. Paris is the great centre of extravagant expenditure; the French are the most frugal of people. Paris is the great solvent of family ties; the French are deeply attached to them. Paris, in fact, if it represents any part of French society at all, represents only one element in it, the young men, for whom indeed it is in some measure a huge university where they go up to graduate in vice....

The great misfortune of France...has been the passion for unity, a passion not shared by the mass of the people, who have always been and still are attached to their homes and their local customs (institutions they have none left), but a passion which, derived form the Catholic Church, has been fostered by French rulers for selfish objects, and by literary men as a subject for vanity and mistaken patriotism. This fatal passion, derived from the teaching of the Church and acting in the name of religious unity, deluged southern France with blood in the too successful effort to stifle religious liberty....

Popular instinct, far wiser than the limited foresight of her politicians, struggles to save France. On one point and on one point only, have Paris and the provinces shown signs of being of one mind: they both wish to be free of one another. A feeling is growing up in both quarters in favour, not of national separation, but of substituting a looser bond of union than that by which both are now cramped and stifled, one which should leave each free to choose its own government for itself....

I have myself asserted that there is no closer natural bond of union between the provinces of France than between those various portions of Italy and Germany which, until lately, were so sadly split asunder, and which have so lately been united amidst universal rejoicing. Why...if once the tight grip of that centralization which holds France together were relaxed, why might not these provinces which differ so much claim different institutions for themselves? Why should not the same liberty be accorded to the other great towns which is accorded to Paris, to make experiments in government and found new institutions for themselves?...Why not? Why should not France try the experiment of federal government if that is in harmony with the wants of the people?

Why should it not go further, and try the experiment of free cities, if by that means free play can be given to the various tendencies of its population and room for the expansion of their differing energies? If the idea seems startling and new it can only be from want of familiarity with history. So far indeed from its being chimerical or utopian, Italy and Germany and Belgium in its most flourishing days, witnessed the sight of great cities, centres of commerce and manufactures, governed, too, by strangely free and republican institutions for their times, planted in the midst of agricultural populations which were subject to princely government. If France as a whole desires a king, why cannot Paris and Lyons (not to speak of Marseilles, which is a seaport) be allowed to live in the midst of the kingdom of France as Bruges and Ghent lived and flourished, and were great centres of commerce....

One reason, apart from the mere repugnance to whatever is unaccustomed, why the idea of a federal France is likely to be rejected by many at first sight is that we have just been all rejoicing at the union of Italy into one nation and acquiescing in, if not rejoicing at, the closer amalgamation that is taking place in Germany. Our sympathies for the present have got into the habit of running into an anti-separatist channel. But...there is no reason at all why European politics should not run in two opposite and parallel currents....We ought to consider that the compact unity of France is premature; it was brought about not by the wishes of the various populations, but by the ambition of sovereigns and the scheming of statesmen....Its full completion is of comparatively recent date, for grinding as in many respects was the despotism of the ancien regime, it was not systematic and it fell far short of the minutely methodic levelling established since the Revolution...it has not lasted long enough to mould the people entirely to itself.

Materially, the centralization of France is probably more complete than the world has ever seen...morally it falls far short of that of Italy....A free nation may retrace the steps which it has taken in a wrong direction, and for France the experiment of federal republics, or of free cities within a monarchy or a federation of sovereigns, would at least have the advantage that it would be clouded with none of those associations of failure which darken the prospects alike of monarchies and republics, empires or constitutional governments, in that country which has shown itself restless under them all.

Government—Elections for Parliament

This letter from Helen Taylor to her step-father John Stuart Mill during the 1868 election campaign is most revealing about the relationship between the two and the pressures of electoral politics. Mill in fact lost that election, ending an eventful and productive three-year Parliamentary career. (He was glad to get back to regular writing and declined opportunities to run again.) The letter shows how isolated and ignorant of the political system even a well-informed woman could be. And, much as Taylor assisted her stepfather in his Parliamentary and other voluntary work, she did nothing to help him in the campaign; indeed she was not even in London but at the Mill-Taylor house in the south of France.

Mill had apparently answered a question about his religious beliefs in a way that riled Taylor. (Normally he refused to answer any questions on his religious beliefs or lack thereof.) Taylor erroneously understood that Mill had expressly denied his atheism and thought that he was capitulating to the religious conservatives. That he had not done so he evidently made clear in several letters back to her, but which are no longer available. Taylor's surviving letters show her to have been both relieved and slightly apologetic for having overreacted.

Note that, while Mill was still "Mr Mill" to her, Taylor was on sufficiently good terms to give him unsolicited advice, draft responses for him to use, berate him for what she thought he had said and to warn him about lost opportunities for the future, should he "attempt to take up a nobler and bolder" position! Mill had to cope with all this while running a difficult election campaign against a big-spending opponent, **W.H. Smith** (he of the book chain), who beat him.

Text: Taylor, Mill-Taylor Collection LIII item 53 folios 149-51:

Avignon, Thursday evening/12th November 1868
Dear Mr Mill:
I am very sorry you should have written such a letter in answer to the question about Bradlaugh as the one you enclose. It seems to me utterly unworthy of you, to speak mildly of it, and not to speak of its imprudence. That you could write such a letter shows how this electioneering, hurry and excitement unfits you for writing, and it seems to me the height of folly to go on varying your replies on such a topic instead of keeping as nearly as possible to one set form to everyone. I do not know which I dislike most—the assertion that to be called an atheist is calumny, that you are as much one as Gladstone is a Catholic, or that dignitaries of the Church of England have spoken for you!!! Surely to use such arguments is to sacrifice all that it is worthwhile to be elected for. Then you go on to say you are no more an atheist than all the working men of Northhampton who support Bradlaugh, and you defy him to find anything in your writings to justify the assertion. I cannot tell you how ashamed I feel. And you actually invite the publication of this letter which makes me literally blush for you and must know the opinion entertained of you by everyone who knows you and sees it.

I beg and entreat of you, refuse utterly to say one word on this topic except what you have already said. Copy as literally as you can the letter I dictated (which I enclose) about Bradlaugh, and what you yourself said at the former election about yourself. Refer people to that and refuse to say anything more. Do not disgrace yourself as an open truthful man; do not shut the door to all future power of usefulness on religious liberty by such mean and wretched subterfuges as this letter. Do not be drawn into saying one *fresh thing* great or small. This is what your opponents want you to do—they want you to go on talking till you have said something they can make use of....

If I speak and feel strongly about this it is because there is work to be done in it in future which you would be particularly fit to do. You ought not in a thoughtless hurry to answer a letter to take up a position which will be justly thrown in your teeth, if at a future time you should attempt to take up a nobler and bolder one.
Your affectionate
Helen Taylor

Taylor was one of the first women in the world to run for Parliament, in 1885, before there was legal provision for women even to vote, let alone serve as MP. (An American woman, **Victoria Woodhull** ran for the presidency of the

United States in 1870.) The campaign poster that is excerpted below is an extraordinary document, a feminist tract in an election in which no women had the vote. As well as giving the legal precedents justifying a woman taking a seat in the House, it gave a resounding endorsement of Taylor as a radical, defender of the poor and oppressed and exposer of corruption. Taylor's record was well known on all these scores from her years of service on the London School Board. Voters were now urged to elect a *woman*, representative of the womanhood of England, half the British people and "utterly unrepresented when laws are made." She would be a voice to demand the repeal of the Contagious Diseases Acts, fight for custody rights for mothers and protection of the victim's name in sexual assault matters.

Text: Jessie Craigen,"Vote for Miss Helen Taylor":

First, that she is a radical, not merely in name, but in heart. During her public career she has been in word and deed always true to the cause of the people. With courage that never quailed before the proudest men, and sincerity that never stooped to selfish ends, she has defended the poor and helpless against the oppressor, be he who he might. With patient labour she has unearthed jobbery [patronage] and corruption wherever she found it and dragged it into the full blaze of day. And what she has done on the School Board she will surely do in the House. Of course it is the interest of all the classes who live upon the labour of the poor to prevent her return by any means however base, but it is the interest of the working classes that she should go in at the head of the poll....

Secondly, return her because she is a *woman*, because while she will be a faithful servant to North Camberwell, she will be the noble and worthy representative of the womanhood of England. Remember that we are *half* the British people, and that we are utterly unrepresented when laws are made, laws which deal with our property, our children and our honour. Many of these laws are a scandal to a Christian country and they are so because no woman's voice is heard....We *need* an advocate in the House of Commons and we could *not* have a braver, a truer or a more eloquent one. In that house womanhood has been outraged by laws which, with cold brutality, made the daughters of the poor mere animal instruments to gratify the lusts of men. That degrading insult to us is still upon the statute book. Send up a woman from North Camberwell to give utterance in the senate for all the womanhood of the land, to the hot shame and anger which every woman feels at it. Give womanhood a voice in the House of Commons to demand the repeal of the Contagious Diseases Acts (Women).

Again, the wedded mother's right to her own child is totally denied by law. Again and again has the attempt to redress this wrong dropped from the nerveless grasp of an assembly of men in which no woman can be heard. Send up a woman from North Camberwell to plead for every married mother in this wide land, with the warm and tender love for little children which Miss Taylor has shown so often in her School Board work, and with the sympathy for women which a woman alone can feel.

Again, if some poor girl is outraged and question in the house is needful for the case...if the member who is to take it up wishes to satisfy himself by personal question of the genuine character of the case the sufferer has to tell her tale, to lay bare her shrinking shame of girlhood to a man. Send up a woman from North Camberwell who can hear the story with a woman's tenderness and speak of it with a woman's feeling of the wrong.

Yet again, working men, did you ever think how the political degradation of women *must* act on men? If the companions of your lives can take no share in your political aspirations, how hard it must be for you to maintain the high level of unselfish patriotism....You chain women to the ground; you chain yourselves to women and you become the prisoners of your own prejudice and folly. *Break* our fetters and you will melt your own....I appeal to you to listen to my words and vote for HELEN TAYLOR at the poll.

Peace, War and Militarism—Organization for Peace

Taylor's short essay, "War and Peace," not included here, dates from the time of the Franco-Prussian War but was only recently published in the *Collected Works of John Stuart Mill* (29:615-17). Her focus was quite different from Nightingale's, raising the need for alternative strategies to war. Means for conflict resolution without war were needed:

> The contemplation of all the brutal horrors of war, as well as of the extremely unsatisfactory way in which after all it settles disputes, irresistibly arouses the question why the disputes of civilized nations cannot be settled as those of private individuals are settled (29:615).

Taylor also refocused the question to that of the attainment of peace rather than avoidance of war, a point that would be frequently made by later pacifist writers. To us now she will seem to have been overly optimistic in her final point, that as plague, pestilence and famine decline, war will appear to be ever more exceptional as a cause of human suffering.

BEATRICE POTTER WEBB/BARONESS PASSFIELD (1858-1943)

The young Beatrice Potter[133] was introduced to sociology by a family friend, the sociologist **Herbert Spencer**. She imbibed his laissez-faire philosophy,

---

[133] On Webb see Dorothy Epstein Nord, *Apprenticeship of Beatrice Webb*; Barbara E. Nolan, *Political Theory of Beatrice Webb*; Lisanne Radice, *Beatrice and Sidney Webb*; Margaret Cole, ed. *The Webbs and their Work*, Carole Seymour-Jones, *Beatrice Webb* and my *Women Founders* 211-28.

shared by her wealthy business family, but changed her mind on acquaintance with the real problems of poverty. After working briefly as a voluntary rent collector for the Charity Organization Society she became a research assistant for the massive survey, *Life and Labour of the People of London*, conducted by **Charles and Mary Booth** (the latter was her cousin). This made Potter a "collectivist" in her terms, or a socialist convinced that profound institutional change was required, including substantial public ownership of industry, especially by municipal governments. This is described in Webb's *My Apprenticeship* as the acquisition of a "craft and creed," sociology and socialism. *My Apprenticeship*, published 1926, covered Webb's life to her marriage to **Sidney Webb** in 1892. *Our Partnership*, published posthumously, relates the years of collaboration from then on. Both are substantially based on Webb's diaries.

The two Webbs published some twenty books and together helped to found the British Labour Party, the London School of Economics and the *New Statesman and Nation*. Beatrice Webb was a dedicated journal keeper throughout her life. Four volumes of her diary have been published and there are separate volumes on the Webbs' travels in Asia, Australia, New Zealand and the United States, mainly based on her journals.[134] Beatrice Webb also assisted her husband in his political career, initially as a London County Councillor, later as a cabinet minister in the first Labour government. He became Baron Passfield to serve as minister; she did not like and did not use the title. The journal records such events as Beatrice Webb and George Bernard Shaw "pulling the vote" on election day. The Webbs worked together on the Minority Report on the Poor Law; she was the appointed member, but he did most of the writing.

Beatrice Webb had worked out her philosophical approach to the social sciences before her marriage to Sidney. Her early methodological papers are available both as appendices to her *My Apprenticeship* and as part of *Methods of Social Study*, edited by Sidney Webb in both their names. A 1906 paper to the Sociological Society in London provides a good statement of her basic principles. She pioneered participant observation in the 1880s.

Government—Labour Legislation

Beatrice Webb made the mistake, as a young woman, of opposing the vote for women. She never did actively work for suffrage although she later acknowledged her error. Instead she served the cause of women by working for protective legislation for women workers. This was then a controversial issue within the women's movement. Liberal women, consistent with their laissez-faire theory, opposed protective factory legislation for depriving women of the

---

[134] *The Diary of Beatrice Webb*; *The Webbs' Australian Diary*; *Visit to New Zealand in 1898*; *Beatrice Webb's American Diary*.

Theorists on Reform/Webb 219

right to compete freely for any job. Webb condemned this position sarcastically as the "high-minded anxiety to secure, for every working woman, the personal liberty of a householder with at least three servants."[135]. Reformers characteristically argue the practicality as well as the morality of their position. Webb insisted that cheap "sweated" labour was not good for the nation as a whole for it depends on its citizens and their children being healthy. In referring to humans being as much a part of a country's capital as its land, machinery and cattle, Webb was using the language of human capital theory before it became fashionable. She gave examples from the textile industry and coal mining, which had been two of the worst, and in which enormous improvements had been made by legislation and collective agreements. Both industries, she observed, expanded and thrived *after* the interventions of government and unions.

Text: Webb, "The Case for the Factory Acts":

It is well to begin this little book with a warning. When modern factory legislation was introduced a hundred years ago women did not concern themselves with such matters. Men did, and it is possible to prove, by the experience of a century, that they began with the best intentions, by making every mistake that could possibly be made on the subject. Now the women of today are no cleverer than the men of that time. The sole advantage they have over the men of the eighteenth century is their knowledge of what has happened during the nineteenth century. Unfortunately, some of the politically active women of today have not acquired that knowledge, do not even know that it is available. They are arguing exactly as the men of their class argued when they, too, had no experience to guide them. Accordingly they are making the same mistakes and laying down the same nihilistic "laws" with the same good intentions, and the same high-minded anxiety to secure, for every working woman, the personal liberty of a householder with at least three servants.

My warning is, then, to form no conclusion until you know the facts....If you try to solve modern industrial problems by simply asking, with regard to each proposal for industrial legislation, is its apparent public principle one of your own private principles you will be doing exactly what has been done before by all the men who have gone hopelessly astray on the subject....Such straying...has led men, and is now leading women, passionately opposed to tyranny and "sweating" to spend their lives in fighting the battle of the tyrant and the sweater against his victims. And it has led...those who, caring less for individual hardships...to resist every measure for the invigoration of England's

---

[135] Webb, "The Case for the Factory Acts" 2.

industrial strength and the raising of her international prestige as an attempt to handicap her in competition with the nations who are still foolish enough to believe that their strength lies in the weakness and degradation of their workers.

At first sight any dictatorial interference by a government official between two private persons making an ordinary contract...seems an intolerable infringement of personal liberty. When the contract is one for the sale and purchase of labour, and the interference goes to the length of preventing the transaction from taking place unless certain conditions are complied with...may easily seem..a denial of [the labourer's] right to work and therefore his right to live. For this view there was, in the eighteenth century, high economic authority. "The patrimony of a poor man," says Adam Smith, "lies in the strength and dexterity of his hands, and to hinder him from employing his strength and dexterity in what manner he thinks proper, without injury to his neighbour, is a plain violation of this most sacred property." [*Wealth of Nations*, ed. J.R. M'Culloch:55]...

All these arguments against factory legislation are as self-evident to the ordinary man and woman of the upper or middle class as the statement that the sun rises in the East and sets in the West is to the man in the street. But exactly as our faith in the Ptolemaic system of the universe has been shattered by a more accurate observation of facts and by unravelling the connections between these facts, so has our faith in the good results of free competition in the labour market been destroyed by a more intimate knowledge of the life and labour of our working people and by a careful analysis of the actual process of bargaining between employer and wage earner. On the facts alone the weight of evidence is overwhelmingly against unfettered competition among wage earners for employment....[Instances of competition being curbed follow]

We must realize the essential and permanent inequality in bargaining power between the individual wage earner and the capitalist employer....The workman's freedom is delusive; where he bargains he bargains at a hopeless disadvantage and on many of the points most vital to his heath, efficiency and personal comfort he is unable to bargain at all (1-7).

If the employers in a particular trade are able to take such advantage of the necessities of their work people as to hire them for wages actually insufficient to provide enough food, clothing and shelter to maintain them and their children in health, if they are able to work them for hours so long as to deprive them of adequate rest and recreation, or if they subject them to conditions so dangerous or insanitary as positively to shorten their lives, that trade is clearly using up and destroying a part of the nation's working capital....Industries yielding only a bare minimum of momentary subsistence are therefore not really self supporting. In deteriorating the physique, intelligence and character of their operatives they are drawing on the capital stock of the nation. And even if the using up is not actually so rapid as to prevent the "sweated" workers from producing a new generation to replace them, the trade is none the less parasitic....

One of the common forms of industrial parasitism is that in which an employer, without imparting any adequate instruction in a skilled craft, gets his work done by boys or girls who live with their parents and work practically for pocket money. Here he is clearly receiving a subsidy...from the parents, that is, from the industry by which the parents live, which gives his process and economic advantage over those worked by fully-paid labour (21-23).

The two great industries which, at the beginning of the nineteenth century, were conspicuous for the worst horrors of sweating were textile manufacture and coal mining. Between 1830 and 1850 Parliamentary inquiries into these trades disclosed sickening details of starvation wages, incredibly long hours and conditions of work degrading to decency and health. The remedy applied was the substitution, for individual bargaining between employer and operative, of a compulsory minimum set forth in common rules prescribing standard conditions of employment [some imposed by legislation, some by collective agreements]....Nor has the remedy for sweating ruined the trades to which it has been applied...but is positively advantageous to the trade concerned....Paradoxical as it may seem, the mere existence of compulsory minimum conditions of employment, below which no employer and no workman may descend, directly improves the employer, improves the operative and improves the processes of manufacture (36-39).

Fabian tracts were an important means of disseminating critical analyses of social problems and new ideas for reform. The Fabian Society itself was formed in 1885 and Sidney Webb was one of the earliest members. Beatrice Webb joined herself and wrote a number of tracts for it. This one, from March 1918, or near the end of the Great War, reflects the Webb interest in "reconstruction." Neither Webb was much involved in issues of the war itself but both were keen to take advantage of the new spirit to bring in fundamental reforms. Beatrice Webb had been a member of the Royal Commission on the Poor Law, 1909. She and Sidney Webb published a famous minority report calling for fundamental reform of the whole approach to social welfare. Here she was returning to a familiar issue but now expecting more support for their ideas.

Webb's opening lines, a paraphrase of Ecclesiastes, urges the timeliness of reform: "For everything there is an appropriate time." Her first argument was that the people should be seen as citizens, not paupers. To replace the Poor Law and its paltry and demeaning handouts there was to be collective provision for all, from schools, books and even food for hungry children, hospitals, maternity and child care institutions and pensions for the aged, all with no stigma of pauperism. Webb then went on to outline the nature of the institutions required. The similarities with Nightingale's (then still unpublished) memorandum on the subject are remarkable. The one area where

Webb has gone further was in provisions for the unemployed (318). She stressed the need (in a section not excerpted here) to bring in the reforms without waiting for the war to end. Timely provision for the unemployed was crucial, for there would be great industrial dislocation as soon as peace was declared.

Text: Webb, "Abolition of the Poor Law"[136]:

The English Poor Law, which dates from 1601, was in its time a notable expression of the right of the individual in distress to be helped by the community, and of the duty of the community to rescue from want even the weakest of its members. But the Poor Law and its administration became subject to grave abuses, which were drastically cut down in 1834. Unfortunately the system then adopted was one of limiting the public assistance to the "relief of destitution," of refusing to help until "destitution" had set in, and of a rigid "deterrence" of all applications for relief by making "pauperism" a disgrace, treating applicants harshly and discourteously, surrounding the relief by deliberately unpleasant conditions, such as "the offer of the workhouse" and the imposition of penal tasks like picking oakum or "the stone yard." The result has been that the Poor Law is universally hated....

Meanwhile there has been growing up, especially under the town councils of the most progressive great cities, another system of meeting our needs, not as paupers eating the bread of charity, but as citizens supplying ourselves collectively with what would be beyond our reach as individuals. Through the Local Education Authority we provide for our children, not only schools and teachers, but also books for them to read, if they are ailing also medical treatment, if they are hungry even food. Through the Local Health Authority we provide hospitals for such of us as are ill and help in maternity and infancy, not as a matter of charity, but as a matter of the public health in which all citizens, rich or poor, are equally concerned. Through the Old Age Pensions Committee we issue pensions (as yet far too small in amount and beginning too late) to such of us over seventy as are in need of them, as matter not of favour but of legal right. In all these and many other municipal services there is no "stigma of pauperism" and nothing disgraceful (3-4).

The Local Government Committee of the Ministry of Reconstruction proposes that: (a) The entire Poor Law, with all the orders of the Poor Law Division of the Local Government Board, the whole system of "deterrence" and all "taint of pauperism" should come to an end; (b) The workhouse, the stone yard and the casual ward should be abolished; (c) The Boards of Guardians should cease to exist...Thus the whole Poor Law system would be wound up and finally got rid of...But we must take care that all the people now

---

[136] Reprinted in Sally Alexander, *Women's Fabian Tracts* 313-23, with another Webb Fabian Tract on women and the factory acts.

dealt with under the Poor Law are provided for, without disturbance or the break of a single day, not only as well as they now are, but better, and that their legal right to maintenance is preserved....

It would be the duty of the town council, acting through its health committee, to take under its care and to provide for under the public health acts...all the sick and infirm persons (including maternity, infancy and the aged needing institutional care) whom the Board of Guardians now provides for....It would be the duty of the town council, acting through its education committee to make...all provision required for the children now under the Poor Law who are able to attend school....It would be the duty of the council, acting through its asylums committee...to make all the necessary provision for persons of unsound mind....

What is now proposed by the Government Committee is that the whole business of dealing with the unemployment problem in each town should be placed, with new statutory powers, in the hands of the town council, which will be required to appoint a "Prevention of Unemployment and Training Committee," *on which organized labour is to have a special right to be represented.* This committee will be expressly empowered to prevent the occurrence of unemployment by keeping the total demand for labour in the town as far as practicable at a uniform level, to find situations for men and women, to provide maintenance and training for any who are unemployed, to provide village settlements if required, to assist towards migration or emigration of families wishing to move elsewhere....As to the workhouse, the casual ward and the stone yard will have come to an end with the Poor Law itself; there can be no reversion to these barbarisms....

There remains the large class of persons in need, for whom the best form of help is a weekly payment to "maintain the home." Widows with young children, old people who cannot get decently looked after, men and women crippled by chronic disease, workers left temporarily without resources through some misfortune, how harshly and cruelly they have often been treated by the Poor Law Guardians...In this way all the people now looked after by the Boards of Guardians under the Poor Law as paupers would henceforth be looked after as citizens by the town council itself through its several committees (5-8).

The *Decay of Capitalist Civilisation*, 1923, is the most theoretical book by the normally practical and applied Webbs. Here they address the flaws of capitalism as a system, or a "civilization" as they put it. They had to convince people not only that capitalism was inadequate as an economic system, but that fundamental, systemic change was possible. That social institutions were not natural and immutable, but human conventions, was a lesson Beatrice Webb learned for herself in the early years of evolving her "craft and creed." To reach this understanding she had first to reject the sociology taught her by her mentor, Herbert Spencer. He had held that government intervention was an unnatural intervention into the workings of society. Webb countered that all social institutions were conventional, economic as much as political.

The Webbs conceded, as had other socialists like Marx and Engels, that capitalism had been materially successful for increasing populations (3). But by the middle of the nineteenth century it had been beaten hopelessly by the social problems of its own creation (4). Decay had begun before capitalism reached maturity. The Webbs could not predict the successful adaptations capitalism would make to compete with the communism of the Soviet Union and China. They unambiguously predicted an end to the capitalism they knew: "History will regard capitalism not as an epoch, but as an episode, and in the main a tragic episode, or Dark Age between two epochs" (94). The Webbs were only partially right in their predictions and dead wrong on some. Capitalism is very different from what it was in their day and nowhere near the centrally-organized socialism they sought but social programs, a strong public sector and (sometimes) Keynesian management of the economy. Environmentalists now would agree with them on the dangers of the profit motive to society, but for different reasons.

Text: Sidney and Beatrice Webb,"The Poverty of the Poor," *Decay of Capitalist Civilisation* 7-12 and 170-74:

The outstanding and entirely unexpected result of the capitalist organization of society is the widespread penury that it produces in the nation. A whole century of experience in the most advanced civilizations of Europe and America alike reveals this widespread penury as the outcome, or at least the invariable concomitant, of the divorce of the mass of the people from the ownership of the instruments of production and of the aggregation, which has everywhere occurred, of this ownership in a relatively small propertied class. It is of course not suggested that a low standard of livelihood and the imminent peril of starvation is peculiar to capitalism. In more primitive communities in which the instruments of production are held in common or are widely distributed among those who gain their livelihood by using them, chronic poverty and recurrent famines have been in the past, and are today, by no means uncommon. But in these backward societies the meagreness and insecurity of livelihood is attributable either to man's incapacity to control the forces of nature, as manifested in droughts, floods and diseases, or to the paucity of natural resources, such as the lack of fertile land and minerals, severity of the climate or the absence of applied science enabling men to use with efficiency the sources of wealth that exist. But the capitalist organization of industry confronts us with a paradox. The countries in which it has been developed in its most complete form enjoy great natural resources and have made great use of science in turning them to the service of man. Taking these nations as wholes, the aggregate wealth thus produced is relatively enormous....

The physical suffering, the accidents and the diseases that have been the concomitants of the capitalist system have not been its biggest evil. It is not in material things only that "the destruction of the poor is their poverty." To the hero on the ice field or the saint in the desert, the lack of adequate means of subsistence, combined with the utmost hardship, may be compatible with spiritual exaltation, individual development and the continuous exercise of personal initiative and enterprise. To the peasant cultivator and master craftsman of primitive communities, a flood, a drought, an epidemic, the murrain or the blight, though it produces devastation and famine, may create fellowship and stimulate energy. What modern industrialism destroyed, generation after generation, in those who succumbed to it, was the soul of the people. There is a moral miasma as deadly as the physical. Right down to our own day the dwellers in the slums of the great cities of Europe and America, actually in increasing numbers as one generation follows another, find themselves embedded, whether they will it or not, in all the ugliness, the dirt and the disorder of the mean streets....The destitution against which the socialist protests is thus a degradation of character, a spiritual demoralization, a destruction of human personality itself....

It is not until the inequalities have gone so far that they are beyond all reason that people begin to suspect that A's degradation is effect and not cause, and B's prosperity is cause and not effect. When a baby in one street owns a million pounds actually before it is born, and a woman who has worked hard from her eighth year to her eightieth is removed from another to die in the workhouse, eighteenth-century optimism begins to lose confidence.

Even when the optimism is staggered it does not surrender. It changes its ground and begins to argue that the poverty of the poor is the inevitable price of a general improvement in the condition of mankind. There seems to be no limit to the willingness of fortunate men, even men of high ideals and great devotion, to accept excuses for the suffering of other people, so long as this suffering seems to be necessary to the maintenance of the position or the interests of their class or race. There were men of exceptionally fine character and intellect among the slave-owning legislators of the Southern states of America who were...passionately convinced that slavery and the slave market formed the only possible basis for the social order that seemed to them indispensable to civilization (7-12).

We are thus brought to the conclusion that the failure of the reign of capitalism, as the principal form of the nation's industrial and social organization, must now be recognized and admitted. It is not merely this or that excess or defect that stands condemned by the world's experience. The making of pecuniary profit has proved to be a socially injurious and even a dangerous stimulus to activity. The very motive of pecuniary gain, on which Adam Smith taught the whole world to rely, is not one by which human action can be safely inspired. After a whole century of trial, the dictatorship of the capitalist for the purpose of private gain has failed to commend itself to the judgment of democracy throughout the world. Today the Christian Church is driven to proclaim its agreement with democracy. Addressing the English Church Congress in 1922 the Archbishop of York thus delivered the Christian judgment on the "vast system of beliefs and practices and policies, industrial, political, international...which we may roughly call Western civilization. It reached its zenith in the last century. It was admirably contrived for the production of wealth and power. With magnificent enterprise it yoked to its service the discoveries of science. It created and satisfied a thousand new demands of comfort and convenience. It called into being a vast industrial population. It stimulated patriotism by its belief in the survival of the strongest. But its motives, governing individuals, classes and states, were non-Christian self-interest, competition, the struggle of rival forces. Now these motives have overreached themselves. They are breaking the fabric which they built. Surely the truth of this is writ large in the outbreak of the Great War and perils of Europe today....If it is to be a blessing, not a blight, to mankind its motives must be transformed"....

The socialist, whilst by no means despising full maintenance for himself and his family (and, in fact, demanding it for everyone), feels a profound dislike for greed of gain as the dominant motive; he demands that the "desire for riches" shall no longer be made the basis of our statecraft, no longer preached to the young as the guide to conduct, no longer applauded and honoured as conducive to the commonwealth....

What the establishment of a genuine co-operative commonwealth requires in the way of an advance in morality is no more than that those who have the gift for industrial organization should be, not saints nor ascetics, but as public-spirited in their work and as modest in their claims to a livelihood as our quite normally human scientific workers, teachers in schools and colleges, our whole army of civil servants of every degree and kind, municipal officers of every grade....This substitution of the motive of public service for the motive of self-enrichment will be imposed on our consciences by the moral revolution, which will make "living by owning" as shameful as the pauperism of the wastrel, and will, moreover, regard the exceptionally gifted man who insists on extorting from the community the full "rent of his ability" as a mean fellow, as mean as the surgeon who refuses to operate except for the highest fee that he can extract....

Even if the evidence on this point were not yet complete, the socialist would still strive for the substitution of fellowship for fighting, of professional ethics for competitive trading, of scientifically audited vital statistics for the test of pecuniary profit, because to him the state of mind that is produced by fellowship and the pursuit of knowledge, the society in which fellowship is the dominant motive and scientific method the recognized way is, whether or not it is materially better provided, infinitely preferable to that produced by the economic war of man against man and the social rancours, national and international, which are the outcome of such warfare (170-74).

This short excerpt from *The Break-up of the Poor Law*, 1909, boldly sets out a central component of the Webb case for the abolition of destitution. From the Minority Report on the Royal Commission on the Poor Laws and the Unemployed, the section presented here delineates an admittedly "utopian" scheme for eradicating unemployment. The Webbs argued no less than that it was "administratively possible...to remedy most of the evils of unemployment," given the will to do so. In the future, people would look back to "ignorant acquiescence" in the starvation and debilitation of the unemployed as their contemporaries looked at slavery, child labour in mines and factories and fever epidemics in slums.

Central to the Webbs' recommendation was the establishment of a National Labour Exchange, reduced hours of work, reduction of child labour and the provision of mothers' allowances. They proposed a works program for reforestation, land reclamation and coastal protection, to even out fluctuations in the demand for labour. Note that this proposal predates **John Maynard Keynes**'s anti-cyclical measures in *General Theory of Employment Interest and Money*, 1936, by a quarter of a century. There would be income support for the maintenance of those unable to obtain work, without loss of the franchise, on condition of their undertaking training. The report advocated eighteen recommendations, several of which are excerpted here. Some of the proposals not included were draconian, for example, detention centres for the reform of men convicted of vagrancy, begging and neglect to maintain their family.

Text: Sidney and Beatrice Webb, The Public Organisation of the Labour Market. *Break-up of the Poor Law*, Pt. II:

We have explained in the Introduction to a companion volume...how it was that a minority of the Royal Commission on the Poor Law and the Unemployed felt compelled to dissent from the conclusions of the majority with regard to the Poor Law and to present an alternative report covering the whole ground, concluding with an alternative scheme of reform. With regard to the unemployed, this minority considered the Majority Report as even more inadequate and reactionary than with regard to the Poor Law. To undo the work of the Unemployed Workmen Act of 1905, and to thrust back the necessitous workmen into the sphere of a resuscitated Poor Law Authority under a new name, seemed no solution of the grave economic and social problem of unemployment....

One thing at once emerges—the remedy will be neither simple nor obvious....It is time to take a lesson from the skilled artisan: to set ourselves really to understand the conditions of the problem and to adopt, deliberately, patiently and persistently, exactly those measures, and all those measures, that are necessary to remedy the evil....It is not too much to say that the morass of under employment and sweating in which the bottom stratum of the population is condemned to live is draining away the vitality and seriously impairing the vigour of the community as a whole. The continued existence and, we fear, the spreading of this morass does not infect alone those unfortunates whom it engulfs, and the rest of the wage-earning class who are always slipping into it. By the heavy charges that it imposes on us for poor relief, hospitals, police and prisons, it lays an unnecessary burden on those who are better off.

To those who look to the substitution of a deliberately ordered co-operative commonwealth for the present industrial anarchy, it will be obvious that no such collectivist community could stand for a year if it did not drain the morass (2:ix-xi). [The Webbs then argued that a nationally-organized labour exchange would be needed whether the economy was centrally-organized, as they hoped, or free market.]

UTOPIAN? This elaborate scheme of national Organisation for dealing with the grave social evil of unemployment, with its resultant able-bodied destitution, and its deterioration of hundreds of thousands of working-class families, will seem to many persons utopian. Experience proves, however, that this may mean no more than that it will take a little time to accustom people to the proposals, and to get them carried into operation. The first step is to make the whole community realize that the evil exists. At present, it is not too much to say that the average citizen of the middle or upper class takes for granted the constantly recurring destitution among wage-earning families due to unemployment, as part of the natural order of things, and as no more to be combated than the east wind. In the same way the eighteenth-century citizen acquiesced in the horrors of the contemporary prison administration and the slave trade, just as, for the first decades of the nineteenth century, our grandfathers accepted as inevitable the slavery of the little children of the wage-earners in mines and factories and the incessant devastation of the slums by "fever." Fifty years hence we shall be looking back with amazement at the helpless and ignorant acquiescence of the governing classes of the United Kingdom, at the opening of the twentieth century, in the constant debasement of character and physique, not to mention the perpetual draining away of the nation's wealth, that idleness combined with starvation plainly causes.

The second step is for the government to make a serious endeavour to grapple with the evil as a whole, on a deliberately thought-out plan. By the Unemployed Workmen Act of 1905, Parliament and the nation have admitted public responsibility in the matter. We may agree that the work of the Distress Committees has resulted in little, but the experiments of the last few years have definitely revealed the nature of the problem and the lines on which it can be dealt with. We have to report that, in our judgement, it is now administratively possible, if it is sincerely wished to do so, to remedy most of the evils of unemployment, to the same extent, at least, as we have in the past century diminished the death rate from fever and lessened the industrial slavery of young children. It is not a valid objection that a demonstrably perfect and popularly-accepted technique, either with regard to the treatment of the unemployed, has not yet been worked out. No such technique can ever be more than foreshadowed until it is actually being put in operation.

Less than a century ago the problem of dealing with the sewage of London seemed insoluble. Half a million separate private cesspools accumulated each its own putrefaction. To combine these festering heaps into a single main drainage system seemed, to the statesmen and social reformers of 1820 or 1830, beyond the bounds of possibility....In the same way, a century ago, no one knew how to administer a fever hospital; the eighteenth century "pesthouse" must, indeed, have killed more people than it cured. Yet it was only by establishing hospitals that we learnt how to make them instruments of recovery for the patients and of a beneficent protection to the rest of the community. To take a more recent problem, less than half a century ago, when millions of children in the land were growing up untaught, undisciplined and uncared for, it would have sounded wildly visionary to have suggested that the remedy was elaborate organization on a carefully thought-out plan. What has been effected in the organization of public health and public education can be effected, if we wish it, in the public organization of the labour market. We therefore recommend:

That the duty of so organizing the national labour market as to prevent or to minimize unemployment should be placed upon a minister responsible to Parliament, who might be designated the Minister for Labour....

That the function of the National Labour Exchange should be, not only (a) to ascertain and report the surplus or shortage of labour of particular kinds, at particular places; and (b) to diminish the time and energy now spent in looking for work, and the consequent "leakage" between jobs; but also (c) so to "dovetail" casual and seasonal employments as to arrange for practical continuity of work for those now chronically under-employed....

That, in order to secure proper industrial training for the youth of the nation, an amendment of the Factory Acts is urgently required to provide that no child should be employed at all below the age of fifteen; that no young person under eighteen should be employed for more than thirty hours per week; and that all young persons so employed should be required to attend for thirty hours per week at suitable trade schools to be maintained by the Local Education Authorities....

That we recommend these reforms for their own sake, but it is an additional advantage that they (and especially the halving of boy labour) would permit the immediate addition to the number of men in employment equal to a large proportion of those who are now unemployed or underemployed (2:323-25).

Government—Socialism in Canada

The short excerpt that follows comes from unpublished material in Webb's diary, from a trip to Canada with Sidney Webb in 1911. It shows that gems remain in the archives, despite the publication of numerous volumes. Webb's direct contact with Canada was limited to this one trip, yet her observations of materialism, Canadians generally, and British Columbia socialists particularly, not only ring true for the time she wrote them, but now, too.

Text: Beatrice Webb Diary:

They gave one the impression that every member of the Canadian Socialist Party was a misfit. How can you hope for a socialist party in a country where every man of ordinary health and capacity is a successful speculator in land values! Such socialists as there are, are of the impossibilist sect—talking loudly of "class consciousness" and revolution, intensely dogmatic and intolerant Marxists refusing to recognize anyone as a socialist that does not believe in a catastrophic revolution. Canada is the most depressing of countries for anyone who is *nothing* but a socialist (July 1911:7735).

What will Canada become? Our impression is that they are a people of more personal charm than the citizens of the United States, less self-assertive, less dogmatic and strident, rather more conscious of others' standards than their own. What they seem to lack is respect for intellect or technical excellences—they are uninterested in public affairs, indifferent to philosophy, somewhat obtuse to the influence of religion, art and music. At present the whole of the inhabitants of Canada seem to be absorbed in acquiring wealth and the future they are looking forward to is the spending of wealth on material pleasure. From the standpoint of collective action the Canadians are, perhaps, at present the most hopeless of any nation....The Canadian does not yet believe that poverty or destitution can exist in Canada any more than he fears the introduction of malaria in the mosquito-haunted districts (August 11 1911:2749-50).

Chapter 5

Theorists on Gender and Violence

"That future peace which we all desire, on the cessation of the present grievous [Boer] war, must be a peace founded on justice, for there is no other peace worthy of the name, and it must be not only justice as between white men, but as between white men and men of every shade of complexion."[137]

"The notion that a man's wife is his PROPERTY...is the fatal root of incalculable evil and misery."[138]

"We cannot think that...any sentient creature was made primarily for another creature's benefit, but first for its own happiness."[139]

JOSEPHINE E. BUTLER (1828-1906)

Butler was born Josephine Grey of Dilston, in the Lake District of England, to a liberal family of Huguenot origin.[140] Her parents knew William Wilberforce,

---

[137] Butler, *Native Races and the War* 3.

[138] Cobbe, "Wife-Torture in England" 62.

[139] Cobbe, "Rights of Man and Claim of Brutes," *Studies New and Old* 251.

[140] The best biography on Butler is E. Moberly Bell, *Josephine Butler*; other good sources are her own *Personal Reminiscences of a Great Crusade*; her *Recollections of George Butler*; George W. Johnson and Lucy A. Johnson, eds., *Josephine Butler: An Autobiographical Memoir*; A.S.G. Butler, *Portrait of Josephine Butler*; Nancy Boyd, *Josephine Butler, Octavia Hill, Florence Nightingale* 23-92; Barbara Caine, "Josephine Butler," in *Victorian Feminists* 150-95; L. Hay-Cooper, *Josephine Butler And Her Work for Social Purity*; in French see: J. de Mestral Combremont, *La noble vie d'une femme*; Anne-Marie Käppeli, *Sublime croisade*. Butler's unpublished papers are mainly in the Fawcett Library; family papers are at Liverpool University. Her papers on the international work are at the Bibliothèque Universitaire de Genève.

the American anti-slavery leader William Garrison and the Italian independence insurgents Garibaldi and Mazzini. Butler's position on the Contagious Diseases Acts reflects this liberal political background rather than the "social purity" concerns of some people in the movement. Indeed Butler warned of the dangers of the "social purity" wing of the repeal movement. She herself always stressed equality for women, opposed the double standard, warned against the dangers of a police state and insisted that all treatment be voluntary.

Butler married the Reverend (later Canon) **George Butler**, a Church of England clergyman. She had two sons who survived and a daughter who died in a tragic fall from a staircase. Her husband's career took her to Oxford University (where she intensely disliked the macho atmosphere), Winchester and then Liverpool, where he was head of a boys' college and she began the voluntary work that led into her political career. On her daughter's death in 1864 Butler immersed herself in charitable work, visiting the unfortunate and bringing "fallen women" into her own home.

In 1869 Butler was asked, thanks to her work with women, to assume leadership of the campaign to abolish the Contagious Diseases Acts, legislation passed by the British Parliament in 1864 to attempt to control syphilis by the compulsory inspection and treatment of infected women prostitutes (see the discussion above on Martineau). She herself experienced a call from God to the work, which she led through suspension of the acts in 1883 and abolition finally in 1886. Public speaking on the issue required great personal courage for crowds were often unruly and pubkeepers/pimps sent hecklers. The women were not a few times threatened with violence and some were beaten up; once a fire was set at a meeting. Butler had to travel in disguise sometimes. Once she was forced to leave her hotel in the middle of the night when the owner found out who she was. Women who worked against the acts were considered "worse than prostitutes." Her husband was thoroughly supportive. He was once howled down trying to read a paper, "The Duty of the Church of England in reference to the Moral State of Society," to Church of England clergy in Oxford.[141]

A massive organization was developed; six hundred towns had committees within a few years of the campaign's launch. Mazzini, who publicly supported the women's cause, urged Butler to go to the working class for support when none was to be had among the usual leaders of society.[142] The abolitionists pioneered intervention in by-elections as a strategy. Butler herself quickly became an inspired speaker. She wrote numerous pamphlets and essays for the cause and assumed major editorial duties for its journal (variously entitled *The*

---

[141] It was published in the association's *The Shield* and reproduced in J. Butler's *Recollections of George Butler* 242-44.

[142] A.S.G. Butler, *Portrait of Josephine Butler* 71.

Shield, The Bell-Storm and *The Dawn*). As well Butler played a leading role internationally, in Europe and India, from 1875 with the founding of the International Abolitionist Federation. She travelled extensively on the Continent speaking and organizing. One of her best writings on the cause was originally a French pamphlet, 1874-75, translated as "A Voice in the Wilderness."

Butler published a large number of books on a diverse range of subjects in addition to her copious writing on the cause. Her first pamphlet, "Education and Employment of Women" appeared in 1868. An edited work, with her introduction, *Women's Work and Women's Culture*, followed in 1869, written just before J.S. Mill published his "Subjection of Women" essay. She published full-length biographies of the mystic/reformer nun Catherine of Siena, Saint Agnes, the Swiss Protestant Jean Frederic Oberlin, her father, sister, and husband. She wrote devotional books, notably *The Lady of Shunem*, 1894, which features inclusive language for God (Great Father-Mother).

Butler's faith was as enthusiastic as any evangelical's but her religious politics were "broad church" and liberal. She knew the Christian socialist leaders Charles Kingsley and F.D. Maurice. She is said to have influenced later Christian socialists.[143] The ideologically liberal Butler belonged in fact to the Women's Liberal Association. She supported the suffrage movement but confined her own work to abolition of the Contagious Diseases Acts. Butler's major essay on Ireland, *Our Christianity Tested by the Irish Question*, is yet another extension of her strong sense of justice, liberty and compassion, reflecting her politico-religious philosophy.

The one obvious blot on the copy book of this redoubtable woman consists of some duplicity (if not the position she took itself) in her book on the Boer War. Yet the book, *Native Races and the War*, 1900, provides an account of South African history enormously sympathetic to the native population and an exemplary statement of the need for racial justice. It contains an excellent refutation of Boer racist theology.

Government—British Rule in Ireland

Josephine Butler's long essay *Our Christianity Tested by the Irish Question* is a most exceptional piece of political commentary. Butler was so audacious as to call for her ostensibly Christian country, whose head of state was "defender of the faith" and head of the established church, to bring Christian principles to bear on public policy! Christian principles should not be applied only to people's "private life" (4). Butler here joins many feminists in arguing explicitly against a separation of public and private, or "state and home" as she put it, with different standards of right and wrong (46). She had herself as a

---

[143] Nancy Boyd, *Josephine Butler, Octavia Hill, Florence Nightingale* 53.

young girl visited Ireland during the famine (44). She reported having seen people literally fall and die of starvation.

Text: Butler, *Our Christianity Tested by the Irish Question*:

There seem to be a number of sincerely Christian people whose rule for private life is the rule of the New Testament, but who have a difficulty in applying the same rule to public and national questions, and in bringing these questions to the test of Christ's teaching. Perhaps it has never occurred to them to do so. They sometimes assert that government could not be carried on, on those high principles; so much the worse for government. At the very bottom of the successive failures and wrecks of governments lies this very fact, that the work of government is carried on on principles which any sincerely good man professing the religion of Christ would be ashamed to permit as a principle of government in his own household....

I have a special interest in addressing myself to my fellow Christians who may hitherto have given little or no thought to the vital question of Ireland's claim to a national existence. The persons to whom I allude have a sincere desire to be "on the side of righteousness," but they have not yet succeeded in taking this question out of the region of expediency, of conflicting interests and selfish passions, and placing it full in the light of God's countenance....

The working people of Great Britain to an overwhelming extent instinctively sympathize with the demand of the Irish for self government, though they have not libraries and leisure to read as the upper classes have, and their knowledge of Ireland's past history may be very defective....They have fought for and obtained the extension of the suffrage for themselves; they have more respect for representative government than the privileged classes have; their position enables them to appreciate the truth of Grattan's words that "Government against the will of the people governed is the very definition of slavery." When they see a large majority of Ireland's chosen representatives persistently demanding a measure of self government they dare not and have no wish to throw these claims to the winds (4-6).

It is worthwhile to note that for several centuries after the introduction of Christianity into Ireland, when the church was in its most healthy condition, it existed very independently of Rome. The early Christian history of Ireland, "the isle of saints," is a beautiful history, and it is that also of a people of a free and independent character. The pope possessed little influence over them. It was not until civil war broke out among them that he began to obtain any influence, but his authority was never generally recognized until the English invaded Ireland. Thus it was the English who, so to speak, thrust Ireland into the arms of the Roman pontiff (8).

Coming down to the time of the Reformation, we see the fact that Ireland was the only one of the northern countries of Europe where the principles of the Reformation took no root. This may be put down by prejudiced persons to sheer bigotry on the part of the Irish, but the true explanation is found in the policy of England towards Ireland. Queen Elizabeth, the representative of Protestantism, with whose reign we justly connect much that was brilliant and memorable for our own people, carried desolation over Ireland. She was zealous to propagate the reformed faith, and this she attempted not by spiritual means but by sheer force. She was also as anxious as most of her successors have been to blot out the nationality of Ireland. In order to bring about the first object she commanded the English church service to be performed everywhere in Ireland, and in order to promote the latter she forbade its being performed in the Irish language....The people, naturally, continued to lean more than ever to their old faith and to regard Protestantism as identified with an alien nation and a rule which they detested.

Cromwell was the next great representative of Protestantism. His protectorate was a great epoch for England in the way of protest against wickedness in high places, and the great revolution of which we are justly proud stamped a character for good on our national institutions....But mark how both in Cromwell's case and in that of William III all that might be called blessing in England turned to cursing in Ireland....If Cromwell's policy had been continued, Catholic Ireland might have been annihilated, extinguished in blood; as it is, it only widened the gulf between the two religions and filled the enslaved Irish with a deeper horror than ever of the conqueror's creed.

William III (of Orange), a monarch of worthy descent and character, deservedly respected in England, is identified in Ireland with the humiliation of the Battle of the Boyne, with the treacherous breaking of the Treaty of Limerick and with the destruction of Irish trade. He, personally, was far more tolerant and enlightened than his followers, and the odious Penal Code under which the Irish were scourged so long was chiefly enacted after his reign (9-10).

Now we come to the Penal Code...an elaborate system which could not have been more ingeniously contrived to demoralize, degrade and impoverish a people. By this code the Roman Catholics of Ireland (who formed three-fourths of the population) were permanently excluded not only from sitting in Parliament but from voting as electors. They were excluded from the magistracy, from corporations, from the bench and from the bar....They were forbidden to act as constables, sheriffs or jurymen, to serve in the army or navy, to become solicitors or even to be gamekeepers or watchmen. Protestant schools were established, of which they might avail themselves for their children; if not they must grow up in ignorance. They were shut out from the university and forbidden under overwhelming penalties from acting as schoolmasters or private tutors, or from sending their children abroad for the education they were excluded from giving them at home.

If a Catholic married a Protestant the marriage was annulled by law and the priest who officiated might be hung. They could not hold life annuities nor leases for more than thirty-one years, nor any lease on such terms that the profits of the land exceeded one-third of the rent....No Catholic could be the guardian of his own children, or of anyone else's....To convert a Protestant to Catholicism was punishable by death....In case of war with a Catholic country the Catholics were forced to reimburse the damage done by the enemies' privateers. Catholic worship was not absolutely suppressed; it was allowed to exist but "stigmatized as a species of licensed prostitution." No priest of rank was allowed to live in Ireland....In every position—in their homes, in business, in their church and in every relation of life Catholics were pursued with relentless restrictions and persecution (10-11).

It is scarcely possible that an English or Irish Protestant of the present day, who is not blinded altogether by religious bigotry, can look back to the past history of Ireland...without a feeling of grief and of shame....No doubt every individual opponent of Ireland's claims at the present moment has the right to say, "I am not personally responsible for all that has been described in the past; these things were done before I was born...." No, we are not personally responsible but nationally we are deeply responsible.... "Thou art weighed in the balances and art found wanting" (17).

It has been said that the annals of persecution contain many more bloodstained pages than those of the persecution of the Irish Catholics, but they contain no instance of a series of laws more deliberately and ingeniously framed to debase their victims, to bribe them either to abandon their convictions or to hold them as rebels do and to crush out hope. The Irish Parliament in the last years of William III was probably one of the most persecuting legislative bodies that ever existed. No impartial reader of Irish history can fail to observe that the times when the Irish Parliament was most persecuting and the Irish Protestants most unjust to their Catholic brethren, were invariably the times when they were most absolutely subservient to foreign, namely English, control (18).

The apostle says to all mature Christians, "Why do ye not *of yourselves judge that which is right.*" "Prove all things; hold fast that which is good." Are questions which vitally concern the happiness and the very salvation in the deepest sense of whole communities to be excluded from the "all things" which we are told to prove and sift? Christians of a certain school do not seem to have yet learned the true largeness of meaning of that test word of the apostle: "Let everyone that nameth the name of Christ stand aloof from injustice"...and this test is equally applicable to the Christian in his family, in the church, in the market and in the state. Some who study to maintain a conscience void of offence in all the details of private life are content to have no conscience at all in greater matters, and by not protesting against—if they cannot actively oppose—public injustice and wrong, they are, in fact, giving an indirect sanction to that wrong. This, a crying evil of our day, is analogous to that which Mr Gladstone ascribed to King Charles, the attempt to separate public and private rectitude, the deviation in official life from justice and positive truth....

The convictions and utterances of every individual of the community contribute to make up the aggregate public opinion of the country on any question of justice and right. Therefore no man, however humble his position, has a right to evade the question: "Why do ye not for yourselves judge that which is right?" (45)

A great act of injustice, as I believe it to be, has been proposed to be carried into effect against Ireland, an act founded on the bad precedent and often repeated evil example of similar acts in the past, only far excelling them all in cruelty, unreasonableness and injustice. How are the Christian people of England at this moment judging it? Do those who truly worship and follow our Lord Jesus Christ form a solid phalanx of opposition to this injustice? (47)

England's denial to Ireland of constitutional weapons by which to defend herself from tyranny and to set wrongs right; England's long-continued refusal to meet the troubles of Ireland with any other measures than those involving the suspension of every charter and every right; the small group of Irish members in the English Parliament forming a wretched minority continually swamped by an English majority; the increasing miseries of the people, their chronic state of famine and pinching poverty, their increasing conflicts for bare life and the bitter sense of the injustice of it all, these have, year by year, driven the Irish to seek fresh resources, to devise fresh artifices for maintaining and defending the poor degree of national life which remained to them, and of forcing the attention of their rulers to their case (48).

Gender—Regulation of Prostitution

Josephine Butler's *Government by Police*, 1879, is a lengthy essay (69 pages) for the abolition of the Contagious Diseases Acts, in the course of which Butler raised more general points about the role of policing in a democratic society. Butler was acknowledged as an expert on the regulation of prostitution but her writing deserves to be read also on these more general issues. After cautioning that tyranny could occur even in liberal democracies, she went on to contrast absolute and freer governments in their policies on policing.

The use of spies by the police was growing in Britain thanks to the Contagious Diseases Acts, a fact that resulted in police corruption. The alternative strategy Butler recommended included municipal control of all police, de-centralization and restriction of the police function to what is legal and constitutional. The police must be civil servants, locally controlled, not "a semi-military force" under central government (53).

Text: Butler, *Government by Police*:

The more absolute a government is, the more will the police be developed, whilst the freer the country is, the more it will follow the principle that everything which can possibly be left to take care of itself should be so left, and the more carefully restricted will be the functions of the police. It is a question whether in free countries a secret police is allowable at all; its place ought to be supplied by public opinion and the liberty of the press....It is a grave question indeed whether by the creation of a vast force including spies and informers...in order to watch over the morality of the public, we are really introducing an influence for good. That that influence is extensive cannot be doubted, but there is every reason to doubt its character, if we judge it not only by the underlying principle involved...but by its effects on the special agents employed and on the population in general...[Butler related increases in police force size for enforcing the acts] (16-17).

We turn now to France. Wherever municipal independence flourishes there a healthy spirit of self government is found in a greater or less degree. A centralized system of bureaucracy is incompatible with the freedom and independent action of provincial authorities....In France where the destruction of municipal freedom was the earliest accomplished we find, as might be expected, the system of centralized bureaucratic rule organized and standing firmly rooted through successive revolutions, through the rise and fall of monarchical and imperialistic regimes, and continuing at this day in spite of the prevalence and strength of republican principles....A monarch may be deposed or a dictator banished—it was comparatively easy to cut off the head of a Stuart king when his rule became intolerable—but it will require a force not yet developed, and perhaps itself too terrible to be invoked except as a last resort, to cut off the hydra head of a vast bureaucracy whose thousand eyes and hands are in every place at every moment, and which...defies the very power which created it.

Whence this immense resistance? There are, in the first place, extensive vested interests involved in the creating of a bureaucracy....Secondly, there is the deplorable result...that a certain mental incompetence, languor, almost atrophy grows upon a people which has continued to be over-ridden by a bureaucracy (19).

Our own government has for some fifteen years past gradually assumed a more extreme and centralized control, both through its unconstitutional police system responsible to the minister alone, and by the modern fashion of the framing and issuing of orders or edicts independently of Parliament....Our government has thus begun to enter on a course of centralization by usurping in fact the functions of Parliament while overriding the independence of municipal and local authorities (23).

We have been familiar with the idea of espionage in Paris, Berlin and Vienna, but we shrink from the approach of this system in England. We now see however that paid employees are becoming more and more the fashion of the day...and that spies can be hired by any body of persons or private person at will....We have in fact a standing army of ten thousand well-drilled soldiers, entirely independent of any annual vote of Parliament, not subject to the

Mutiny Act, but practically in the pay and under the control of the Home Secretary (37).

The history of France proves that one of the results of such centralization would be the crushing out of all life and vigour in the conduct of local affairs, leaving our hitherto active provincial functionaries as mere puppets in the hands of government officials. It would be a death blow to English independence of character and to that strength and self reliance of which we have hitherto been accustomed to boast as characteristics of our countrymen. A full-blown system of espionage, both for private and political purposes would quickly follow such a state of things (44).

In Paris and every bureaucratically-governed capital we have the fullest proofs that not only is a state police apt to fail in its duty of protecting the persons of the citizens, but that its agents become themselves the violators of personal liberties, the assailants of the modesty and chastity of women and the cause, frequently, of public disorders....The danger of this growing tyranny on the part of the police is so much the greater now for us in England because of the introduction of that very element which has so rapidly and so deeply corrupted the personnel of the police in many other capitals, that is the constituting of a portion of the metropolitan force as an organized body of women-hunters, with the most frightfully arbitrary and irresponsible powers to pursue, to accuse, to condemn and to hurry off to the most horrible and unnatural form of punishment any woman who may be an immoral person or not, or to whom they may have a personal enmity (45-46).

What reforms do we propose?...What measures shall we adopt in order to counteract the prevailing tendency?...*First*, the placing of all police under municipal control. *Secondly*, its decentralization, not only by removing it from the direct control of the central government, but by relegating certain duties now combined under one great organization to other persons and offices, and by inviting and encouraging as much as possible the action of the citizens themselves....*Thirdly*, the restriction of the functions of the police to what is essentially legal and constitutional, and the guarding against that needless and mischievous multiplication of laws enacted year by year, whereby the police service and staff are necessarily greatly increased and its functions enormously enlarged beyond what is good or safe for the public (50-51).

A military police immediately under the control of government produces...a double evil, by placing in the hands of the executive government which already possesses the army another power more formidable than the army itself....In the capital itself a military state police is more especially dangerous; it is a Damocles' sword constantly suspended over the city.... "Such a force is more terrible in Paris for a coup d'état than twenty regiments of infantry; it disperses itself among the masses, lays traps for them and by exciting the people's anger eventually drives them to violence. The army may be won over to a just popular cause, but not so the police; whilst the one is seen, the other remains invisible"....

The police in a free country must therefore be placed under the strict control of a body of distinctly popular constitution, independent of the central executive, for all history teaches that as soon as it becomes the agent of a central power its mission gradually becomes political and...it soon loses its efficiency for the very object for which it was instituted, namely that of watching over the security of the citizens. The police must in future be civil servants, under local control and not a semi-military force acting under government (52-53).

Butler was inexperienced in speaking when she gave her evidence to the royal commission at the House of Lords in 1871. She was the only woman present, and all but one of the members of the commission were known to support the acts. It was an ordeal for her, but she, and others, did succeed in raising doubts about the legislation and even changing some supporters' opinions. There was a minority report. The royal commission had been called by the government on the defeat in a by-election of a Liberal MP who was a visible and staunch supporter of the acts (as Governor of Malta he had been responsible for administering them). The excerpts from Butler's testimony are terse but revealing. She insisted on equality in the law between men and women, both as regards inspections for disease (nothing compulsory for men) and for street solicitation for purposes of prostitution. Butler notably won over **F.D. Maurice**, the Christian socialist leader, suffragist and promoter of education for women. That even such a feminist as Maurice was initially in favour of the acts shows how very little support the repealers had. Many women, including **Elizabeth Garrett**, a well-known physician, supported the acts, too. J.S. Mill was a solid and principled abolitionist who gave evidence on the principles of security of the person and equality of the sexes to this commission.[144] The royal commission itself was deeply divided on the issue. Its recommendations take up two pages, the dissents and provisos (some for more stringent measures, some for more limited) eleven pages.[145] Butler's remarks on equal laws on solicitation for purposes of prostitution for the two sexes remind of debates in Canada in the 1980s, when in fact the Criminal Code was changed to make the offence applicable to either sex, prostitute or customer.

---

[144] Mill testimony 728-35, also in Mill, *Collected Works* 29:349-71.

[145] Amos, *Comparative Survey* 482-96.

Text: Butler testimony to U.K. House of Lords Contagious Diseases Commission March 18 1871:xxxiv-xxxv:

Witness considers the examination of women a lowering of the moral standard in the eyes of the people. No alteration in the acts could reconcile her to them. She would be satisfied with nothing but entire repeal. The association to which she belongs has many suggestions by which the state might check profligacy as well as cure disease....Seduction must be punished, law of bastardy altered, legislation must deal equally with both sexes, a higher standard of morality of men must be enforced, and the law directed against vice itself, not merely its physical effects.

Women are not always tempted to this career by seduction. Various causes are at work: crowding and want of decency in their homes, where girls are often violated by a drunken father; the negligence or wickedness of parents who sometimes sell them; and especially the want of industrial training, leading often to positive starvation.

This evil cannot be reached by legislation alone; the law must be aided by moral influence. The law is protective of vice, recognizing prostitution as a necessity. This she denies. She doubts "in a considerable degree" that every effort is made, as is alleged by the supporters of the acts, to reclaim women. But if they reclaim ninety per cent, her opposition remains, because you still stimulate vice in men, and if some women are reclaimed, the stream is kept up. The evil far more than counterbalances any good the acts may have done....

Witness belongs to an organization spreading over England and embracing working men. The movement is led by temperance men and old political reformers—educated men. They object to the acts as "sex legislation." They object to a woman's character being referred to so arbitrary and inadequate a tribunal as one magistrate, without a jury. They object to the power the acts give any man to injure a woman's reputation. These men are mostly married and are of good character. She thinks the moral tone of the working classes on this subject is higher than that of gentlemen. She has heard university men say that it would be better to dispense with marriage, never heard a working man say this....

She would think it right to detain a small-pox patient for cure. She is in favour of voluntary lock hospitals, not of detention by law. In the Liverpool voluntary hospital the patient signs an agreement to stay until cured. Asked if she does not see that a bond without a penalty is useless, replies that what they would chiefly make a point of is an equal law for males and females....There should be equal laws to check solicitation in the streets by either sex....

Witness would approve of persons with any infectious disease being detained in hospital, but the rule must be very carefully framed, to check the tendency of doctors to despotism....She does not want reclamatory measures from government; she wants preventive measures....She considers any reformations under the acts accidental and doubts whether, as brought about by the acts, reformation is a benefit....She does not believe that young women are saved by the acts from falling into vice.

Peace, War and Militarism—the Boer War

Butler's motives in writing *Native Races and the War* were obviously mixed. She supported British prosecution of the war against the Boers.[146] Her book was critical of British neglect in South Africa, but far more a condemnation of Boer racism. (Its publication was subsidized by someone sympathetic to the Africans.) It reviewed the history of white settlement, recalling that the purpose of the first great trek by the Dutch was to keep their slaves (34). Butler refuted Boer theological justifications for their treatment of Africans with a string of Biblical citations on paying the wages of one's labourers, whether fellow citizens or aliens, paying without delay—and woe to those who do not (134). The work ended with a quotation from Isaiah: to loose the bonds of injustice, let the oppressed go free and break every yoke.

ELIZABETH BLACKWELL (1821-1910)

Blackwell[147] was British born but emigrated as a child with her family to the United States and became an American citizen. She studied medicine in New York, and midwifery at La Maternité in Paris to become the first woman doctor on the English Medical Register. In 1852 she published *The Laws of Life, with special reference to the physical education of girls*, work republished with further material in 1902 as *Essays in Medical Sociology*. In 1859 she gave a series of lectures in England advocating the entry of women into medicine. She and Nightingale had become friends, each visiting the other, although they differed on the question of women in medicine (Nightingale tried to recruit her to head *nursing* services at St Thomas's Hospital).[148] They shared a religious philosophy of faith informing practical service. Blackwell was later involved in the struggle against the Contagious Diseases Acts, writing for Josephine Butler's association for repeal.

During the American Civil War she helped organize medical/nursing relief services for the North. Blackwell helped to institute sound sanitary measures for the Northern side. Freshly back from England and acquainted with Nightingale, she called a meeting April 25 1861 in New York City to mobilize

---

[146] Unpublished correspondence shows that Butler would have come out more explicitly for the British, but her European colleagues fighting the Contagious Diseases Acts were pro-Boer; see June 20 1900 letters to Fawcett Items 4632 and 4633.

[147] Mary St. J. Fancourt, *They Dared to be Doctors, Elizabeth Blackwell, Elizabeth Garrett Anderson*.

[148] On the complicated relationship see Lois A. Monteiro, "On Separate Roads: Florence Nightingale and Elizabeth Blackwell."

women for this purpose. Only after they had formed a Ladies' Central Relief Committee did the women contact the American government to regularize their services.[149]

Government—Christian Socialism

Bumper stickers inform us that "THE CHRISTIAN RIGHT IS NEITHER." Yet by the late twentieth century the Christian right had become so powerful and pervasive that the fact of a Christian left with a substantial history will be news to some. Elizabeth Blackwell wrote her "Christian Socialism" for the Easter season of 1882 and included it in her 1902 anthology, *Essays in Medical Sociology*. It refers to the work of the founders of English Christian socialism, F.D. Maurice and **Charles Kingsley**.[150] Christian socialism was known as the "social gospel" movement in the United States and Canada.[151] It was a minority movement wherever it formed, in the Church of England and the dissenting churches. It fed into the Workers' Education Association, the establishment of producers' co-operatives and the university settlements of the late nineteenth century. Its advocates supported the vote for women and measures for government intervention now associated with the welfare state.

Christian socialism was a significant element in the formation of the British Labour Party, the Co-operative Commonwealth Federation in Canada (the predecessor of the New Democratic Party) and social democratic parties in Europe. Its philosophy has been important in the making of the welfare state, especially public health care. **Tony Blair**, whose Labour government was elected in 1997, is a member of the Christian Socialist Movement.

Text: Blackwell, "Christian Socialism." *Essays in Medical Sociology* 2:151-71:

About thirty years ago a little band of ardent and earnest men joined themselves together as Christian Socialists, under the guidance of the Rev. F. Maurice, Rev. Charles Kingsley and other able and hopeful leaders. They shared in a high degree that ardent desire after "practical Christianity," that embodiment in every act of daily life of the spirit of our Master's teachings,

---

[149] Stanton et al., *History of Woman Suffrage* 2:15.

[150] On the movement see F.D. Maurice, *Kingdom of Christ, Politics for the People* and *The Workman and the Franchise*; Frederick Maurice, ed., *Life of Frederick Denison Maurice*; Charles E. Raven, *Christian Socialism*; Maurice B. Reckitt, *Maurice to Temple*; Max Beer, *History of British Socialism*.

[151] Walter Rauschenbusch, *Christianity and the Social Crisis, Selected Writings* and *New Evangelism*; Richard T. Ely, *The Social Law of Service* and *The Strength and Weakness of Socialism*; James Dombrowski, *The Early Days of Christian Socialism in America*; George D. Herron, *Between Caesar and Jesus*.

which has always existed in the Christian Church and which can only cease with the disappearance of the Christian faith.

The grand idea of human brotherhood is a vital principle of our Lord's teaching. It is the foundation on which He builds His church, but practical Christianity cannot exist unless political and social economy are founded upon this principle. Trade and manufactures, agriculture and education, national government and the individual home are not Christian unless they are inspired by this central principle, laid down by our divine Master, and reiterated in every page of His wonderful life, namely that we must live as brethren under the inspiration of a wise and loving Father.

Attempts to realize more fully this fundamental position of the Christian faith...have always been observed in every age. From those early times when the disciples laid their offerings at the apostles' feet and strove to "have all things in common," to the present day, the attempt to secure higher ends by the power of combination, a combination inspired by the highest idea of right, is always going on. Christian socialism, therefore, is no new idea; it is as old as our faith. It is the shaping of actual daily life on the principle of Christian brotherhood. It enters in some degree into every association: church, chapel or society of any kind whatsoever which seeks to embody an unselfish or a higher spiritual idea, but the Christian socialist believes that the structure of society in every part should be moulded by the idea of united interests....The Christian socialist believes that many principles on which a better society must be founded have come into clearer light during the past thirty years and have been, and are being, tested by varied and valuable experiment....

Reverently and heartily a Christian must accept the rule and guide of life so emphatically laid down by our Master, namely that in eating and drinking, in buying and selling, at home and abroad, we are to act for our brethren, not for ourselves alone. We are to seek, first of all, righteousness. The problem we have to face is the ever-increasing amount and variety of evils which we see around us and to ascertain how far this is caused by the present selfish structure of society, by the false individualism which hypocritically asks "Am I my brother's keeper?"

Evils now increase upon us more rapidly than we can remove them. Pauperism and vice, drunkenness and crime, Mammon worship and frivolity, dishonesty and corruption are all bred by ourselves. They are largely produced by the conditions of the society into which children are born and by which they are moulded [Blackwell next recounted problems of industrial society and attempts at change] (151-55).

The following are some of the chief applications of the principle of Christian brotherhood, which we believe will remould the structure of future society:

1. The repurchase of land by Christian joint-stock companies in order that its control and management may henceforth belong to those who live upon it and use it. The absolute irresponsible individual possession of land becomes, as

society advances, contrary to the best interests of a nation. The soil, which is limited in quantity, but indispensable to the maintenance and welfare of the people, should not be treated as an individual, selfish speculation, regardless of its most advantageous use and of the needs of those who may live upon it....Health, convenience, human welfare in its necessities and interlinkings are never thought of, or are entirely secondary to gain. A showy neighbourhood for the rich, yielding the highest rents that can be screwed out and a crowded neighbourhood for the poor, with still higher proportionate rents, are created. Gardens disappear in the dreary mass of showy, badly-constructed...dreary quarters....It is the irresponsible individual possession of land, with the speculation which such a method of holding gives rise to, which is the principle always ultimately injurious to society.

2. Economy in distribution and management. A rational economy in the retail distribution of products, in the domestic arrangements of our homes, in the official management of local and general government, will set free an immense number of persons whose time is now needlessly occupied. The talent and energy of this wasted multitude should be turned to increase of production and other necessary and valuable employment, under the wise freedom of united interests.

3. A fair share of profits to all workers. This is a most important principle which can only be solved under the guidance of Christian brotherhood. In the increased production which will result from wise economy in distribution, management and government, an equitable division of profits between capital, ability and labour must be arranged....

4. The formation of insurance funds which will secure aid to every worker in sickness or old age....

5. An arrangement of dwellings which will facilitate communication, domestic service and supply, sanitary arrangement, the education of children and municipal government.

6. The entire abolition of all trade in the human body....The buying and selling the human body is a natural wrong. The fearful evils, moral and physical, which result from such trade prove its inherent iniquity....As a striking contrast to growing immorality, the possibility and incalculable benefit of equal purity for boys and girls, for men and women, is the great truth which is springing into vigorous life in this nineteenth century. A new world of hope and freedom opens to women, a new realm of energy to men, from the consecration of this mighty power of sex, which is descending upon our age as a great guide for the future (160-64).

There are large numbers of sincere followers of our spiritual Guide who clearly perceive the radical evils above referred to...but these earnest seers are scattered far and wide; they require the indispensable strength of union. A grand work is before all the churches to join their members together under the noble banner of Christian socialism....The meaning of the Easter season is the arising of Christianity from the grave, that grave where it lies bound in darkness, corrupting in worldliness, dying through selfishness, but, thank God! not yet dead. May our religious people awake from their fatal lethargy and roll away the stone from the sepulchre by the establishment of a true Christian society! (171)

Gender Roles—Regulation of Prostitution

Blackwell actively supported the campaign for the repeal of the Contagious Diseases Acts. She also opposed the supposedly voluntary system of control in use in Scotland.[152] The government had early on attempted to co-opt women physicians in the compulsory examination of prostitutes. The journal of the Ladies' National Association for the Repeal of the Contagious Diseases Acts called this adding "insult to injury to propose that any woman should be used to further the degradation of her sister."[153] Elizabeth Blackwell contributed a short article, "The True Attitude of Women Physicians in regard to Venereal Disease," which insisted on the principle of voluntary treatment and denounced the double standard:

> The most degraded or criminal woman who, of her own free will, comes to her professional sister for medical assistance, will be kindly and skillfully aided to recover her health of body and mind. But directly a woman is taken by the administration as one of its recognized traders in vice, and compelled to submit to medication in order if possible to make the trade healthy, the whole attitude towards the physician is changed.
>
> The effect of legal interference in regulating female vice, instead of checking male and female fornication, is disastrous. The woman is hardened by compulsion, the man is encouraged in vice, society is demoralized by the perversion of law, and Christ's method of healing is destroyed (13).

Blackwell's *Essays on Medical Sociology* include two articles on prostitution and one on medical aspects of the Contagious Diseases Acts. The item excerpted below, a lecture to a conference of rescue workers in 1881, offered a very different approach to legislation. Since society had the right to prevent any individual from harming another it should prohibit sexual intercourse by persons suffering from venereal disease, but not impose compulsory inspection. Insisting on the principle of voluntary treatment, Blackwell pointed out the need for greater access to facilities, without a social stigma. In a section not excerpted here she cautioned against anything that

---

[152] Mahood, *The Magdalenes* 146-47.

[153] *The Dawn*, No. 27, May 1895:13.

would facilitate prostitution. Rescue workers should offer remunerative, alternative occupations.

Text: Blackwell, "Rescue Work," *Essays in Medical Sociology* 1:124-28:

I do not advocate letting disease and vice alone. There is a right way as well as a wrong way of dealing with venereal disease. I consider that legislation *is* needed on this subject. It is unwise to propose to do nothing because legislation has unhappily done wrong....All legislation upon the diseases of vice which can be durable, that is which will approve itself to the conscience of a Christian people, must be based upon two fundamental principles: the principles namely of equal justice and respect for individual rights. These principles are both overturned in the Contagious Diseases Acts, acts which are, therefore, sure to be abolished in a country which, however many blunders it makes, is equally distinguished for its love of justice and liberty. Respect for individual rights will not allow compulsory medical examination and treatment. The right of an adult over his or her own body is a natural fundamental right....

Society, however, has undoubtedly the right to prevent any individual from injuring his neighbour. Interference to prevent such injury is just. The same sacredness which attaches to individual right over one's own person exists for one's neighbour over his or her own person. Therefore, no individual suffering from venereal disease has a right to hold sexual intercourse with any other person. In doing so he goes outside his individual right and injures his neighbour....Society has a right to stop any person who is spreading venereal disease, but it has no right to compel such a person to submit to medical treatment. It is of vital importance to recognize the broad distinction between these two fundamental points, namely the just protection which society must exercise over its members and the inherent right of self-possession *in* each of its members....

A law which makes it a legal offence for an individual suffering from venereal disease to hold sexual intercourse with another person, and a ground for separation, is positively required....Secondly, a necessary regulation to be established in combating the spread of this disease is its free treatment in all general dispensaries and hospitals supported by public or charitable funds. Such institutions have hitherto refused to receive persons suffering from disgraceful diseases, or have made quite insufficient provision for them. This refusal or neglect has left venereal diseases more uncared for than ordinary diseases....

The rigid exclusion in the past of venereal diseases from our general medical charities, on the ground of their disgraceful nature, has done great mischief by producing concealment or neglect of disease. This mischief cannot be repaired in the present day by establishing special or so-called "lock hospitals." A strong social stigma will always rest on the inmates of special venereal hospitals, a stigma we ought not to insist upon inflicting....These hospitals are established for the purpose of relieving human suffering and such suffering constitutes a rightful claim to admission, not to be set aside.

FRANCES POWER COBBE (1822-1904)

The fifth child to a "gentry" Anglo-Irish family, Cobbe was largely educated at home, then sent to school for two years in Brighton, aged fourteen to sixteen. The family was clerical, including several bishops, her father a priest; an ancestor helped to arrange the first performance of Handel's Messiah in Dublin. Cobbe was brought up in a cheerful (Arminian) evangelical version of Christianity, but experienced doubt on her mother's death. By age twenty she considered herself to be an agnostic. Her views next evolved into theism—belief in God, but without any institutional expression—she did not like the Unitarian church. Religion nevertheless remained a major preoccupation of her life. Her first book, published in 1855, was an *Essay on Intuitive Morals*.

Cobbe inherited an income of £200 yearly on her father's death; the substantial property and its income went to her brother. In 1857-58 she travelled to Paris, Italy, Egypt, Palestine, Greece and Turkey. She did not want to be dependent on her brother so she left the family estate and moved to England, initially living and working in Bristol with **Mary Carpenter** and her "ragged schools." The experience acquainted her with the problems of women, including wife beating, on which she later wrote. Cobbe moved to London and became a successful journalist, writing anonymous leaders for major newspapers and publishing her own books and essays. Later in life colleagues raised an annuity for her so that she would not have to continue to write for money and permitting her to retire to Wales.

Cobbe supported the central concerns of the women's movement of her time, suffrage[154] and access to education, but her most significant contribution was on the less travelled issues. In 1862 she gave a paper at the Social Science Congress advocating the opening of university examinations to women. (At the time, women at Oxford and Cambridge could attend classes, but not sit the examinations and obtain a degree.) She was the first person publicly to advocate this next and obviously important step. Her article, "Criminals, Idiots, Women and Minors," published 1868 in *Fraser's Magazine*, made the legal case for women's rights, with typically strong language. It has been reprinted in, and used as the title for, an anthology by Susan Hamilton, 1995.

Cobbe's most successful advocacy on the cause of women was on wife beating, or "wife torture" as she called it in the article excerpted here. Legislation was actually adopted to implement her chief recommendations,

---

[154] See her two articles in Jane Lewis, *Before the vote was won*, and "The Final Cause of Woman," in Josephine Butler, *Woman's Work and Woman's Culture* 1-26.

making it possible for an abused wife to cease co-habiting with her husband, obtain custody of her children and maintenance in a separate domicile.

Cobbe wanted to do as much for "brutes"—non-human animals—as she had for women. She was moved by the horrors of vivisection on the Continent, a practice increasingly being taken up by physiologists and medical researchers/professors in Britain. Cobbe founded and edited the *Zoophilist*, the journal of the Victoria Street Society, in 1881. Much of the work she did for animal welfare was behind the scenes, using more eminent men to front the cause. Thus she would organize a meeting, recruit and brief the speakers; **Cardinal Manning** or **Lord Shaftesbury** would then take the chair or lead the delegation. She published her own two-volume memoirs, *Life of F.P. Cobbe* in 1894. There has yet to be a full-scale biography.[155]

Gender—Violence against Women

Cobbe wrote "Wife-Torture in England" in 1878, three years after a Home Office report on "brutal assaults" had documented the high number of aggravated assaults on women and children and the futility of existing laws to deal with the problem.[156] A sympathetic MP, Colonel Egerton Leigh, had spoken movingly on the subject in 1874, prompting the prime minister, Disraeli, to promise action. Leigh then withdrew his motion, with a joke, Cobbe noted. The Home Office conducted a thorough review of the available police and court data, but did nothing by way of remedy. Cobbe estimated that an additional 6000 women and children were brutally assaulted in the years of inaction after the report's publication. Her article was immediately successful. Published in the progressive *Contemporary Review* in April 1878, legislation was introduced the following month and passed by Parliament without opposition.

The very term "wife torture" startles, as it was intended (although Mill used the term "torture" in a speech in 1867[157]). Cobbe analyzed the causes of the violence as well as describing its prevalence. She acknowledged that wife-beating existed in the middle and upper classes but dealt in detail only with the much more prevalent, and more dangerous, violence of the artisans and labourers. Violence against wives was worse in the industrial North, especially in Liverpool, than in London. Cobbe asked what conditions of life there led to such deeds. She found her answer in the appalling working conditions and

---

[155] Good articles are: Barbara Caine, "Frances Power Cobbe;" Jennie Chappell, "Frances Power Cobbe," in *Women of Worth* 93-134; Olive Banks, "Cobbe, Frances Power," *Biographical Dictionary of British Feminists*. Her correspondence and most papers are in the Huntingdon Library; some letters are at the Bodleian Library, Oxford University.

[156] Carol Bauer and Lawrence Ritt, "A Husband is a Beating Animal."

[157] Hansard, May 20 1867:826 and Mill, *Collected Works* 21:349-71.

degraded physical environment of the industrial revolution—Blake's "dark satanic mills."

Cobbe's essay ended with a draft bill (not included here) prepared by a Birmingham justice of the peace, "An Act for the Protection of Wives whose Husbands have been convicted of Assaults upon them." Its provisions would protect the earnings and property of assaulted wives, prohibit their husbands from visiting them without their consent, give the women legal custody of their children, with maintenance payments both for themselves and their children. So much of the discussion on what Cobbe saw as needing to be done will seem familiar to feminist activists a century later. Passage of the Act to Amend the Matrimonial Causes was the work that gave Cobbe the most satisfaction of her life.[158]

Text: Cobbe, "Wife-Torture in England":

How does it come to pass that while the better sort of Englishmen are thus exceptionally humane and considerate to women, the men of the lower class of the same nation are proverbial for their unparalleled brutality, till wife-beating, wife-torture, and wife-murder have become the opprobrium of the land? How does it happen...that the same generous-hearted gentlemen, who would themselves fly to render succour to a lady in distress, yet read of the beatings, burnings, kicking and "cloggings" of *poor* women well-nigh every morning in their newspapers without once setting their teeth, and saying "This must be stopped! We can stand it no longer"?

The paradox truly seems worthy of a little investigation. What reason can be alleged, in the first place, why the male of the human species, and particularly the male of the finest variety of that species, should be the only animal in creation which maltreats its mate, or any female of its own kind?[159] To get to the bottom of the mystery we must discriminate between assaults of men on other men, assaults of men on women who are not their wives and assaults of men on their wives.

I do not think I err much if I affirm that, in common sentiment, the first of these offences is considerably more heinous than the second—being committed against a more worthy person (as the Latin grammar itself instructs boys to think) and, lastly, that the assault on a woman who is *not* a man's wife is worse than the assault on a wife by her husband. Towards this last or *minimum* offence a particular kind of indulgence is indeed extended by public opinion. The proceeding seems to be surrounded by a certain halo of jocosity which inclines people to smile whenever they hear of a case of it (terminating

---

[158] Cobbe, *Life of F.P. Cobbe* 2:223.

[159] Cobbe footnoted the possible exception of seals.

anywhere short of actual murder), and causes the mention of the subject to conduce rather than otherwise to the hilarity of a dinner party (56-57).

Wife-beating exists in the upper and middle classes rather more, I fear, than is generally recognized, but it rarely extends to anything beyond an occasional blow or two of a not dangerous kind. In his apparently most ungovernable rage, the gentleman or tradesman somehow manages to bear in mind the disgrace he will incur if his outbreak be betrayed by his wife's black eye or broken arm, and he regulates his cuffs or kicks accordingly. The dangerous wife-beater belongs almost exclusively to the artisan and labouring classes (58).

There are also various degrees of wife-beating in different localities. In London it seldom goes beyond a severe "thrashing" with the fist—a sufficiently dreadful punishment, it is true, when inflicted by a strong man on a woman—but mild in comparison of the kickings, tramplings and "purrings" with hob-nailed shoes and clogs of what we can scarcely call the "dark and true and 'tender' North." As Mr Serjeant Pulling remarks, "Nowhere is the ill-usage of woman so systematic as in Liverpool, and so little hindered by the strong arm of the law, making the lot of a married woman whose locality is the 'kicking district' of Liverpool simply a duration of suffering and subjection to injury and savage treatment, far worse than that to which the wives of mere savages are used." It is in the centres of dense mercantile and manufacturing populations that this offence reaches its climax.

What are the conditions of life among the working classes in those great "hives of industry" of which we talk so proudly? It is but justice that we should picture the existence of the men and women in such places before we pass to discuss the deeds which darken it. They are lives out of which almost every softening and ennobling element has been withdrawn, and into which enter brutalizing influences almost unknown elsewhere. They are lives of hard, ugly, mechanical toil in dark pits and hideous factories, amid the grinding and clanging of engines and the fierce heat of furnaces, in that Black Country where the green sod of earth is replaced by mounds of slag and shale, where no flower grows, no fruit ripens, scarcely a bird sings, where the morning has no freshness, the evening no dews, where the spring sunshine cannot pierce the foul curtain of smoke which overhangs these modern cities of the plain, and where the very streams and rivers run discoloured and steaming with stench, like Styx [the river around Hades]...through their banks of ashes. If "God made the country and man made the town," we might deem...that here we had at last found the spot where the Psalmist might seek in vain for the handiwork of the Lord (59).

These, then, are the localities wherein wife-torture flourishes in England: where a dense population is crowded into a hideous manufacturing, mining or mercantile district. Wages are usually high though fluctuating. Facilities for drink and vice abound, but those for cleanliness and decency are scarcely attainable. The men are rude, coarse and brutal in their manners and habits, and the women devoid, in an extraordinary degree, of all the higher natural attractions and influences of their sex. Poor drudges of the factory, or of the crowded and sordid lodging-house, they lose, before youth is past, the freshness, neatness and gentleness, perhaps even the modesty of a woman, and present, when their miserable cases come up before the magistrate, an aspect so sordid and forbidding that it is no doubt with difficulty he affords his sympathy to them rather than to the husband chained to so wretched a consort.

Given this direful "milieu," and its population, male and female, we next ask what are the immediate incitements to the men to maltreat the women?...First, the whole relation between the sexes in the class we are considering is very little better than one of master and slave. I have always abjured the use of this familiar comparison in speaking generally of English husbands and wives, because as regards the upper orders of society it is ridiculously overstrained and untrue. But in the "kicking districts," among the lowest labouring classes, Legree himself might find a dozen prototypes, and the condition of the women be most accurately matched by that of the Negroes on Southern plantation before the war struck off their fetters.

To a certain extent this marital tyranny among the lower classes is beyond the reach of law, and can only be remedied by the slow elevation and civilization of both sexes. But it is also in an appreciable degree, I am convinced, enhanced by the law even as it now stands, and was still more so by the law as it stood before the Married Women's Property Act put a stop to the chartered robbery by husbands of their wives' earnings. At the present time, though things are improving year by year, thanks to the generous and far-seeing statesmen who are contending for justice to women inside and out of the House of Commons, the position of a woman before the law as wife, mother and citizen remains so much below that of a man as husband, father and citizen that it is a matter of course that she must be regarded by him as an inferior, and fail to obtain from him such a modicum of respect as her mental and moral qualities might win did he see her placed by the state on an equal footing.

I have no intention in this paper to discuss the vexed subject of women's political and civil rights, but I cannot pass to the consideration of the incidental and minor causes of the outrages upon them without recording my conviction that the political disabilities under which the whole sex still labours...presses down more and more heavily through the lower strata of society in growing deconsideration and contempt, unrelieved (as it is at higher levels) by other influences on opinion. Finally at the lowest grade of all it exposes women to an order of insults and wrongs which are never inflicted by equals upon an equal, and can only be parallelled by the oppressions of a dominant caste or race over their helots [serfs]. In this as in many other things the educating influence of law immeasurably outstrips its direct action (60-61).

The general depreciation of women as a *sex* is bad enough but...the special depreciation of *wives* is more directly responsible for the outrages they endure. The notion that a man's wife is his PROPERTY, in the sense in which a horse is his property (descended to us rather through the Roman law than through the customs of our Teuton ancestors), is the fatal root of incalculable evil and misery. Every brutal-minded man, and many a man who in other relations of life is not brutal, entertains more or less vaguely the notion that his wife is his *thing*, and is ready to ask with indignation...of anyone who interferes with his treatment of her, "May I not do what I will *with my own?*" It is even sometimes pleaded on behalf of poor men, that they possess *nothing else* but their wives, and that, consequently, it seems doubly hard to meddle with the exercise of their power in that narrow sphere! (62-63)

I have called this paper English wife-torture because I wish to impress my readers with the fact that the familiar term "wife-beating" conveys about as remote a notion of the extremity of the cruelty indicated as when candid and ingenuous vivisectors talk of "scratching the newt's tail" when they refer to burning alive, or dissecting out the nerves of living dogs, or torturing ninety cats in one series of experiments.

Wife-*beating* is the mere preliminary canter before the race—the preface to the serious matter which is to follow. Sometimes, it is true, there are men of comparatively mild dispositions who are content to go on beating their wives year after year, giving them occasional black-eyes and bruises, or tearing out a few locks of their hair and spitting in their faces, or bestowing an ugly print of their iron fingers on the woman's soft arm, but not proceeding beyond these minor injuries to anything perilous....But the unendurable mischief, the discovery of which has driven me to try to call public attention to the whole matter, is this: wife-*beating* in process of time and in numberless cases advances to wife-*torture*, and wife-torture usually ends in wife-maiming, wife-blinding or wife-murder. A man who has "thrashed" his wife with his fists half a dozen times becomes satiated with such enjoyment as that performance brings, and next time he is angry he kicks her with hob-nailed shoes. When he has kicked her a few times standing or sitting, he kicks her down and stamps on her stomach, her breast or her face. If he does not wear clogs or hob-nailed shoes, he takes up some other weapon—a knife, a poker, a hammer, a bottle of vitriol or a lighted lamp—and strikes her with it or sets her on fire—and then, and then only, the hapless creature's sufferings are at an end (72-73).

Finally, a most important reason for adopting such a measure is, that it—or something like it—is indispensable to induce the victims of such outrages to apply for legal redress. The great failure of justice...is chiefly due...to the fact that the existing law *discourages* such applications—and in like manner must every projected law do so which merely adds penalties to the husband's offence without providing the suffering wife with any protection from his renewed violence when that penalty has been endured. Under the Wives Protection Bill, should it become law, the injured wife would have the *very thing she really wants*, namely, security against further violence, coupled with the indispensable custody of her children (without which, no protection of herself would offer a temptation to the better sort of women), and some small (though probably precarious) contribution to their maintenance and her own. With this real relief held out to them by the law, I should have little doubt that we should find the victims of brutal assaults and of repeated aggravated assaults very generally coming forward to bear testimony and claim their release, and the greatest difficulty attendant on the case would be at an end (84).

Nature and Society—the Anti-Vivisection Movement

Vivisection (the dissection of living animals, then without painkillers) had been practised in Britain from the seventeenth century, although less so than on the Continent. It only came into frequent use in the nineteenth century with the advent of physiology. Public reaction against the practice was prompted by the callousness of European vivisectors. This resulted in the establishment of a royal commission that tried to mediate between the scientific/medical advocates of vivisection and their opponents. Cobbe tried first to interest the large and well established Royal Society for the Prevention of Cruelty to Animals. It, however, gave only cautious support and she decided that a society dedicated to the issue was needed. On enlisting the support of Lord Shaftesbury and Cardinal Manning the Victoria Street Society for the Protection of Animals Liable to Vivisection was born.[160]

In 1876 Parliament actually passed legislation *legalizing* vivisection, amending a bill originally intended to limit it. The newly formed Victoria Street Society then worked for amended legislation, initially seeking restriction only, after 1878 total prohibition. It quickly became the largest and politically most influential anti-vivisection society, thanks to Cobbe's ability to recruit big names. Apart from numerous bishops, archbishops and the lord chief justice, there were the poets Byron and Tennyson and other well-known writers such as J.S. Mill, Benjamin Jowett and Thomas Carlyle. Cobbe was honourary secretary from the society's inception until her retirement to Wales in 1884. She remained the dominant person on the executive until outmanoeuvred by a protegé in 1898. She then founded another, totally abolitionist society, the British Union for the Abolition of Vivisection. Both societies remain in existence, as does vivisection, although now with more concern for pain control.

Cobbe for decades led the movement against vivisection in Britain. She accepted the conventional hierarchy of value favouring humans; some animals were evidently intended to be our servants. This statement she then immediately qualified: all creatures were meant to be happy and every creature's first purpose was its own happiness. Brute animals complement

---

[160] On Cobbe's role in the anti-vivisection movement see: Richard D. French, *Antivivisection and Medical Science in Victorian Society* and Carol Lansbury, "Gynaecology, Pornography and the Antivivisection Movement."

humans and so are our "fellow creatures." When we use them we must do so without cruelty. Humans have obligations as sovereigns over subjects, to be responsible as "viceregents of God" and therefore merciful. This paper was first published in 1863 in the progressive *Fraser's Magazine* and republished in her own collection, *Studies New and Old* (from which the excerpt was taken). Cobbe in her autobiography claimed that it was "as far as I know the first effort made to deal with the moral questions involved in the torture of animals either for the sake of science or therapeutic research, or for the acquirement of manipulative skill."[161] For Cobbe what made it such a "portentous" fact was that it was justified cruelty, a new vice from our highest culture, approved by the "educated classes." She blamed Darwinism for supplying the excuse for all sorts of villainy.

It is no coincidence that Cobbe worked both on violence against women and cruelty to (non-human) animals. It has been argued that large numbers of women were drawn to the anti-vivisection movement precisely because they saw the parallels between the abusive treatment of women (especially poor women) as gynecological patients, their portrayal in pornography and the vivisection of non-human animals.[162] Ovariotomy has even been considered as a form of vivisection because its use, which was extensive, was experimental, more directed to scientific inquiry than treatment. The unifying factor was the strapping/binding of the victim/patient on a board—very similar as between the vivisected animal, the gynecological patient and the pornographic subject positioned for a flogging.

From Cobbe's extensive publication on vivisection two items have been selected, her pioneering article from 1863 in *Fraser's Magazine*, and a pamphlet from 1891 by the Victoria Society for the Protection of Animals Liable to Vivisection.

Text: Cobbe, "The Rights of Man and the Claims of Brutes," *Studies New and Old* 251-54:

There remains one grave and solemn side of this question which we have some hesitation in approaching. Man and brutes are not mere creatures of chance. Sentiments of pity are not matters of arbitrary taste. Moral laws do not alone bind us with a sacred obligation of mercy. The Maker of man is also the Maker of all the tribes of earth and air and waters. Our Lord is their Lord also. We rule the animal creation not as irresponsible sovereigns but as the viceregents of God.

The position of brutes in the scale of creation would appear to be that of the complement of the mighty whole. We cannot suppose that the material

---

[161] Cobbe, *Life of F.P. Cobbe* 2:247.

[162] Carol Lansbury, "Gynaecology" 413-37.

universe of suns and planets was created for irrational and unmoral beings, but rather to be the habitation of various orders of intelligences endowed with that moral freedom by which they may attain to virtue and approach to God in ever-growing likeness and love. If we may presume to speculate on the awful designs of the supreme Architect, we almost inevitably come to this conclusion, that these world houses were all built to be, sooner or later, in the million millenniums of their existence, the abodes of living souls. Be this as it may regarding the other worlds in the universe, we must at least believe that here, where such beings actually exist, their palace home of plains, hills, woods and waters, with all its libraries of wisdom, its galleries of beauty, has been built for them and not for their humble fellow lodgers, the brutes, fowls, insects and fish. They are, we must conclude, the complement and filling up of the great design.

Some of them are the servants appointed for our use; all of them are made to be happy, to fill the world with their innocent delight. We cannot think that any of them, any sentient creature, was made primarily for another creature's benefit, but first for its own happiness, and then afterwards to "second too some other use." Thus we believe the world was made for man, the end of whose creation is virtue and eternal union with God, and the complement of the plan are the brutes, whose end is such happiness as their natures may permit.

If this be so, our relation to the whole animal creation is simply that of *fellow creatures*, of a rank so much higher that our interests must always have precedence. But to some orders of animals we are in a much nearer relation, for these are the servants given us expressly by God, and fitted with powers and instincts precisely suiting them to meet our wants. The camel, horse, ass, elephant, cow, sheep, goat, dog, cat and many species of fowls, are all so constituted as to supply us with what we need in the way of services, food, clothing and protection. Our use or misuse of these servants is a matter in which it is impossible to conceive that we are irresponsible, or that we do not offend the merciful Creator when, instead of profiting by His gifts, we use our superior power to torture and destroy the creatures He has made both to serve us and to be happy also.

If there be one moral offence which more than another seems directly an offence against God, it is this wanton infliction of pain upon His creatures. He, the good One, has made them to be happy, but leaves us our awful gift of freedom to use or to misuse towards them. In a word, He places them absolutely in our charge. If we break this trust and torture them, what is our posture towards Him? Surely as sins of the flesh sink man below humanity, so sins of cruelty throw him into the very converse and antagonism of Deity; he becomes not a mere brute but a fiend.

These would seem to be the simple facts of our relation to the animals, viewed from the religious point of view, on the hypothesis that our usual ideas concerning the lower creation are correct, that brutes have no germ of a moral nature, no prospect of immortality, and that between us and them there are no other ties but those of fellow creaturehood. It may be that a more advanced mental philosophy, and further researches in science, may modify these ideas. It may be that we shall come to see that sentient life and consciousness and self-consciousness are mysterious powers working upward through all the orders of organic existence, that there are rudiments in the sagacious elephant and the affectionate dog of moral faculties which we need not consign hopelessly to annihilation. It may be that we shall find that man himself, in all the glory of his reason, has sprung, in the far-off ages of the primeval world, not from the "clod of the valley"...but from some yet-undiscovered creature which once roamed the forest of the elder world, and through whom he stands allied in blood to all the beasts of the field.

It may be we shall find all these things, and finding them we shall not degrade man but only elevate the brute. By such ideas, should science ever ratify them, we shall certainly arrive at new and vivid interests in the animal creation, and the brutes will receive at our hands (we must needs believe) some more tender consideration. But these are, as yet, all doubtful speculations, and we do not need to rest a feather's weight of argument upon them to prove that as religious beings we are bound to show mercy to all God's creatures.

Text: Cobbe, "The significance of Vivisection":

The most portentous fact concerning vivisection is not that it is a cruel practice but that it is a *justified cruelty*. It is not the lingering relic of old barbarism, condemned by every enlightened and educated mind, but the upspringing of a new vice in the hotbeds of our highest culture. In every age and country cruel men and women have existed, and in ancient times and savage lands no public opinion condemned them. But that *now* and *here*, where the tide of human sentiment has reached a higher level than ever before on the globe, there should arise and flourish a practice involving the extremest cruelty and that that practice should be largely approved by the educated classes of the community—this is a fact assuredly fraught with terrible significance.

How has this paradox come to pass? How is it that we see multitudes of well-meaning persons exhibiting maudlin anxiety lest the most ferocious criminals should taste any degree of bodily pain, and when no government would have power to restore to the statute book a single one of the older and severer penalties, even for a wholesale murder of shiploads or trains-full of human beings, how is it, we ask bewildered, that in such an age, and in England, the very focus of zoophily, the vivisection of unoffending animals is not only practiced, but tolerated, justified and approved?

When the agitation against scientific cruelty began sixteen years ago, the practice was regarded generally as a frightful *exception* to the regular progress of humanity which had prevailed since the beginning of the century, a back water and eddy in a narrow reach of the great onflowing current. We deemed—sanguine men, women that we were—that the evil might be shortly and sharply checked. One good act of Parliament, such as was Lord Carnarvon's, as sketched at the committee table of the Victoria Street Society and before 3000 doctors eviscerated it, would, we confidently trusted, eliminate the transitory, accidental evil, put a stop to the vile new fashion and restore English scientists to the ranks of English humanitarians. It was not to be.

The distinctive feature of our time is not that men are selfish, but that they now justify and systematize selfishness. Darwinism seems to have supplied those who wished for it with a sort of philosophy of selfishness, which enables them to formulate without a blush principles of action which, heretofore, even when acted upon, were decently cloaked in some travesty of regard for honour or probity....Now we have selfishness *pur et simple*, rough and ready, cowardly and cruel, having this earthly life for its alpha and omega, yet, for all its unqualified earthiness, appealed to by the host of advocates of vivisection as if it were the recognized law of humankind, as of the beasts of prey! We are formally invited, having it is presumed quitted the schools of Kant, Plato, Paul and Christ, to take lessons from those humble vivisectors, polecats and wasps....

To contend against vivisection is, then, to contend not against any exceptional or transitory evil but against those besetting sins of the age...selfishness, cowardice and the pitilessness characteristic of cowards, over estimate of the body compared to the soul, over estimate of knowledge as compared to love.

Chapter 6

Theorists on Peace, War and Militarism

"Always the other side that wishes war! Always the other one who is accused of resolving that might shall overcome justice...a much higher plane would be reached if every war were recognized as a war of mankind against mankind."[163]

The women theorists related in this chapter were all highly involved in the women's peace movement (although some of their contributions are on social policy and government). Accordingly a brief introduction on their common themes seems appropriate. This will give an opportunity also to relate the theme of peace, war and militarism to that of the nature of the social bond discussed in Chapter 2. The existence of a distinctive women's peace movement may even be seen to be a logical progression of the distinctive position women have tended to take with regard to basic human nature and the social bond.

That women have been disproportionately involved in the modern peace movement is a matter of fact. So is it that women are less supportive of military expenditures and more favourable to measures for disarmament, both of nuclear and conventional weapons. There are still women's peace organizations that draw on women's traditional concerns as bearers and nurturers of children. As late as the Afghan War of the 1980s Soviet mothers demonstrated, held hunger strikes, gave refuge to soldiers and demanded compensation and alternative service. As recently as the 1995 war in Chechnya

---

[163] Von Suttner, *"Ground Arms!"* 127.

organizations of soldiers' mothers demonstrated in Russian and Chechnya to demand an end to the war.[164]

The "gender gap" on war and militarism, however, must not be exaggerated. Most women have supported their countries' wars and some have led them (Margaret Thatcher's Falklands War is a recent example). Many women's peace initiatives foundered when their country actually declared war and prominent women pacifists later changed their minds. **Agnes Macphail**, Canada's first woman MP, voted for the declaration of war in 1939, although she had been a strong peace advocate until then; her socialist colleague **J.S. Woodsworth** was the only MP to vote against. **Nellie McClung**, stated in 1915 that there would be no war if women had the vote, but later supported participation in World War I.[165] The British women's suffrage movement split on the Boer War at the end of the nineteenth century and later again on World War I. In the United States *A History of Woman Suffrage* reported proudly on women's efforts in the Civil War. In World War I a suffrage convention sent President Wilson a unanimous message of support for the war.[166]

Along with the literature relating women as peace makers there is a counter-literature insisting on no particular proclivity.[167] Historian Mary Beard described how women in World War II both bragged about women's active participation in the war, yet blamed men for the war. The same Carrie Chapman Catt who, as president of the national suffrage organization, led the support for war just described, in World War II declared it to be women's task to stop war, that "men have made all the wars in history."[168] The literature includes a number of anthologies,[169] and numerous histories of women in war, as war production workers and as victims of war, too numerous to cite. As well there are, again too numerous to cite, a sizable number of memoirs, biographies and analyses by advocates of peace.

---

[164] Metta Spencer, "The Russian Peace Movement and its Western Friends."

[165] McClung, *In Times Like These* and see R.F. Warne, "Nellie McClung and Peace" in Janice Williamson and Deborah Gorham, *Up and Doing* 35.

[166] Ida Husted Harper, in Stanton et al. eds., *History of Woman Suffrage* 5:518.

[167] See especially Jean Bethke Elshtain, *Women and War*.

[168] Beard, *Woman as Force in History* 48.

[169] Carol R. Berken and Clara M. Lovett, *Women, War and Revolution*; Cambridge Women's Peace Collective, *My Country is the Whole World*; Daniela Gioseffi,ed., *Women on War*; Nancy Loring Goldman, *Female Soldiers--Combatants or Noncombatants?*; Margaret Randolph Higonnet et al., *Behind the Lines*; Sharon Macdonald et al., *Images of Women in Peace and War*; Ruth Roach Pierson, *Women and Peace*; Judith Stiehm, *Women and Men's Wars*; Arthur H. Westing, *Cultural Norms, War and the Environment*.

Given the availability of a rich and growing literature on the subject my purpose is properly limited and modest: to show the logical culmination of women's broader theoretical contributions to the subjects of peace, war and militarism over the centuries, reported in Chapters 2 to 5. The theorists discussed in this chapter, who were pioneers of a distinctly *women's* focus, nonetheless built on a theoretical perspective developed over the centuries, at least from Christine de Pisan on. Thus we examine the work of Jane Addams, Bertha von Suttner, Olive Schreiner, Catherine Marshall and Emily Greene Balch, aware of the groundwork laid by the theorists who challenged militarism and refused to glorify war, and who held to a different, more benign view of human nature in the seventeenth and eighteenth centuries.

Acknowledging the important role women theorists have played in questioning militarism and de-glorifying war is not to argue any automatic relationship between gender and advocacy of peace or war, or to deprecate the role men have played as peace advocates. Still, to some extent, a gender gap remains. The different position that so many women theorists have taken on underlying human nature, the positive approach to a social bond over a hostile social contract would seem to contribute as well. This last substantive chapter then goes back to several of the earliest themes of the book.

JANE ADDAMS (1860-1935)

Jane Addams[170] was part of the first generation of American women to obtain a university degree, from Rockford College, Illinois. She established the first American settlement house, Hull-House, in Chicago in 1892, after visiting the prototype university settlement in London, Toynbee Hall. Hull-House, however, was less hierarchical and more practical than the men's settlements. Its philosophy was in the social gospel tradition, but none of the women were clerics. Hull-House was both a home for its core group of women residents and a social service centre with a research wing. *Hull-House Maps and Papers*, 1895, reports the first research conducted by the residents, work that reflects the influence of Booth's *Life and Labour* survey.

Addams and her colleagues were well aware that they were upper middle class visitors to an inner city, largely immigrant area. She took the precaution of taking someone from the area with her when lecturing on the settlement to ensure that she represented it fairly. Addams became a prominent speaker and writer for a number of causes: the profession of social work as well as the settlement house movement, the vote for women, other political rights and access to education and occupations. She encouraged union organization,

---

[170] On Addams see her own two memoirs, *Twenty Years at Hull-House* and *The Second Twenty Years at Hull-House*; biographies John C. Farrell, *Beloved Lady* (with a full bibliography); Allen F. Davis, *American Heroine*; Mary Jo Deegan, *Jane Addams and the Men of the Chicago School*, Jean Elshtain, "Self/Other, Citizen/state: G.W.F. Hegel and Jane Addams," in *Meditations on Modern Political Thought* 71-84 and my *Women Founders* 228-38.

fought municipal corruption and promoted child labour legislation. Unlike her contemporary (and acquaintance) Beatrice Webb she did not seek socialist organization of the economy, but she did want a substantial welfare state, including both extensive social services and income support measures. Hence she supported the Progressive Party on its founding.

Much of her life was devoted to the women's peace movement. Addams led the American delegation to the first women's congress on peace at The Hague and was the founding president of the Women's International League for Peace and Freedom, formed at that congress. She was awarded the Nobel Peace Prize in 1931 for this work in the peace movement.

Government—Minimum Standards Legislation

Two selections deal with social and economic issues, one from early in her life, on trade unions, the second from late in her life, on the role of government more generally. Addams was a life-long collectivist, advocate of public measures for social security, education, public health and protective labour legislation in a society and a time in which individualism was a patriotic duty and public measures were suspiciously un-American. In speeches and essays throughout her life she tried to persuade other citizens of the practicality of using government measures to provide important community benefits. She frequently cited European examples to show that what was proposed had been tried in other countries and had been proven to be effective.

In "Unions and Public Duty" Addams had the burden of defending unions in the country (still) most hostile to them. Her Chicago settlement, Hull-House, actively supported union organization, loaning the premises for meetings and encouraging people to join as a means of improving their wages and working conditions. *Hull-House Maps and Papers* includes a chapter, written by Addams, on union organization. Her focus in the essay excerpted here was on the particular role they have played more broadly in society, in effect taking on public duties such as securing protective legislation for children and obtaining shorter working hours and other protective measures for the weakest members of society.

Although the essay was published in 1899 it is clear that unions still play that role and still are treated derogatively as if they were working only for their narrow self-interest. Addams remarked at the harshness with which union failures are judged and the undue stress laid on the violence and disorder that sometime accompany union efforts.

She sympathetically discussed six measures commonly condemned by the public: harsh treatment of non-union labour in a strike, the activities of paid union officers, boycotts, insistence on shorter hours, limitation of apprentices and the sympathy strike. She likened the sympathy strike to major state actions such as war, even the civil war that ended American slavery. "We condemn in trades unions what we praise when undertaken by the state" (459).

Text: Addams, "Trade Unions and Public Duty":

In this paper I have assumed that the general organization of trades unions and their ultimate purposes are understood, and also that we recognize that the public has a duty toward the weak and defenceless members of the community. With these assumptions granted, two propositions are really amazing: first that we have turned over to those men who work with their hands the fulfillment of certain obligations which we must acknowledge belong to all of us, such as protecting little children from premature labour and obtaining shorter hours for the overworked, and second that, while the trades unions, more than any other body, have secured orderly legislation for the defence of the feeblest, they are persistently misunderstood and harshly criticized by many people who are themselves working for the same ends. The first proposition may be illustrated by various instances in which measures introduced by trades unions have first been opposed by the public and later have been considered praiseworthy and valuable when the public as a whole has undertaken to establish and enforce them.

For years trades unions have endeavoured to secure laws regulating the occupations in which children may be allowed to work, the hours of labour permitted in those occupations and the minimum age below which children may not be employed....The regulation of child labour is one of the few points in which society as a whole has made common cause with the voluntary efforts of trades unions, but the movement was initiated and is still largely carried forward by them (448-49).

For many years I have been impressed with the noble purposes of trades unions and the desirability of the ends which they seek. At the same time I have been amazed at the harshness with which their failures are judged by the public and the undue stress which is laid upon the violence and disorder which sometimes accompany their efforts....Scenes of disorder and violence are enacted because trades unions are not equipped to accomplish what they are undertaking; the state alone could accomplish it without disorder. The public shirks its duty and then holds a grievance toward the men who undertake the performance of that duty. It blames union men for the disaster which arises from the fact that the movement is a partial one....

We may consider half a dozen measures which trades unions have urged, and concerning which the community has often been stirred by indignation and find that, when the public undertakes to enforce identical or similar measures, they are regarded with great complacency...*first*, the harsh treatment of a non-union labourer during a strike; *second*, the dictatorship of the walking delegate [union agitator]; *third*, the use of the boycott; *fourth*, the insistence upon shorter hours of labour; *fifth*, the limitation of apprentices; *sixth*, the sympathetic strike. It is quite possible to compare all of these to national measures of which we approve and concerning which we are a part, but which the community as a whole undertakes to enforce. [Addams made the comparisons, only the last of which is included here.]

We see a great sympathetic strike ramifying throughout the entire unions of a trade and its allied trades; we suddenly hear of men all over the country leaving their work, places which they may have held for years, which they know that it may be difficult and perhaps impossible again to secure. They certainly do this under some dictate of conscience and under some ethical concept that stands to them as a duty. Later many of them see their wives and children suffer and yet they hold out for the sake of securing better wages for workmen whom they have never seen....We say the men are foolish and doomed to fail....We study other great movements toward human freedom and fail to comprehend that the consciences of our contemporaries are aroused to a participation in the same great struggle.

We condemn in trades unions what we praise when undertaken by the state when it enters into a prolonged civil war to rid itself of slavery....After all, the state, the nation, as Mazzini pointed out, represents no more than a mass of principles in which the universality of its citizens were agreed at the time of its foundation. But we would not have the state remain motionless and chained to the degree of civilization attained at the moment the state was founded. We would have a rational development of the truths and principles which gave vitality to the state at first. If the objects of trades unions could find quiet and orderly expression in legislative enactment, and if their measures could be submitted to the examination and judgment of the whole without a sense of division or of warfare, we should have the ideal development of the democratic state....

One might almost generalize that the trades-union movement, as such, secures its lower objects best where there is a well-defined class feeling among the proletarians of its country, but that it accomplishes its highest objects in proportion as it is able to break into all classes and seize upon legislative enactment. A man who is born into his father's trade, and who has no hope of ever entering into another, as under the caste system of India or the guilds of Germany, is naturally most easily appealed to by the interests within his trade life. A workingman in America, who may become a carpenter only as a stepping-stone toward becoming a contractor and capitalist, as any ambitious scholar may teach a country school until he shall be fitted for a college professorship, does not respond so easily to measures intended to benefit the carpenter's trade as he does to measures intended to benefit society as a whole....

That all its citizens may be responsible is, then, perhaps the final reason why it should be the mission of the state to regulate the conditions of industry....This is the attempt of factory legislation. It is concerned in the maintenance of a certain standard of life and would exercise such social control over the conditions of industry as to prevent the lowering of that standard....Is it too much to hope that in time other citizens, as well as trade unionists, may be educated to ask themselves: "Does our industrial machinery, or does it not, make for the greatest amount and the highest quality of character?" And that when it is answered...that the state does not concern itself with the character of the producer but only with the commercial aspects of the product, is it again too optimistic to predict that those other citizens will feel a certain sense of shame and recognize the fact that the trades unions have undertaken a duty which the public has ignored?

Her second essay in this section was first published in Charles Beard's *A Century of Progress*, 1932. (Other essays in the collection include Henry Ford on industry and Grace Abbott on women, as well as Beard himself on the idea of progress.) "The Process of Social Transformation" was written in the early period of the Great Depression before **F.D. Roosevelt's** New Deal. (Addams died in 1935.) It is old-fashioned institutional analysis, interweaving geographical conditions, economic attitudes and technological change into historical explanation. The main object was to explain why the United States, by 1890, was a generation behind England and the Continent in social legislation. Central to her analysis was the attitude of "native Americans" (meaning earlier waves of northern Europeans) towards more recent immigrants. She described how "overwhelming admiration" for American individualism made it "patriotic" to oppose government measures for old-age security, because they would lessen the independence of workers (247). At the time of this essay the full scope of the Depression had not yet been realized. Addams insisted on the economic interdependence of all countries; neither the tariff nor any other political device could keep the United States from sharing in a worldwide Depression.

Text: Addams, "The Process of Social Transformation" 234-52:

Harsh conditions obtained within as well as without in the newly-opened territories [of the United States], for although philosophers had arrived in Boston to resurrect a belief in man's inherent worthiness, the soothing doctrine had not yet reached the sturdy men and women who occupied the great stretches of country to the west and south....The reverse of this doctrine, that rewards come only to virtue, was easily transformed into the belief that the man successful in dollars thereby established his right to all the honours due to virtue itself, and this social tenet became more widely held than the theological doctrine. This may have been because it fell in quite easily with the economic theory of laissez-faire which at that moment ruled the English-speaking world. Never was a doctrine better fitted to the predilections of these pioneer agriculturalists lately emerged from the covered-wagon stage and with government free land still available for its surplus population....

By the early 1860s, when machine industry began to invade the Mississippi valley, all the orthodox beliefs of church and state protected it from "interference" of either industrial or fiscal legislation. As one after another of these industries attained giant proportions in Chicago, they claimed and received the adulation of a population....The individualistic farmer, made even more independent by the ownership of a harvester, was to be placated as a buyer and the Western rancher as a seller of raw material. In any case the farmer and rancher cared little for the problems of the European workman and considered both trade unions and governmental control over conditions in industry as subversive of American principles. The United States was therefore inevitably slow in any attempt to regulate industry in the interest of the workers, although there were other reasons as well [notably the movement to abolish slavery]. By the time the abolition of slavery had been accomplished public-spirited citizens were obliged to deal with another social problem which long absorbed their energy [political corruption].

For many reasons, therefore, the period of social reconstruction in the United States was postponed until the 1890s, by which time the situation had grown correspondingly acute, and by 1890 we were well behind England and the Continent in all types of social legislation designed to safeguard the health of labouring men and their standards of life.

It was quite obvious by this time that the attitude of native Americans toward immigrants, who have always composed so large a proportion of those engaged in performing the rough labour of the nation, was a factor in our delayed manifestation of social compunction....From the very beginning of the 1830s to the opening of the [First] World War, there had been an ever-increasing number of immigrants, until in 1913 the annual arrivals were more than a million. Because these immigrants were associated with the unskilled and undesirable labour of building railroads and opening coal mines, there gradually developed a superior attitude toward them, resulting in a tendency to exalt the Yankee and to put immigrants into a class by themselves. Naturally every approach to labour problems had to do with immigrants, and it is quite likely that Americans were less concerned for the well being of aliens than they would have been for their own kinsfolk. This was perhaps inevitable, for as the immigrants increased in numbers they tended more and more to live in colonies by themselves and, separated in many cases by religion and almost always by language and customs, Americans had naturally few contacts with them....[Addams then recounted the use of settlement houses as a means of integrating immigrants.]

Just when usages long established come into collision with new standards, resulting in a moral revolution, it is hard to say. Certainly the first decade of the new century exhibited features of such a coming revolution....The Progressive Party was organized in 1912. Many people throughout the country, social workers among them, had become convinced that certain industrial evils could not be corrected unless they were considered a national responsibility and treated from a broader scope than any one state could furnish. It was also believed that only a nation-wide discussion of these social needs would arouse an enthusiasm and understanding adequate to secure national measures. In August 1912 a platform was adopted in the Coliseum of Chicago by the newly-organized Progressive Party, which expressed the stirring hope of thousands of citizens....The platform formulated in political terms remedies for the industrial situation, believing that the United States...might now attain the standards of protective legislation adopted by other great industrial countries....

The Progressive Party campaign was spirited and doubtless of educational value, but it was apparently premature. It was unfortunate, too, that its plans for the future were cut across by the volcanic eruption of the World War....Some of the measures advocated by the Progressive Party and others that had been enacted into laws by the various state legislatures were declared unconstitutional by the Supreme Court of the United States and thus made inoperative...[e.g. maximum hours of work].

Perhaps it was because mass production had so raised the standards of living that more and more people lived in much the same sort of essential material comfort, resulting in a pressure to make them take on a like similarity mentally and spiritually. It is hard to tell what actually produced such a situation—doubtless fear of Russia was an element in it—but certainly for a decade after the war there was less scope for individual self-expression within the ordered framework of the state than there had ever been before on American soil. Yet this widespread desire for conformity was accompanied by such an overwhelming admiration for our early individualism, that it was considered patriotic to oppose governmental measures for old-age security, for instance, because they would lessen the sturdy independence of the working man.

A tendency always present in America, thus intensified, resulted in a dogmatic nationalism which inevitably bred new intolerance toward immigrants....But because the Simon-pure American made an exception of himself—what was good for the immigrant was not necessarily good for him—he exempted himself from laws which he would like to see enforced upon others, with the result that the individual often voted for laws that he himself had no intention of obeying. For instance, the Southern man voted for the Eighteenth Amendment [prohibition of alcohol] because he wanted to keep drink from the Negro, the Northern man because he wished sober immigrant labour and so on (245-48).

Government—British Rule in Ireland

Addams's involvement with Ireland occurred through appointment to an American commission of leading (Protestant) citizens to investigate alleged atrocities, a "pogrom," on the part of the British government in 1920. The seven Americans sought information on both sides, but the British government refused to co-operate. The commission's goal was to place before public opinion—English, Irish and American—the facts of the latest phase of the "troubles," with the hope that causes might be revealed which would in turn lead to a cure. The commission found excesses by the British Army, atrocities comparable to those alleged by Belgium to have been committed by the Germans in World War I. It did not consider that religious differences were the obstacle.

Text: Addams et al, *American Commission on Conditions in Ireland: Interim Report*:

Unless moral force could prevail to end the terror in Ireland, physical force seemed to us bound to continue both to deny the possibility of peace in Ireland, and to diminish the possibility of non-intervention of our government in the struggle. It seemed to us that we could best serve the cause of peace by placing before English, Irish and American public opinion the facts of the situation, free from both agonized exaggeration and merciless understatement; for a knowledge of the facts might reveal their cause, and recognition of that cause might permit its cure by those whose purpose was not to slay but to heal.

The facts available to us for investigating the situation were the atrocities caused by it. We therefore sought evidence of these atrocities from both sides, in the hope that we could make clear to the English on the one hand and to the Irish on the other, our desire to do them the service our common civilization required as a right, our common humanity as a duty (2).

It would appear to your commission that the official campaign of murder, arson and repression has had an unfortunate effect upon the moral fibre of the forces engaged in it. Lord Mayor O'Callaghan [of Cork] and others testified that it has been fashionable for the soldiers and police, careening through cities and villages, to hang over the sides of lorries, their rifles pointed at the passers-by. Apart from any deliberate intention to shoot the citizenry, this bullying practice would seem to us contrary to British tradition. Deaths result from it. And sometimes these deaths seem scarcely accidental....Numerous examples of wanton slaying or wounding were brought before us, including the shooting even of dumb animals, dogs and cattle (79).

It would appear to your commission that the Imperial British Army in Ireland has been guilty of proved excesses, not incomparable in degree and kind with those alleged by the Bryce Report on Belgium atrocities to have been committed by the Imperial German Army. It would further appear that the Imperial British Government have created and introduced into Ireland, a country in area less than the state of Maine, a force of at least 78,000, many of whom were boys and some of them convicts, has incited them to slay, burn and loot, has armed them for the task and has tempered with terror and alcohol this chosen instrument to fit it for the appointed purposes of the Imperial British Government in Ireland. It would seem to us that the moral responsibility for the crime of this instrument rests on those who fashioned and used it.

We would extend our sympathy to the great British people. The army which is the instrument of their Government in Ireland would also seem to be the instrument of the destruction of that moral heritage which was their glory....The sun of that glory seems finally to have set over Ireland; British "justice" has become a discredited thing. The official Black and Tans in Ireland compete for the dishonour of Anglo-Saxon civilization with our unofficial lynch mobs. Decent folk everywhere are shamed and scandalized that such things can still be in their day and generation (98).

Summary

1. Outside of a part of Ulster, Catholics and Protestants live in peace and harmony and their political opinions are not primarily a matter of religion.
2. Even in Ulster religious bigotry is not by any means wholly spontaneous, but is artificially stirred up by those whose economic and political interests are served by dividing the people.
3. While it obviously lies beyond our province to pass final judgment upon the various aspects of the Ulster issue, we have not only a right but a duty as American Protestants to denounce the degradation of religion by such pogroms as occurred last summer. Upon this subject we owe it to our fellow religionists both in America and in Ulster to speak plainly (116).

Government—Role of Women

Addams's "Woman's Part in Managing the City," 1912, was originally produced for the National American Woman Suffrage Association as part of its justification for the municipal franchise for women. Addams confronted the rationale for excluding women on the basis of their not being in the military. Now that cities did not settle their disputes by force of arms other criteria for citizenship were needed. Since many of the functions of modern municipal government have been the traditional responsibility of women: health care, schools and child care, women should be admitted to the franchise.

Text: Addams, "Woman's Part in Managing the Modern City" 322-29:

It has been well said that the modern city is a stronghold of industrialism quite as the feudal city was a stronghold of militarism, but modern cities fear no enemies and rivals from without and their problems of government are solely internal. Affairs for the most part are going badly in these great new centres in which the quickly congregated population has not yet learned to arrange its affairs satisfactorily. Unsanitary housing, poisonous sewage, contaminated water, infant mortality, the spread of contagion, adulterated food, impure milk, smoke-laden air, ill-ventilated factories, dangerous occupations, juvenile crime, unwholesome crowding, prostitution and drunkenness, are the enemies which the modern cities must face and overcome, would they survive. Logically, their electorate should be made up of those who can bear a valiant part in this arduous contest, those who in the past have at least attempted to care for children, to clean houses, to prepare foods, to isolate the family from moral dangers, those who have traditionally taken care of that side of life which inevitably becomes the subject of municipal consideration....To test the elector's fitness to deal with this situation by his ability to bear arms is absurd. These problems must be solved, if they are solved at all, not from the military point of view, not even from the industrial point of view, but from a third, which is rapidly developing in all the great cities of the world, the human welfare point of view.

There are many evidences that we are emerging from a period of industrialism into a period of humanitarianism, and that personal welfare is now being considered a legitimate object of government. The most noticeable manifestation of this civic humanitarianism is to be found in those cities where the greatest abuses of industrialism and materialism exist....

A city is in many respects a great business corporation, but in other respects it is enlarged housekeeping. If American cities have failed in the first, partly because office holders have carried with them the predatory instinct learned in competitive business, and cannot help "working a good thing" when they have an opportunity, may we not say that city housekeeping has failed partly because women, the traditional housekeepers, have not been consulted as to its multiform activities? The men of the city have been carelessly indifferent to much of its civic housekeeping, as they have always been indifferent to the details of the household. They have totally disregarded a candidate's capacity to keep the streets clean, preferring to consider him in relation to the national tariff or to the necessity for increasing the national navy, in a pure spirit of reversion to the traditional type of government, which had to do only with enemies and outsiders. It is difficult to see what military prowess has to do with the multiform duties which, in a modern city, include the care of parks and libraries, superintendence of markets, sewers and bridges, the inspection of provisions and boilers and the proper disposal of garbage....

Because all these things have traditionally been in the hands of women, if they take no part in them now they are not only missing the education which the natural participation in civic life would bring to them, but they are losing what they have always had....From the days of the cave dwellers, so far as the home was clean and wholesome it was due to their efforts....From the period of the primitive village the only public sweeping which was performed was what they undertook....Most of the departments in a modern city can be traced to woman's traditional activity, but, in spite of this, so soon as these old affairs were turned over to the care of the city they slipped from woman's hands....

What would the result have been could women have regarded the suffrage not as a right or a privilege, but as a mere piece of governmental machinery, without which they could not perform their traditional functions under the changed conditions of city life?...We are at the beginning of a prolonged effort to incorporate a progressive, developing city life, founded upon a response to the needs of all the people....To be in any measure successful, this effort will require all the intelligent powers of observation, all the sympathy, all the common sense which may be gained from the whole adult population....

Out of the medieval city, founded upon militarism, there arose in the thirteenth century a new order, the middle class, whose importance rested, not upon birth or arms, but upon wealth, intelligence and organization. They achieved a sterling success in the succeeding six centuries of industrialism because they were essential to the existence and development of the industrial era. Perhaps we can forecast the career of woman the citizen, if she is permitted to bear an elector's part in the coming period of humanitarianism, in which government must concern itself with human welfare. She would bear her share of civic responsibility not because she clamours for her rights, but because she is essential to the normal development of the city of the future.

Addams was a staunch supporter of the Progressive Party, which lived up to its name by being the advocate of welfare state measures and the vote for women. In the speech reported below she seconded the nomination of **Theodore Roosevelt** for President of the United States. This must have posed some problem for the peace advocate, for Roosevelt was a "cheerful warrior" with an enormously positive view of war's potential for developing manliness. Roosevelt in fact lost the election to **Woodrow Wilson**, who was then president during World War I, and the president whom Addams herself had to lobby on peace measures for the Women's International League for Peace and Freedom.

Text: Addams, Appendix to the Congressional Record. House of Representatives August 12 1912:

I rise to second the nomination, stirred by the splendid platform adopted by this convention. Measures of industrial amelioration, demands for social justice, long discussed by small groups in charity conference and economic associations, have here been considered in a great national convention and are at last thrust into the stern arena of political action.

A great party has pledged itself to the protection of children, to the care of the aged, to the relief of overworked girls, to the safeguarding of burdened men. Committed to these humane undertakings it is inevitable that such a party should appeal to women, should seek to draw upon the great reservoir of their moral energy, so long undesired and unutilized in practical politics—one the corollary of the other—a program of human welfare, the necessity for women's participation....

We ratify this platform not only because it represents our earnest convictions and formulates our high hopes, but because it pulls upon our faculties and calls us to definite action. We find it a prophecy that democracy shall not be actually realized until no group of our people—certainly not

10,000,000 so sadly in need of reassurance—shall fail to bear the responsibilities of self-government and that no class of evils shall lie beyond redress.

The new party has become the American exponent of a world-wide movement toward juster social conditions, a movement which the United States, lagging behind other great nations, has been unaccountably slow to embody in political action. I second the nomination of Theodore Roosevelt because he is one of the few men in our public life who has been responsive to the social appeal and who has caught the significance of the modern movement. Because of that, because the program will require a leader of invincible courage, of open mind, of democratic sympathies, one endowed with power to interpret the common man and to identify himself with the common lot, I heartily second the nomination.

Peace, War and Militarism—The Women's Peace Movement

The last four items are the work largely of Jane Addams, three written jointly with other members of the Women's International League for Peace and Freedom (WILPF). Addams herself was the founding president of the League, which still has active chapters in many countries. Her chief intellectual sources were **Jesus** (she had a life-long faith but resisted "evangelical conversion") and **Leo Tolstoy** (who reproached her for her decadent lifestyle when she visited him in Russia). Her first writing on peace dates from 1907 and she continued to write, speak and organize on peace until her death in 1935. Both Addams and Emily Greene Balch, her co-author on two of the items excerpted below, were awarded the Nobel Peace Prize, in 1931 and 1947 respectively.

The WILPF was formed in World War I with the hope of bringing the war in Europe to an early end. Addams at the same time worked with other Americans to keep the United States out of the war, which it joined only in 1917. The League's first meeting was held at The Hague in 1915 as the "International Congress of Women;" its initial name was the Committee of Women for a Permanent Peace.[171] (The current name was adopted at the second congress, in 1919.) Addams led the large American delegation, presided over the congress (selected because she was from a neutral nation) and was elected president of the ongoing organization. The resolutions adopted are both a cogent statement of abhorrence of war, stressing women's particular vulnerability as victims of sexual assault, and an argument for an alternative, negotiated peace based on justice. Woodrow Wilson's Fourteen Principles are believed to have been influenced by the women's analysis. The resolutions are noteworthy for offering practical proposals to ensure that the peace, whenever achieved, would be lasting.

---

[171] On the WILPF see Bussey and Tims, *Women's International League for Peace and Freedom*; Jill Liddington, *The Road to Greenham Common*.

The women at The Hague conference were rightfully aware of the extent to which the profit motive fuelled, and continues to fuel, the arms race. They sought to eliminate the profit factor by advocating state control of the arms industry and trade, a remedy which, with the benefit of hindsight, we know is not enough. Delegates from the women's conference, selected to include both belligerent and non-belligerent countries, carried the message to all the nations of Europe and the United States. Addams took part in meeting with President Woodrow Wilson on her return.

The second women's congress, in Zürich in 1919, was convened and took place fortuitously the week the Treaty of Versailles was published. The women were the first to react to the harshness of the terms when they were announced. They condemned the terms for condoning secret diplomacy and the "spoils to the victor" approach. They correctly predicted the creation of animosities which would lead to future wars. They not only condemned the economic blockade that led to serious hunger and disease in the losing nations, but many of the women, notably Addams, worked for food relief. With the benefit of hindsight it could not be more obvious that the women were right.

Text: From Bussey and Tims, *Women's International League for Peace and Freedom* 31:

The International Congress of Women expresses its deep regret that the terms of peace proposed at Versailles should so seriously violate the principles upon which alone a just and lasting peace can be secured, and which the democracies of the world had come to accept.

By guaranteeing the fruits of the secret treaties to the conquerors, the terms of peace tacitly sanction secret diplomacy, deny the principles of self-determination, recognize the rights of the victors to the spoils of war and create all over Europe discords and animosities which can only lead to future wars. By the demand for the disarmament of one set of belligerents only, the principle of justice is violated and the rule of force is continued. By the financial and economic proposals a hundred million people of this generation in the heart of Europe are condemned to poverty, disease and despair, which must result in the spread of hatred and anarchy within each nation.

With a deep sense of responsibility, this Congress strongly urges the Allied and Associated Governments to accept such amendments of the terms as shall bring the peace into harmony with those principles first enumerated by President Wilson, upon the faithful carrying out of which the honour of the Allied peoples depends.

Like so many activists in the peace movement today, Addams believed that women have a particular role to play because their roles as mothers make them highly sensitive to human life. In her address to the founding congress of the Women's Peace Party, 1915, she did not assert any innate superiority of women, but rather the closer involvement of women in the protection, nurture and conservation of human life. She predicted that Europe at the end of the war would be generations behind in its social and economic goals, which was indeed the case. Addams next argued that women's heightened sensitivity for human life carried with it an obligation to act. She described how, historically, women had stopped the practice of child sacrifice and urged women to protest the war in the light of their consciences.

Text: Addams, Address to the Women's Peace Party January 10, 1915:

After the eloquent speeches you have heard from women who have come from the field of battle, as it were, a speech from one representing American women thousands of miles away from the devastation and carnage must seem tame and scarcely deserving a hearing. But there are certain things now being destroyed by war in which from the beginning of time women, as women, have held a vested interest, and I beg to draw your attention to three or four of them.

One thing war is now destroying and which is being "thrown back" in the scientific sense, is the conception of patriotism gradually built up during thousands of years. Europe has had one revolution after another in which women as well as men have taken part, that a patriotism might be established which should contain liberty as well as loyalty. At the present moment, however, thousands of men marching to their death are under compulsion, not of this higher type of patriotism, but of a tribal conception which ought to have left the world long since.

A state founded upon such a tribal ideal of patriotism has no place for women within its councils, and women have a right to protest against the destruction of that larger ideal of the state in which they had won a place, and to deprecate a world put back upon a basis of brute force, a world in which they can play no part. Women also have a vested right in the developed conscience of the world. At this moment, because of war, the finest consciences in Europe are engaged in the old business of self-justification, utilizing outgrown myths to explain the course of action which their governments have taken.

Last, shall we not say that that sensitiveness to human life so highly developed in women has been seriously injured by this war? Thousands of people in the United States and Europe had become so convinced that the sanctity of life was an accepted tenet of civilization that they deemed war had become forever impossible. That belief has been rudely overturned and we are now at the foot of the ladder, beginning again to establish the belief that human life is sacred above all else that the planet contains. I do not assert that women are better than men—even in the heat of suffrage debates I have never maintained that—but we would all admit that there are things concerning which women are more sensitive than men, and that one of these is the treasuring of life. I would ask you to consider with me five aspects concerning this sensitiveness which war is rapidly destroying.

The first is the *protection* of human life. The advanced nations know very accurately, and we had begun to know in America, how many children are needlessly lost in the first years of infancy. Measures inaugurated for the prevention of infant mortality were slowly spreading from one country to another. All that effort has been scattered to the winds by the war....

The second aspect is the *nurture* of human life. From the time a soldier is born to the moment he marches in his uniform to be wantonly destroyed, it is largely the women of his household who have cared for him. War overthrows not only the work of the mother, the nurse and the teacher, but at the same time ruthlessly destroys the very conception of the careful nurture of life.

The third aspect is the *fulfillment* of human life. Every woman who cares for a little child fondly throws her imagination forward to the time when he shall have become a great and heroic man. Every baby is thus made human and is developed by the hope and expectation which surrounds him. But no one in Europe in the face of war's destruction can consider any other fulfillment of life than a soldier's death.

The fourth aspect is the *conservation* of human life, that which expresses itself in the state care of dependent children, in old-age pensions, the sentiment which holds that every scrap of human life is so valuable that the human family cannot neglect the feeblest child without risking its own destruction. At this moment none of the warring countries of Europe can cherish the aged and infirm. The state cannot give care to its dependents when thousands of splendid men are dying each day. Little children and aged people are dying, too, in some countries in the proportion of five to one soldier killed on the field, but the nation must remain indifferent to their suffering.

Last of all is that which we call the *ascent* of human life, that which leads a man to cherish the hope that the next generation shall advance beyond the generation in which he lives, that generous glow we all experience when we see that those coming after us are equipped better than we have been. We know that Europe at the end of this war will not begin to build where it left off; we know that it will begin generations behind the point it had reached when the war began.

If we admit that this sensitiveness for human life is stronger in women than in men because women have been responsible for the care of the young and the aged and those who need special nurture, it is certainly true that this sensitiveness, developed in women, carries with it an obligation. Once before in the history of the world, in response to this sensitiveness, women called a halt to the sacrifice of human life, although it then implied the abolition of a religious observance long believed to be right and necessary. In the history of one nation after another it was the mothers who first protested that their children should no longer be slain as living sacrifices upon the altars of the tribal gods, although the national leaders contended that human sacrifice was bound up with traditions of free religion and patriotism and could not be abolished.

Women led a revolt against the hideous practice which had dogged the human race for centuries, not because they were founding a new religion, but because they were responding to their sensitiveness to life. When at last a brave leader here and there gave heed to the mother of the child, he gradually found that courage and religion were with the abolition of human sacrifice, and that the protesting women had anticipated the conscience of the future.

Many of us believe that throughout this round world of ours there are thousands of men and women who have become convinced that the sacrifice of life in warfare is unnecessary and wasteful. It is possible that if women in Europe—in the very countries which are now at war—receive a message from the women of American solemnly protesting against this sacrifice, that they may take courage to formulate their own....We believe that we are endeavouring to express that which is grounded in the souls of women all over the world, that when this war is over—as in time it must be, if only through the exhaustion of the contending powers—there will be many men to say, "Why didn't women call a halt before thousands, and even millions, of men had needlessly lost their lives?" Certainly, if women's consciences are stirred in regard to warfare, this is the moment to formulate a statement of their convictions.

In "The Hopes We Inherit" Jane Addams and Emily Greene Balch gave a more academic analysis of war than that provided in the resolutions from The Hague. The essay clearly stated the religious foundations of the authors' commitment to peace: the dream of a warless world in Messianic prophecy. They noted that the "swords into ploughshares" contrasted with Greek classical myths of a golden past. They credited the "dynamic teaching of Jesus" for the next step forward. They related the good early start of the Church on the issue; Christians refused to take part in war just as they had rejected the human sacrifices of the Roman religion.

Addams and Balch succinctly traced the teachings on peace by Mennonites, Quakers and such philosophers as Grotius and Kant, through the Enlightenment, French Revolution, Napoleonic Wars and on to Tolstoy. They set out the first practical steps to peaceful dispute settlement in The Hague Court of Conciliation and Arbitration. They next asserted the political conditions required for peace, consistent with the resolutions the women's peace movement had evolved. They believed that it was as practicable to abolish war as it had been to abolish slavery in the nineteenth century.

Text: Addams and Balch, "The Hopes we Inherit," *Women at the Hague*:

The hopes we inherit are manifold for during many centuries no generation has failed to bear testimony to that unfulfilled desire for universal peace which torments mankind like an unappeased thirst. Sometimes this testimony has been borne by small groups of humble people, or embodied in the schemes of a great monarch or able statesman, at other times it has broadened into political or religious organizations carrying the ardent consent of whole populations. While this desire is always in the hearts of men it is never so widespread, so driven by remorse, so restless for expression, as after a great war. It is of course impossible to survey more than a few of the historic efforts which carried forward these hopes which have never yet been fulfilled....These futile attempts give at least a certain dignity and traditional background to contemporaneous endeavour and even suggest an accumulation of moral energy which in the end cannot be withstood.

The best known and perhaps most beautiful expression of this dream of a warless world is the great Messianic prophecy of Isaiah, who foretold a reign of peace both outward and inner, resulting from righteousness and goodwill. Isaiah's prophecy was remarkable in that it looked forward rather than backward, for the mythology of the ancients, including the dreams of the Greeks and Romans, had always placed the era of peace in the past, in a golden age of long ago which had been followed by other ages, each harder than the last, until men fell upon the iron age of the present. Such a traditional view naturally supplied little stimulus for endeavours to bring about better conditions until into this apathy came the dynamic teaching of Jesus. The kingdom of God is indeed within, but the sons of the kingdom are themselves to do the will here and now.

Courage, for Aristotle a purely martial virtue, took a new form in passive resistance of violence. Many of the early Christians, endeavouring to keep themselves unspotted from the world, refused to take part in war as they refused to burn incense before the image of a deified emperor. Certainly Tertullian, Clement, Origen and Basil held that no Christian could properly be a soldier or keep a magisterial office in which he would have to inflict the death penalty. This position was gradually abandoned, and only a few later bishops endorsed Ambrose in forbidding bloodshed in self defence.

A change of view was indeed inevitable as the church became powerful in the state and the question of war in relation to Christianity took on a political aspect. When the great St Augustine himself distinguished just and unjust wars and did not condemn the former the road was opened for so-called Christian wars. The double organization of Christendom under medieval theory, the emperor to be the representative of God upon earth for secular matters as the pope for those of religion, resulted in various peace plans and experiments in the endeavour to limit the plague of private feudal wars....

The movement that culminated in the Reformation included at least one unobtrusive revolt against war when Mennonites began to preach their doctrine of nonresistance....The idea of putting an end to the wars that devastated Europe by organizing a confederation of states was urged in a more practical shape than ever before by the famous Huguenot financier and statesman,

Sully....His great design was not wholly a peace plan, but it was international in scope and contained some very wise observations upon war. One of them, that the victor may suffer quite as much as the vanquished, has a very modern sound.

William Penn, follower of George Fox, the founder of the Society of Friends, was not only a religious pacifist but also, like Sully, an active statesman and administrator and the author of a project for international organization for peace. The gist of both plans was a parliament of powers to maintain justice. In Pennsylvania the Quakers exemplified their beliefs in practice and at least their fair and friendly dealings with the Indians were extraordinarily successful. For the most part they bore a consistent testimony against war and succeeded in getting recognition for their conscientious objection to military service. Since then no war has been without the testimony of those who, whether Quakers or not, have refused to take part in war for conscience's sake.

The legal aspect of the peace movement, the great conception of a body of laws recognized by all nations, had its most striking formulation in Hugo Grotius of the Netherlands, by his great book *On the Rights of War and Peace* [1620] (3-7).

The eighteenth century, which seemed to make a great advance toward peace, was marked by its enthusiasms for large and generous ideas and its belief that man by the use of his reason could make over the world. The idea of a Europe organized for peace...found many supporters....It was largely in the cosmopolitan salons of Paris where Jefferson, Franklin and Thomas Paine met other thinkers of the day...that the ideas that underlay the overthrow of imperialism in American and of feudalism in France were kindled and spread abroad....But the very success of these ideas brought on the struggle with outgrown institutions...a struggle which was accompanied by violence and the ugly intolerance that violence breeds....

The wars of Napoleon, however, through the combinations of allied nations who waged the last campaign against him...were responsible for a notable experiment in peace, the Holy Alliance. This remarkable organization testified to the spirit of "never again," which fills the hearts of men as they call upon high heaven to witness their efforts to make another war impossible. The periodical meetings of rulers and statesmen provided for in the Holy Alliance were but a sorry substitute for the brotherhood of man so loudly acclaimed in the eighteenth century, but they at least established the system of an international concert and disclosed the honest belief that an enduring peace would result from "a just redistribution of political forces."...

Unhappily the nineteenth century saw a long series of wars, large and small, wars for independence as in Greece and Italy, wars of diplomacy as in the Crimea, wars of expansion and empire as in the Franco-Prussian War, the Boer War or our own [American] war in Mexico. But the belief in "progress" was paramount throughout the century and men seeking to realize it in the most diverse fields became impatient with the barbarism of war and the interruption it brought to their plans....

The movement for the abolishment of war became organized into definite peace societies as early as 1815, reflecting doubtless the high hopes of the peace of Vienna...Formal peace societies were founded in the United States and in England...In 1849 a general Peace Congress met in Paris under the presidency of Victor Hugo and in 1867 Hugo and Garibaldi founded a League of Peace and Liberty in Geneva. Only three years later the clash of Prussian and Napoleonic imperialism again sowed the dragon's teeth of war and then nations of Europe...conscripted whole populations and prepared for a coming struggle for power which they deemed inevitable. The civilized world lived in the shadow of the threat of a war which, as Bismarck prophesied, would "bleed Europe white."

In the midst of this apprehension Baroness von Suttner's novel *Throw Down Your Arms* was to the peace movement something of what *Uncle Tom's Cabin* was to the antislavery cause....Even deeper and stronger than this appeal to pity and horror was Tolstoy's challenge to the Christian conscience. He called upon all who accepted the teachings of the sermon on the mount "to resist not evil"....There resulted for the moment such a revolt against war in the ranks of sensitive Christians...as foreshadowed a return to the early Christian position. At least thousands of Christians ceased to say that the abolition of war was impossible....

From Russia also came the next great impetus toward peace in its political aspect. The czar...called a peace conference at The Hague in 1899, followed by another in 1907. The two great policies brought forward at these conferences were arbitration and disarmament....The Hague Court of Arbitration functioned satisfactorily for fifteen years, during which period many cases were formally arbitrated and others were adjusted by conciliation....Since the [First] World War militarism has invaded new territory. Fear, which far more than courage is the mother of wars, obsesses whole peoples, most of all the victorious ones....Fear that a social revolution may spread from Russia fills the possessing classes with panic and intolerance. There seems to be an increased willingness to resort to violence and in many countries, including the United States, there is an unprecedented development of training for military service (7-14).

Through it all, however, the problem of peace and war—for it is a problem—begins to be better understood. We see that for its solution certain conditions are necessary which the older peace movements necessarily lacked: the first is technical, the possibility of rapid and universal intercourse. This now exists and there is constant progress in this field....The second is psychological; peace can come only if men are determined to have it...there must be a widespread desire for peaceful solutions of difficulties, fair to both sides, and a willingness patiently to endeavour to find such solutions....The third condition of a world at peace is political. Orderly methods of doing what is now done by war, that is settling clashes between nations, must be organized....Arbitration treaties, a world court, an association of nations preventing aggression at once by world opinion and by providing non-violent methods of securing fair demands—these are parts of the necessary machinery of world peace. The League of Nations, even to those who do not believe that the United States should enter it, must appear as the most important experiment in this direction that ever has been made....

It is as practicable to abolish war as it was to abolish the institution of chattel slavery which also was based on human desires and greed. These are still with us, but slavery has joined cannibalism, human sacrifice and other once sacred human habits as one of the shameful and happily abandoned institutions of the past. It is quite possible to reduce war to the present status of chattel slavery, a moribund survival, occurring only in backward parts of the earth, no longer accredited, honoured, regulated by law, deliberately fostered and prepared for, approved by the churches, beautified by literature and considered inevitable although deplorable by conscientious statesmen. A great kingdom of peace lies close to hand, ready to come into being if we would but turn toward it (15-18).

Text: Addams and Balch, "Resolutions adopted by the International Congress of Women," *Women at the Hague.* Appendix II, 150-59:

We women, in international congress assembled, protest against the madness and the horror of war, involving as it does a reckless sacrifice of human life and the destruction of so much that humanity has laboured through centuries to build up. This International Congress of Women opposes the assumption that women can be protected under the conditions of modern warfare. It protests vehemently against the odious wrongs of which women are the victims in time of war, especially against the horrible violation of women which attends all war....

The congress...urges the governments of the world to put an end to this bloodshed and to begin peace negotiations. It demands that the peace which follows shall be permanent and therefore based on principles of justice...namely: that no territory should be transferred without the consent of the men and women in it, and that the right of conquest should not be recognized, that autonomy and a democratic parliament should not be refused to any people; that the governments of all nations should come to an agreement to refer future international disputes to arbitration or conciliation and to bring social, moral and economic pressure to bear upon any country which resorts to arms; that foreign politics should be subject to democratic control; that women should be granted equal political rights with men.

This International Congress of Women resolves to ask the neutral countries to take immediate steps to create a conference of neutral nations which shall without delay offer continuous mediation...[and] that a third Hague Conference be convened immediately after the war.

This International Congress of Women urges that the organization of the Society of Nations should be further developed on the basis of a constructive peace, and that it should include:
(a) as a development of the Hague Court of Arbitration, a permanent International court of Justice;
(b) a permanent International Conference holding regular meetings, in which women should take part, to deal not with the rules of warfare but with practical proposals for further international cooperation among the states....This International Conference shall appoint a permanent Council of Conciliation and Investigation for the settlement of international differences arising from economic competition, expanding commerce, increasing population and changes in social and political standards.

The International Congress...urges...that all countries...take over the manufacture of arms and munitions of war and should control all international traffic in the same. It sees in the private profits accruing from the great armament factories a powerful hindrance to the abolition of war. The International Congress of Women urges that in all countries there shall be liberty of commerce, that the seas shall be free and the trade routes open on equal terms to the shipping of all nations....

This International Congress of Women demands that all secret treaties shall be void and that for the ratification of future treaties the participation of at least the legislature of every government shall be necessary. This congress recommends that national commissions be created and international conferences convened for the scientific study and elaboration of the principles and conditions of permanent peace, which might contribute to the development of an International Federation....

To urge the governments of the world to put an end to this bloodshed and to establish a just and lasting peace, this International Congress of Women delegates envoys to carry the message expressed in the congress resolutions to the rulers of the belligerent and neutral nations of Europe and to the President of the United States.

As other committed pacifists, Addams had often to answer the sneering question, "Are pacifists cowards?" the title of a speech made shortly before American entry into the Great War. She was keen to show that those against war, or American participation in it, did not lack higher ideals. The people who first demanded change always excited opposition; it took courage to oppose war.

Text: Addams, "Are Pacifists Cowards?"

When as pacifists we urge a courageous venture into international ethics, which will require a fine valour as well as a high intelligence, we experience a sense of anti-climax when we are told that because we do not want war we are so cowardly as to care for "safety first," that we place human life, physical life, above the great ideals of national righteousness. But surely that man is not without courage who, seeing that which is invisible to the majority of his fellow countrymen, still asserts his conviction and is ready to vindicate its spiritual value over against the world. Each advance in the zigzag line of human progress has traditionally been embodied in small groups of individuals who have ceased to be in harmony with the status quo and have demanded modifications. Such modifications did not always prove to be in the line of progress but, whether they were or not, they always excited opposition, which from the nature of the case was never so determined as when the proposed changes touched moral achievements which were greatly prized and had been secured with much difficulty.

Bearing in mind the long struggle to secure and maintain national unity the pacifist easily understands why his theories seem particularly obnoxious just now, although in point of fact our national unity is not threatened and would be finely consummated in an international organization.

With visions of international justice filling our minds, pacifists are always a little startled when those who insist that justice can only be established by war, accuse us of caring for peace irrespective of justice. Many of the pacifists in their individual and corporate capacity have long striven for social and political justice with a fervour perhaps equal to that employed by the advocates of force, and we realize that a sense of justice has become the keynote to the best political and social activity in this generation....

We believe that the ardour and self sacrifice so characteristic of youth could be enlisted for the vitally-energetic role which we hope our beloved country will inaugurate in the international life of the world. We realize that it is only the ardent spirits, the lovers of mankind, who will be able to break down the suspicion and lack of understanding which has so long stood in the way of the necessary changes upon which international good order depends, who will at last create a political organization enabling nations to secure without war those high ends which they now gallantly seek to obtain upon the battlefield.

With such a creed can the pacifists of today be accused of selfishness when they urge upon the United States not isolation, not indifference to moral issues and to the fate of liberty and democracy, but a strenuous endeavour to lead all nations of the earth into an organized international life worthy of civilized men?

BERTHA VON SUTTNER (1843-1913)

Von Suttner was a member of an impecunious noble Austrian family.[172] Forced to work, she took a position in Paris, 1875, as secretary—for one week!—for

---

[172] On her life see Caroline E. Playne, *Bertha von Suttner* and Beatrix Kempf, *Woman for Peace*.

Alfred Nobel. She returned to Vienna to marry for love, against her family's wishes. Von Suttner kept in touch with Nobel until the end of his life, keeping him up to date on activities of the peace movement. He gave money to it at various stages before making the legacy in his will that became the Nobel Peace Prize. Von Suttner herself received the tenth award in 1905. She shared Nobel's view that the money should go to an individual, not an organization (these provisions were not followed) and that it should be substantial enough to represent a "handsome reward" for effort and a "useful instrument of action."[173]

Bertha von Suttner had only been involved in the peace movement a few years when she published, in 1889, her famous *Lay Down Your Arms*.[174] It became an instant best seller, was translated into sixteen languages and sold more than a million copies. The last popular edition, 200,000 copies, came out in 1914. A film was made from the book, to be launched at a peace conference in 1914, but the conference was cancelled with the outbreak of World War I. Von Suttner herself died that year. *Lay Down Your Arms* was an action-packed page turner. Ostensibly it is the story of a young woman who lost her first husband in the Italian campaigns, whose second husband escaped death in the Danish-German wars and joined her in peace work. In the course of the book there is considerable discussion of ideas both on the causes of war and the measures required to secure peace. Leo Tolstoy likened it to Harriet Beecher Stowe's *Uncle Tom's Cabin* and hoped that it would lead to the abolition of war as Stowe's had to the abolition of slavery.[175]

Text: von Suttner, *Ground Arms!* [Lay Down Your Arms]:

History is responsible for this training of youth to the idea of the glory of war. From baby days it is stamped upon the impressionable childish mind that the God of battles has ordained wars, and that this divine ordinance regulates the history of nations, that these are engaged in the fulfillment of immutable decree, a law of nature, like tornadoes and earthquakes, which from time to time will not be stemmed, that though atrocities and wickedness, sorrow and heart-breaking anguish are bound up therewith, these cannot be avoided and must be recognized as a portion of the inevitable. The magnitude of the result attained for the advantage of the many justifies the sacrifice of the happiness, interests or the very life of the individual. Is there a nobler death than comes

---

[173] Cited from unpublished correspondence, Irwin Abrams, "Bertha von Suttner and the Nobel Peace Prize" 301.

[174] The translation by Abbott used here is entitled *Ground Arms!* For a good introduction see Irwin Abrams, introduction to the Holmes' translation, *Lay Down Your Arms*.

[175] Abrams, Introduction, *Lay Down Your Arms* 10.

in the line of duty on the field of honour—a more enviable immortality than that of the heroic soldier? (13)

Always the other side that wishes war! Always the other one who is accused of resolving that might shall overcome justice. An "unholy war," because it was "German against German." Quite right; it is a step forward when above Prussia and Austria the appeal to Germany is made. But a much higher plane would be reached if every war were recognized as a war of mankind against mankind, that is, civilized man against civilized man, and were regarded as an unholy fratricidal contest. And of what use to summon before the judgment seat of history? History as hitherto written gives judgment to the victor. Around the conqueror falls the golden halo of history, and he becomes the great promoter of civilization.

And before the judgment seat of God, the Almighty? Is He not the same who is always represented as the Lord of Hosts, and is the outbreak as well as the termination of every war other than the result of the immutable will of this same Almighty? Oh, contradiction upon contradiction! Where shall we find the truth under all these conventional phrases, where two antagonistic principles—war and justice, international hatred and love of humanity, the God of Love and the God of Battles—are set against each other as equally holy (127).

On the nineteenth of July, the French ambassador in Berlin presented the formal declaration of war to the Prussian government. A declaration of war! We speak of it so coolly. What does it mean? The beginning of an action, the result of political intrigue and incidentally the sentence of death of half a million human beings. This document I copied into my red note-book:
"The government of his Majesty, the Emperor of the French, could only consider the elevation of a Prussian prince to the throne of Spain as an undertaking dangerous to the territorial security of France, and has therefore found it necessary to demand of the King of Prussia the assurance that a similar combination will not receive his support in the future. Since his Majesty declined to give this assurance, and, on the contrary, declared to our ambassador that he reserved to himself the right of inquiry into such possible events, the imperial government must recognize in this declaration of the King a suppressed intention, which is threatening to France and the balance of power in Europe (there it is again, this famous balance of power). This declaration has become of more serious character through the report communicated to the ministry of the refusal to receive the Emperor's plenipotentiary and enter into further discussion of the subject (so it seems that a more or less friendly intercourse between regents and diplomatists settles the fate of peoples). As a result of this course the French government considers it its duty without delay to think of the defence (yes, yes, defence—never attack) of its outraged dignity and its outraged interests. Determined to adopt all measures to this end, which are offered it by existing circumstances, it considers itself from now on in the condition of war with Prussia." Condition of war! Does he who sitting at the

diplomatic table sets this word down on paper realize that he has dipped his pen in flames, in bloody tears, in the poison of disease?... (251-52)

The Emperor Napoleon on his part issued the following proclamation: "Because of the arrogant claims of Prussia we were obliged to protest. These protests have been met with ridicule. Events followed which indicated a contempt for us. Our country has been deeply incensed thereby and instantly the battle-cry has been heard from one end of France to the other. There is nothing to be done except to consign our fate to the lot drawn by war. We do not war against Germany, whose independence we respect. We have the most earnest desire that the people who compose the great German nation may be the arbiters of their own destiny. What we desire is the establishment of a condition of things which will insure our present security and make our future safe. We desire a permanent peace, founded upon the true interests of peoples; we wish that this miserable condition should end and that all nations use all possible means to secure general disarmament."

What a lesson, what a striking lesson this document is when we consider it in connection with the events that followed. In order to be sure of safety, in order to attain permanent peace this war was begun by France. And what was the result?—"the terrible year" and enduring hatred. No, no; one does not use charcoal to paint a thing white, nor asafoetida to perfume a room, nor war to secure peace (254).

Possibly the prince or the statesman is now alive who will figure in all future history as the most famous, the most enlightened, because he will have brought about this general laying down of arms. Even now the insane idea is dying out, notwithstanding that diplomatic egotism attempts to justify itself by its assertion, the insane idea that destruction of one person is the security of another. Already the realization that justice must be the foundation of all social life is glimmering upon the world and, from an acknowledgement of this truth, humanity must gain a nobler stature (286).

OLIVE SCHREINER (1855-1920)

Schreiner was a prominent South African author (known especially for *The Story of an African Farm* and her classic book of feminist economic analysis, *Woman and Labor*, 1911), suffragist and peace advocate. As a South African she had been greatly influenced by the Boer War and wrote a novel on it, *Trooper Peter Halket*. That war also marked the first use of concentration camps for civilians—the wives and children of Boer guerrilla fighters.

Peace, War and Militarism—Gender Roles

Schreiner's "Woman and War" is perhaps the best formulation of the feminist perspective on war from the period before World War I. Neither it nor Jane Addams's rested on differences in biological makeup between the sexes. Rather women's role in child bearing and rearing made them care more than men. Women knew the cost of producing human life and would be less reckless in sacrificing lives. Schreiner observed, undoubtedly correctly for the time, that women paid more in "bloodshed and anguish" in giving birth than men did by dying in battle. For lengthy wars women were called on to maintain a nation's numbers by increased childbearing and rearing. This amounted to a "war tax" on women heavier than any borne by men. Schreiner, as so many other suffragists, thought that when women had the vote they would use it for peace. Women would not carelessly sacrifice lives but would turn to arbitration and compensation as better means of solving international disputes.

Text: Schreiner, "Woman and War," *Woman and Labor*:

Our relation to war is far more intimate, personal and indissoluble than [men's]. Men have made boomerangs, bows, swords, or guns with which to destroy one another; we have made the men who destroyed and were destroyed! We have in all ages produced, at an enormous cost, the primal munitions of war, without which no other would exist. There is no battle field on earth, nor has ever been howsoever covered with slain, which it has not cost the women of the race more in actual bloodshed and anguish to supply than it has cost the men who lie there. *We pay the first cost on all human life* (174).

On that day when the woman takes her place beside the man in the governance and arrangement of external affairs of her race will also be that day that heralds the death of war as a means of arranging differences. No tinsel of trumpets and flags will ultimately seduce women into the insanity of recklessly destroying life, or gild the wilful taking of life with any other name than that of murder, whether it be the slaughter of the million or of one by one (176).

It is not because of woman's cowardice, incapacity, nor, above all, because of her general superior virtue, that she will end war when her voice is fully and clearly heard in the governance of states—it is because, on this one point...she knows the history of human flesh; she knows its cost; he does not....Men's bodies are our woman's works of art. Given to us power to control, we will never carelessly throw them to fill up the gaps in human relationships made by international ambitions and greed....Arbitration and compensation would as naturally occur to her as cheaper and simpler methods of bridging the gaps in national relationships....

In nations continually at war, incessant and unbroken child-bearing is by war imposed on all women if the state is to survive; and whenever war occurs, if numbers are to be maintained, there must be an increased child-bearing and rearing. This throws upon woman as woman a war tax, compared with which all that the male expends in military preparations is comparatively light....It is our intention to enter into the domain of war and to labor there till in the course of generations we have extinguished it (178-84).

CATHERINE E. MARSHALL (1880-1961)

Marshall came into the peace movement in 1915 after years of virtual full-time organizing for the non-militant wing of the British women's suffrage movement.[176] Marshall herself took part in the planning of the first women's conference at The Hague, 1915, but the English delegates to the conference were prevented, by their own government, from attending it. She and others initially tried to get the National Union of Women's Suffrage Societies to support the peace cause. **Millicent Fawcett**, its president, however, was strongly pro-war (as she had been on the Boer War). The executive split; Marshall and half its members left to form their own organization. Marshall's biographer reports that **Bertrand Russell** was himself "favourably impressed" with the position taken by the women, that it was often preferable to the "idealistic theorizing" which often contented the Union for Democratic Control.[177] Marshall in fact recruited Russell to work for the No Conscription Fellowship, the organization that defended conscientious objectors. The short excerpt that follows is from a 1915 pamphlet, one of the only two that Marshall published (she wrote for years on the practical aspects of the movement: minutes, memoranda, letters to politicians, et cetera). The other pamphlet, only very briefly excerpted here, is "The Future of Women in Politics," which argued that such future depended on whether the war resulted in the discrediting of militarism or its intensification. As had Schreiner, Marshall held that women had a special role from their everyday lives (he brings home the game, earns the wages, builds the house; she cooks and distributes food, spends money on the household and transforms the house into a home):

> If you regard getting and holding as the chief business of life it is natural to regard your neighbours as rivals and competitors, whom you must fight and outwit...To a woman every man is a mother's son, not as her possession, but as her gift of great price which must not be wasted, her great adventure on which she has staked her all. This view involves a revaluation indeed, based not on power or on wealth but on humanity, not getting but on giving, not on domination, but on service (48-49).

Text: Marshall, "Women and War," in Kamester and Vellacott, *Militarism versus Feminism* 37-41:

It is true that the peoples have not wanted war, but they have not willed peace. They have been content if their rulers have avoided *making war*; they have not

---

[176] Jo Vellacott, *From Liberal to Labour with Women's Suffrage*. Marshall's papers are housed in the Cumbria Record Office. Copies of some are in the Bertrand Russell Collection at McMaster University.

[177] Jo Vellacott, *Bertrand Russell and the Pacifists in the First World War* 23.

insisted that they should positively and constructively *make peace*—make the conditions that promote mutual trust and co-operation instead of acquiescing in conditions that promote mutual suspicion and enmity. If the peoples had cared enough for peace they would have known no rest until they had established such relations between the civilized countries as would have made a disaster like the present war impossible. For the choice with which our men are faced today need not have been the only choice; the sacrifices each nation is making need not have been necessary sacrifices....Honour does *not* demand that destruction or bloodshed shall be the only means of fulfilling...obligations.

What contribution has...awakened womanhood to offer for the solution of the great problems of reconstruction that the civilized world has got to face? Women in all countries have proved the value of their service in relieving the suffering and mitigating the material evils caused by war, and the most valuable qualities they have brought to this work have been the qualities of imagination, of faith, of dauntless love, their habit of regarding people under all circumstances as human beings, and not merely as ciphers in an Army estimate or a census return...in presiding over the mutual relations of the separate human units of which a family or a household is composed, adjusting the claims and needs of its various members with their different temperaments, their different stages of growth, in such a way that each may develop all his powers to the full and use them for the common good. In some instances women's very inexperience has been of value; it has made them refuse to be daunted by difficulties which to men, tired and discouraged by former failures, had appeared unsurmountable....

I believe that just as women can do much for the healing of the physical wounds which men are inflicting on one another, so they can do much also for the healing of the deeper and more disastrous spiritual wounds which nation is inflicting on nation. I believe that women, if they turn their minds in that direction, are more likely than men to find some other way of seeing international disputes than by an appeal to force, partly because that is an appeal which is not open to them as women, and they have, therefore, never been accustomed to rely upon it....Above all I believe that on women rests a large share of the responsibility for providing the motive power which alone can make all these things possible, and without which the most perfect machine in the world will not work. And I believe that this motive power is to be found in the deep horror of war which has entered for the first time into the soul of an organized women's movement.

EMILY GREENE BALCH (1867-1961)

Balch was both a sociologist and economist who pursued an academic career until she lost her position at Wellesley College for her pacifist, and generally left-leaning politics.[178] She was, like Addams, a co-winner of the Nobel Peace Prize (1947). In addition to the material on peace already excerpted, co-authored with Addams, Balch wrote on race, ethnicity and anti-semitism. In 1910 she published a major scholarly work on the Slavs, *Our Slavic Fellow Citizens* and in 1927 *Occupied Haiti*, a plea for its independence. As a professor she had taught a course on immigration. In the 1930s she worked assiduously for European Jews seeking asylum in the United States, against the "narrow minded and pusillanimous" State Department (60). The pamphlet abridged below came out in 1939 and contributed to the liberalization of American attitudes to refugees. As well as issuing a moral challenge it used political arguments (refugees are often good democrats) and economic arguments (they create more jobs than they take and are good consumers).

Government—Rights and Liberties

Text: Balch, "Refugees as Assets," *Beyond Nationalism* 60-62:

When a town finds that it is growing in numbers through newcomers, this is generally taken as a sign of prosperity and the local Chamber of Commerce boasts of it. Yet when newcomers add to our national population people are apt to feel displeased. Is this because in the one case the mind is fixed on the idea of fresh customers, clients and tenants, and in the other on that of new competitors for non-existent jobs or additional applicants for relief?

Historically, certain immigration movements are regarded as having been morally and economically advantageous, especially those due to religious or political conscience as, for instance, the coming of the Huguenots after 1665 [revocation of the Edict of Nantes] or of the Germans after the liberal movements of 1848. On the other hand, the influx in the 1830s and 1840s of literal paupers shipped by English Poor Law authorities was soon stopped by law. From the 1880s for a number of decades there was a very heavy immigration of manual labourers. These two phases of immigration made a disproportionate impression and helped to create a tradition of anti-foreignism and contempt for immigrants, which tended to overshadow the fact that the United States developed and prospered very largely precisely through its immigrants....Throughout all our history the great mass of poor, hardworking, adventurous newcomers, seeking to achieve a new life for themselves, have helped to make America, both economically and culturally. It would be impossible to list the industrial organizers, inventors, writers, ministers and

---

[178] On Balch see Mercedes M. Randall, *Improper Bostonian: Emily Greene Balch* and the introduction to and bibliography in Balch, *Beyond Nationalism*. For a recent perspective on her work see Anne Marie Pois, "Foreshadowings: Ecofeminist/Pacifist Feminism of the 1980s."

priests, artists, musicians, philanthropists and philosophers sprung from this group.

An interesting case is that of the east-side Jews who came to New York some fifty years ago from the miserable ghetto slums of Russia, fleeing from bloody pogroms. Ignorant, fanatical, poverty-stricken, they appeared singularly unpromising human material. Yet they created the great garment-making industry which ended the sweat shop, organized its labour relations on an exemplary footing, gave Americans perhaps the best and cheapest ready-made clothing in the world and raised themselves to a cultural level of which the Yiddish theatre and the recent Broadway success *Pins and Needles* are symptoms.

It is simply not true, as often assumed, that the more men and women of working age the fewer the chances of a job for each. Everyone, children and all, is a consumer, a unit of the home market and in so far givers of work. As producers they come not only to be job takers but to be self-employers or to employ others. Often they bring valuable new inventions or patents or originate new businesses....

The refugees now coming to us as fast as our rigid restrictionist laws permit are not of the pauper type or unskilled labourers, nor are they alien in tradition or political convictions. Many of them have proved themselves courageous defenders of democratic and liberal principles and of both Catholic and Protestant Christianity. They include men of worldwide reputation in most diverse fields. There is good reason to be convinced that they are bringing to us more than they ask of us....A horse or a cow has value. In the days of slavery, when a price was put on men, they were naturally far more valuable than animals. A free man is not worth less as an economic asset than a slave. His non-economic value is one for which money has no measure. May we ourselves be worthy of the refugee. And to him, may his enforced change of country with all its pain and loss be in the end blessed also.

International Government

Balch's paper on internationalizing the waterways dates from 1947 but is an evolution of ideas advanced by the original members of the Women's International League for Peace and Freedom as early as the Hague conference, 1915. As well as recommending provisions to "internationalize" the world's oceans and seas, in aid of preventing war, it proposes various measures for their management, for meteorological observations and support services for maritime commerce. It anticipates the "global commons" conceptualization of the World Commission on Environment and Development in *Our Common Future*, 1987. Her analysis is part of a more general argument for increasing recourse to the United Nations; Balch herself wrote on strategic bases and aviation.

Text: Balch, "Internationalization of Waterways," *Beyond Nationalism* 169-73:

The United Nations is in an early stage. It may be cut off by untimely catastrophe or frustrated by the inability of those curious entities that we call national states to make the adjustments necessary for the abolition of war. But the abolition of war is a "must" if civilization is to persist. With this imperative in mind, I will say that *as*—not *if*—the United Nations develops there will be before it various possibilities as regards the character and direction of its further growth. With my best hopes I look for an extension of the United Nations and its constituent bodies through a widening of administrative powers.

As regards the waters of the world the field, old as it is, is still relatively open and it seems that a measure of actual internationalization might be relatively easy to realize....If the history of air power is short, that of sea power is long, and it is one that clearly demonstrates the need for wide and wise organization. For it is a story of anarchy, broken by periods of the temporary supremacy of imperial powers. For ages water-borne traffic was a matter of small vessels at the wind's mercy and of voyages which necessarily hugged the shore as much as possible. As navies evolved, one power after another rose and secured, in some sense, command of the seas. The breakup of the Roman Empire with its Pax Oceanica was followed by a period of raiding and of complete insecurity, both for peaceful shipping and for the unhappy populations within reach of the water.

As Europe became more highly organized in the modern period, anarchy was replaced by a great struggle for sea power between a relatively few great states, till Britannia succeeded in ruling the waves. Her power has had its beneficent side. She took it on herself to keep order and put down piracy. In this period the seas were surveyed and charted by modern methods; lighthouses and buoys multiplied and in times when no war was in progress the seas were in practice open.

Whatever the merits of the naval peace maintained by Britain, conflict was always implicit in it as to rights at sea in time of war. Students of international law debated, statesmen quarreled and naval commanders shed the blood of their men over the rights of neutral vessels, neutral cargoes, the right of search and blockades, especially in connection with narrow waterways like the Dardanelles and the Suez Canal. The whole complex of problems implied in the term "freedom of the seas" was an endless source of trouble.

Moreover, naval supremacy, however temperately employed, was increasingly felt as a provocation by other powers. Germany's effort to make herself an effective rival played a major part in the outbreak of war in 1914 and Japan's resentment of her naval inferiority played its part [in World War II]. The United States also, with its growing naval power was increasingly a challenge to British supremacy until in 1922 Britain, with her extraordinary genius for political realism, accepted the shift of power and agreed to parity with the United States. Neither Germany nor Japan was pleased with this solution.

As to the conception of freedom of the seas, the international ideas of President Wilson injected an entirely new element....In a speech on May 27 1916 he put forward a concept which foreshadowed the League of Nations. His proposal included a suggestion for "universal association of the nations to maintain the inviolate security of the highway of the seas for the common and unhindered use to all the nations of the world." In formulating the Fourteen Points he demanded "absolute freedom of navigation upon the seas, outside territorial waters, alike in peace and in war, except as the seas may be closed in whole or in part by international action for the enforcement of international covenants." This point rests, of course, upon the fundamental proposal of "a general association of nations."

Britain, still mistress of the seas, was not then ready to accept freedom of the seas in Wilson's sense nor to entrust the protection of her interest at sea to any power but her own and the United States—not ready even to enter the League of Nations, on which Wilson's proposals were based, on Wilson's terms....

The General Assembly of the United Nations should appoint a Maritime Authority, superseding any existing body of the sort, with wide powers covering all the waterways of the world which have an international character, including the oceans, narrow seas such as the Mediterranean, straits, canals such as Suez, Kiel and Panama and so far as may seem indicated, international rivers such as the Rhine and Danube, although very possibly the latter might be best left to a purely European authority. The International Maritime Authority should be charged with the following functions:

1. The making of maritime surveys covering the main international waterways of the world as well as scientific studies of currents and other aspects of oceanography.
2. Weather reporting and meteorological research.
3. The care of lighthouses, buoys and in general whatever is necessary to render navigation safe and convenient.
4. The control of fisheries, whaling and sealing in the interests of fair play and productiveness and to prevent denudation of fishing grounds and wasteful and destructive whaling and sealing practices.
5. Provisions looking to safety at sea, including iceberg patrol.
6. The establishment and maintenance of free ports or foreign trade zones where vessels engaged in foreign trade can transship, sort, rearrange or store cargoes without going through customs as long as the goods do not leave the specified zone....

The advantages of the plan, if it could be realized, are important. It would take the poison out of the strategic problem of the Mediterranean, especially the Dardanelles....It would facilitate trade, navigation and use of natural resources, including fisheries. It would prevent the development of a naval race to fill any vacuum caused by shifts in naval policy and would make it easier to lessen naval establishments pending disarmament. Incidentally, it would offer opportunity for distinguished service on a national plane for ex-navy officers.

It would increase the prestige and usefulness of the United Nations and build up consciousness of the globe as one world. It ought to be self-supporting and no burden on national exchequers....A major crux is the relation of the maritime Authority to armed naval forces until such time as national navies may be superseded, if that consummation is achieved....If such a system develops, the globe will be irregularly spotted with international footholds, which might come to have considerable significance psychologically in the development of world mindedness.

Chapter 7

An Afterword

The contention made in the introductory chapter was that the social sciences would be different today if the work of these women theorists had been given its due. Readers can judge for themselves, using the work reported in the substantive chapters just completed. I believe that the case has been made for a distinctive contribution as well as that of valuable writing unjustly neglected, whose inclusion would enrich the literature of both sociology and political science.

Returning to the criteria suggested in Chapter 1, I suggest that the excerpts given show (1) that theory on the origins of society, especially of moral rules, would be different if the literature stressing the positive bonds between mother and children (du Châtelet, Grouchy de Condorcet, Macaulay, de Staël) had been paid more heed. For the same reason less credit would have been given to Hobbes's portrayal of life as "solitary, poor, nasty, brutish and short."[179] (2) Following from this the literature on war and peace would have shown less glorification of war, more scepticism as to its benefits and exposure of its untoward results in anti-democratic institutions, if the women theorists (especially de Staël, Wollstonecraft, von Suttner, Addams and Balch) had been given greater attention.

(3) In political and social analysis generally there would have been less emphasis on the dramatic extremes (à la Rousseau) and more on the middle ground if the women theorists (de Staël, Macaulay, Taylor, Butler) had been taken more seriously. Perhaps compromise and negotiated settlements would have become more respectable pursuits, the practical solving of problems of government praiseworthy. The sharp accusations against the theory of "possessive individualism" would have been more nuanced if the work on obligation (beginning with Astell) had been routinely read. Utility theory

---

[179] Hobbes, *Leviathan* 186.

would have become less harsh, and moved further to including non-human species, if Macaulay's version had been paid more heed than Bentham's.

(4) More attention would have been accorded the bio-physical environment in sociological analysis if the examples of Macaulay, Nightingale, Cobbe and Martineau had been followed. Ecologists would have had less cause to condemn sociologists for excessive anthropocentrism, or the failure to see human life as part of a web, with continuities between human and non-human species.

(5) More attention would have been paid, earlier, to stratification by gender as well as by class if the analysis by Astell, Macaulay and Wollstonecraft had been taken up seriously by political scientists and sociologists. Analysis on gender roles, too, would have progressed more rapidly if the early work of Nightingale, Webb and Addams had not been effectively lost. A feminist perspective in midwifery might have been accepted much earlier if Nightingale's approach had been adopted.

(6) Medical sociology, health promotion and preventive medicine might have developed much earlier if the pioneering examples of so many women theorists had not disappeared (from Astell and Wortley Montagu's work on smallpox inoculation to Nightingale's many studies).

It is suggested that the differences in methodology would have been no less significant, although this facet has been given less attention here.[180] (1) The integration of quantitative and qualitative work would have seemed natural if Webb's advice had been taken. The denigration of quantitative techniques might not have happened if the enormous usefulness of empirical work for women's betterment (notably Nightingale on mortality in childbirth) had been seen. Nor might it if de Staël's eloquent advocacy of rigorous, quantitative research had been heeded.

(2) Applied sociology generally might have developed earlier and with more enthusiasm if the work of so many of these women theorists had been esteemed and emulated. (3) Statistical evaluation of new programmes might have become more widespread if the recommendations of Nightingale and Webb had been followed (they both had recommended routine evaluation). (4) The field of public administration would have progressed earlier if the very practical work of a number of these women had been given due credit. All of the above examples argue for the inclusion of women theorists (and their research and research methods) in mainstream sociology and political science.

It remains to consider for a moment what other material there is and where people concerned with women's writing on society and politics might go from here. At various places in the preceding chapters reference was made, on a particular point, to other women scholars whose work otherwise was not

---

[180] The distinctive contributions of women in both theory and methodology are treated further in McDonald, "Classical Social Theory with the Women Founders Included," in Camic, *Reclaiming the Sociological Classics*, 1998.

Afterword 297

included. As well, reference was made in Chapter 1 to a number of women theorists who were included here, but who deserve much more attention, in my view—even the publication of a collected works of their writing. The work anthologized in *Women Theorists on Society and Politics*, it should be clear, is a selection from a much larger body of writing that deserves to see the light of day.

If space had permitted it might have been interesting to include a few other early women writers, for example **Catherine of Siena (1347-80)** and the Puritan **Mary Cary Rande**. Both of these women wrote on religion rather than political or social theory, but there are some gems with strong political content. Both women, for example, gave toughly-worded, unsolicited, advice to the political authorities of their day. Advice to princes was a genre of political expression for men theorists for a number of centuries. Why not for women too?

Catherine of Siena, in a letter to Charles V of France, advised:

Hold your kingdom as something lent to you, not as if it were your own. For you know well that life, health, wealth, honour, status, dominion—none of these belongs to you....Uphold holy justice. Let it not be adulterated by selfish love for yourself or by flattery or by human respect. Don't pretend not to see if your officials are inflicting injustice for money, denying the poor their rights. No, be a father to the poor as a dispenser of what God has given you. And see to it that any wrongs in your kingdom are punished, and virtue honoured. For this is the work of divine justice.[181]

One of the many tracts by Cary Rande, 1653, urged England's governors:

That you seriously and in good earnest lay to heart the condition of the poor, and make it your care to provide for the supply of their wants, and that consideration be had of their condition before any rich man's case whatsoever be taken into consideration, how nearly soever related to you or any of you...for certainly the crying of the poor and the sighing of the needy maketh a louder noise in the ears of the Lord of Sabbath than the complaints of any rich man whatsoever, and His ear is more open to their cries and should not yours? Those passages (Deut 24 10-end) where there are several laws made by God, in which He maketh provision for the poor and needy, have taken great impression upon my heart, especially considering that it is He that requires His people to do so in behalf of the distressed, and tells His people that when they are compassionate and

---

[181] Catherine of Siena, *Letters of St. Catherine of Siena* 238.

show acts of mercy and goodness towards the poor, that He will bless them for it in all the work of their hands."[182]

Cary Rande added that these admonitions were especially directed to "those that have most power to help the poor." A further stipulation was:

> That you having first provided for the very poorest sort, then next that you consider the conditions of such as are next them and are in a mean condition, though not in so mean a condition as to want bread, and to stand in need of alms. The consideration you are to have of their condition is to provide that if they be wronged or defrauded by any that you do them right, or appoint some to do them right, before you do such acts of justice for persons of greater estates (10).

This provision was obviously intended to counter the usual situation, "that the rich man's cause is heard before the poor's," calling for an end to such "corruption." "Let the richest of all be relieved last of all, because...the richest are better able to bear delays than meaner people are" (10).

Many women could have been added from the late nineteenth century, such as **Matilda Joslyn Gage (1826-98)** and **Charlotte Perkins Gilman (1860-1935)** with a slight change in the terms of reference. These two, however, are being given increased attention as feminist writers and their work hardly needs to be rescued from obscurity. **Marianne Weber (1870-1954)** like Gilman and Gage published mainly on what we would call women's studies rather than mainstream social or political theory, but some of her writing treats these wider issues. Translation of more of her work into English would be most welcome.

Three nineteenth-century African-American women, one Northern and two Southern, wrote important work on slavery, race and gender: **Maria W. Stewart (1803-79)**,[183] **Anna Julia Cooper (1858-1964)**,[184] and **Ida B. Wells-Barnett (1862-1931)**.[185] In all cases this work is more advocacy and less theoretical than that sought for this book, but the analysis is excellent and the writing vigorous. The recent re-publication and new publication of selections will facilitate study of these important contributors. *Women Theorists on Society and Politics*, it is hoped, will prompt both more work on the women selected for inclusion in it and this wider group of estimable women writers.

---

[182] Mary Cary Rande, *Proposals to the Supreme Governours*, 8.

[183] Stewart, *Maria W. Stewart, America's First Black Woman Political Writer*.

[184] Cooper, *A Voice from the South*.

[185] See especially Wells-Barnett, *Selected Works of Ida B. Wells-Barnett* and *Crusade for Justice: the Autobiography of Ida B. Wells*.

Manuscript Sources

Butler, Josephine E., Correspondence with Fawcett at the Fawcett Library, Guildhall University, London.
Craigen, Jessie, "Vote for Miss Helen Taylor." Pamphlet, Mill-Taylor Collection, British Library of Political and Economic Science, London.
Martineau Manuscripts, University of Birmingham.
Nightingale, Florence. Add Mss references are all to manuscripts in the Nightingale Collection, British Library. The Wellcome Trust references are of copies held at the Wellcome Institute for the History of Medicine, London. References to the Woodward Biomedical Library are for the Charles Woodward Memorial Room, Woodward Biomedical Library, University of British Columbia, Vancouver.
Taylor, Helen, Correspondence, Mill-Taylor Collection, British Library of Political and Economic Science, London.
Webb, Beatrice, Diary in Passfield Papers, British Library of Political and Economic Science, London.

Bibliography

Abel-Smith, Brian, *The Hospitals 1800-1948: A Study in Social Administration in England and Wales*. London: Heinemann 1964.
Abrams, Irwin, "Bertha von Suttner and the Nobel Peace Prize," *Journal of Central European Affairs*. 22 (3) October 1962.
Addams, Jane, ed., *Hull-House Maps and Papers*. New York: Crowell 1895.
* "Trade Unions and Public Duty." *American Journal of Sociology*. 4 (4)   January 1899:448-62.
* *Twenty Years at Hull-House*,1909-1929. New York: Macmillan 1910.
* "Woman's Part in Managing the Modern City." *Woman's Athenaeum*. 9. 1912:320-329.
*   Address given at the Organization Conference of the Women's Peace Party. Washington, DC., January 10 1915.
* "Are Pacifists Cowards?" Address to the City Club, Chicago, 15 May 1917. *Unity* 19 July 1917:331.
* et al., *American Commission on Conditions in Ireland: Interim Report*. March 21 1921.
* *The Second Twenty Years at Hull-House*. New York: Macmillan 1930.
* "The Process of Social Transformation." In *A Century of Progress*, ed. Charles A. Beard. New York: Books for Libraries Press 1932:233-252.
* and Emily G. Balch and Alice Hamilton, eds., *Women at the Hague*. New York: Garland reprint 1972 [1915].
*   and Emily Greene Balch, "What Concern has America with World Peace: The Hopes we Inherit." *Building International Goodwill*. New York: Macmillan 1927:3-18.
Alexander, Sally, ed., *Women's Fabian Tracts*. London: Routledge 1988.
Amos, Sheldon, *A Comparative Survey of Laws in Force for the Prohibition, Regulation, and Licensing of Vice in England and Other Countries*. London: Stevens 1877.

Armogathe, Daniel, "Flora Tristan, féministe et socialiste." In Fini le féminisme? *Compte rendu du colloque international Féminisme et socialismes*, Paris: Choisir 1983 58-73.

Astell, Mary, *A Serious Proposal to the Ladies*. London: J.R. 1701 2nd ed. and Source Book reprint 1970 [1694].

* In John Norris. *Letters concerning the Love of God*. London: Manship & Wilkin 1695.
* *Some Reflections upon Marriage*. London: Parker: 1730 4th ed. [1700].
* *The Christian Religion*. London: R. Wilkin 1705.
* *The First English Feminist: Reflections upon Marriage and other Writings*, ed. Bridget Hill. Aldershot: Gower 1986.

Badinter, Elisabeth, *Emilie, Emilie: l'ambition féminine au XVIIIe siècle*. Paris: Flammarion 1983.

Baelen, Jean, *La vie de Flora Tristan: socialisme et féminisme au 19e siècle*. Paris: Seuil 1972.

Balayé, Simone, *Madame de Staël: lumières et liberté*. Paris: Klincksieck 1979.

Balch, Emily Greene, *Beyond Nationalism: The Social Thought of Emily Greene Balch*, ed. Mercedes M. Randall. New York: Twayne 1972.

* ed., *Occupied Haiti*. New York: Garland 1972 [1927].

Ballard, George, *Memoirs of Several Ladies of Great Britain*. Oxford: W. Jackson 1752 and ed. Ruth Perry. Detroit: Wayne State University Press 1985 reprint.

Banks, Olive, "Cobbe, Frances Power," *Biographical Dictionary of British Feminists*. New York University Press, 1985 1:53-55.

Bauer, Carol and Lawrence Ritt, "A Husband is a Beating Animal: Frances Power Cobbe Confronts the Wife-Abuse Problem in Victorian England." *International Journal of Women's Studies*. 6 (2) March/April 1983:99-118.

Beard, Mary R., *Woman as Force in History*. New York: Collier 1946.

Beccaria, Cesare de, *On Crimes and Punishments*, trans. Henry Paolucci. New York: Bobbs-Merrill 1963 [1764].

Beer, Max, *History of British Socialism*. 2 vols. London: Bell 1929 [1919].

Bell, E. Moberly, *Josephine Butler: Flame of Fire*. London: Constable 1962.

Bell, Susan Groag, "Christine de Pizan: Humanism and the Problem of a Studious Woman." *Feminist Studies 3 (3/4) (spring summer 1976):173-84*.

Bentham, Jeremy, *Collected Works of Jeremy Bentham*, ed. Stephen Conway. Oxford: Clarendon 1987.

Berkin, Carol R. and Clara M. Lovett, eds., *Women, War and Revolution*. New York: Holmes & Meier 1980.

Besser, Gretchen Rous, *Germaine de Staël Revisited*. New York: Twayne 1994.

Besterman, Theodore, *Voltaire Essays*. London: Oxford University Press 1962.

Blackwell, Elizabeth, *Essays in Medical Sociology*. (2 vols. in 1) New York: Arno Reprint 1972 [1902].

* *The Laws of Life, with special reference to the physical education of girls*. New York: Putnam 1852.

Bibliography 303

Booth, Charles, *Life and Labour of the People in London*. 17 vols. London: Macmillan 1892-1902.
Boxer, Marilyn J. and Jean H. Quataert, eds., *Socialist Women: European Socialist Feminism in the Nineteenth and Early Twentieth Centuries*. New York: Elsevier North Holland 1978.
Boyd, Nancy, *Josephine Butler, Octavia Hill, Florence Nightingale: Three Victorian Women Who Changed Their World*. London: Macmillan 1982.
Burke, Edmund, *Reflections on the Revolution in France*, ed. L.G. Mitchell. London: Walter Scott 1780 and Oxford University Press 1993.
Busmann, Johanna, *Feminismus und Sozialismus in den Schriften Flora Tristan*. Hamburg 1984.
Bussey, Gertrude and Margaret Tims, *Women's International League for Peace and Freedom 1915-1965*. London: Allen & Unwin 1965.
Butler, A.S.G., *Portrait of Josephine Butler*. London: Faber & Faber 1954.
Butler, Josephine E., ed., *Woman's Work and Woman's Culture*. London: Macmillan 1869.
* *Government by Police*. London: Dyer 1879.
* *Our Christianity Tested by the Irish Question*. London: Fisher Unwin 1887.
* ed., *The Dawn*. Ladies' National Association for the Abolition of State Regulation of Vice. London: May 1888.
* ed., *The Shield*. Official Organ of the British Committee of the Federation for the Abolition of State Regulation of Vice.
* *Recollections of George Butler*. Bristol: Arrowsmith 2nd ed. [1892].
* *Native Races and the War*. London: Gay & Bird 1900.
* *Personal Reminiscences of a Great Crusade*. Westport, CT: Hyperion reprint 1976 [1911].
* *Josephine Butler: An Autobiographical Memoir*, ed. John W. Johnson and Lucy A. Johnson. Bristol: Arrowsmith 1912.
Caine, Barbara, ed., *Victorian Feminists*. Oxford University Press 1992.
Cambridge Women's Peace Collective, *My Country is the Whole World: An Anthology of Women's Work on Peace and War*. London: Pandora 1984.
Camic, Charles, ed., *Reclaiming the Sociological Classics*. Oxford: Blackwell 1998.
Carpenter, Mary, *Juvenile Delinquents*. London: Cash 1853.
Catherine of Siena, *The Letters of Catherine of Siena*, trans. Suzanne Noffke. Binghamton NY: Medieval & Renaissance Texts 1988.
Chappell, Jennie, "Frances Power Cobbe," in *Women of Worth*. London: Partridge 1908:93-134.
Child, Lydia Maria, *An Appeal in favor of Americans called Africans*. New York: Arno 1968 [1833].
Clark, Lorenne M.G. and Lynda Lange, eds., *The Sexism of Social and Political Theory*. Toronto: University of Toronto Press 1979.
Clémenceau-Jacquemarie, Madeleine, *Life of Madame Roland*, trans. Laurence Vail. London: Longmans, Green 1930.

Cobbe, Frances Power, *Studies New and Old of Ethical and Social Subjects*. London: Trübner 1860.
* "Workhouse as an Hospital." London: Emily Faithfull 1861.
* "Female Education and how it would be affected by University Examinations." Paper read at the Social Science Congress, London 1862.
* "Wife-Torture in England." *Contemporary Review 32*. 1878:57-87.
* "The significance of Vivisection." Victoria Society for the Protection of Animals from Vivisection. Pamphlets, vol. 2 1891.
* *Life of F.P. Cobbe*. 2 vols. Boston: Houghton 1894.
* "Ethics of Zoophily." reprint of *Contemporary Review*. October 1895.
Colbourn, H. Trevor, *Lamp of Experience: Whig History and the Intellectual Origins of the American Revolution*. Chapel Hill NC: University of North Carolina Press 1964.
Cole, G.D.H., *History of Socialist Thought*. 5 vols. London: Macmillan 1953-60.
Cole, Margaret, ed., *The Webbs and their Work*. London: Muller 1949.
Condorcet, Sophie Grouchy de, *Théorie des sentiments moraux et huit lettres sur la sympathie*. 2 vols. Paris: Buisson 1798.
* *Huit lettres sur la sympathie*, ed. Jean-Paul de Lagrave. Montréal: L'Etincelle 1994.
Cook, E.T., *The Life of Florence Nightingale*. 2 vols. London: Macmillan 1913.
Coole, Diana H., *Women in Political Theory: From Ancient Misogyny to Contemporary Feminism*. New York: Harvester Wheatsheaf, 2nd ed. 1993 [1988].
Cooper, Anna Julia, *A Voice from the South*. New York: Oxford University Press 1988.
Cross, Maire and Tim Gray, *The Feminism of Flora Tristan*. Oxford: Berg 1992.
Davis, Allen F., *American Heroine: The Life and Legend of Jane Addams*. New York: Oxford University Press 1973.
Deegan, Mary Jo, *Jane Addams and the Men of the Chicago School*. New Brunswick NJ: Transaction 1988.
Desanti, Dominique, *A Woman in Revolt. A Biography of Flora Tristan*, trans. Elizabeth Zelvin. New York: Crown 1976 [1972].
* ed., *Flora Tristan: oeuvres et vie mêlées*. Union générale d'éditions 1973.
De Staël, Germaine Necker, *Letters on the Works and Character of J.J. Rousseau*. London: G.C.J. & J. Johnson 1789 [1788].
* *Treatise on the Influence of the Passions*. London: Cawthorn 1798 [1796].
* *Considerations on the Principal Events of the French Revolution*. 3 vols. London: Baldwin, Craddock 1818.
* *Oeuvres complètes*. 17 vols. Paris: Treuttel & Würtz. 1820-21.
* *Circonstances actuelles*. Paris: Fischbacher 1906.
* *Circonstances actuelles*, ed. Lucia Omacini. Geneva: Droz 1979.
* "Unpublished Correspondence of Mme de Staël with Thomas Jefferson," ed., trans. Marie G. Kimball. *North American Review*. 1918: 208 (752) 63-71.
* *Madame de Staël on Politics, Art, Literature, and National Character*, ed. & trans. Morroe Berger. London: Sidgwick & Jackson 1964.
* *Unpublished Correspondence of Madame de Staël and the Duke of Wellington*, trans. Harold Kurtz. London: Cassell 1965.

Bibliography

* *Major Writings of Germaine de Staël*, ed. & trans. Vivian Folkenflik. New York: Columbia University Press 1987.

Diesbach, Ghislain de, *Madame de Staël*. Paris: Perrin 1983.

Dombrowski, James, *The Early Days of Christian Socialism in America*. New York: Columbia University Press 1936.

Donovan, Josephine, *Feminist Theory*. New York: Ungar 1985.

Drysdale, Susan Hoecker, *Harriet Martineau: First Woman Sociologist*. Oxford: Berg 1992.

Du Châtelet, Emilie, trans., *Principes mathématiques de la philosophie naturelle*. 2 vols. Paris: Desaint and Saillant 1759.

* *Doutes sur les religions révélées*. Paris: 1792.
* "Discours sur le bonheur," ed. Robert Mauzi, Paris: Belles Lettres 1961.

Ducpétiaux, Edouard, *Statistique comparée de la criminalité en France, en Belgique, en Angleterre et en Allemagne*. Brussels: Haumann 1835.

Ehrman, Esther, *Mme du Châtelet*. Leamington Spa: Berg 1986.

Elshtain, Jean Bethke, *Public Man, Private Woman: Women in Social and Political Thought*. Princeton NJ: Princeton University Press 1981.

* *Meditations on Modern Political Thought*. New York: Praeger 1986.
* *Women and War*. New York: Basic Books 1987.

Ely, Richard T., *The Strength and Weakness of Socialism*. New York: Chautauqua 1894.

* *The Social Law of Service*. Toronto: Briggs 1896.

Engels, Friedrich, *Condition of the Working Class in England*, trans. W.O. Henderson & W.H. Chaloner. Oxford: Blackwell 1971 [1845].

Falco, Maria J., ed., *Feminist Interpretations of Mary Wollstonecraft*. University Park PA: Pennsylvania State University Press 1996.

Fancourt, Mary St. J., *They Dared to be Doctors, Elizabeth Blackwell, Elizabeth Garrett Anderson*. London: Longmans Green 1965.

Farrell, John C., *Beloved Lady: A History of Jane Addams' Ideas on Reform and Peace*. Baltimore, MD: Johns Hopkins Press 1967.

Ferguson, Moira and Janet Todd, *Mary Wollstonecraft*. Boston: Twayne 1984.

Flexner, Eleanor, *Mary Wollstonecraft: A Biography*. New York: Coward, McCann & Geoghegan 1972.

French, Richard D., *Antivivisection and Medical Science in Victorian Society*. Princeton NJ: Princeton University Press 1975.

Gilbert, Marc Jason, "An Eminent Victorian as Outsider: Florence Nightingale and Indian Politics." unpublished paper 1991.

Gilligan, Carol, *In a Different Voice: Psychological Theory and Women's Development*. Cambridge MA: Harvard University Press 1982.

Gioseffi, Daniela, ed., *Women on War: Essential Voices for the Nuclear Age*. New York: Touchstone 1988.

Goldman, Nancy Loring, ed., *Female Soldiers—Combatants or Noncombatants?* Westport CT: Greenwood 1982.

Goldsmith, Margaret L., *Seven Women Against the World*. London: Methuen, 1976 [1935].
Grimshaw, Jean, *Philosophy and Feminist Thinking*. Minneapolis: University of Minnesota Press 1986.
Grogan, Susan K., *French Socialism and Social Difference: Women and the New Society 1803-44*. Basingstoke: Macmillan 1992.
Guerry, A.M. *Essai sur la statistique morale de la France*. Paris: Crochard 1833.
Gutwirth, Madelyn et al. eds., *Germaine de Staël: Crossing the Borders*. New Brunswick NJ: Rutgers University Press 1991.
Guyot, Charly, *Plaidoyer pour Thérèse Levasseur*. Neuchatel: Ides et Calendes 1962.
Halsband, Robert, *Life of Mary Wortley Montagu*. Oxford: Clarendon 1956.
Hamilton, Susan, ed., *Criminals, Idiots, Women and Minors: Victorian Writing by Women on Women*. Peterborough: Broadview Press 1995.
Hay-Cooper, L., *Josephine Butler And Her Work for Social Purity*. London: SPCK 1922.
Hays, Mary, *Letters and Essays, Moral and Miscellaneous*. London: Knott 1793 and reprint, ed. Gina Luria. New York: Garland 1974.
* *An Appeal to the Men of Great Britain in Behalf of Women*. London: J. Johnson 1798 and reprint, ed. Gina Luria. New York: Garland 1974.
* *Memoirs of Emma Courtney*. 2 vols. 1796 and reprint New York: Garland 1974.
* *Female Biography*. 6 vols. London: Phillips 1803.
Held, Virginia, *Feminist Morality: Transforming Culture, Society and Politics*. Chicago: University of Chicago Press 1993.
Helvétius, Claude, *Oeuvres complètes*. 7 vols. Paris: Deux Ponts 1784.
Herold, J. Christopher, *Mistress to an Age*. A Life of Madame de Staël. London: Hamilton 1959 [1958].
Herron, George D., *Between Caesar and Jesus*. New York: Crowell 1975 reprint [1899].
Higonnet, Margaret Randolph, et al., eds. *Behind the Lines: Gender and the Two World Wars*. New Haven: Yale University Press 1987.
Hill, Bridget, *Republican Virago: The Life and Times of Catharine Macaulay, Historian*. Oxford: Clarendon 1992.
Hirschmann, Nancy J. *Rethinking Obligation: A Feminist Method for Political Theory*. Ithaca: Cornell University Press 1992.
Hobbes, Thomas, *Leviathan*, ed. C.B. Macpherson. London: Pelican 1968.
Holbach, Paul Thiry d' *Système de la nature*, ed. Denis Diderot. 2 vols. Paris: Ledoux 1821 [1770].
Hume, David, *Philosophical Works of David Hume*. Boston: Little Brown 1864.
* *Enquiry concerning the Principles of Morals*, ed. Selby-Bigge. Oxford: Clarendon, 1920 [1751].
Hunt, Margaret, et al., eds. *Women and the Enlightenment*. Institute for Research in History/Haworth 1984.
Hutcheson, Francis, *A System of Moral Philosophy*. 2 vols. Hildesheim: Georg Olms 1969 reprint of 1755

Bibliography

Hutchinson, John, *Champions of Charity: War and the Rise of the Red Cross*. Boulder: Westview 1996.
International Statistical Congress, *Proceedings of the Second Section*. London 1860.
Jacobs, Jane, *Cities and the Wealth of Nations: Principles of Economic Life*. New York: Random House 1984.
Jones, Kathleen B. and Anna G. Jonasdottir, eds., *The Political Interests of Gender: Developing Theory and Research with a Feminine Face*. London: Sage 1985.
Jowett, Benjamin, *"Dear Miss Nightingale." A Selection of Benjamin Jowett's Letters to Florence Nightingale 1860-1893*, ed. Vincent Quinn and John Prest. Oxford: Clarendon 1987.
Jump, Harriet Devine, *Mary Wollstonecraft Writer*. New York NY: Harvester Wheatsheaf 1994.
Kamester, Margaret and Jo Vellocott, eds., *Militarism versus Feminism: Writings on Women and War*. London: Virago 1987.
Kandal, Terry R., *The Woman Question in Classical Sociological Theory*. Miami: Florida International University Press 1988.
Käppeli, Marie, *Sublime croisade: éthique et politique du féminisme protestant, 1875-1928*. Geneva: Zoé 1990.
Kempf, Beatirx, *Woman for Peace: The Life of Bertha von Suttner*, trans. R.W. Last. Park Ridge NJ: Noyes 1973.
Kennedy, Ellen and Susan Mendus, eds., *Women in Western Political Theory: Kant to Nietzsche*. New York: St. Martin's Press 1987.
Keynes, John Maynard, *The General Theory of Employment Interest and Money*. London: Macmillan 1936.
Kinnaird, Joan K., "Mary Astell and the Conservative Contribution to English Feminism," *Journal of British Studies*. 19 1979: 53-75.
La Méttrie, Julien de, *L'homme machine*, ed. Aram Vartanian. Princeton NJ: Princeton University Press 1960 [1747].
Lansbury, Carol, "Gynaecology, Pornography and the Antivivisection Movement." *Victorian Studies* 28 (3) spring 1985:413-37.
Larg, David Glass, *Madame de Staël: Her Life as Revealed in her Work*. Paris: Champion 1926 [1924].
Lawrence, John, "On the Rights of Beasts," *A Philosophical and Practical Treatise on Horses, and on the Moral Duties of Man Towards the Brute Creation*. 2 vols. London: Longman 1796.
Lee, Gerhard, *Flora Tristan, la révolte d'une pariah*. Paris: Atelier 1994.
Leprohon, Pierre, *Flora Tristan*. Antony: Corymbe 1979.
Lewis, Jane, ed., *Before the vote was won: arguments for and against women's suffrage*. New York: Routledge & Kegan Paul 1987.
Liddington, Jill, *The Road to Greenham Common: Feminism and Anti-militarism in Britain since 1820*. Syracuse NY: Syracuse University Press 1989.
Locke, John, *Two Treatises of Government*, ed. Peter Laslett. Cambridge: Cambridge University Press 1960 [1690].

Macaulay, Catharine, *The History of England from the Accession of James I to the Brunswick Line*. 8 vols. London: Nourse 1763-83.
* *Loose Remarks on Hobbes's Philosophical Rudiments*. London: Davies 2nd ed. 1769 [1767].
* *Observations on the Cause of the Present Discontents*. 5th ed. London: Dilly 1770.
* *An Address to the People of England, Scotland, and Ireland*. Bath: Cruttwell 1775.
* *The History of England from the Revolution to the Present Time*. London: Cruttwell 1778.
* *Observations on the Reflections of the Rt. Hon. Edmund Burke on the Revolution in France*. London: Dilly 1790.
* *Letters on Education: With Observations on Religious and Metaphysical Subjects*. New York: Garland reprint, 1974 [1790] and London 1989.

Macdonald, Sharon, Pat Holden and Shirley Ardener, eds., *Images of Women in Peace and War: Cross-Cultural and Historical Perspectives*. London: Macmillan 1987.

Macpherson, C.B., *Political Theory of Possessive Individualism*. Oxford: Clarendon 1962.

Mahood, Linda, *The Magdalenes: Prostitution in the 19th Century*. London: Routledge 1990.

Maier, Pauline, *From Resistance to Revolution: Colonial Radicals and the Development of American Opposition to Britain*. New York: Knopf 1972.

Mandeville, Bernard, *Fable of the Bees*, ed. Phillip Harth. Harmondsworth: Penguin 1970 [1732].

Marshall, Catherine, C.K. Ogden and Mary Sargant Florence, *Writings on Women and War*, ed. Margaret Kamester and Jo Vellacott. London: Virago 1987 [1915].

Martineau, Harriet, *Illustrations of Political Economy*. 9 vols. London: Charles Fox 1834 [1832].
* *Society in America*, ed. S.M. Lipset. Garden City NY: Anchor 1962 [1837].
* *How to Observe Morals and Manners*, ed. Michael R. Hill. New Brunswick NJ: Transaction 1989 [1838].
* *Retrospect of Western Travel*. 3 vols. London: Saunders & Otley 1838.
* "The Martyr Age of the United States." *London and Westminster Review*. December 1838 32 (no. 1).
* *History of the Thirty Years' Peace: A.D. 1816-1846*. 4 vols. London: Bell, rev. ed. 1877 [1849].
* ed. and trans., *The Positive Philosophy of Auguste Comte*. 2 vols. London: Kegan Paul 1895 [1853].
* *British Rule in India: A Historical Sketch*. London: Smith, Elder 1857.
* *Suggestions Towards the Future Government of India*. London: Smith, Elder 1858.
* *England and her Soldiers*. London: Smith Elder 1859.
* "The Negro Race in America." *Edinburgh Review*. 119 (243) January 1864:203-42.
* *The Contagious Diseases Acts, as applied to Garrison Towns and Naval Stations*. Liverpool: Brakell 1870.
* *Autobiography*. 3 vols. London: Smith Elder 1877.
* *Selected Letters*, ed. Valerie Sanders. Oxford: Clarendon 1990.

Bibliography

Marx, Karl and Friedrich Engels, *The Holy Family, or Critique of Critical Critique*, trans R. Dixon. Moscow: Foreign Languages Publishing House 1956.

Masham, Damaris Cudworth, *Occasional Thoughts in reference to a vertuous or Christian Life*. London: A. & J. Churchill 1705. Maurice, F.D., *Kingdom of Christ*. 2 vols. London: Rivington 1842.

* *Politics for the People*. London: John Parker 1848.

* *The Workman and the Franchise*. New York: Kelly 1970 reprint [1866].

Maurice, Frederick, ed., *Life of Frederick Denison Maurice*. London: Macmillan 1884.

May, Gita, *Madame Roland and the Age of Revolution*. New York: Columbia University Press 1970.

Mayhew, Henry, *London Labour and the London Poor*. 4 vols. London: Mark Cass 1967 [1861].

McDonald, Lynn, *Early Origins of the Social Sciences*. Montreal: McGill-Queen's University Press 1993.

* *Women Founders of the Social Sciences*. Ottawa: Carleton University Press 1994.

Mestral, Julie Combremont de, *La noble vie d'une femme: Josephine Butler*. Lausanne: Payot 1929 [1927].

Michaud, Stéphane ed., *Un fabuleux destin: Flora Tristan*. Editions Universitaires de Dijon 1984.

Miles, Angela R. and Geraldine Finn, eds., *Feminism from Pressure to Politics*. Montréal: Black Rose 1989 2nd ed. [1983].

Mill, J.S. *Collected Works of John Stuart Mill*, ed. John Robson. 33 vols. Toronto: University of Toronto Press 1981-91.

Mitford, Nancy, *Voltaire in Love*. London: Hamish Hamilton 1957.

Monteiro, Lois A., "On Separate Roads: Florence Nightingale and Elizabeth Blackwell." *Signs*. (spring 1984) 9 (3) 520-33.

Moreau-Christophe, L.M., *Du problème de la misère et de sa solution*. 3 vols. Paris: Guillamin 1851.

Morris, M.C.F., *Francis Orpen Morris: A Memoir*. London: Nimmo 1897.

Nevill, John Cranstoun, *Harriet Martineau*. London: Muller 1943.

Nield, Keith, ed., *Prostitution in the Victorian Age: Debates on the Issue from 19th Century Critical Journals*. Farnborough Hants: Gregg International Publishers 1973.

Nightingale, Florence, "Hospital Statistics" and "Letter from Miss Nightingale," Proceedings of the Second Section of the International Statistical Congress, London 1860.

* Note on the Supposed Protection afforded against Venereal Disease. London 1862.

* Observations by Miss Nightingale on the Evidence contained in Stational Returns...by the Royal Commission on the Sanitary State of the Army in India. November 21 1862.

* *How People may Live and not Die in India*. London: Victoria Press 1863.

* *Introductory Notes on Lying-in Institutions*. London: Longmans Green 1871.

* "The People of India," *Nineteenth Century*. 4 (18) 1878:193-221.

* *Cassandra*, ed. Myra Stark. Old Westbury CT: Feminist Press 1979.

* *Ever Yours, Florence Nightingale*, ed., Martha Vicinus and Bea Nergaard. Cambridge MA: Harvard University Press 1990.
Nixon, Edna, *Mary Wollstonecraft*. London: Dent 1971.
Nolan, Barbara E., *Political Theory of Beatrice Webb*. New York: AMS 1988.
Nord, Dorothy Lepstein, *Apprenticeship of Beatrice Webb*. London: Macmillan 1985.
Nye, Andrea, *Feminist Theory and the Philosophies of Man*. New York: Routledge 1988.
Okin, Susan Moller, *Women in Western Political Thought*. Princeton NJ: Princeton University Press 1979.
Oldfield, Sybil, *Women against the Iron Fist: Alternatives to Militarism*. London: Blackwell 1989.
Osborne, Martha Lee, ed., *Woman in Western Thought*. New York: Random House 1979.
Pateman, Carole, *The Sexual Contract*. Stanford CA: Stanford University Press 1988.
* and Elizabeth Gross, eds., *Feminist Challenges: Social and Political Thought*. Boston: Northwestern University Press 1986.
Pearson, Karl, ed., *Life, Letters and Labours of Francis Galton*. 3 vols. Cambridge: Cambridge University Press 1924.
Pellikaan-Engel, Maja, ed., *Against Patriarchal Thinking: A Future Without Discrimination?* Amsterdam: VU University Press 1992.
Perry, Ruth, *The Celebrated Mary Astell: An Early English Feminist*. Chicago: University of Chicago Press 1986.
Pichanick, Valerie Kossew, *Harriet Martineau*. Ann Arbor: University of Michigan Press 1980.
Pierson, Ruth Roach, ed., *Women and Peace: Theoretical, Historical and Practical Perspectives*. London: Croom Helm 1987.
Pisan, Christine de, *The Epistle of the Prison of Human Life*, ed. Josette A. Wisman. New York: Garland 1984 [1410].
* *Book of Fayttes of Armes and of Chyvalrye*, trans. William Caxton. London: Oxford University Press 1971 [1489].
* *Writings of Christine de Pizan*, ed. Charity Cannon Willard. New York: Persea 1994.
Playne, Caroline E., *Bertha von Suttner and the Struggle to Avert the World War*. London: Allen & Unwin 1936.
Pois, Anne Marie, "Foreshadowings: Ecofeminist/Pacifist Feminism of the 1980s," *Peace and Change*. October 1995 20 (4):439-65.
Pomeau, René, ed. *Voltaire en son temps*. 5 vols. Oxford: Voltaire Foundation 1985-94.
Puech, Jules-L., *La vie et l'oeuvre de Flora Tristan: 1803-44*. Paris: Rivière 1925.
Quesnai, François, *Quesnay's Tableau économique*, ed. Marguerite Kuczynski & Ronald L. Meek. London: Macmillan 1972 [1758].
* *Oeuvres économiques et philosophiques*, ed. Auguste Onken. Aalen: Scientia reprint 1965 [1888].
Quetelet, L.A.J., "Du Nombre des Crimes et des Délits dans les provinces," *Correspondance mathématique et physique* (1829) 5:177-87.

Bibliography

* *Traité sur l'homme et le développement de ses facultés*. Paris 1835.
* *Physique sociale*. 2 vols. Brussels: Muquardt 2d. 1869.
* Radice, Lisanne. *Beatrice and Sidney Webb: Fabian Socialists*. London: Macmillan 1984.

Randall, Mercedes M., *Improper Bostonian: Emily Greene Balch*. New York: Twayne 1964.

Rande, Mary Cary, *Proposals to the Supreme Governours of the three Nations now assembled at Westminster*. London: Henry Hills 1653.

Rauschenbusch, Walter, *New Evangelism* 1904.
* *Christianity and the Social Crisis*. New York: Harper & Row 1964 [1907].
* *Selected Writings*, ed. Winthrop S. Hudson. New York: Paulist Press 1984.

Rauschenbusch-Clough, Emma, *A Study of Mary Wollstonecraft*. London: Longmans Green 1898.

Raven ,Charles E., *Christian Socialism*. London: Macmillan 1920.

Rawls, John, *A Theory of Justice*. Cambridge MA: Belknap 1971.

Rawson, W., "An Inquiry into the statistics of crime in England and Wales," *Journal of the Statistical Society*. (1839) 2:316-44.

Reckitt, Maurice B. *Maurice to Temple: A Century of Social Movement in the Church of England*. London: Faber & Faber 1947.

Roland, Marie-Jeanne Phlipon, Lettre de M Roland, *Histoire parlementaire de la révolution française*. Paris: Paulin. 15 1792:39-45.
* *Oeuvres de J.M. Ph. Roland*. 2 vols. Paris: Bidault 1796.
* *The Works*. London: J. Johnson 1800.

Rossi, Alice S., ed., *The Feminist Papers: From Adams to de Beauvoir*. New York: Columbia University Press 1973.

Rousseau, Jean-Jacques, *Social Contract*, trans. and ed. Maurice Cranston. Harmondsworth: Penguin 1968 [1755].
* *Oeuvres complètes*, ed. B. Gagnebin and Marcel Raymond. Paris: Bibliothèque de la Pléiade 1969.

Saxonhouse, Arlene W., *Women in the History of Political Thought: Ancient Greece to Machiavelli*. New York: Praeger 1985.

Schneir, Miriam, ed., *Feminism: The Essential Historical Writings*. New York: Random House 1972.

Schreiner, Olive, *Trooper Peter Halket of Mashonoland*. London: Fisher Unwin 1927 [1897].
* *Woman and Labor*. New York: Stokes 1911.

Seymour-Jones, Carole, *Beatrice Webb: Woman of Conflict*. London: Allison & Busby 1992.

Siltanen, Janet and Michelle Stanworth, eds., *Women and the Public Sphere: A Critique of Sociology and Politics*. London: Hutchinson 1984.

Smith, Adam, *Theory of Moral Sentiments*, ed. D.D. Raphael and A.C. Macfie. Oxford: Clarendon 1976 [1759].
* *Wealth of Nations*, ed. Edwin Cannan. New York: Modern Library 1937 [1776].

Smith, F.B., "Ethics and Disease in the Later Nineteenth Century: the Contagious Diseases Acts." *Historical Studies.* 15 (1971):118-35.
Smith, Florence M., *Mary Astell.* New York: AMS 1966 [1916].
Sophia, *Woman not Inferior to Man.* London: Hawkins 1739.
Sparks, Jared, ed., *Correspondence of the American Revolution,* ed. Jared Sparks. Boston: Russell, Shattuck and Williams.
Spencer, Metta, "The Russian Peace Movement and its Western Friends," *Peace Magazine.* November/December 1995 11 (6)16-17.
Spender, Dale, *Women of Ideas and what men have done to them.* London: Routledge & Kegan Paul 1982.
* ed., *Feminist Theorists: Three Centuries of Key Women Thinkers.* New York: Pantheon 1983.
Stanton, Elizabeth Cady, Susan B. Anthony and Matilda Joslyn Gage, eds., *History of Woman Suffrage.* 6 vols. New York: Arno and New York Times, 1969 [1882].
Stewart, Maria W., *Maria W. Stewart,* America's First Black Woman Political Writer: Essays and Speeches, ed. Marilyn Richardson. Bloomington: Indiana University Press 1987.
Stiehm, Judith, ed., *Women and Men's Wars,* Oxford: Pergamon 1983.
Strumingher, Laura S. *The Odyssey of Flora Tristan.* New York: Peter Lang 1988.
Sunstein, Emily W. *A Different Face: The Life of Mary Wollstonecraft.* New York: Harper & Row 1975.
Taylor, Helen, "Personal Representation." *Westminster Review* 84 (old series)/28 (new series) No. 165. October 1865:145-54.
* "Paris and France." *Fortnightly Review* 15 old series (9 new series) April 1871:451-58.
* "Land for the People," *Northern Daily Telegraph,* November 4 1886 and *The Darwen News,* November 5 1886.
Thomas, Gillian, *Harriet Martineau.* Boston: Twayne 1985.
Thompson, Dorothy, *The Chartists.* London: Temple Smith 1984.
* ed., *Over Our Dead Bodes: Women Against the Bomb.* London: Virago 1983.
Tomalin, Claire, *Life and Death of Mary Wollstonecraft.* New York: Mentor 1974.
Tristan, Flora, *The London Journal of Flora Tristan,* trans. Jean Hawkes. London: Virago 1982 [1840] .
* *Workers' Union,* trans. Beverley Livingston. University of Illinois Press 1983 [1844].
* *Lettres,* ed. Stéphane Michaud. Paris: Seuil 1980.
Tuana, Nancy, *Woman and the History of Philosophy.* New York: Praeger 1992.
Turgot, A.R.J., *Oeuvres de Turgot,* ed. Gustave Schelle. 5 vols. Paris: Alcan 1913.
Tuson, Penelope, ed., *Queen's Daughters: An Anthology of Victorian Feminist Writings On India, 1857-1900.* Reading: Ithaca Press 1995.
United Kingdom. Army Medical Department, *Statistical, Sanitary, and Medical Reports.* 1860. HMSO 1862. WO 33/12:12.
* Report of the Royal Commission on the Sanitary State of the Army in India. 2 vols. 1863.
* House of Lords. Contagious Diseases Commission. Analysis of Evidence.

Bibliography 313

Vaillot, René, *Avec Mme du Châtelet*. vol. 2 of René Pomeau, *Voltaire en son temps*. Oxford: Voltaire Foundation 1988.

Vellacott, Jo, *Bertrand Russell and the Pacifists in the First World War*. Brighton: Harvester 1980.

* *From Liberal to Labour with Women's Suffrage: The Story of Catherine Marshall*. Montreal: McGill-Queen's University Press 1993.

Voltaire, François Arouet de, *Lettres philosophiques ou lettres anglaises*. Paris: Garnier 1962 [1733].

Von Suttner, Bertha, *"Ground Arms!" The Story of a Life*, trans. Alice A. Abbott. Chicago: McClurg 1892 [1889].

* *Lay Down Your Arms*, trans. T. Holmes. New York: Garland reprint 1972 from the 2nd ed., 1894.

Wade, Ira O., *Voltaire and Madame du Châtelet*. Princeton: Princeton University Press 1941.

* ed., *Studies on Voltaire With some Unpublished Papers of Mme du Châtelet*. Princeton University Press 1947 and reprint New York: Russell & Russell 1967.

Walkowitz, Judith R., *Prostitution and Victorian Society: Women, Class and the State*. Cambridge: Cambridge University Press 1980.

Wardle, Ralph M., *Mary Wollstonecraft*. A Critical Biography. Lawrence: University of Kansas Press 1951.

Washington, George, *Writings of George Washington*, ed. Jared Sparks. 12 vols. Boston: Russell, Shattuck & Williams 1836.

Webb, Beatrice, "The Case for the Factory Acts." London: 1901:1-38.

* "Methods of Investigation." London Sociological Society 1906.
* "The Abolition of the Poor Law," London: Fabian Tract No. 185 (March 1918).
* *Our Partnership*, ed. Barbara Drake and Margaret I. Cole. New York: Longmans 1948.
* *My Apprenticeship*. 2 vols. London: Longmans, Green 1950 [1926].
* *Visit to New Zealand in 1898: Beatrice Webb's Diary*. Wellington, NZ: Price, Milburn 1959.
* *Beatrice Webb's American Diary*, ed. David A. Shannon. Madison: University of Wisconsin Press 1963.
* *The Diary of Beatrice Webb*, ed. Norman and Jeanne Mackenzie. 4 vols. London: Virago and LSE 1982-85.
* and Sidney Webb, *The Break-up of the Poor Law*. 2 vols. London: Longmans Green 1909.
* and Sidney Webb, *Decay of Capitalist Civilisation*. London: Allen & Unwin/Fabian Society 1923.
* and Sidney Webb, *Methods of Social Study*. LSE/Cambridge University Press 1975 [1932].
* *The Webbs' Australian Diary*, ed. A.G. Austin. Melbourne: Pitman 1965.

Webb, R.K., *Harriet Martineau: A Radical Victorian*. London: Heinemann 1960.

Wells-Barnett, Ida B., *Crusade for Justice: The Autobiography of Ida B. Wells*, ed. Alfreda M. Duster. Chicago: University of Chicago Press 1970.
* Selected Works of Ida B. Wells-Barnett, comp. Trudier Harris. New York, NY: Oxford University Press 1991.

Westing, Arthur H., ed., *Cultural Norms, War and the Environment*. Oxford University Press 1988.

Wheatley, Vera, *Life and Work of Harriet Martineau*. London: Secker & Warburg 1957.

Willard, Charity Cannon, *Christine de Pizan*. Her Life and Works. New York: Persea 1984.

Willcocks, Mary Patricia, *Madame Roland*, trans. Joseph Thérol. Paris: Hachette.

Williamson, Janice and Deborah Gorham, eds., *Up and Doing: Canadian Women and Peace*. Toronto: Women's Press 1989.

Wollstonecraft, Mary, *A Vindication of the Rights of Men*. Gainesville FL: Scholars' reprint 1960 [1790].
* Review of Macaulay, *Letters on Education*, in *Analytical Review*. 8 (November 1790):241-54.
* *A Critical Edition of Mary Wollstonecraft's Vindication of the Rights of Woman*, ed. Ulrich H. Hardt. Troy NY: Whitston 1982 [1792].
* *An Historical and Moral View of the Origin and Progress of the French Revolution*. London: J. Johnson 1795 [1794].
* *Original Stores*. London: Henry Frowde 1906.
* *The Works of Mary Wollstonecraft*, ed. Janet Todd and Marilyn Butler. New York: New York University Press 1989.
* *Political Writings*, ed. Janet Todd. Toronto: University of Toronto Press 1993.
* *A Vindication of the Rights of Men and A Vindication of the Rights of Woman*, ed. Sylvana Tomaselli. Cambridge: Cambridge University Press 1995.

Woodham-Smith, Cecil, *Florence Nightingale 1820-1910*. London: Constable 1950.

World Commission on Environment and Development, *Our Common Future*. Oxford: Oxford University Press 1987.

Wortley Montagu, Mary, *The Nonsense of Common-Sense*, ed. Robert Halsband. Evanston IL: Northwestern University Press 1947 [1737-38].
* *Complete Letters of the Lady Mary Wortley Montagu*, ed. Robert Halsband. 3 vols. Oxford: Clarendon 1965-67.

Young, D.A.B., "Florence Nightingale's fever." *British Medical Journal* 311 (7021) December 25-30 1995:1697-1700.

Young, Thomas, *An Essay on Humanity to Animals*. London: T. Cadell 1798.

Index

Abbott, Grace, 265
Abel-Smith, Brian, 167n
abolition, of slavery, 87, 118-20, 139, 140-49, 184, 198, 266, 283
Adams, John Quincy, 140
Addams, Jane, life 261; writing 262-82; 1, 2, 8, 285, 289, 295, 296
Addams and Balch, 276-81, 289, 295
Africa, 117-20, 144; see also South Africa
African-American women, 298
agriculture, 41, 77, 84, 85, 100, 104, 105, 124, 155, 157, 185, 213, 244, 265
Alexander, Tsar, 120
American Revolution, 3, 4, 5-6, 61-68
anarchy, 88, 101, 228, 273, 291
ancient (times, civilization) 11, 14, 37, 38, 50, 51, 54, 55, 69, 81, 89, 96, 113, 150, 257, 277
animals, animal welfare, 4, 22, 23, 29-30, 32, 35, 50, 74-75, 81, 92-93, 110, 155, 184, 206-07, 268, 290; see also justice
Anne, Queen, 15, 73-74
anthropocentrism 22, 296
applied sociology 4, 296
Aristotle, 277
Astell, Mary, life 15-16; writing, 16-23; 1, 2, 5, 8, 35, 42, 43, 45, 53, 295, 296
Augustine, bishop, 10, 277
Badinter, Elisabeth, 24n

Balch, Emily Greene, life, 288-89; writing, 289-93; 2, 3, 261, 272, 276, 295
Balch and Addams, 276-82
Ballard, George, 15n
Banks, Olive, 249n
Beard, Charles, 265
Beard, Mary, 260
Beccaria, Cesare de, 52, 54, 55
Bentham, Jeremy, 16, 17, 18, 41, 42, 296
Besterman, Theodore, 24n
Bible, 15, 17, 84, 242
birds, bird protection, 92, 155-58, 251
Bismarck, Chancellor, 191, 193, 194, 279
Blackwell, Elizabeth, life, 242-43; writing, 243-47; 1, 2, 18, 202
Booth, Charles and Mary, 218, 261
Blair, Tony, 243
bourgeoisie, 137, 138
Britain, 2, 18, 24, 61-65, 82, 87, 97, 117, 130-35, 139, 140, 141, 155, 156, 158, 159, 180, 192, 195, 204, 216, 232, 242, 249, 254, 287, 291, 292
British Army, 166, 173-74, 179, 188, 268
British Columbia, 230
British Constitution, 88-89
British imperialism, 3, 4, 184, 238, 268, 278
British Labour Party, 204, 218, 243

315

British rule of India, 4, 139, 166, 182, 182-87
British rule of Ireland, 4, 233-37, 268
brutes, brute creation, 23, 40, 50, 74-76, 93, 248, 254-57
Buckle, H.T., 204
Buddha, 184
Burke, Edmund, 54, 56-60, 78, 80
Bussey, Gertrude, 273-74
Bute, Lady Mary, 38
Butler, George, 232
Butler, Josephine E., life, 231-33; writing, 233-42; 2, 158, 161, 163, 202, 295
Camic, Charles, v, 4n, 296
Canada/Canadian, 7, 18, 230, 240, 243, 260
capitalism, capitalists, 131-32, 135, 187, 220, 223-25, 264
Carlyle, Thomas, 254
Carpenter, Mary, 131n, 248
Catherine of Siena, 233, 297
Catt, Carrie Chapman, 260
Caxton, William, 10
Chadwick, Edwin, 173, 180
Charles V, 297
Chartists, Chartism, 130, 131-33
Chicago, 261, 262, 266, 267
Child, Lydia Maria, 104n
child, children, 10, 12, 26, 29-35, 42-44, 50-52, 55, 79, 80, 108, 110, 125, 181, 182, 190, 193, 194, 197, 216, 217, 219, 220, 221, 223, 228, 236, 244, 245, 258, 249, 250, 262, 274, 269, 270, 271, 275, 276, 286, 290, 295-96
childbirth, 166, 296
child labour, 227, 261-63, 267
children, education of, 56, 70, 71, 72, 74-75, 93, 136-37, 146, 157, 171-72, 176-79, 193, 222, 229, 235, 245

Christ/Christian/Christianity, 15, 16, 17, 19-22, 29, 32, 73, 84, 87, 118, 119, 164, 179, 191, 216, 226, 233-37, 248, 258, 290; see also Jesus
Christianity and prostitution, 159, 246-47
Christianity and slavery, 118-19
Christianity and war, 14, 190-91, 276-77, 279
Christian socialism, 18, 233, 240, 243-46
Church of England, 15, 215, 232, 243
Clark, Lorenne, 3n
Cobbe, Frances Power, life, 248-49; writing, 249-58; 1, 2, 168, 296
Colbert, 105
compassion, 21, 22, 24, 31, 32, 156, 233, 297; see also passion, sympathy
Comte, Auguste, 139
Condorcet, marquis de, 125
Condorcet, Sophie Grouchy de, life, 125; writing, 125-27; 52, 98, 110, 295
Contagious Diseases Acts, 6, 139, 158-64, 166, 181, 195-202, 203, 216, 232, 233, 237-42, 246-47
Cook, E.T., 182n
Cooper, Anna Julia, 298
co-operative commonwealth, 226-28, 243
co-operatives, 131, 187, 228, 243
corruption, 20, 21, 30, 35, 67, 82, 93-96, 99, 100, 127, 134, 144, 149, 237-39, 244, 246
corruption, political, 35-37, 40, 63, 67-72, 86, 216, 261, 266, 298
Corsica, 67, 70-72
crime, criminals, 32, 33, 34, 52, 55, 69, 87, 96, 103, 113, 114, 116,

Index

117, 119, 130, 131-32, 146, 176, 179, 180, 188, 244, 248, 257, 269
crime and prostitution, 4, 240
Cromwell, Oliver, 47, 235
Curie, Marie, 7n
Darwin, Charles, 139, 194
Darwinism, social, 255, 258
debt, 37, 153, 183, 187
debt, national, 65, 88, 90, 113, 151, 153
Declaration of Independence, 146
Declaration of the Rights of Man, 76, 82, 84, 86, 98, 102, 136
declaration of war, 191, 260, 284
deficit, 88, 90, 151
de Gouges, Olympe, 6
de Grey, Lord, 199, 201
democracy, democratic institutions, 3, 16, 17, 41, 42, 46, 57, 59, 60, 61, 105, 120, 175, 193, 204, 205, 226, 237, 264, 271, 272, 273, 280, 282, 287, 289, 290, 295
democratic government, 66, 69-72, 206
de Staël, Germaine de, life, 107-08; writing, 108-25; 1, 2, 6, 8, 42, 43, 52, 54, 94, 193, 211, 295, 296
disease, 4, 130, 150, 153, 155, 166, 172, 174, 179-81, 196, 223-25, 247, 273, 285; see also Contagious Diseases
division of labour, 129, 130, 132, 133
double (sexual) standard, 4, 6, 159, 232, 246
Drysdale, Susan Hoecker, 138n
du Châtelet, Emilie, life, 24; writing, 24-35; 1, 2, 5, 6, 18, 42, 44, 52, 110, 295
Dunant, Henri, 187, 188
ecologists 296

education, 22, 27, 34, 38, 41, 53, 54, 56, 69, 71, 93, 140, 145, 146, 150, 164, 169, 175-77, 183, 185, 193, 206, 222-23, 229, 235, 244, 245, 248, 262, 267, 270
education, for women, 7, 15-18, 48, 70, 72, 73, 94, 95, 97, 139, 150, 233, 240, 242, 248, 261
education, military, 97
education of working-class children, 136-37, 243
Elizabeth I, 235
Elshtain, Jean Bethke, 260n
Engels, Friedrich, 131; see also Marx and Engels
England, 17, 36, 41, 47, 48, 56, 57, 61-66, 68-70, 73, 82, 92, 107, 108, 117-22, 129-38, 145, 148, 154, 162, 164, 170, 173, 175-77, 183, 186-87, 188-89, 191, 193, 196, 202, 205, 206, 208-11, 216, 219, 235-42, 249-53, 257-58, 265-66, 279, 297; see also Britain, Church of England
environment, 5, 48, 155-56, 171, 187, 224, 249, 290, 296; see also ecologists
equality, 3, 19-21, 45, 47, 49, 51, 58, 59, 67, 68, 70, 72, 76, 77-79, 83-86, 88, 89, 90, 99-102, 112, 114, 115, 120, 126-27, 130, 132, 205, 208, 220, 222, 225, 247, 281
equality rights for women, 4, 6, 15-17, 38, 40, 41, 48, 97, 139, 166, 204, 232, 240-41, 245, 252, 280
ethics, 5, 17, 108, 226, 264, 281
Europe, 60, 61, 65, 66, 68, 70, 78, 82, 95, 97, 100, 116-17, 134, 135, 142, 152, 186, 188, 190, 211, 214, 224, 225, 226, 235, 254, 289, 291, 292

Europe, abolition of slave trade in, 117-19, 140-41, 142, 144-46
Europe and Contagious Diseases Acts, 158, 233
Europe and India, 153-54
Europe and Napoleon, 121-23
Europe, social policy in, 243, 262, 266
Europe, wars in, 186-91, 194, 272-81, 284
family, 1, 15, 18, 26-29, 32, 34, 57, 73, 79, 80, 86, 94, 96, 97, 107, 129, 130, 132, 133, 152, 155, 212, 223, 226-28, 236, 270, 275, 288
famine, 11, 52, 150, 156, 217, 224, 224
famine in India, 165-66, 184, 186
famine in Ireland, 234, 237
Farr, William, 177
Fawcett, Millicent, 24n, 287, 231
federalism, 5, 121, 142, 211, 213, 214
federal government (U.S.), 143, 145, 147, 148
feminist critique, 41, 44
feminist demands, 203, 216
feminist theory/analysis 1-3, 6, 17, 18, 48, 76, 93, 97, 98, 125, 167, 168, 233, 240, 250, 285, 298
feminist theory of war, 285, 287-88
Fox, George, 278
France, 8, 9, 13, 48, 65, 71, 78, 82, 112, 123, 124-25, 130, 131, 138, 157, 186, 189, 203, 207, 208, 211-14, 238-39, 276, 278, 284, 297; see also War, Franco-Prussian
France, Contagious Diseases Acts in, 158, 195-96, 198, 199, 233
French Enlightenment, 2, 5, 24, 98, 276

French Revolution, 3, 4, 5, 6, 48, 56-61, 66-68, 70, 76-90, 94, 98, 105, 107-08, 110-17, 118, 121-22, 137, 276
Franklin, Benjamin, 48, 56, 62
Gage, Matilda Joslyn, 298
Garrett, Elizabeth, 163, 202, 240
gender roles, 1, 4, 5, 6, 10, 94, 157, 158, 195, 231, 237, 246-47, 296, 298
gender and violence, 5, 249-53
gender and war, 10, 90, 97, 260-61, 285-86
general will, 54, 99
Geneva Convention, 187-89
George III, 63
Galton, Francis, 175, 177-78
Garibaldi, 232, 279
Garrison, William Lloyd, 140
George, Henry, 208
Germany, 107, 121, 122, 123, 191, 193-94, 211, 213, 214, 264, 268, 283-85, 289, 291, 292
Ghokale, Gopale Krishna, 184
Gilligan, Carol, 108
Gilman, Charlotte Perkins, 298
Gladstone, W.E., 163, 164, 194, 197, 198, 199, 215, 237
God, 10, 11, 12, 13, 14, 15, 16, 17-23, 30, 31, 36, 37, 50, 51, 80, 123, 131, 136, 144, 181, 189, 191, 198, 211, 232, 233, 234, 246, 248, 251, 275, 277, 297
God and animals, 75, 92, 254-57
God and war, 10-14, 118, 283-85
government, 1, 3, 4, 5, 20, 21, 22, 35-37, 44-45, 47, 49, 50-52, 53, 54-59, 61, 68-73, 76-77, 78, 81-83, 86-90, 94-106, 108, 110-14, 16, 119, 121-25, 133, 138, 139, 143, 144, 151, 152, 157, 163, 164, 166-81, 191, 192, 201,

Index

205, 206, 207, 210, 212-14, 218-24, 228, 233-41, 243-45, 246, 257, 259, 262-63, 265-69, 272-73, 274, 280, 281, 284, 287, 295
government, international, 290-93
government of India, 181-88, 191, 193, 195, 201, 204-17, 218, 220
government, U.S. 61-68, 195; see also federal government
government, women in 269-71
Greece/Greece, 51, 82, 94, 276, 277, 278
Grimké, Angelina, 140, 141
Grotius, Hugo, 276, 278
Guerry, A.M., 131n
Hamilton, Susan, 7n, 248
happiness, greatest happiness, 14, 16-18, 20, 29, 33, 54-56, 64, 66, 67, 71, 73, 74, 75, 78, 81, 83, 88-90, 95, 99, 100, 103, 111, 113-16, 117, 118, 120, 125, 126, 207, 211, 231, 236, 254, 256, 283
Hays, Mary, life 93; writing, 94-97; 2
health, 136, 211, 219-23, 245, 266, 297
health and local government, 181
health, in British Army, 173-74, 197
health, in India, 153-54, 181-83
health, in U.S. Army, 148-49
health promotion, 4, 178, 296
health, public, 3, 130, 167-73, 179, 229, 243, 269, 292
Helvétius, Claude, 25, 55
Herbert, Sidney, 153, 175, 189, 200
Hill, Bridget, 18, 23, 48, 62
Holbach, Paul T. d', 25
hospitals, 110, 135, 165, 171, 173, 201, 221, 222, 228, 229
hospitals, army, 148, 153, 170, 174, 181, 190, 195,
hospitals, field, 189-90, 192

hospitals, "lock," 158, 161, 195-201, 241, 242, 247
hospital statistics, 178-180
hospitals, workhouse, 170-73
housing, 169, 171, 269
Hugo, Victor, 179
Hull-House, 261-262
Hume, David, 16, 24, 47, 52, 62, 74, 75, 88
Hutcheson, Francis, 16, 52
hygiene, 174, 176; see also health
immigrants, 261, 265, 266-67, 289
India, 3, 4, 87, 139, 149-55, 166, 175, 177, 181-87, 195, 198, 199, 200, 233, 264; see also government, health, British rule
Indians (North American) 265, 266, 278,
industry, industrialist, 42, 77, 84, 85, 100, 104-05, 120, 129, 131-35, 151, 219-21, 222, 224, 225, 241, 244, 249, 251, 264-67, 269-71, 273, 289, 290
industry, public ownership of, 208, 218-19
international relations, 3, 4, 188, 219, 226, 227, 278, 281, 282, 284, 286, 288; see also government, international
International Abolitionist Federation, 233
International Congress of Women, 272-73, 280-81
international statistics, 149, 178-80
Ireland, Irish, 3, 4, 61, 63, 136, 184, 233-37, 267-69,
Italy/Italian, 121, 122, 123, 165, 193, 211, 213, 214, 232, 248, 278, 283
Jacobs, Jane, 211
Jefferson, Thomas, 2, 62, 121-24, 278

Jesus, 272, 276-77; see also Christ
Jews, 29, 74, 289, 290
Jowett, Benjamin, 175, 193, 254
justice, 10, 13, 14, 16-22, 39, 42-45, 50, 56, 64, 65, 69, 80, 85-87, 95, 97, 99, 102, 104, 107, 110, 113-14, 118-19, 125-27, 130, 133, 185, 187, 201, 231, 233, 236-37, 242, 247, 251, 252, 253, 259, 269, 271, 272, 273, 278, 280-85, 297, 298
justice, for animals, 5, 74-75, 93
justice, courts of, 72, 133, 169, 281
justice, criminal, 130, 132
justice, international 281-82
justice, racial, 233
justice, theory of, 44-45
juvenile crime, 269
Kant, Immanuel, 108, 258, 276
Keynes, John Maynard, 224, 227
Kingsley, Charles, 233, 243
labour, labouring classes, 3, 7, 85, 100, 106, 131, 133, 136, 138, 142-43, 147, 162, 169, 172, 177, 179, 187, 190, 216-21, 223, 227-29, 242, 245, 249, 251-52, 261, 266, 267, 289, 290; see also British Labour Party, division of labour
labour, child, 227, 261-63
labour legislation, 218-19, 261-62
labour theory of value, 3, 18, 79, 130, 138, 155
la Fayette, General de, 122
la Méttrie, Julian O. de, 25
land tenure reform 72, 150, 203, 208
law, 16, 18, 20, 25-27, 30, 31, 42, 43, 47, 48-59, 68-70, 72- 73, 81-84, 86, 87, 92 95, 99-104, 106, 110, 114-15, 118-19, 124, 127, 132-35, 144, 155, 178, 184, 187, 206-07, 209-11, 216, 219, 236, 239-41, 246, 247, 249, 251-53, 255, 258, 263, 267, 278, 280, 290, 291; see also Poor Law
law, Contagious Diseases Acts, 158-64, 195, 197, 199, 201, 240-41
law, divine/God's, 13, 14, 17, 21, 80, 297
law, physical 113, 165, 168, 175, 242, 283
law and war, 13-14, 187, 278, 280, 283
lawyers, 54, 68, 69, 209
Lévasseur, Thérèse, 110n
Lewis, George, 199
Lewis, Jane, 7n
liberty, 6, 36, 37, 55, 60, 63, 65, 66, 70, 71, 73, 76-77, 82-83, 86-90, 98-100, 102, 106, 112, 115, 117, 121-25, 140, 147, 159, 169, 194, 213, 215, 219, 220,, 223, 238-39, 247, 274, 279, 282, 289
liberty, civil, 82-84, 86, 94-97, 162
Lincoln, Abraham, 142-43, 147
Lipset, S.M., 139, 140
Locke, John, 3, 16, 17, 18, 24, 26, 30, 41, 42, 44, 76, 82
London, 28, 129, 131, 135, 149, 158, 172-73, 178, 185-86, 192, 193, 203, 214, 216, 218, 229, 249, 251, 261
Longmore, Thomas, 188-89
Louis XIV, 134, 192
Louis XVI, 100, 107, 120, 121
Louis Napoleon, 191, 285
Lowe, Robert, 201
love, 6, 11, 13-15, 19, 21, 25-26, 29-37, 45, 49, 52, 78, 80, 95, 99, 100, 103, 108, 121, 167, 190, 193, 217, 247, 255, 258, 282-84, 288, 297
love, maternal, 35, 50, 110

Index

Macaulay, Catharine, life 47-48; writing, 48-75; 1, 2, 6, 8, 42, 43, 44, 77, 79, 84, 93, 94, 110, 111, 295, 296
Macphail, Agnes, 260
Macpherson, C.B., 41-44
Maine, Henry, 209
Mahood, Linda, 246n
Mandeville, Bernard, 6, 24-35
Manning, Henry, 249, 254
marriage, 15-16, 18-19, 22, 23, 73, 206, 236, 241
Martineau, Harriet, life, 138-39; writing, 140-64; 1, 2, 5, 8, 129, 173, 195, 232, 296
Martineau and Nightingale, 139, 148-49, 150, 153, 158-63, 173, 183, 195, 198-202
Martineau, James, 139
Marx, Karl, 131
Marx and Engels, 136, 138, 224
Masham, Damaris, 22, 23
mathematics, 24, 82, 126
Maurice, F.D., 233, 240, 243
Mayhew, Henry, 131
Mazzini, Guiseppe, 232, 264
medical sociology, 242-43, 246-47, 296
medical statistics, 153
medicine, medical, 15, 148, 153, 154, 159, 165, 166, 172, 173, 174, 181, 192, 196, 197, 199-202, 222, 242, 246-47, 249, 254
medicine, preventive, 4, 148, 296
medicine, women in, 242
Middle Ages, 118, 134, 135
Middle East, 139
middle class, 79, 129, 132, 164, 220, 228, 249-50, 261, 271
militarism, 4-6, 9-14, 37-41, 90-92, 97, 124-25, 187-95, 217, 242, 259-92

military, 4, 6, 37-41, 71, 76, 84-85, 90-92, 97, 107, 113, 133, 143, 148, 149, 153, 154, 182, 188, 193-95, 197, 237, 239, 240, 259, 269, 276, 278-79, 286; see also British Army
Mill, Harriet Taylor, 98, 202-03
Mill, James, 204
Mill, J.S., 3, 41-42, 98, 167, 169, 173, 202-04, 208, 214-17, 233, 240, 249, 254
Mitterand, François, 7n
monarchical government, 94, 96, 116, 238
monarch/monarchy, 41, 47-52, 60-64, 94, 96, 105, 106, 111-12, 116, 119, 122, 212, 214, 235, 277
moral philosophy, 16, 18, 26, 52
moral rules, 17, 26, 110, 295
moral sentiments, 6, 44, 109-09, 125-27
morality, 4, 24, 25, 26, 30, 36, 44, 50, 52, 91, 108, 111, 112, 114, 116, 125, 126, 159, 162, 163, 176, 196, 200, 201, 219, 226, 238, 241
Moreau-Christophe, L.M., 131
mortality, 74, 146, 147, 153-54, 166, 174, 179-80, 183
mortality, infant, 269, 275
mortality, maternal, 166, 296
mothers, 6, 12, 34-35, 42, 43, 44, 50, 80, 110, 125, 203, 209, 216, 227, 233, 252, 259, 273, 275-76, 287, 295; see also mortality, maternal, family
Napoleon (Bonaparte) Napoleonic, 107, 108, 117, 121-24, 132, 276, 278, 279

nature, 13, 22, 25, 31, 35, 39, 50, 77-79, 81, 83, 85, 86, 87, 120, 127, 203, 224, 283
nature, human, 5, 6, 25, 28-33, 49, 71, 83, 92, 109-10, 194, 207, 212, 259, 261
nature/social difference, 3, 4, 5, 6, 22-23, 74-75, 92-93, 108, 155-58, 254-58, 259
nature, state of, 6, 29, 42-44, 48, 50, 52, 54, 76, 77, 110
Newton, Isaac, 24, 38, 178
Nightingale, Florence, life, 165-66; writing, 167-202; 1, 2, 5, 6,8, 17, 110, 129, 155, 217, 221, 242, 296
Nightingale and Martineau, 139, 148-49, 150, 153, 158-63
Nobel, Alfred, 283
Nobel Peace Prize, 262, 272, 283, 289
nobles, nobility, 11, 12, 14, 61, 80, 84, 85, 87, 101, 102, 107, 111, 123, 133, 137, 138
Norris, John, 15
nurses, nursing, 165-66, 168, 170-73, 181, 188-90, 192, 242, 275
nutrition, 155, 171
occupations, for women, 7, 38, 139, 165, 261
O'Connell, Daniel, 136, 184
pacifists/pacifism, 8, 89, 217, 260, 278, 281-82, 288
Paine, Thomas, 125, 278
Paoli, General, 67, 70-73
Paris, 7, 30, 56, 61, 96, 103, 104 118, 121, 125, 162, 189, 190, 191, 192-93, 201, 211-24, 238-39, 242, 248, 278, 279, 282
Parliament, 5, 14, 36, 37, 39, 41, 59, 61, 63, 68-69, 70, 84, 86, 106, 132-34, 150, 152, 155, 159- 63, 166, 167, 172, 173, 177, 184, 185, 194, 197, 201, 208, 210, 214, 221, 228, 229, 232-39, 249, 254, 257, 278, 280
Parliament, women and, 203, 215
passions, 19, 23, 26, 29-35, 43-44, 53, 58, 61, 71, 77, 78,81, 83, 84, 92, 100, 102, 107-11, 114-16, 149, 161, 164, 213, 219, 234; see also compassion, love
Pateman, Carol, 3n, 41
Paul, apostle, 258
paupers/pauperism, 141, 146, 167-72, 177, 185, 193, 221-23, 226, 244, 289, 290; see also poverty, Poor Law
peace, 4, 5, 6, 9-14, 37-41, 44, 53, 55, 65, 72, 78, 81, 83, 88-92, 95, 97, 103, 108, 113, 117, 118, 122, 124-25, 132, 133, 134, 139, 141, 142, 174, 187-95, 217, 222, 231, 242, 259-93, 295
peace movement, 5, 259, 262, 272-81, 283, 287
Pearson, Karl, 175, 178
Penn, William, 278
Perry, Ruth, 15n
physicians, 46, 174, 246,
physicians, women, 240, 246
Pisan, Christine de, life, 9; writing, 9-14; 1, 2, 5, 26, 261
Pitt, William, 118, 119, 124
Plato, 14, 258
police, 71, 73, 130, 132, 134, 153, 158, 161-62, 196-99, 201-02, 228, 232, 237-40, 249, 268
political economy/ists 79, 90, 139, 150, 153, 155
political science 1, 4, 8, 77, 83, 206, 295, 296
Poor Law, 167-71, 184, 186, 218, 221-23, 227-28, 289; abolition, of Poor Law 222-23

Index

possessive individualism, 41-43, 48, 295
poverty, 58, 99, 131, 134, 137, 167, 185, 186, 217, 224, 225, 230, 237, 273, 290; see also paupers, Poor Law
progress, progressive, 3, 9, 24, 25, 54, 76, 79, 83, 88-89, 95, 96, 98, 105, 109, 115, 125, 129, 135, 139, 157, 174, 175, 194, 197, 204, 205, 207, 208, 211, 212, 222, 249, 254, 257, 259, 265, 270, 278, 279, 282
Progressive Party, 262, 266-67, 271
property, property rights, 18, 21, 43, 57, 69, 70, 72, 78- 80, 82, 86, 87, 89, 90, 99, 100, 102, 111, 120-21, 127, 138, 186, 204, 207, 209-11, 212, 216, 220, 231, 250
property, married women's, 6, 252
prostitution, 4, 5, 6, 34, 130, 158-63, 195-202, 232, 236, 237-42, 246-47, 269; see also Contagious Diseases Acts
Protestant/ism, 6, 15, 111, 165, 233, 235-36, 267, 269, 290
public opinion, 62, 101, 112, 181, 185, 186, 237, 238, 250, 257, 267, 268
Puritans, 41, 54, 68, 297
Quakers, 140, 159, 276, 278
Quesnai, François, 104
Quetelet, L.A.J., 178, 180
radical/s, 16, 25, 48, 61, 62, 73, 84, 93, 122, 125, 131, 132, 159, 167, 173, 203, 216
Rande, Mary Cary, 54, 68, 296
Rathbone, William, 170
Rauschenbusch, Walter, 243n
Raven, Charles E., 243n
Rawls, John, 45
Rawson, W., 131n

Red Cross, 187-92
refugees, 192-93, 289-90
republic/an, 4, 41, 47-48, 56-57, 61-62, 71-73, 105, 106, 111-16, 121, 122, 125, 141-45, 147, 211-14, 238
revolution, 1, 5, 41, 47, 57, 60, 62, 69, 73, 76, 88, 89, 94, 96, 98, 104, 112, 114, 116-17, 120, 124, 129, 131, 132, 136, 146, 147, 208, 211-12, 226, 230, 235, 238, 249, 266, 274, 279; see also American Revolution, French Revolution
Robespierre, 122
Roland, Marie-J. de, life, 98; writing, 98-106; 1, 2, 6, 112
Roman Catholic, 115, 213, 215, 235-36, 269, 290
Roosevelt, F.D., 265
Roosevelt, T. 271-72
Rousseau, J.J., 3, 4, 6, 26, 48, 54, 77, 91, 105, 110, 295
royal commissions 163, 184, 202, 240, 254
Royal Commission on Sanitary Condition of Army, 150, 166, 173-74, 182
Royal Commission on India, 150, 153, 166, 182-83, 195
Royal Commission on Poor Law, 221, 227
Russell, Bertrand, 287
sexism/sexist bias, 1, 44n
sexist language, 7
sexual contract, 41
Shaftesbury, Lord, 178, 249, 254
slaves/slavery, 1, 3, 16, 19, 37, 64, 65, 77, 78, 79, 81, 83, 84, 86, 87, 98-100, 106, 113, 114, 117, 120, 122, 123, 125, 130, 131, 132, 135, 136, 137, 140-49, 184,

204, 209, 225, 227, 228, 229, 232, 234, 242, 252, 262, 264, 266, 276, 279, 283, 290, 298; see also abolition
slave trade, 87, 108, 117-19, 143, 144, 185-86, 228
smallpox vaccination, 15, 201, 296
Smith, Adam, 24, 25, 44, 52, 108, 109, 125-27, 220, 225
Smith, W.H., 175, 215
social bond, 1, 5, 6, 16, 24, 27, 41, 44, 48, 76, 108, 125, 259, 261
social contract, 1, 3, 4, 5, 6, 8, 26, 41, 44, 48, 52, 54, 105, 110, 261
social democrat, 204, 243
social gospel 243, 261; see also Christian socialism
socialism/ist, 1, 3, 4, 130, 136, 236, 203, 208, 212, 218, 224-26, 230, 260, 261; see also Christian socialism
sociology, sociologist, 1, 2, 5, 8, 129, 139, 217-18, 223, 288, 295, 296; see also applied sociology, medical sociology
soldiers, 11, 33, 38-39, 90, 91, 100, 110, 119, 124, 125, 133, 134, 142-43, 145, 148-49, 154, 159-61, 173, 174, 182, 187, 195, 197, 201, 239, 259, 268, 275, 277, 284
Sophia, life 38; writing, 39-41; 97
South Africa, 233, 242, 285
Spencer, Herbert, 217, 223
Spender, Dale, 1
Stanley, Lord, 182, 198
Stanton, Elizabeth Cady, 243n, 260n
Stewart, Maria W., 298
Stowe, Harriet Beecher, 283
suffrage, 130, 132, 133, 134, 205, 212
suffrage, women's, 6, 139, 159, 166, 168, 203, 218, 233-34, 248, 260, 269, 270, 274, 287

Sutherland, John, 199
sweating industry/sweat shop, 219-221, 228, 290
sympathy, 6, 17, 18, 43, 44, 52-53, 77, 92, 94, 97, 109, 111, 115, 116, 125-27, 145, 147, 159, 189, 192, 207, 214, 217, 233-34, 242, 252, 262-64, 269, 271, 272; see also compassion
taxes/taxation, 11, 58, 61-65, 69, 72, 76, 84-85, 88, 90, 95, 105, 106, 133, 135, 150-53, 156, 166, 169, 175, 177, 185-86, 210, 286
tax, single, 105, 208
Taylor, Helen life, 202-03; writing, 203-17, 1, 2, 5, 295
Thatcher, Margaret, 260
Tolstoy, Leo, 276, 272, 279, 283
trade unions, 130, 159, 167, 169, 219, 261-65, 266; see also Workers' Union
Tristan, Flora, life 129-39 writing, 130-38; 2, 5
Turgot, A.R.J. 48, 56, 104, 105
Twining, Louisa, 168
tyranny/tyrants, 18, 51, 59, 63, 84, 92- 94, 98, 99, 107, 114, 117, 119, 121, 125, 134, 142, 144, 169, 194, 219, 237, 239, 252
unemployed/ment, 129, 130, 137, 168, 221-23, 227-29
unemployment insurance, 3, 130
United Nations, 4, 290, 291-93,
United States, 18, 47, 48, 56, 61-62, 105, 117, 121-23, 139, 140-42, 145-46, 148, 195, 216, 218, 230, 242, 243, 265-67, 271, 274, 279-82, 289, 291-92; see also American Revolution, Civil War,
university, 2, 62, 138, 145, 146, 159, 175, 177, 213, 235, 241, 243

Index

university settlements, 243, 261
university, women and 248, 261
University, Oxford, 175-76, 232, 248
utility theory/utilitarianism, 16, 17, 18, 23-25, 42-44, 48, 52, 74-75, 86, 126, 200, 206; 295
Vellacott, Jo, 287
Verney, Harry, 180-81, 189-92, 200-02
Victoria, Queen, 158, 159, 182, 190
violence, 5, 21, 29, 40, 42, 53, 88-101, 106, 118, 124, 141, 172, 211, 240, 262, 263, 277, 278, 279, 280
violence against women, 4, 5, 34, 231-32, 249-53, 255
virtue, 23, 24-35, 39, 43, 52-53, 55, 60, 65, 66, 68, 69, 71, 73, 75, 78, 79, 91, 93, 95, 98, 99, 100, 103, 106, 108-09, 111, 114, 115-16, 127, 164, 184, 255, 256, 265, 286, 297
vivisection, 198, 248, 254-58
virtue and vice, 13, 73, 126
virtue, military, 4, 90-91, 277
Voltaire, 24, 25, 26, 27
von Suttner, Bertha, life, 282-83; writing, 283-85; 2, 261, 279, 295
vote, 36, 59, 70, 72, 198, 267; see also suffrage
vote, for women, 7, 158, 166-67, 169, 203, 204, 215-17, 218, 243, 260, 261, 271, 286
Wade, Ira O., 24n, 27
Walkowitz, Judith, 158n
War, abolition, of, 279-81, 283, 291
War, Afghan, 259
War, American Civil, 3, 123, 145, 148, 195, 242, 260, 262, 264
War, Boer, 233, 242, 260, 278, 285, 287

War, Crimean, 148, 165-66, 170, 173, 178, 182, 188, 192, 195, 278
War, Falklands, 260
War, French Civil, 9-12, 26, 101, 103, 111, 123, 124
war, just, 9-10, 14, 277
War, Franco-Prussian, 166, 187-95, 211, 217, 278
War, Hundred Years, 9
War, World War I, 5, 260, 266-68, 271-72, 279, 283, 285
War, World War II, 1, 4, 260, 291; see also Christianity and war, declaration of war, Europe, feminist theory, gender and war, God and war, law and war
Warren, Mercy Otis, 63
Washington, George, 2, 48, 62-63, 66-68, 71
Washington (Government) 142, 143, 149,
Webb, Beatrice, life, 217-18; writing, 218-30; 1, 2, 5, 8, 261, 296
Webb, Sidney, 218, 221-29
Weber, Marianne, 298
welfare state, 1, 3, 4, 167, 243, 261, 271
Wellington, Duke of, 108, 123, 124
Wells-Barnett, Ida, 298
West Indies, 117
Wilberforce, William, 87, 108, 117-19, 184, 231,
William III, 235, 236
Williams, Helen Maria, 56n
Wilson, Woodrow, 260, 271-73, 292
Wollstonecraft, Mary, life, 76; writing, 76-93; 1, 2, 42, 43, 44, 48, 59, 94, 111, 295, 296
women workers, 218-19; see also occupations for women

Women's International League for Peace and Freedom, 262, 271, 272-73, 290
women's movement, 48, 218, 248, 288
women's studies, 1-6, 298; see also feminism
Woodhull, Victoria, 215
Woodsworth, J.S., 260
Workers' Union, 130, 136-38
workhouse, 130, 167-72, 177, 222, 223, 225
working class, 130, 131-38, 192, 204-06, 216, 232, 241, 251; see also women workers
World Commission on Environment and Development, 290
Wortley Montagu, Mary, life, 35-36; writing, 36-38; 2, 15, 296